Lecture Notes in Artificial Inte

Edited by J. G. Carbonell and J. Siekmann

Subseries of Lecture Notes in Computer Science

Mohamed Chetouani   Amir Hussain
Bruno Gas   Maurice Milgram
Jean-Luc Zarader (Eds.)

Advances in Nonlinear Speech Processing

International Conference
on Nonlinear Speech Processing, NOLISP 2007
Paris, France, May 22-25, 2007
Revised Selected Papers

 Springer

Series Editors

Jaime G. Carbonell, Carnegie Mellon University, Pittsburgh, PA, USA
Jörg Siekmann, University of Saarland, Saarbrücken, Germany

Volume Editors

Mohamed Chetouani
Bruno Gas
Maurice Milgram
Jean-Luc Zarader
Université Pierre et Marie Curie
Institut des Systèmes Intelligents et de Robotique (ISIR)
3 rue Galilée, 94200 Ivry-sur-Seine, France
E-mail: {mohamed.chetouani, bruno.gas, maurice.milgram, jean-luc-zarader}@upmc.fr

Amir Hussain
University of Stirling
Department of Computing Science & Mathematics
Stirling FK9 4LA, Scotland, UK
E-mail: ahu@cs.stir.ac.uk

Library of Congress Control Number: 2007941810

CR Subject Classification (1998): I.2.7, J.5, C.3

LNCS Sublibrary: SL 7 – Artificial Intelligence

ISSN   0302-9743
ISBN-10   3-540-77346-0 Springer Berlin Heidelberg New York
ISBN-13   978-3-540-77346-7 Springer Berlin Heidelberg New York

Springer is a part of Springer Science+Business Media

springer.com

© Springer-Verlag Berlin Heidelberg 2007
Printed in Germany

Typesetting: Camera-ready by author, data conversion by Scientific Publishing Services, Chennai, India
Printed on acid-free paper   SPIN: 12206032   06/3180   5 4 3 2 1 0

Preface

We present in this volume a collection of revised selected papers from the ISCA Tutorial and Research Workshop on Nonlinear Speech Processing (NOLISP 2007) held in Paris, France, 22–25 May, 2007. NOLISP 2007 was organized by the University Pierre and Marie Curie (UPMC) with the generous support of ISCA (International Speech Communication Association), EURASIP and the IEEE. NOLISP 2007 was the first follow-on workshop to a series of three earlier events related to nonlinear speech processing, that were organized within the framework of the European COST action 277 Nonlinear speech processing (2001–2005). The financial support of ISCA enabled the attendance of leading researchers from various parts of the world.

The exciting field of speech processing has witnessed tremendous development over the past 20 years or so, thanks to both technological progress and to the growing focus of research on a number of key application areas. However, some specificities of the speech signal are still not well addressed by the currently available models. Hence, new nonconventional models and processing techniques need to be investigated in order to foster and/or accompany future progress, even if they do not match immediately the level of performance and understanding of the current state-of-the-art approaches.

The purpose of NOLISP is to present and discuss novel ideas, work and results related to such alternative techniques for speech processing, which depart from mainstream approaches. It declared its intent to be an interdisciplinary forum, intertwining research in different fields of speech processing with its growing applications in everyday practice.

One of the special characteristics of the NOLISP volumes is that the authors usually propose new improvements for speech processing by drawing inspiration from other exciting fields including, amongst others, statistical signal processing, pattern classification, multi-modal processing, perceptual-based criteria, auditory processing and machine learning-based approaches.

This volume contains a collection of revised and selected papers presented at NOLISP 2007. After a thorough review process, 24 papers were accepted for publication, including the contribution of three invited speakers. A total of 8 sessions containing 32 papers were accepted for presentation, covering specific aspects such as speaker recognition, speech analysis, voice pathologies, speech recognition, speech enhancement, audio and visual speech processing and applications.

In this book, the papers have been divided into the following sections:

- Nonlinear and Nonconventional Techniques
- Speech Synthesis
- Speaker Recognition
- Speech Recognition

– Speech Analysis
– Exploitation of nonlinear techniques

Finally, we would like to express our gratitude to members of the NOLISP Organizing Committee, and to all the people who participated in the event (delegates, invited speakers, scientific committee members). The editors would also like to address a special mention to the people who helped in the peer-review process as special or additional reviewers.

October 2007

Mohamed Chetouani
Amir Hussain
Bruno Gas
Maurice Milgram
Jean-Luc Zarader

Organization

NOLISP 2007 was organized by the Institute of Intelligent Systems and Robotics (CNRS FRE2507), University Pierre and Marie Curie (Paris-6).

Scientific Committee

Frédéric Bimbot	IRISA, Rennes (France)
Mohamed Chetouani	UPMC, Paris (France)
Gérard Chollet	ENST, Paris (France)
Tariq Durrani	University of Strathclyde, Glasgow (UK)
Marcos Faundez-Zanuy	EUPMt, Barcelona (Spain)
Bruno Gas	UPMC, Paris (France)
Hynek Hermansky	OGI, Portland (USA)
Amir Hussain	University of Stirling, Scotland (UK)
Eric Keller	University of Lausanne (Switzerland)
Bastiaan Kleijn	KTH, Stockholm (Sweden)
Gernot Kubin	TUG, Graz (Austria)
Petros Maragos	Nat. Tech. Univ. of Athens (Greece)
Stephen McLaughlin	University of Edinburgh (UK)
Kuldip Paliwal	University of Brisbane (Australia)
Bojan Petek	University of Ljubljana (Slovenia)
Jean Rouat	University of Sherbrooke (Canada)
Jean Schoentgen	Univ. Libre Bruxelles (Belgium)
Isabel Trancoso	INESC (Portugal)

Organizing Committee

Mohamed Chetouani	UPMC, Paris (France)
Bruno Gas	UPMC, Paris (France)
Amir Hussain	University of Stirling, Scotland (UK)
Maurice Milgram	UPMC, Paris (France)
Michèle Vie	UPMC, Paris (France)
Jean-Luc Zarader	UPMC, Paris (France)

Sponsoring Institutions

University Pierre and Marie Curie (Paris-6)
International Speech Communication Association (ISCA)
European Association For Signal, Speech And Image Processing (EURASIP)
IEEE UKRI Industry Applications Society Chapter

Table of Contents

Speech Recognition

Speech Analysis

Exploitation of non-linear techniques

Phase-Based Methods for Voice Source Analysis

Christophe d'Alessandro[1], Baris Bozkurt[2], Boris Doval[1], Thierry Dutoit[3],
Nathalie Henrich[4], Vu Ngoc Tuan[1], and Nicolas Sturmel[1]

[1] LIMSI-CNRS Orsay, France
[2] Izmir Institute of Technology, Izmir, Turkey
[3] TCTS-FPMs, Mons, Belgium
[4] DPC-GIPSA-Lab Grenoble
cda@limsi.fr, barisbozkurt@iyte.edu.tr, boris.doval@limsi.fr,
thierry.dutoit@fpms.ac.be, Nathalie.Henrich@gipsa-lab.inpg.fr,
vnt@limsi.fr, sturmel@limsi.fr

Abstract. Voice source analysis is an important but difficult issue for speech processing. In this talk, three aspects of voice source analysis recently developed at LIMSI (Orsay, France) and FPMs (Mons, Belgium) are discussed. In a first part, time domain and spectral domain modelling of glottal flow signals are presented. It is shown that the glottal flow can be modelled as an anticausal filter (maximum phase) before the glottal closing, and as a causal filter (minimum phase) after the glottal closing. In a second part, taking advantage of this phase structure, causal and anticausal components of the speech signal are separated according to the location in the Z-plane of the zeros of the Z-Transform (ZZT) of the windowed signal. This method is useful for voice source parameters analysis and source-tract deconvolution. Results of a comparative evaluation of the ZZT and linear prediction for source/tract separation are reported. In a third part, glottal closing instant detection using the phase of the wavelet transform is discussed. A method based on the lines of maximum phase in the time-scale plane is proposed. This method is compared to EGG for robust glottal closing instant analysis.

1 Introduction

Voice source analysis is an important issue for speech and voice processing, with many applications such as source tract decomposition, formant estimation, pitch synchronous processing, low-rate speech coding, speaker characterisation, singing, speech synthesis, phonetic and prosodic analyses, voice pathology and voice quality evaluation, etc.

However, voice source analysis is also a difficult issue for speech processing. There is generally no measurable reference to the "true" source and vocal tract components. Speech and voice signals are rapidly time-varying, and subject to large individual and inter-subject variations. Finally source tract interactions are not well known to date, but they may render voice source decomposition questionable in the situations where strong interactions are likely to occur (e.g. source-tract adjustments in singing).

The aim of this tutorial is to present some aspects of the authors' recent works in the domain of voice source analysis. A common feature of this line of research is the specific attention paid to the phase structure of the voice source signal. Two aspects

M. Chetouani et al. (Eds.): NOLISP 2007, LNAI 4885, pp. 1–27, 2007.

of the voice source phase are explored: the spectral phase of the glottal pulse itself and cross-scale instantaneous phases in a time-scale space. This paper presents the concepts without much technical details. The general reader will get the main ideas out of this paper. As the most significant references to published literature are pointed out at the beginning of each section, the interested reader will easily find more detailed presentations of the material described herein.

1.1 Definitions of Phase

"Phase" is a highly polysemic word in the general language. In signal processing also, the meaning of "phase" is manifold (for a review, see Alsteris & Paliwal, 2007). Starting from the more basic periodic signals, sine waves, phase is defined as the argument of the sinusoidal function. This first definition of phase, in time domain, or "instantaneous phase" is useful for dealing with waveforms. For instance maxima of sine waves are located at phases $\pi/2$ modulo 2π, Mathematically, instantaneous phase and instantaneous envelopes are defined using the Hilbert Transform. They are useful for describing the time evolution of signals. This first definition of phase can be extended to time-frequency or time-scale representations. This will be used below for time-scale analysis of the glottal closings instants of the voice source.

As spectral representation is a decomposition of the signal on a basis of complex exponentials (i.e. sine and cosine waves), a second definition of phase is the argument of the complex spectrum. This "spectral phase" or "phase spectrum" is often difficult to deal with. On the one hand, spectral phases computed using the Fourier transform are obtained modulo 2π and must be unwrapped. On the other hand, even the smallest delay in the signal changes dramatically the phase spectrum, because it introduces a linear component (note that the phase spectrum derivative in frequency, or group delay, is a more robust representation (Yegnanarayana & Murthy, 1992). This second definition of phase will be used below for glottal flow analysis and synthesis.

1.2 Phase Structure of the Glottal Pulse

Let's write the linear speech production model of voiced speech, in the time domain and in the spectral domain:

$$s(t) = e(t) * v(t) * l(t) = (\sum_n \delta(t - nTo) * g(t)) * v(t) * l(t) \tag{1}$$

$$S(f) = E(f) \times V(f) \times L(f) = (\sum_n \delta(f - nFo) \times G(f)) \times V(f) \times \tag{2}$$

Where: t represents times, f frequency, s the speech signal, e the voiced excitation component, v the vocal tract impulse response, l the lip radiation component, T_0 (F_0) the fundamental period (frequency) and g the glottal flow component.

Depending on the application, the time domain (1) or spectral domain (2) model is preferred. But it goes generally unnoticed that time domain and spectral domain approaches may not be equivalent, because of a different underlying phase structure implicitly assumed for the glottal flow component. Let us examine this point in more detail.

In the early years of the source-filter theory of speech production, the effect of the voice source was mainly studied in the spectral domain, like in Equation (2): the glottal flow signal being considered as the output of a low-pass system to an impulse train. For instance, in a transmission line analogue (Fant, 1970) four poles (*sr1, sr2, sr3, sr4*) on the negative real axis were used, with $|sr1| = |sr2| = 2\pi 100Hz$, and $|sr3| = 2\pi 2000Hz$, $|sr4| = 2\pi 4000Hz$. Note that two poles are low pass (we shall interpret these poles later on in terms of "glottal formant"), and that two poles (*sr3* and *sr4*) are fixed (we shall interpret these poles later on in terms of "spectral tilt"). This simple form entailed important practical consequences, because it has been used (for discrete time signals) for deriving the linear prediction equations (see for instance Markel and Gray, 1976). In this later case, only two poles are used, because the linearity of this acoustic model only holds for frequencies below about 4000 Hz.

$$G(z) = 1/(1 - pz^{-1})(1 - p^*z^{-1}) \qquad (3)$$

The corresponding impulse response, magnitude and phase spectra of are plotted in Fig 1.

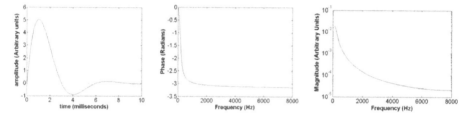

Fig. 1. All pole glottal flow model, as assumed by the Linear Prediction synthesis model. From left to right: glottal waveform, spectral phase and spectral magnitude.

On the other hand, for e.g. formant synthesis, the time domain model like in equation (1) is generally preferred, using time domain models of the glottal flow component. A neglected dimension of this glottal flow component is its phase structure. In time-domain models, glottal flow models are generally not viewed as filters or linear systems, but are rather described by ad hoc equations (based on polynomials or trigonometric functions). An example of such a model is the KLGLOTT88 model (Klatt & Klatt, 1990), described by the following equations (when there is no additional spectral tilt component):

$$Ug(t) = \begin{cases} at^2 - bt^3 & 0 < t < OqTo \\ 0 & OqTo < t < To \end{cases} \qquad (4)$$

The corresponding impulse response, magnitude and phase spectra of are plotted in Fig 2.

Note that, as far as spectral magnitude is concerned, Figure 1 and Figure 2 are very close (the same glottal flow parameters being used). However, both waves are reversed in time, or equivalently, their phases are opposed in sign (corresponding to a symmetry

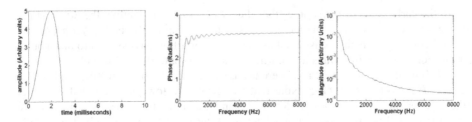

Fig. 2. KLGLOTT88 glottal flow model, as assumed by the Klatt synthesizer (Klatt & Klatt, 1990). From left to right: glottal waveform, spectral phase and spectral magnitude.

relative to the glottal closing instant (GCI)). Then it is argued in the following that the specific phase structure of glottal flow models can be used for source/tract separation and for designing new linear glottal flow models. Section 2 give details on the spectrum of glottal flow models, and presents a new model: the Causal-Anticausal Linear model. In Section 3 a new method that takes advantage of this causal-anticausal model is presented, along with some application to voice source analysis.

1.3 Glottal Pulse Phases in the Time-Scale Space

A second noticeable aspect of the phase of the voice source signals is the instant of glottal excitation or glottal closing. According to Equation (1) the source component can be split in two parts: (1) a linear (and thus linearly predictable using a small set of preceding samples) glottal flow filter and (2) excitation by a train of Dirac pulses (which is not linearly predictable at all using a small set of preceding samples) at the GCI. GCIs correspond to singularities in the signal. Time-scale representation using the wavelet transform is well suited to the problem of singularity detection. However, in the case of glottal pulses, the phase structure of the glottal pulse also influences instantaneous phases in the time-scale domain. A specific method for following the phases across scales is proposed: the lines of maximum amplitude (LOMA) of the wavelet transform. This method is applied to GCI detection, and compared to direct GCI measurement using electroglottography (EGG) in Section 4. Finally, Section 5 summarizes the main results obtained.

2 Time-Domain and Spectral Glottal Flow Models[1]

2.1 Glottal Source

Several mathematical "glottal flow models", abbreviated as GFM hereafter, have been proposed over the past decades, such as the well-known LF model (Fant & Liljencrants, 1985), the KLGLOTT88 model (Klatt & Klatt, 1990), the Rosenberg's models (Rosenberg, 1971) or the R++ model (Veldhuis, 1998). Figure 3 gives a typical example of a glottal flow model and its time derivative.

---

[1] The main references for this Section are: Doval, d'Alessandro, Henrich, 2006; Doval, d'Alessandro, Henrich., 2003.

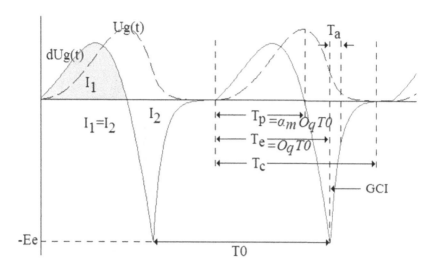

Fig. 3. Example of glottal flow model (top) and differential glottal flow mode (bottom). See text for explanation of the symbols (from Sturmel et al., 2007).

Generally, voice quality is better described by spectral parameters, such as the spectral tilt, the relative amplitude of the first harmonics (Hanson, 1997), the harmonic richness factor (Childers, 1991), the parabolic spectral parameter (Alku et al, 2002). A remarkable spectral feature of GFM is the spectral peak that can be observed on the glottal flow derivative spectrum in the region of the first harmonics. This peak has been coined the "glottal formant", although it is not a resonance, like vocal tract formants.

The link between spectral voice quality and glottal source parameters has not previously been addressed systematically. For answering this problem, one must study the position, variation and properties of the glottal formant and derive closed-form equations for relating time-domain glottal flow parameters to the glottal formant. This work has been conducted in (Doval et al., 2006), with the following aims:

- Studying the spectral behavior of the most common glottal flow models
- Deriving the relationships between time-domain parameters and spectral parameters
- Providing some hints for spectral estimation or modification of glottal flow parameters

2.2 Glottal Flow Models

Among the GFMs proposed in the literature, we have studied the following ones (the parameters mentioned in this paragraph are explained later in the paper):

- KLGLOTT88 model (Klatt & Klatt, 1990): the glottal flow is modelled by a third order polynomial which is possibly smoothed using the low-pass filter method. There are four parameters: A_v, T_0, O_q and TL which is the attenuation in dB of the low-pass filter at 3000 Hz. Notice that the asymmetry of the flow cannot be changed and is always: $\alpha_m = 2 / 3$.

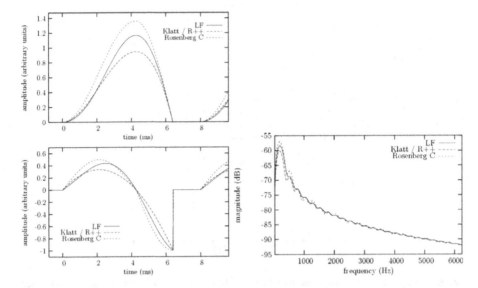

Fig. 4. Comparison of several glottal flow models in time and magnitude spectral domains. Left, top: GFM waveform. Left, bottom: GFM derivative waveform. Right: GFM Magnitude spectrum (from Doval et al., 2006).

- R++ model (Veldhuis, 1998): the glottal flow is composed of a fourth order polynomial for the open phase followed by an exponential return phase. There are five parameters: K (an amplitude coefficient), T_0, T_e, T_p and T_a. The glottal flow is computed so that it returns exactly to 0 at the end of the cycle.
- Rosenberg C (Rosenberg, 1971): the glottal flow is composed of two sinusoidal parts. The 4 parameters are: A_v, T_0, T_p and $T_n = T_e - T_p$. Noticed that the smooth closure case is not handled.
- LF model (Fant & Liljencrants, 1985): the glottal flow derivative is modelled by an exponentially increasing sinusoid followed by a decreasing exponential. There are five parameters: $E_e = E$ (the maximum excitation), T_0, T_e, T_p, T_a. The glottal flow is computed so that it returns exactly to 0 at the end of the cycle. For that, two implicit equations must be solved.

Figure 4 shows an example of the four GFMs (left, top) and their derivatives (left, bottom) with abrupt closure and with a common set of parameters: $T_0 = 8ms$, $O_q = 0.8$, $\alpha_m = 2/3$ and $E = 1$. KLGLOTT88 and R++ models are identical for this parameter set. Note that A_v differs between models when E and the other parameters are fixed. However these differences are hardly audible. All GFMs share some common time-domain features:

- the glottal flow is always positive or null
- the glottal flow and its derivative are quasi-periodic
- during a fundamental period, the glottal flow is bell-shaped: it increases, then decreases, then becomes null

- during a fundamental period, the glottal flow derivative is positive, then negative, then null.
- the glottal flow and its derivative are continuous and differentiable functions of time, except in some situations at the glottal closing instant.

Furthermore, GFMs are described in terms of phases in the time domain:

- the opening phase: the glottal flow increases from baseline at time 0 to its maximum amplitude A_v also called "amplitude of voicing" at time T_p.
- the closing phase: the glottal flow decreases from A_v to a point at time T_e where the derivative reaches its negative extremum E. T_e is the glottal closing instant (GCI) and E is called the "maximum excitation".
- the open phase: it consists of the opening and closing phases, characterized by the open quotient $O_q = T_e / T_0$. The ratio between the opening phase duration and the open phase duration is called "asymmetry coefficient" and noted α_m.
- the closed phase: in the situation of "abrupt closure" there is a discontinuity in the glottal flow derivative which instantaneously reaches 0 after maximum excitation. The glottal flow is null between $O_q T_0$ and T_0. In the situation of "smooth closure" the glottal flow derivative is continuous and exponentially returns to 0 at time T_c. This phase is called "return phase" and the exponential time constant is noted T_a. It can also be characterized by the relative parameter $Q_a = T_a / [(1 - O_q)T_0]$ which takes its value between 0 and 1. The smooth closure case can be modelled in two different ways: either a time-domain decreasing exponential (leading to the return phase as described above) noted "return phase method" or a low-pass first (or second) order filter applied to the whole open phase noted "low-pass filter method".

2.3 Spectral Properties of Glottal Flow Models: The Glottal Formant

Since the early years of the source-filter theory of speech production, it is well known that the effect of the glottal flow in the spectral domain can be approximated by a low-pass system. When considering the GFM derivative spectrum, one can show that it behaves like a band-pass filter, and a spectral peak appears in low frequencies, the so-called "glottal formant". Figure 4 shows the magnitude spectra of the four GFM derivatives (phase spectra are also similar for the four models). Closed-form equations for the GFM spectra and the GFM derivative spectra are given in (Doval et al., 2006).

Figure 5 shows the magnitude spectrum of a GFM derivative and a straight line stylization of this spectrum. The glottal formant is clearly visible in this log-log representation. Again, "glottal formant", does not refer in this case to a resonance in the speech apparatus but only to a maximum in the spectrum.

Figure 5 shows that the glottal formant frequency is slightly higher than the asymptotes crossing point. Its amplitude is also different from the crossing-point amplitude. However, straight line stylisation gives a good approximation of the glottal formant position, and it can be computed from the glottal flow parameters (see Doval et al., 2006).

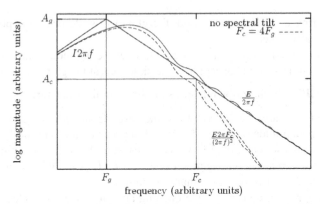

Fig. 5. Magnitude spectrum of a GFM derivative (in a log-log representation), and straight line stylization (from Doval et al., 2006)

2.4 Effects of Open Quotient and Asymmetry Coefficient on the Glottal Formant

The glottal formant frequency is mainly inversely proportional to the open quotient. It depends only marginally on α_m. The glottal formant is roughly found between the first and the 4th harmonics. Its relative amplitude depends mainly on α_m An example of synthetic speech is given in Figure 6.

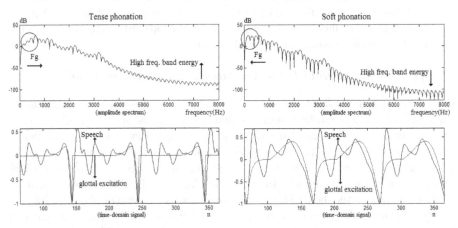

Fig. 6. Glottal formant and open quotient (synthetic speech). Top row: magnitude spectrum of the speech signals. Bottom row: time domain signals, with glottal excitation superimposed to speech (arrows are showing the corresponding waves). Left column: small open quotient (tense phonation); right column: large open quotient (lax phonation) (from Bozkurt, 2005).

Figure 7 (right panels) shows the influence of O_q (4th column right) and α_m (3rd column right) on the GFM (3rd row) and the GFM derivative (4th row) spectra. Several points may be observed:

- the mid and high frequency spectral energy is not much modified by α_m and O_q variations

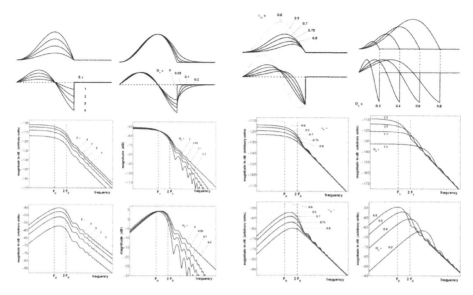

Fig. 7. Effect of amplitude of voicing, spectral tilt, asymmetry and open quotient on the waveform and spectra of GFM and GFM derivatives. Top row: GFM; Second row; GFM derivative; Third row GFM log-log magnitude spectrum; Bottom row: GFM derivative log-log magnitude spectrum. First column: effect of amplitude of voicing; Second column: effect of the return phase and spectral tilt; Third column: effect of GFM asymmetry; Last column: effect of open quotient (from Doval et al., 2006).

- O_q mainly changes the glottal formant frequency
- α_m mainly changes the glottal formant amplitude (or rather its bandwidth)

2.5 Spectral Tilt

The voice spectral tilt describes the GFM spectral profile in mid to high frequencies. It is related to the return phase in the case of smooth closure of the vocal folds. From a modelling point of view, two methods can be applied: either a time-domain decreasing exponential (leading to the return phase as described above) noted "return phase method" or a low-pass first (or second) order filter applied to the whole open phase noted "low-pass filter method". For example, R++ and LF are using the "return phase method" while KLGLOTT88 is using the low-pass filter method. The spectral tilt parameter is Q_a. Its main effect is to add an additional -6dB/oct attenuation above the cut-off frequency F_c . Figure 7 (second column) illustrates the effect of Q_a. The main vocal quality effect of spectral tilt is voice loudness: a low or null Qa corresponds to a minimum spectral tilt and a loud voice. Conversely, a high (close to 1) Q_a corresponds to a high spectral tilt and a weak voice.

2.6 Causal-Anticausal Glottal Flow Model and Application to Speech Synthesis

The preceding discussion shows that the source log magnitude spectrum can be stylized by three linear segments with +6dB/octave, -6dB/octave and -12dB/octave (or sometimes

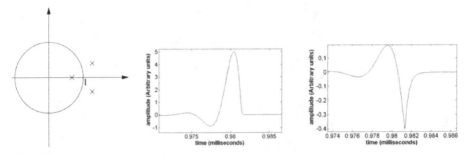

Fig. 8. Poles pattern (left).for the Causal-Anticausal Linear Model (left). Corresponding: GFM (middle) and GFM derivative (right).

-18dB/oct) slopes, respectively, like in Figure 5. The two breakpoints in the spectrum correspond to the glottal spectral peak and the spectral tilt cut-off frequency.

For synthesis in the spectral domain, it is possible to design an all-pole filter which is comparable to e.g. the LF model. This filter is a 3rd order low-pass filter, with a pair of conjugate complex poles, and a simple real pole. The simple real pole is given directly by the spectral tilt parameter. It is mainly effective in the medium and high frequencies of the spectrum. The pair of complex-conjugate poles is used for modelling the glottal formant (see Figure 8). If one wants to preserve the glottal pulse shape, and thus the glottal flow phase spectrum, it is necessary to design an anticausal filter for this pole pair. The spectral model is then a Causal (spectral tilt) Anti-causal (glottal formant) Linear filter Model (CALM, Doval et al. 2003). This model is computed by filtering a pulse train by a causal second order system, according to the frequency and bandwidth of the glottal formant, whose response is reversed in time to obtain an anti-causal response. Note that if one wants to preserve the finite duration property of the glottal pulse, it is necessary to truncate the impulse response of the filter. Otherwise, the decay of the filter response may continue longer than a single period and get mixed with the next period. Spectral tilt is introduced by filtering this anti-causal response by the spectral tilt component of the model. The waveform is then normalized in order to control accurately the intensity parameter E. The CALM has been recently used successfully for real-time gesture-controlled voice synthesis (D'Alessandro et al., 2007).

3 Zero of the Z-Transform (ZZT) Representation of Speech [2]

3.1 Principle of the ZZT

ZZT is a new representation of signals. ZZT means Zeros of Z-Transform and is defined by the set of roots of the Z-transform of any signal frame. Mathematically speaking, if $x(n)$, $n=0...N-1$ is a signal frame, its ZZT is the set of N complex roots (or zeros) Z_m of its Z-transform X(z):

---

[2] The main references for this Section are: Bozkurt, 2005, Bozkurt, Doval, d'Alessandro, Dutoit, 2005, Sturmel, d'Alessandro, Doval, 2007.

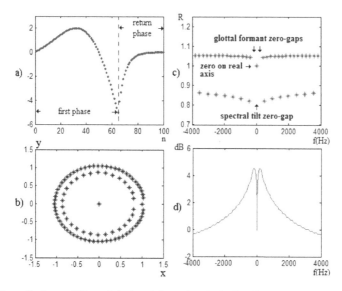

Fig. 9. ZZT, applied to a differential glottal flow signal. a) signal; d) corresponding magnitude spectrum; c) Zeros of the Z transform in Cartesian coordinates; b) Zeros of the Z transform in polar coordinates (from Bozkurt et al, 2005).

$$X(z) = \sum_{0}^{N-1} x(n) \, z^{-n} = x(0)z^{-N+1} \prod_{1}^{N-1} (z - Z_m) \tag{5}$$

The ZZT is then an all-zero representation of the Z-Transform. It can be represented on the complex plane either in the classical Cartesian coordinates (see Figure 9c) or in the more readable polar coordinates (see Figure 9b).

To compute the ZZT, an algorithm for polynomial root extraction is needed, like such as the "root" function in Matlab™, since it is known that there is no general closed-form expression to calculate the roots of a polynomial whose degree is larger than 5 from its coefficients (Galois' theorem).

3.2 ZZT and the Linear Speech Production Model

The ZZT and the source-filter model have strong relationships. The ZZT shows different patterns for each contribution of the source/filter model, and particularly for each part of the glottal flow signal; the speech signal is simply the union of the ZZT of each contribution. These results indicate that ZZT is well-suited for source/filter deconvolution, and especially for the study of the source parameters. Let us consider the LF GFM, with equations:

$$g(t) = E_0 e^{\alpha} \sin(\omega_g t), 0 \le t \le t_e \tag{6}$$

$$g(t) = -\frac{E_e}{\varepsilon_a} \left[e^{-\varepsilon(t-t_e)} - e^{-\varepsilon(t_c-t_e)} \right] t_e \le t \le t_c \le T_0 \tag{7}$$

$$g(t) = 0, t_c \leq t \leq T_0 \tag{8}$$

The corresponding ZZT patterns are displayed in Figure 9. Two rows of zeros are obtained, one for the causal part, and the other for the anticausal part. Gaps appear in each row, corresponding to the poles of the CALM model.

According to Equation 1, a voiced speech frame $s(n)$ can be written as the convolution product of an impulse train (excitation signal) $e(n)$ by the differential[*] glottal flow waveform $g(n)$ followed by the vocal tract filter with impulse response $v(n)$. As usual for source-filter model, the lip radiation contribution is approximated as a derivation and is incorporated into the source contribution as a differentiation. Therefore it is the differential glottal flow rather than the glottal flow itself which is represented. An example is given in Figure 10.

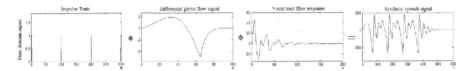

Fig. 10. A pictorial view of the speech production model of Equation 1 (from Bozkurt, 2005)

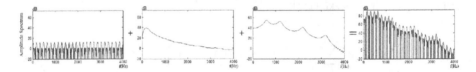

Fig. 11. A pictorial view of the speech production model of Equation 2 (from Bozkurt, 2005)

It is well known that the magnitude spectral representation (in dB) transforms the convolution into a sum :

$$\log(|S(v)|) = \log(|E(v)|) + \log(|V(v)|) + \log(|L(v)|) \tag{9}$$

For instance, this is the first step of cepstrum source/filter deconvolution. An example is given in Figure 11.

In contrast, the ZZT representation transforms the convolution into a union:

$$ZZT\{S\} = ZZT\{E\} \cup ZZT\{V\} \cup ZZT\{L\} \tag{10}$$

This can be clearly seen on Figure 12, where the sets of zeros of each contribution (left three plots) are simply "copy-pasted" in the speech signal ZZT (right plot).

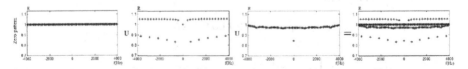

Fig. 12. A pictorial view of the speech production model in terms of ZZT (from Bozkurt, 2005)

Let us describe more precisely the different ZZT patterns encountered in each part of the source-filter model (like in Figure 12):

- For the impulse train (left plot), the ZZT pattern is a set of regularly spaced zeros on the unit circle, with a gap at each multiple of the fundamental frequency. Since the magnitude spectrum is the modulus of the Z-Transform taken on the unit circle, one can observe the effect of these zeros as spikes on the spectrum between the harmonics (Figure 11, left).
- For the differential glottal flow (left middle plot), the ZZT pattern is the union of a row of zeros lying outside the unit circle and of a row of zeros inside the circle. The outside row shows a gap between the zero which is on the real axis and the others. This corresponds to the glottal formant which can be seen as a local maximum in the low-frequency region on the spectrum representation (Figure 11, left middle plot). On the other hand, the zero gap on the inside row corresponds to the "spectral tilt" which can be seen as a global slope on the spectrum representation.
- For the vocal tract (right middle plot), the ZZT pattern is a row of zeros lying inside the unit circle. Gaps appear in this row, each one corresponding to a (vocal tract) formant.

Finally, the ZZT pattern of the speech signal (right plot) is the union of all the zeros that appear in each part of the source-filter model. This is the key to source/filter deconvolution using separation of the zeros into two subsets.

3.3 Source Parameter Estimation Using the ZZT

An interesting property of ZZT decomposition is that it can distinguish between the minimum and maximum phase parts of a signal. Note that the glottal formant is maximum phase: this can be seen on the group delay because the corresponding peak is negative, or on the ZZT because the corresponding zeros are outside the unit circle (Bozkurt et al., 2004), or on the CALM model where the corresponding poles are outside the unit circle. Since all other speech components are minimum phase (or causal), the outside zeros belong to the glottal flow component. Therefore they can be extracted to estimate the glottal flow component and the glottal formant frequency. Using this position, the open quotient can be deduced using the theory exposed in Section 2 (Henrich et al., 2001).

Figure 13 gives an example of open quotient estimation using ZZT. This example is a natural vowel changing from lax to pressed voice quality. It has been recorded together with the EGG signal in order to extract the open quotient Oq [3]. For a pressed voice, the open quotient is low. Figure 13 shows the estimated glottal formant frequency Fg, together with a curve proportional to $1/Oq$ (the value of k has been chosen to fit the first part of the Fg curve) and the fundamental frequency (which is

---

[3] The EGG signal is proportional to the electrical current across the vocal fold. When the glottis is open this current is relatively weak, conversely when the glottis is closed this current is relatively strong. The variation of the EGG current is more important at the GCI than at the opening instant. In the derivative of the EGG current, a large peak indicates the closing instant and a smaller peak indicates the opening instant (Henrich et al. 2004). Notice that these two peaks have opposite signs.

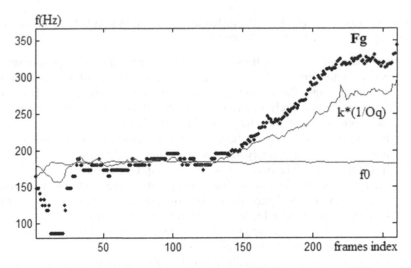

Fig. 13. Open quotient estimation using the ZZT (from Bozkurt, 2005)

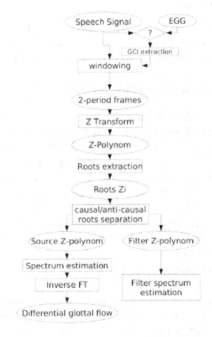

Fig. 14. Source-tract decomposition using ZZT (from Sturmel et al., 2007)

approximately constant). Fg follows well the curve in $1/Oq$, which shows that ZZT is a promising means of estimating Oq. Experiments on synthetic signals have shown that Fg can be estimated with good precision if it does not coincide with the first formant (Sturmel et al. 2006).

3.4 Source-Tract Deconvolution Using the ZZT and Comparative Evaluation with Inverse Filtering

Source-filter deconvolution using ZZT is explained in Figure 14 (Bozkurt et al. 2004, Sturmel et al. 2006). The principle is to compute the ZZT of a speech frame, to separate its zeros in two sets according to their radius, and then to compute two components from these sets of zeros. These two components correspond to the "source dominated" and "vocal tract dominated" signals.

According to ZZT theory, the zeros outside the unit circle correspond to the anticausal part of the speech signal. The source-filter model predicts that the anticausal part corresponds to the glottal formant. However, spectral tilt corresponds to a causal signal (a decreasing exponential in the time-domain). Then the ZZT decomposition method separates the glottal formant contribution from the vocal tract and spectral tilt contributions. Figure 15 shows an example of decomposition.

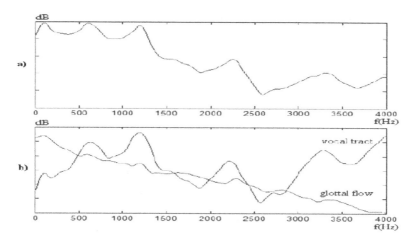

Fig. 15. Source tract decomposition using the ZZT (from Bozkurt, 2005)

The top plot shows the spectrum of a speech frame where formants can be seen at around 600Hz, 1200Hz, 2300Hz, 3300Hz and 4000Hz. The bottom plot shows the spectra of the two signals obtained from ZZT decomposition: one mainly corresponds to the vocal tract response showing the formants, the other corresponds to the glottal flow spectrum showing the glottal formant and a global spectral slope.

It must be pointed out that ZZT decomposition and inverse filtering are based on different principles. Inverse filtering requires the vocal tract filter identification, and is based on passing the speech signal through the inverse filter. Inverse filtering achieves source-filter decomposition mainly on the basis of properties of the filter. On the contrary, the ZZT representation is based on a very specific property of the source, i.e. its mixed-phase nature. Therefore, source tract decomposition using ZZT is not another inverse filtering method.

Four state-of-the-arts commonly used inverse filtering methods have been compared to ZZT for source filter separation (Sturmel et al., 2007). All methods are based on LP (Markel & Gray, 1976), the last one requiring additional processing steps. All these methods are well documented in the literature: (1) Linear prediction, autocorrelation method (unlike ZZT, Autocorrelation is an asynchronous method), (2) linear prediction, covariance (like ZZT, covariance LP is a pitch synchronous method); (3) Linear prediction, lattice filter (asynchronous method based on the Burg's algorithm, which ensures a stable lattice filter; this is an asynchronous method); (4) Iterative Adaptive Inverse Filtering (IAIF, asynchronous method; Alku, 1992).

As the source signal is unknown in natural speech, the evaluation procedure is mainly based on analyzing synthetic speech in a first part, and then on simultaneous recording of natural speech and electroglottographic signals (that give partial information on the voice source). The synthetic speech database contains a large number of test signals. Automatic procedures for comparisons of synthetic and estimated voice sources are also proposed.

More formal evaluation, with the help of a spectral distance were conducted, using a large number of experimental conditions

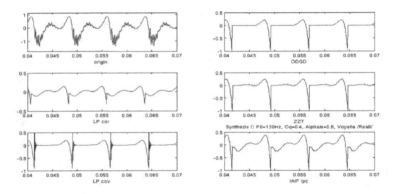

Fig. 16. Comparison of ZZT and LP inverse filtering for source-tract decomposition of a synthetic speech signal. Top Left, synthetic speech. Top right, synthetic differential glottal flow. Middle left, LP correlation, Middle right: ZZT; bottom left: LP covariance, bottom right IAIF (from Sturmel et al., 2007).

Source estimation examples are presented in figures 16 and 17. Figure 16 presents the estimated source waveforms for a synthetic speech signal /a/. Note that the original synthetic source is known, and can be compared directly to the estimated source waveforms. Figure 17 presents source estimations for a real speech signal. Both glottal flow and its derivative are shown for each method. An electroglottographic reference is available for this example, showing that the open quotient is about 0.5 (i.e. the closed phase of the source is about half of the period). In the example, the ZZT is the only method giving a closed phase of about 0.5.

Spectral distance results and visual inspection of the waveforms lead to the following conclusions:

   o   The pitch synchronous covariance linear prediction seems the worst differential glottal wave estimator. Since it is performed on a very short signal segment, the autoregressive filter order may probably be too small for accurate estimation of the vocal tract filter. Nevertheless, the overall low frequency restitution of the glottal formant seems realistic.

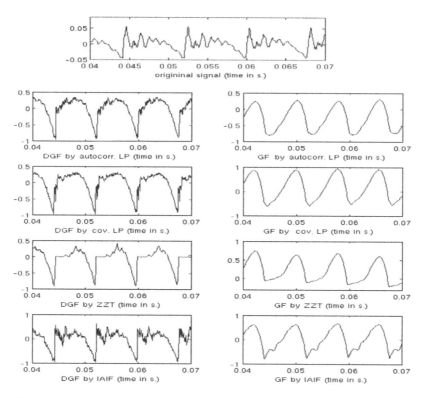

Fig. 17. Comparison of ZZT and LP inverse filtering for source-tract decomposition of a natural speech signal. Top center: natural speech (vowel /a/). Left column: estimated differential glottal flow. Right column: estimated glottal flow.

o — The IAIF method seems the most robust one tested in the sense that it gives good results in almost every case : the adaptive part of the algorithm appears to be useful for fitting even the most difficult signals. However noise and ripples on the estimated differential glottal waveform make it hardly suited to parameter extraction or analysis.

o — The auto-correlation linear prediction is surprisingly the best LP-based source estimation in this benchmark. However, tests on signals are using long analysis windows, exploiting the time invariance assumed by the method. This is not always realistic for actual time-varying real speech signals. Furthermore, we observed that the worst cases are those where the pre-emphasis does not completely suppress the glottal formant :low Oq values leading to a glottal formant at two or three times $F0$, and low values for αm leading to a more resonant formant.

o — The ZZT inverse filtering outperforms LP-based methods both in spectral measurements and time-domain observations. The absence of ripples in the glottal closed phase together with the very good benchmark results are the strongest arguments in favour of this method. On real signals, it is the only one to present a clearly visible closed phase on glottal flow waveforms (figure 17). The low error values achieved during benchmark make ZZT the best choice for glottal parameter estimation by model fitting. However, the method relies heavily on precise glottal closing instants determination, and it seems also relatively weak for low signal to noise ratio. Computational load is heavier than for LP based methods, because it is based on roots extraction from a high degree polynomial.

4 Lines of Maximum Amplitude of the Wavelet Transform[4]

4.1 Glottal Closing Instants for Soft and Strong Voices

In this section another aspect of the phase of the glottal source is explored. The periodicity of the voice source signal is defined by the positions in time of the GCI. In addition to periodicity, another important prosodic parameter is the degree of voicing (in the simplest form, a voiced/unvoiced decision). For speech synthesis, the GCI are needed in methods based on pitch period or pitch synchronous processing. The preceding discussions also pointed out that the GCI is important for determining the "anticausal" and the "causal" parts of the glottal source signals.

Glottal closings are often points of sharp variations, or singularities in the speech signal. This is particularly the case for abrupt glottal closings, when there is no additional spectral tilt component. In this situation, GCI are corresponding to a discontinuity in the glottal flow derivative, and methods for discontinuity detection would be desirable.

On the other hand, for soft voices with low vocal effort, the glottal closing instants do not correspond to well-marked discontinuities in the glottal flow derivative. The waveform is smooth, and the spectral tilt is large. The waveform resembles a sine wave. Then instead of searching for discontinuities in the signal, it seems more important to follow the signal instantaneous phase.

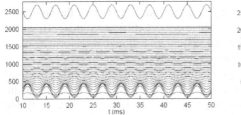 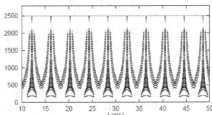

Fig. 18. Signal analysis using a non-uniform filterbank. Two extreme situations for glottal excitation signals (signal at the top of the Figures), and time-scale analysis. Left panel: sinusoidal excitation, without any singularity at glottal closing. Right panel: impulsive excitation.

The Wavelet Transform demonstrates excellent capabilities for detection of singularities in signals (Mallat & Wang, 1992). This feature has been applied to pitch detection (Kadambe and Boudreaux-Bartels, 1992). Their work is based on the dyadic

---

[4] The main references for this section are: Vu Ngoc Tuan & d'Alessandro, 1999, 2000.

wavelet transform of the speech signal. This transform is computed only for two or three small scales (high frequencies), typically 2^4, 2^5 and 2^6. Then, GCI are detected by locating the local maxima of the transform which are above a threshold level across two dyadic scales. This method works well when the speech signal contains singularities at glottal closing (Figure 18, right panel). This is not always the case, and the singularity detection is questionable for quasi-sinusoidal voice (Figure 18, left panel).

When voiced speech is seen using a non-uniform filterbank, characteristic tree-like patterns were obtained for voiced, as can be seen in Figure 18. Long lines pointing to the singularities are obtained for strong voices or signal containing singularities. On the contrary, only the first filters give a significant response to soft voice, or smooth signals. However both situations are actually encountered in speech. This is an indication that one could take advantage of the length of lines in the time-scale space for improving GCI detection.

A new algorithm for GCI detection with the help of the wavelet transform has been presented (Vu Ngoc Tuan & d'Alessandro 1999). Contrary to previous works, all the scales are actually used for analysis. Then, the high frequency features related to abrupt closures as well as low-pass quasi-sinusoidal speech signals of soft voices can be analyzed with accuracy. This is achieved by a new concepts, the lines of maximum amplitude (LOMA), which are linking amplitude maxima across scales in the wavelets transform domain.

4.2 Line of Maximum Amplitude of the Wavelet Transform

A wavelet filter-bank (6 band-pass filters centered on 4000, 2000, 1000, 500 250 and 125 Hz), with bandwidths proportional to center frequencies is used for signal decomposition. The purpose of the filter-bank is to detect the most important periodic peaks. Small peaks due to noise are present only in few high frequency (HF) filters, and are uncorrelated. On the contrary, large periodic peaks are likely to produce large amplitudes for filters at all scales. Lines of maximal amplitude (LOMA) are defined by following the amplitude maxima of the filter responses, starting at HF filters and ending at low frequency (LF) filters. The LOMA for voiced and unvoiced segments have rather different shapes. Unvoiced segments result in short HF lines. On the contrary, voiced segments are represented by long lines starting from HF filters and ending at the LF filters. For each voicing period, the LOMA are drawing a kind of tree pattern. The GCI for each period is associated to the position of the principal LOMA, taken in the highest filter. The analysis algorithm can be summarized as follows:

1. Compute a wavelet transform. The basic wavelet is chosen in such a way that the transform is equivalent to a zero-phase filter-bank. Each filter is a band-pass filter with a bandwidth proportional to its center frequency. The wavelet transform (WT) can be considered as the convolution between the signal and a dilated/compressed mother wavelet. Let x(t) be the speech signal, its WT $y_i(t)$ at scale i is given by:

$$y_i(t) = x(t) * h(\frac{t}{S_i}) \qquad (11)$$

The mother wavelet is a band-pass impulse response in the form:

$$h(t) = -\cos(2\pi f_0 t)\exp(-\frac{t^2}{2\tau^2}) \tag{12}$$

Note the minus sign in the cosine. Then the wavelet analysis will have a maximum response to negative peaks. The filters impulse responses are not causal, because this is a zero-phase filter-bank. Thus, the signal and its response are in phase, and the phase of the signal can be read in the phases of the filters, at each scale. The filters frequency responses are displayed in Figure 19.

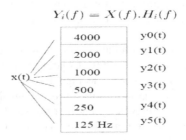

Filterbank

$$Y_i(f) = X(f).H_i(f)$$

4000	y0(t)
2000	y1(t)
1000	y2(t)
500	y3(t)
250	y4(t)
125 Hz	y5(t)

x(t)

Filter Transfert Function

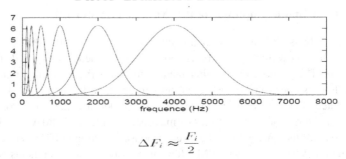

$$\Delta F_i \approx \frac{F_i}{2}$$

Fig. 19. Wavelet filterbank

The frequency response of the mother wavelet is:

$$H(\nu) = |H(\nu)| = \frac{\tau}{\sqrt{1 + (2\pi(\nu - f_0)\tau)^2}} \tag{13}$$

2. Signals at the output of these filters have local maxima (see Figure 21). These maxima are tracked across scales, starting from the highest frequency (HF=4000 Hz) towards the lowest frequencies (BF=125 Hz). Several LOMA are starting from the highest filter in a period (the number of LOMA at a given scale is roughly equal to the center frequency of this scale). However, all these lines are joined together at a unique instant in the lowest filter, for each voicing period, as there is one LOMA "tree" per period. Thus, one can gather these lines into groups, with only one group per period of voiced

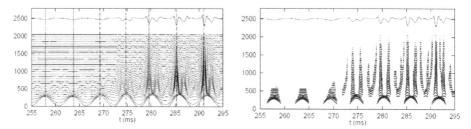

Fig. 20. Filterbank output (right panel: positive amplitudes only) for a consonant-vowel transition. More filters are used for the sake of display (from Vu Ngoc Tuan & d'Alessandro, 1999).

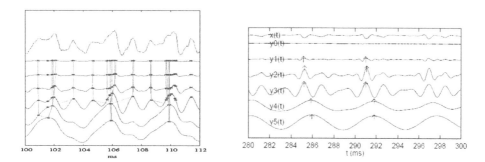

Fig. 21. Lines of Maximum Amplitude across scales. All the lines are displayed in the left panel. In the right panel, the optimal line for each period are shown.

signal. In each group, the strength of each LOMA is computed by adding all the amplitudes along the lines. Optimal selection of maxima across scale is achieved using a dynamic programming algorithm. Then the set of optimal LOMA for a period is computed.

3. The line with the highest cumulated amplitude is then chosen for representing the period. The GCI is then computed as the instant where the selected line starts at the smallest scale (highest frequency) (see Figure 21, right panel).

4.3 Comparison with Electroglottography

For GCI detection algorithm evaluation, a reference is needed. The electroglottographic (EGG) reference is chosen, because it is an accurate and non-invasive GCI measurement method. A database of speech including various productions like vocal fry, modal and falsetto voices, spontaneous and read speech, male and female voices, has been recorded.

Most of the GCI peaks in the EGG derivative signal are well-defined, but some of them are too close: the time interval between two successive peaks is shorter than the period of the highest possible fundamental frequency. So we developed a simple algorithm for selection of the most prominent peaks that represent GCI. The EGG signal and the EGG derivative signal are represented in Figure 22.

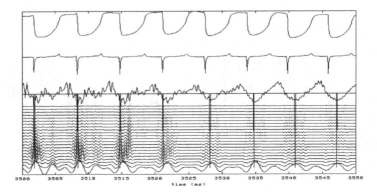

Fig. 22. Simultaneous EGG and acoustic signals analyses. EGG and DEGG (top panels), acoustic signal (middle panel), and response of the wavelet filterbank (from Vu Ngoc Tuan & d'Alessandro, 2000).

For experiments, the speech signal is sampled, and discrete-time signals are analyzed. Then the GCI cannot be determined with accuracy greater than the sampling period, and there is a slight difference between the discrete-time signal maximum and the corresponding continuous-time signal maximum. To increase time-domain accuracy, parabolic interpolation is used. Near a GCI, a parabola passing by this maximum and two adjacent points is computed. The GCI is taken at the parabola maximum. Parabolic interpolation is applied to both methods.

Acoustic signals were recorded in a sound-proof room, using a condenser microphone (Brüel & Kjær 4165) placed at 50 cm from the speaker's mouth, a preamplifier (Brüel & Kjær 2669) and a conditioning amplifier (Brüel & Kjær NEXUS 2690). EGG signals were recorded simultaneously, using a two-channel electroglottograph (EG2). The data were digitally recorded (one channel for the acoustic signal and the other one for the EGG signal). Four subjects have been recorded (two males and two females).The speakers were asked to read 3 short stories, with normal voices, then with a high pitch using falsetto, and then with a very low pitch using vocal fry. Sustained vowels and spontaneous speech (an informal conversation on daily life matters) were also recorded.

The data-base has been analyzed using both algorithms. The GCI obtained with the DEGG signals are taken as reference measures. As a matter of fact, visual inspection shows that this is true in almost all cases: when a pitch period (or a vocal pulse in case of vocal fry) is visible on the speech signal, then there is a peak in the DEGG signal.

The GCI obtained in the speech signal are delayed from the DEGG peaks, mainly because of the sound propagation time. This delay depends on the distance between the lips and the microphone, on the vocal tract group delay and on the electronic delay of the measurement apparatus. The delay is almost constant for each recording (except for the time-varying vocal tract group delay). For comparing the GCI detected by the two algorithms, the DEGG and speech analyses must be resynchronized by delaying the DEGG. This is achieved by the following procedure:

1. The DEGG signal is delayed by Td ms.
2. GCI are detected using DEGG.
3. GCI are detected using LOMA.

4. The mean difference between both sets of GCI is computed (Dm)
5. The procedure is repeated, varying Td.

The optimal delay Do between the DEGG and the speech signal is obtained for the value of Td corresponding to minimum Dm. The results of this analysis are summarized in Table 1 for 8 sustained vowels:

Table 1. Comparison of GCI detection using the EGG and LOMA (from Vu Ngoc Tuan & d'Alessandro, 2000)

Tr (s)	Do (ms)	Dm (ms)	N Degg	% diff	N Speech
1.3	0.4	-0.039	206	1.9	210
2.5	2.2	0.011	349	O.8	346
1.8	1.4	0.012	175	0.5	176
3.0	3.2	-0.003	474	1.2	480
1.8	0.6	-0.038	380	0.2	379
1.5	0.1	-0.010	282	7.8	306
3.0	1.8	-0.132	517	2.1	506
2.3	0.2	-0.010	599	34.0	908

Where Tr represents the sentence duration, Ndegg is the number of GCIs detected on the DEGG signal, Nspeech is the number of GCIs detected using wavelets, and %diff the percentage of difference between the two measures.

Except for the last example Ndegg and Nspeech are generally very close. In the last example, in many cases the second harmonic (octave) is much stronger than the first harmonic (fundamental frequency). In this situation, the wavelet algorithm tends to detect two peaks for each voicing period, instead of only one. When fundamental frequency is known (which is actually the case), these extra peaks are removed by a simple post-processing procedure. After this procedure the mean value of Dm is -0.028 ms (standard deviation 0.3 ms). This indicates that the LOMA method correctly detects the GCI, when peaks due to the second harmonic are removed by post processing.

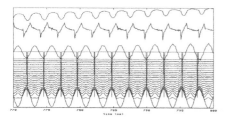 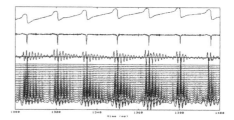

Fig. 23. Examples of EGG and wavelet GCI detection. Left panel: soft voice, "head" register, female voice, right panel, "chest" register, male voice (from Vu Ngoc Tuan & d'Alessandro, 2000).

Figure 23 is presents short segments extracted from sentences in the data-base. All the figures are presented in the same way, from top to bottom: EGG signal, DEGG signal, speech signal, wavelet filter-bank output, with a line indicating the position of the GCI detected using LOMA. The right panel Figure 23 shows a male voice, in modal register (which is the normal register for this speaker). The algorithm takes advantage of small scales (high frequencies) for accurate GCI detection. Figure 23 shows another female speaker, using her normal ("head") voice register. In Figure 23 (left), GCI detection takes advantage of large scales (low-pass frequencies).

4.4 LOMA and Glottal Flow Parameters

In general, the LOMA are not straight lines. Figure 24 shows 7-bands decomposition for a (derivative) glottal flow with open quotient 0.8 (left panel) and 0.3 (right panel). LOMA differ between these two conditions, and then glottal flow parameter analysis using LOMA should in principle be possible. It is straightforward to obtain a first parameter: amplitude of voicing. Amplitude of voicing is computed using the energy carried by the best LOMA of each tree. When the signal is unvoiced, the lines carry very little energy: this is because in this situation, amplitude maxima are not well-organized in the time-scale space, and no strong and long lines are likely to occur. The energy is spread in a wide tree, with no strong trunk and many small branches. On the contrary, the best LOMA (i.e. the strongest trunk) corresponding to a period of voicing carries a large amount of the signal energy. The voiced/unvoiced decision can be carried out by using a simple threshold on the amplitude carried by the trunk of each tree. This simple measure is surprisingly robust.

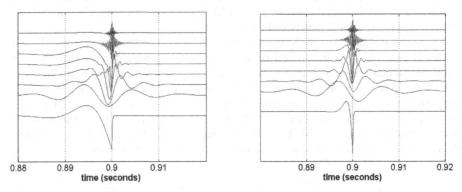

Fig. 24. Analysis of glottal pulses with different open quotients (left panel: Oq=0.8, right panel, Oq=0.3)

In future work, LOMA will be used to investigate the shape of speech signal periods, particularly near GCI. It is well known that the shape of glottal closing is a strong correlate of spectral tilt and is important for studying voice quality. LOMA will also be used for speech signal modification (e.g. time and pitch scaling).

5 Conclusions

In this article recent work by the authors on voice source analysis and synthesis using methods based on the spectral phase or instantaneous phase are presented. The main results obtained are the following:

- detailed and careful consideration of the glottal flow shows that glottal flow models can be represented by causal-anticausal (mixed phase) filters
- the link between time-domain and spectral domain parameters can be worked out, equations are available for most time domain glottal flow models
- a new glottal model in the spectral domain is proposed for speech synthesis (Causal-Anticausal Linear Model, or CALM).
- Taking advantage of the mixed-phase nature of glottal flow models, a new speech representation method is proposed, the Zero of the Z Transform (ZZT). Speech analysis and synthesis using the ZZT is achieved using a simple (although computationally heavy) algorithm.
- Comparison of the ZZT and inverse filtering for source-tract decomposition indicates better performances for the ZZT, in terms of waveform and spectral distance.
- The ZZT is also useful for estimation of open quotient and asymmetry coefficient of the voice source
- Glottal closing instants correspond to specific patterns of instantaneous phases and amplitudes in the time-scale domain. These patterns can be analyzed in terms of lines of maximum amplitude (LOMA) across scales. LOMA are also providing information on the energy of the corresponding speech periods, and may be useful for further analysis of the glottal waveforms properties.
- A comparison of glottal closing detection using LOMA and EGG shows that the method performs reasonably well

References

1. Alku, P.: Glottal wave analysis with pitch synchronous iterative adaptive inverse filtering. Speech Communication 11, 109–118 (1992)
2. Alku, P., Bäckström, T., Vilkman, E.: Normalized amplitude quotient for parametrization of the glottal flow. J. Acous. Soc. Am. 112(2), 701–710 (2002)
3. Alsteris, L.D., Paliwal, K.K.: Short-time phase spectrum in speech processing: A review and some experimental results. Digital Signal Processing 17, 578–616 (2007)
4. Bozkurt, B., Doval, B., d'Alessandro, C., Dutoit, T.: Improved differential phase spectrum processing for formant tracking. In: Interspeech 2004-ICSLP. 8th International Conference on Spoken Language Processing, Jeju Island, Korea, October 4-8, 2004, 4 pages (2004)
5. Bozkurt, B., Doval, B., d'Alessandro, C., Dutoit, T.: Appropriate windowing for group delay analysis and roots of z-transform of speech signals. In: EUSIPCO 2004. 12th European Signal Processing Conference, EURASIP, Vienna, Austria, September 6-10, 2004, 4 pages (2004)

6. Bozkurt, B., Doval, B., d'Alessandro, C., Dutoit, T.: A method for glottal formant frequency estimation. In: Interspeech 2004-ICSLP. 8th International Conference on Spoken Language Processing, Jeju Island, Korea, October 4-8, 2004, 4 pages (2004)

7. Bozkurt, B., Doval, B., d'Alessandro, C., Dutoit, T.: Zeros of Z-Transform (ZZT) decomposition of speech for source-tract separation. In: Interspeech 2004-ICSLP. 8th International Conference on Spoken Language Processing, Jeju Island, Korea, October 4-8, 2004, 5 pages (2004)

8. Bozkurt, B.: Zeros of z-transform(ZZT) representation and chirp group delay processing for analysis of source and filter characteristics of speech signals, PhD Thesis, Université Polytechnique de Mons, Belgium and LIMSI-CNRS, France (October 2005)

9. Bozkurt, B., Doval, B., d'Alessandro, C., Dutoit, T.: Zeros of Z-transform representation with application to source-filter separation in speech. IEEE Signal Processing Letters 12(4), 344–347 (2005)

10. Childers, D.G., Lee, C.K.: Voice quality factors: analysis, synthesis and perception. J. Acoust. Soc. Am. 90(5), 2394–2410 (1991)

11. d'Alessandro, N., Doval, B., Le Beux, S., Woodruff, P., Fabre, Y., d'Alessandro, C., Dutoit, T.: Realtime and Accurate Musical Control of Expression in Singing Synthesis. Journal on Multimodal User Interfaces 1(1), 31–39 (2007)

12. Doval, B., d'Alessandro, C., Henrich, N.: The voice source as a causal/anticausal linear filter. In: Proc. Voqual 2003. Voice Quality: Functions, analysis and synthesis, ISCA workshop, Geneva, Switzerland, pp. 15–20 (August 2003B)

13. Doval, C.D., Henrich, N.: The spectrum of glottal flow models. Acustica united with Acta Acustica 92, 1026–1046 (2006)

14. Fant, G.: Acoustic theory of speech production, Mouton De Gruyter, Revised edn. (January 1970)

15. Fant, G., Liljencrants, J., Lin, Q.: A four-parameter model of glottal flow. STL-QPSR 4, 1–13 (1985)

16. Hanson, H.M.: Glottal characteristics of female speakers: Acoustic correlates. J. Acous. Soc. Am. 101, 466–481 (1997)

17. Henrich, N., d'Alessandro, C., Doval, B.: Spectral correlates of voice open quotient and glottal flow asymmetry: theory, limits and experimental data. In: Eurospeech 2001, Aalborg, Denmark (September 2001)

18. Henrich, N., d'Alessandro, C., Castellengo, M., Doval, B.: On the use of the derivative of electroglottographic signals for characterization of nonpathological phonation. J. Acoust. Soc. Amer. 115(3), 1321–1332 (2004)

19. Kadambe, S., Boudreaux-Bartels, G.F.: Application of the wavelet transform for pitch detection of speech signals. IEEE trans. on IT 38(2), 917–924D (1992)

20. Klatt, D., Klatt, L.: Analysis, synthesis, and perception of voice quality variations among female and male talkers. J. Acous. Soc. Am. 87(2), 820–857 (1990)

21. Mallat, S., Hwang, W.L.: Singularity detection and processing with wavelets. IEEE trans. on IT 38(2), 617–943 (1992)

22. Markel, J.D., Gray Jr., A.H.: Linear Prediction of Speech. Springer, Berlin (1976)

23. Rosenberg, E.: Effect of glottal pulse shape on the quality of natural vowels. J. Acous. Soc. Am. 49, 583–590 (1971)

24. Sturmel, N., d'Alessandro, C., Doval, B.: A spectral method for estimation of the voice speed quotient and evaluation using electroglottography. In: 7th Conference on Advances in Quantitative Laryngology, Groningen, The Netherlands, October 6-7, 2006 (2006)

25. Sturmel, N., d'Alessandro, C., Doval, B.: A comparative evaluation of the Zeros of Z Transform representation for voice source estimation. In: Proceedings of Interspeech 2007, Antwerp, Belgium (August 27-31, 2007)
26. Veldhuis, R.: A computationally efficient alternative for the Liljencrants-Fant model and its perceptual evaluation. J. Acous. Soc. Am. 103, 566–571 (1998)
27. Tuan, V.N., d'Alessandro, C.: Robust Glottal closing Detection using the Wavelet Transform. In: Proceedings of Eurospeech 1999 Budapest, Hungary, vol. 6, pp. 2805–2808 (1999)
28. Tuan, V.N., d'Alessandro, C.: Glottal closing Detection using EGG and the Wavelet Transform. In: Advances in Quantitative Laryngoscopy, Voice and Speech Research Proceedings of the 4th International Workshop, Jena, Germany, pp. 147–154 (2000)
29. Yegnanarayana, B., Murthy, H.A.: Significance of group delay functions in spectrum estimation. IEEE Trans. Signal Process. 40(9) (1992)

Some Experiments in Audio-Visual Speech Processing

G. Chollet[1], R. Landais[1], T. Hueber[1,2], H. Bredin[1], C. Mokbel[4], P. Perrot[1,3], and L. Zouari[1]

[1] CNRS LTCI/TSI Paris, 46 rue Barrault, 75634 Paris Cedex 13 - France
[2] Laboratoire d'Electronique - ESPCI - 10 rue Vauquelin - 75005 Paris - France
[3] Institut de Recherche Criminelle de la Gendarmerie Nationale (IRCGN), 93110, Rosny sous bois, France
[4] University of Balamand, Po Box 100, Tripoli, Lebanon

Abstract. Natural speech is produced by the vocal organs of a particular talker. The acoustic features of the speech signal must therefore be correlated with the movements of the articulators (lips, jaw, tongue, velum,...). For instance, hearing impaired people (and not only them) improve their understanding of speech by lip reading. This chapter is an overview of audiovisual speech processing with emphasis on some experiments concerning recognition, speaker verification, indexing and corpus based synthesis from tongue and lips movements.

1 Introduction

A talking face is more intelligible, expressive, recognisable, attractive than acoustic speech alone. Natural speech is produced by the vocal organs of a particular talker. The acoustic features of the speech signal must therefore be correlated with the movements of the articulators (lips, jaw, tongue, velum,...). For instance, hearing impaired people (and most of us) improve their understanding of speech by lip reading. Lip reading also increases understanding in adverse environment. All these reasons motivate the research done on audiovisual speech processing.

This chapter is an overview of audio-visual speech processing. The combined use of facial and speech information improves speech recognition, identity verification and robustness to forgeries. Multi-stream models of the synchrony of visual and acoustic information have applications in the analysis, coding, recognition and synthesis of talking faces. SmartPhones, VisioPhones, WebPhones, SecurePhones, Visio-Conferences, Virtual Reality worlds are gaining popularity. This defines several applications of audiovisual speech processing, e.g:

- Audio-Visual speech recognition : Automatic lip-reading to help understanding in adverse environment like a cocktail party, ...
- Audio-Visual speaker verification : Detection of forgeries
- Speech driven animation of the face : Could we look and sound like somebody else ?

M. Chetouani et al. (Eds.): NOLISP 2007, LNAI 4885, pp. 28–56, 2007.

– Speaker indexing : Who is talking in a video sequence ?
– OUISPER : a silent speech interface : Corpus based synthesis from tongue and lips movements

This chapter reviews some of the signal processing techniques which have been developped and experimented for these applications. It is organised as follows : features extraction techniques, for face and speech are first analysed, followed by an overview of modelling and classification techniques. It is shown within this chapter how similar techniques may be used in the framework of five different applications. The experimental results of these applications are detailed and finally, conclusions and perspectives are given.

2   Features Extraction

Audiovisual applications analyse video data and take benefit from information extracted from the two available signals: the audio and the visual signals. Features extraction from these two signals is the preliminary step to any further analysis. The most common features used in the five applications mentionned previously are detailed here. Apart from the description of the features, this section also addresses issues related to temporal and spatial segmentation, to the sampling of signals and to the dimension of features vectors.

2.1   Temporal Segmentation

One of the main difference between the audio and the visual signal extracted from a video stream is the temporal sampling : while the visual stream is divided into frames which could be directly handled, audio samples are generally grouped together to form larger units which allow to extract reliable features. Audio samples can be grouped using a sliding analyis window (e.g of 10ms). This window moves over the signal (overlapping may be allowed) and each position leads to the extraction of relevant audio features to characterize the temporal segment attached to the window.

As speech oriented applications are considered, the basic signal unit is the phone (or a subword based unit as speech synthesis is concerned). Phonetic segmentation is generally performed in the same time as their recognition. For example, phones are modeled into three to five states within a Hidden Markov Models (HMM) framework, and the features extracted from a sliding window are used as observations to estimate the current state. Whenever the signal leaves the last state of a given phone, a phonetic temporal boundary is added. More details are further given concerning HMM and speech recognition in section 4.2.

Whenever phonetic modeling is adopted, all or a part of speech training databases must be manually segmented into phones. Unfortunately, such a manual phonetic segmentation of the speech signal is difficult and time consuming. For applications where text output is not needed, an alternative segmental decomposition of speech, called ALISP (Automatic Language Independant Speech

Processing techniques), has been introduced in [1]. This decomposition is computed in three main steps. First, speech signal is decomposed into variable length units using the temporal decomposition algorithm described in [2]. This algorithm is based on the detection of quasi-stationary segments in the parametric representation of the signal. Then, unit classes are built by gathering together acoustically similar speech segments using an unsupervised vector quantization algorithm [3].

This decomposition is driven only by the data and is independent from the language and from the text, but correspondence of ALISP segmentation with phonetic transcriptions has been studied [4]. A consistent mapping was found, which was however far from a one to one correspondence. Applications using the ALISP segmentation are discussed later.

2.2   Managing Sampling Rates and Alignement

Two issues arise when first comparing an audio stream with a visual one: the difference in sampling rates and the alignement. Concerning sample rates, any easy solution to recover a common sampling rate is to choose for a reference which may be the audio rate or the visual one. In the first case, the visual signal must be over sampled. For instance, if a sliding window of 10ms is considered to produce audio observations while video frames are observed every 40 ms, interpolation must be provided to produce "new" visual features leading to the same number of frames per second (cf 4.2, 4.3).

Another problem is alignement. Audio and visual streams may not be synchronised at a particular time due to co-articulation effects and articulator inertia. In fact, the articulators sometimes move in anticipation of a phonetic event before the phone is produced. In these cases, the visual information may be available before the acoustic evidence. Many methods for modelling audio-visual asynchrony have been proposed and are detailed in section 3.

2.3   Spatial Segmentation

Prior to any feature computation stage, video frames are usually spatially segmented in order to focus on particular regions of interest. Applications reported in this chapter mainly deal with speech processing. Most of these regions of interest are therefore related to faces; that is either faces or face features like eyes or lips.

In most of the cases, face features are localized within a face area which has been previously determined. A complete survey about face detection may be found in [5].

Two face detection systems have been experimented. The first one, the Viola and Jones algorithm [6], may be qualified as a "classical" one, considering that its use is widely spread over the community. It is based on the estimation of a "strong" classifier composed of a cascade of many weak classifiers, each of these weak classifiers being attached to a particular Haar feature. A stage of learning is thus required to produce this "strong" classifier. The nature of the data included in the learning base then influences the type of faces which can be correctly detected afterwards. As a consequence, different cascades must be learnt to allow the detection of faces under different orientations. Typically, a cascade is dedicated to frontal faces detection and another one to profile faces detection. This system has been used in the framework of the VMike project concerning audiovisual speech recognition (cf section 4.2). Faces are first extracted thanks to a frontal cascade. A *mouth* cascade (that is to say a classifier which has been learnt over a database containing samples of mouth), is applied on the lower part of the detected face.

The second system may be considered as a probabilistic equivalent of the Viola and Jones method [7]. While this system still relies on the estimation of a strong classifier, the difference is that the underlying classifier function is then used to estimate the distribution of the object of interest (faces in our case), that is to model the generation of such objects within images (such a model is called a *"generative model"*). As this distribution is computed, many partitions of the input images are considered and the patches they are composed of are assigned a label (*"object of interest"* versus *"background"*) depending on the estimation of likelihoods. As for the Viola and Jones method, any object may be considered. A two stage process then allows to detect faces and eyes within faces.

This algorithm has been applied prior to features extraction within the framework of asynchrony detection 4.3 and within the framework of face verification. Concerning the asynchrony detection application, eyes position allows to determine a region of interest where to look for the mouth knowing the geometrical structure of the human face. Then, the actual mouth detection step is performed using a *Viola and Jones* detector [6]: it was developped by *Castrillón et al.* [8] and is freely available on the internet for download.

A different kind of face features is used on ultrasound images within the framework of the OUISPER project (section 4.4). In that context, objects of interest are the lips, the jaws and the tongue. A classical approach to characterize such local objects is to extract their contours using automatic methods.

Fully automatic methods use classical edge-detection method, basically Canny's one or its variations to segment an object in the image. Such methods are easy to use and require no a priori knowledge on the object shape. However, non relevant contours could also be extracted and a post-processing is often needed to remove them. Furthermore, the parametrization of extracted contour is a difficult task. Active contours (also known as Snakes), introduced by Kass [9], are semi-automatic methods to track edges in image sequences. They are based on the assumption that the edge is smooth and that the object is well contrasted with respect to the background. Here, the contour is initialized manually and its motion is driven by the image data, minimizing a potential, which can embed a priori knowledge on the object shape and on its motion. In order to track an object in sequence, the contour found in the current frame can be used to initialize the contour in the next frame.

2.4   Faces Normalization and Selection

Once eyes position is obtained within a face, a geometrical normalization is performed in order to make the line between the eyes horizontal. Then, a mask

Fig. 1. Face detection and normalization

is applied in order to remove artifacts that might appear at the border of the face. Finally, image pixels are normalized by histogram equalization. Figure 1 shows an example on a face from the BANCA database (see section 4.1).

Given that the rotation of the face, its (partial) occlusion or bad lightning conditions can lead to a poor quality detected face whose features are not representative of the person, a method has been designed to keep only the *best* faces. This selection is obtained by removing all detection results that might lead to degraded results regarding the aimed application (e.g: authentication). For each frame f of the video, a reliability score $r(f)$ is computed as the inverse of the euclidean distance between the detected face and its projection into the *eigenface* space (see figure 2).

Consequently, a threshold is applied on $r(f)$ in order to keep only the *best* faces within the video sequences:

$$\text{Face } f \text{ is selected if and only if } r(f) > \alpha \cdot \max_{f' \in N_f} r(f') . \qquad (1)$$

where N_f is the set of all faces detected in the video sequence. $\alpha = \frac{2}{3}$ has been used in our experiments. Only the selected faces are then used for authentication. Figure 3 shows an example of the application of this method.

2.5   Audio Features

Most speech recognition and speaker verification systems use short-term cepstral features. The two most popular sets of features are cepstrum coefficients obtained with a Mel-frequency cepstrum coefficient (MFCC) [10] analysis and the ones whose computation relies on a perceptual linear predictive (PLP) [11] analysis. In both cases, a short-term power spectrum is estimated on a fixed frame (20-30 milliseconds), with the most used frame rate being 100 hz.

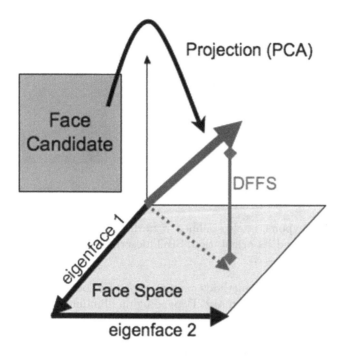

Fig. 2. Reliability based on the distance from face space

To get MFCC coefficients, a cosine transform is applied to the log power spectrum. A root-linear prediction cepstral coefficient (LPCC) analysis is used to obtain the PLP cepstrum parameters.

2.6   Visual Features

A difference must be made between **local** features which are attached to a particular set of points within the region of interest that must be characterized ; and **global** which produce a new representation of the region of interest treating it as a whole. Both features are detailed thereafter.

Local features. *SIFT* (Scale Invariant Feature Transform) descriptors [12] are known to be among the best local descriptors [13]. Their extraction can be coarsely summarized into three stages: extraction of keypoint candidates, filtering and descriptors calculation.

Keypoint candidates extraction relies on the scale-space theoretical background [14,15]. Once these candidates are extracted, their location is refined and their scale is determined. Keypoints are then filtered according to some constraints on contrast and geometrical properties (ratio of principal curvatures). Each remaining keypoint is finally represented by a 128 dimensional vector by computing gradient orientation and magnitude over its neighbourhood and by quantizing values spatially (reducing to a 4x4 array) and regarding orientation

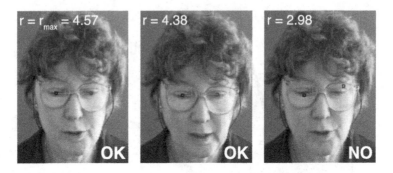

Fig. 3. Face with maximum r (left), selected (center) and rejected face (right)

(8 bins). Each keypoint is also defined regarding three other data: its spatial location, its scale and its orientation. SIFT descriptors have been used for face verification (cf section 4.3).

Global features. Local methods require a precise localization of particular points within the region of interest. Depending on illumination, occlusions, such a localization may not be easily obtained. Global methods then allow to overcome this drawback.

The first kind of global features rely on the *Discrete Cosine Transformation* (DCT) which are used for asynchrony detection (cf section 4.3) and audiovisual speech recognition (cf section 4.2). Their extraction is illustrated in figure 4.

Only the 28 coefficients corresponding to the low spatial frequency are kept, as shown in figure 5.

The *eigenfaces* method [16] may also be used to code the relevant information in the region of interest. The main principle is to project face images (viewed as intensity vectors) in a space where data scattering is maximized. Such a space is obtained by applying Principal Component Analysis (PCA) over a training set composed of numerous face images. Its direction vectors are called *eigenfaces* as they refer to eigenvectors of the training data covariance matrix.

Such a method may easily be extended to any visual object given that enough learning data are available. It has thus been applied to lips (*eigenlips) and tongues (*eigentongues) within the framework of our experiments concerning audiovisual speech recognition (OUISPER project).

The control points of the optimal snake are good features of the object edges.

2.7   Audiovisual Features and Decision Fusion

Each of the audiovisual applications detailed in the next sections are related to an underlying decision process: transcribing speech, deciding whether a person claiming he/she is person λ is effectively λ, deciding whether an audio stream is synchronised with the visual one, etc. All these decision processes may take benefit from considering in the same time audio features vectors and visual ones.

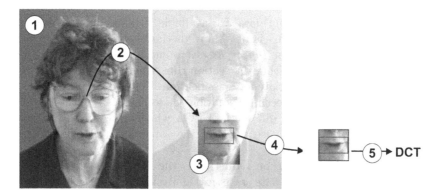

Fig. 4. Visual speech features extraction. 1– Eyes detection. 2– Selection of the region of interest where to look for the mouth. 3– Mouth detection. 4-5– DCT coefficients computation.

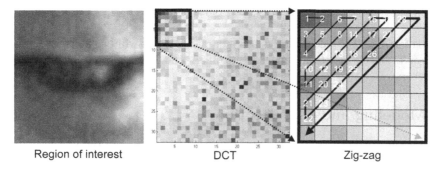

Fig. 5. Visual speech features extraction. 28 low spatial frequency DCT coefficients are extracted, in a zigzag manner.

Two main approaches may then be adopted. The first one is called *early fusion* and is based on the computation of audiovisual features vectors from audio and visual features vectors (for instance concatenation). The second one is called *late fusion* and relies on the fusion at the decision level. Many different methods may be applied to combine the outputs of all the classifiers used in the modeling process [17]: majority voting, max, min, sum, ... We will also mention here the use of Support Vector Machines *SVMs* to perform fusion at the score level (e.g for audiovisual identity verification involving scores given by each modality.

Early and late fusion methods have been experimented within the framework of several audiovisual applications and are detailed thereafter.

2.8   Dimension Reduction

The size of the learning databases required to compute models is a function of the dimension of the feature vectors chosen to represent audio segments/visual regions. As a consequence, handling high dimensional feature vectors may be difficult if not enough learning data are available. Dimension reduction may then be used to overcome this issue. Many methods are available: *Principal Component Analysis* (PCA) or *Linear Discriminant Analysis* (LDA), ... PCA has already been presented within the section concerning *eigenfaces*.

LDA is much more appropriate for classification. Typically, its properties are interesting for audiovisual speech recognition (cf section 4.2) since classes are then known (phones). On the difference of PCA which tends only to maximize intra-classes scattering, LDA also tends in the same time to minimize inter-classes scattering.

Another method for dimension reduction is the *Co-Inertia Analysis* (CoIA [18]). This method is a multivariate statistical analysis that aims at jointly transforming two signal (the acoustic and the visual one when performing audiovisual synchrony analysis) in order to maximise their covariance. Denoting $X \in \mathbb{R}^n$ and $Y \in \mathbb{R}^m$ the acoustic and visual features vectors, CoIA can be summarized by the following equation (**a** and **b** are column vectors of **A** and **B** optimal projection matrices):

$$(\mathbf{a}, \mathbf{b}) = \underset{(\mathbf{a} \in \mathbb{R}^n, \mathbf{b} \in \mathbb{R}^m)}{\operatorname{argmax}} \operatorname{cov}\left(\mathbf{a}^t \cdot X, \mathbf{b}^t \cdot Y\right) \tag{2}$$

Details for **A** and **B** calculation can be found in [18]. It will be shown in section 4.3 how to derive synchrony measures from **A** and **B** matrices using their first K vectors.

3   Modeling and Classification

Once features vectors have been extracted from the audio and the video stream, a modeling stage is applied to compute representations which will be used to make the final decision. Most of the time these models are statistics. For instance, *Gaussian Mixture Models* model the distribution of observation vectors as a combination of gaussian distributions. These models may be used for modeling phones observation distribution, as the speech of a given speaker (see sections 4.2,4.3). *Hidden Markov Models* (HMMs) then allow to model a statistical process involving different states.

These models are at the heart of many audiovisual applications and are detailed in this section.

3.1   Gaussian Mixture Models

As already mentionned, GMM distribution is a mixture whose components are classical Gaussian distributions. This results in the following form for the GMM distribution:

$$p(\underline{X}) = \sum_{k=1}^{K} w_k N_k(\underline{X}, \underline{\mu}_k, \underline{\underline{\Gamma}}_k) = \sum_{k=1}^{K} w_k (2\pi)^{-p/2} \left\| \underline{\underline{\Gamma}}_k \right\|^{-1/2} e^{-\frac{1}{2}(\underline{X}-\underline{\mu}_k)^T \underline{\underline{\Gamma}}_k^{-1} (\underline{X}-\underline{\mu}_k)}$$

$$\tag{3}$$

where K, $\underline{X}$, w_k, $\underline{\mu}_k$, $\underline{\Gamma}_k$ are respectively the number of components in the GMM, the speech feature vector, the weight of the kth component in the mixture (i.e. its probability of appearance), the mean vector and the covariance matrix of this k^{th} Gaussian component. Given a GMM to model the speech, a sequence of T speech feature vectors will have the following likelihood:

$$p(\underline{X}_1, ..., \underline{X}_T) = \prod_{T}^{t=1} p(\underline{X}_t) \qquad (4)$$

This supposes that the speech feature vectors are independent given the GMM model. Therefore the same likelihood will be obtained if we take a random order of the same sequence of T vectors. Large GMM distributions have been used to represent speech in general in speaker recognition systems [19]. The number of components K can take large values, sometimes more than 2048.

Given a set of feature vectors the estimation of the GMM parameters, i.e. the components weights w_k and the mean and covariance matrices $(\underline{\mu}_k, \underline{\Gamma}_k)$ does not have a direct analytical solution. The estimation of the distribution parameters is then based on the Estimation-Maximization (EM) algorithm. It is an iterative algorithm that adjusts in each iteration the model parameters while ensuring a non-decrease of the likelihood of the training data.

In some cases, the amount of data available for training is not large enough to estimate the GMM parameters. A constrained training is applied and is called adaptation. Actually, starting from an existing GMM, the parameters are adjusted in order to better describe, based on a criterion, the training data. The adjustment is constrained either by an a priori distribution function like in the Maximum A Priori (MAP) or Bayesian adaptation or by a transformation function applied on the models parameters like in the Maximum Likelihood Linear Regression (MLLR) adaptation. A unified adaptation theory has been proposed in [20].

3.2   Hidden Markov Models

A Markov Model is a finite state machine composed of N states. It changes state once every time unit. In Hidden Markov Models states are not observed and each time a state is entered, it emits an observation according to a state-specific probability distribution.

Formally, an HMM is defined as :

$$\lambda = (s_i, a_{ij}, b_j)$$

s_i state $i_{i=1,2,..,N}$
a_{ij} transition probability between i and j
$b_i(o_k)$ emission probability of observation o_k at state i

Looking at a series of observations $O = o_1, o_2, ..o_T$ does not directly indicate the sequence of states $S = s_1, s_2, .., s_N$ which are hidden. However, knowing the emission probabilities $b_i(o_k)$ and the transition probabilities a_{ij} allows to

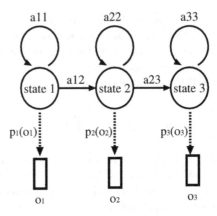

Fig. 6. Example of a HMM model with three states

estimate the associated states sequence thanks to the *Viterbi* algorithm [21]. All these probabilies are thus required to compute the sequence of hidden states. The very first stage is then to estimate them using the *Baum-Welch* algorithm over a training set.

3.3   HMMs Extensions

Two other kinds of statistical models may be derived from the classical HMMs to facilitate audiovisual process modeling, namely the *Multistream HMMs* and the *coupled HMMs* (CHMMs) [22,23,24].

Multistream HMMs may be considered as a *late fusion* method. In this approach, each modality (here the audio one and the visual one) is independently processed and pre-classified. The final classification is based on the fusion of the outputs of both modalities. Multistream HMMs derive the most likely class by taking the product of the likelihoods of the two single-modality classifier decisions, using appropriate weights λ. The models for each mode are estimated separately.

In the case of state-synchronous decision fusion, the scores (weighted likelihoods) are multiplied after eachtime unit in order to find a new audio-visual likelihood of the observation being generated by a state :

$$P(o_{av,t}|s) = P(o_{a,t}|s)^{\lambda_a} P(o_{v,t}|s)^{\lambda_v}$$

An advantage of *decision fusion* over *early fusion* is the possibility of weighting the importance of the two modes independently: the weights λ_a and λ_v may be chosen so as to model the reliability of each modality. However, assigning the good weights to different streams is a critical step and if the weights are not chosen properly, the system might perform poorly. In fact, the weights can be defined in a static manner by using a-priori knowledge or they can be estimated and learned on a validation dataset. For a more complete description of this dynamic weighting technique, we refer the reader to [25] in which multi-stream combination is used to improve the noise robustness of automatic speech recognition (ASR) systems.

It has already been explained that audio and visual streams may not be synchronised at a given time due to co-articulation effects and articulator inertia. Many methods for modelling audio-visual asynchrony have been proposed in the literature including multistream HMMs we presented above, product HMMs and coupled HMMs. The product HMM is a generalisation of the state-synchronous multistream HMMs that combines the stream log-likelihoods at an higher level. A CHMM [24] can be considered as a set of HMMs in which each HMM is dedicated to one stream. In the common topology of coupled HMM, the discrete nodes at time t for each HMM are conditionned by the discrete nodes at time $t-1$ of all the HMMs of the set. Thanks to this property, CHMM can model the audio and visual state asynchrony while preserving their natural correlation over time.

4   Applications

Four main on-going experimentations will be detailed afterwards: audiovisual speech recognition, audiovisual identity verification, speaker indexing, and speech reconstruction from silent-speech. All these applications make use of the features and models which have been presented in the previous section.

4.1   The BANCA Database

The BANCA database [26] has been used for our experiments concerning audiovisual speech recognition and for our audiovisual identity verification system. Here is a brief overview of its content.

The BANCA database contains audiovisual recordings of 52 persons talking in front of a camera equipped with a microphone. Two disjoint groups (G1 and G2, of 26 persons each) are made of 13 females and 13 males. Each person recorded 12 sessions divided in 3 different conditions. In each session, one true and one false identity claims were recorded. The difference between true and false identity claims only stays in what the person says: his/her name and address and a personal PIN for true identity claims, and the name and address and the personal PIN of the target for false identity claims.

Concerning identity verification, seven evaluation protocols for identity verification are defined for the BANCA database. The Pooled protocol, which contains 232 client accesses and 312 impostor accesses per group, from any recording conditions has been chosen for our evaluation.

4.2   Speech Recognition

Most state-of-the-art Automatic Speech Recognition (ASR) systems make use of the acoustic signal only and ignore visual speech cues while visual information has been shown to be helpful in improving the quality of speech recognizers, especially under noisy conditions [27,28,29]. The system described in this section involves information extracted from both modalities to improve recognition performances.

Audiovisual recognition units: Audio only ASR systems generally use phones as basic recognition units. As the visual signal only provides partial information about the underlying sequence of phones as all the articulators are not visible (usually only the lips), various sets of phones that are acoustically distinct may be visually indistinguishable. A possible solution is to consider "*visemes*" (the linguistically minimal units which are visually distinguishable). However, having different classes in the audio and the video system components complicates audiovisual integration: identical classes for both modalities will then be used afterwards and both components will recognize phones.

Audiovisual integration: The concept behind bimodal ASR is to combine the information from each mode in order to increase performances which could be obtained considering each mode separately [29,30,31]. Both *early* and *late* fusion have been tested.

Early fusion: the vectors of each single mode are concatenated. Given time-synchronous audio and visual feature vectors $o_{a,t}$ and $o_{v,t}$, feature fusion considers $o_{av,t} = [o_{a,t}, o_{v,t}] \in R^{l_{av}}$, where $l_{av} = l_a + l_v$ as the joint audio-visual observation. So a single classifier is trained on the concatenated vector. It is also possible to process the concatenated vectors with any transformation (such as Linear Discriminant Analysis LDA) in order to reduce the increased number of coefficients and facilitate classification (see Figure 7).

Late fusion: as already explained, multistream HMMs derives the most likely speech class by taking the product of the likelihoods produced using models learned for each mode. The final likelihood is then:

$$P(o_{av,t}|s) = P(o_{a,t}|s)^{\lambda_a} P(o_{v,t}|s)^{\lambda_v}$$

Experiments:

Data and features. This work is done within the framework of the VMike project [32]. VMike is a video microphone, which includes both a microphone and an optical retina. Experiments have been led on the BANCA database: 208 subjects were recorded in three different scenarios, controlled, degraded and adverse over 12 different sessions. During each recording, the subject was prompted to say a random 12 digit number, his/her name, address and date of birth. In the scope of this work, only the 12 digit sequences of the scenario "controlled" are extracted. In order to test the performance of the developed audiovisual speech system under noisy conditions, those utterances are combined with samples of babble noise at several signal to noise ratios (SNR). The babble sample is taken from the NOISEX database [33].

The retina has been simulated for evaluation. First, a detection algorithm is applied on every frame and outputs the position of the mouth as an image of

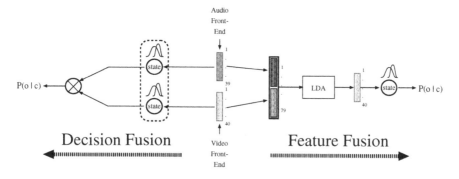

Fig. 7. Example of discriminative feature fusion and state-synchronous multistream integration

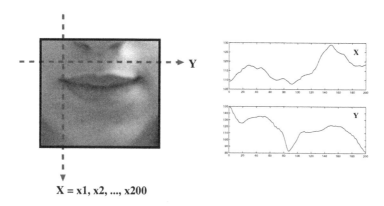

Fig. 8. Horizontal and vertical profiles

size 200x200 (thanks to the Viola&Jones mouth detector described in section 2.3). Horizontal and vertical projection profiles are then computed (cf fig. 8). The 200 projections along the X axis and 200 projections along the Y axis are concatenated to a single vector whose dimension is reduced to 40 using an LDA after a feature mean normalization. So as to capture dynamic speech information, each vector is then extended by concatenating its 7 chronologically preceding and the 7 following vectors. The resulting 600 features per sample are finally transformed into vectors of 40 using LDA.

In order to compare these features to state-of-the-art features, DCT coefficients of the detected mouths are also computed (these zones are firstly scaled to a 64x64 image) and the 100 most energetic coefficients are then selected. The same process as the one described for profiles features is then applied resulting in a DCT feature vector of size 40. The computation of all the visual features is summarized in figure 9:

Concerning the audio features, 13 feature-mean-normalized MFCC coefficients are extracted and extended with first and second derivatives of each coefficient. In order to obtain audio and visual features synchronicity, a simple element-wise

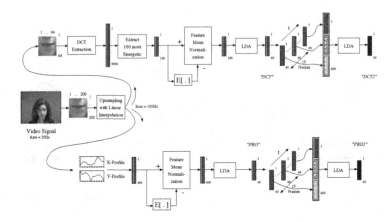

Fig. 9. Visual features extraction process

linear interpolation of the visual features to the audio frame rate is applied. From the up-sampled pictures the Discrete Cosine Transform (DCT) coefficients and *profiles* are extracted.

Models and Fusion. The acoustic models are context-independent. Each monophone consists of 3 states, which are modeled by 16 Gaussians each. The HTK Toolkit [34] software is used for model training and testing.

For the feature fusion, the 39-dimensional audio vectors are simply concatenated with the 40-dimensional visual features (DCT or profiles respectively). The combined vectors are then LDA transformed before being used for model estimation. Decision fusion is obtained by combining separately trained models for the audio and the visual coefficients to *two-stream* models, with specific weights on each stream. We assume state-synchronous fusion for combining the stream likelihoods. The optimal weighting is found through by trial-and-error.

Results. Two speech recognizers are then evaluated : *video-only* and *audio-visual*. The terminology for the different visual features is the following (see figure 9): DCT/PRO and DCT2/PRO2 correspond to the features without and with dynamic concatenation respectively.

1. **Visual-only speech recognition:** the results of all four different parametrization experiments do not exceed 45% accuracy (Fig.10). Using 15 consecutive vectors to include feature dynamics, did not improve performance. The results for single (DCT/PRO) and for concatenated (DCT2/PRO2) vectors respectively do not differ significantly.
2. **Audio-visual speech recognition:** figure (a) in fig. 11 shows the performance for all decision fusion recognizers at -5 db. Both *DCT2* and *PRO2* improve word recognition, but only *DCT2* does so *significantly* compared to the audio-only system. When feature fusion is applied (figure (b) in fig. 11) under noisy conditions, the recognition is improved by up to 12 percent with respect to audio-only recognition.

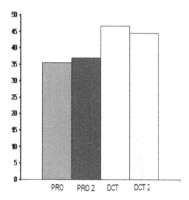

Fig. 10. Visual-only ASR

4.3   Audiovisual Identity Verification

Biometrics identity verification systems have been proven to be much more effective when information extracted from several modalities are merged together [35]. The system presented in this section relies on the fusion of three different modalities: the visual modality based on face verification, the audio one based on speaker verification and the synchrony modality based on the analysis of the correspondence between the audio and the visual stream (in a region located around the lips). We will also deal with the issue of speech conversion which may be considered as a high-effort attack against the verification system.

Face verification. Face verification may rely either on global face features (as in the *eigenfaces* approach [16]) or on local ones (approach using facial keypoints). The latter are able to capture geometrical relations between particular parts of the face and are thus more efficient when geometrical distortions occur. On the other hand, global features are easier to compute and takes the whole face into account: no information is lost. We propose to benefit from the complementarity of these two approaches in a fusion framework, where two algorithms based on global and local features respectively will be fused at scores level. The first algorithm uses classical *eigenfaces* global features (cf section 2.6) and the second one involves local *SIFT* descriptors (cf section 2.6). The comparison stage is the same for both type of features and is based on an SVD-matching process [36,37].

   SIFT descriptors have already been used together with the SVD based matching method in [38] which deals with object matching. Concerning face authentication in particular, *SIFT* descriptors have been tested in [39] where the matching between two images relies on the minimum euclidian distance between their *SIFT* descriptors. Unfortunately, this method relies on a manual registration of the different images. The main advantage of our method is then to propose an end-to-end system which does not suppose to know the position of faces before applying verification.

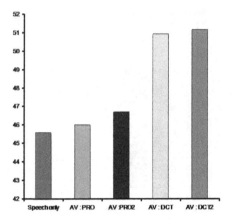

(a) Audio-visual decision-fusion results at -5db

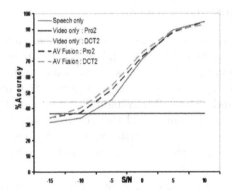

(b) Audio-visual parameter-fusion results

Fig. 11. Audiovisual ASR results

SVD-based matching method was introduced for spatial matching between keypoints [36] and relies on the *proximity* and *exclusion* principles enunciated by *Ullman* [40], which impose one-to-one correspondences.

Let us consider two sets of keypoints and R be the distance matrix between them. The matching consists in searching for pairs (i, j) that minimize R_{ij}. Searching for one-to-one correspondences may be facilitated if some projection matrix Q allows to make R closer to the identity matrix I. Such a problem is referred as the *orthogonal procrustes problem*: find the orthogonal matrix Q that minimizes $\|R - IQ\|$ [41]. It is proven that Q can be computed as follows:

1. Compute R Singular Values Decomposition (SVD): $R = UDV'$
2. Replace D by the identity I to get Q: $Q = UV'$

The last step is then to extract good pairings (i, j) searching for the elements of Q that are the greatest both of their row and their column.

This main principle is further improved by using a gaussian-weighted distance to compute the proximity matrix $G_{ij} = \exp\left(-R_{ij}/2\sigma^2\right)$ where σ quantifies the maximal tolerated distance between two keypoints. This parameter is known to have very little influence on the final results [42] and will be set to $1/8$ of the width of the image as this value has been already successfully tested [42]. A first extension was defined in [42] to take local descriptions around keypoints into account. SVD is then performed on the matrix G defined as $G_{ij} = f(C_{ij})g(R_{ij})$ where C_{ij} denotes the correlation between gray-levels around i and j keypoints, and where g is the gaussian function previously defined. Two different f functions may be used [37]:

$$\text{Exponential: } f(C_{ij}) = \exp(-(C_{ij} - 1)^2/2\gamma^2) \, . \tag{5}$$

$$\text{Linear: } f(C_{ij}) = (C_{ij} + 1)/2 \, . \tag{6}$$

where $\gamma = 0.4$ [37]. A second improvement has been experimented in [38] where gray-level correlation is replaced with *SIFT* descriptors correlation (only the linear form for f function is tested).

At test time, pairings (i, j) are filtered according to their associated correlation C_{ij} and the number of pairings with $C_{ij} > \text{Corr}_{th}$ is taken as the authentication score.

Considering a video as a set of faces, the same SVD matching process is used to search for correspondences between two videos whatever face representation is used (the global one based on *eigenfaces* or the local one using *SIFT* descriptors). Concerning *SIFT* matching, our system is the same as the one in [38]. Position vectors (used to compute R proximity matrix) include the spatial location, the scale and the orientation of *SIFT* descriptors.

A $\{\epsilon - \lambda\}$ test will refer afterwards to an authentication test involving two videos: V^ϵ of a person ϵ claiming she/he is person λ and V^λ, the enrollment video of person λ. Let then N_f^{SIFT} be the number of detected faces selected (cf section 2.4) in each video. *SIFT* descriptors are extracted from each of these faces. Resulting video representations will be denoted afterwards as follows: $\{S_k^\epsilon\}_{k\in[1...N_f^{\text{SIFT}}]}$ and $\{S_k^\lambda\}_{k\in[1...N_f^{\text{SIFT}}]}$, where $S_k^\epsilon = \{s_i^{\epsilon,k}\}_{i\in[1...N_{\text{desc}}^k]}$. N_{desc}^k represents the number of 128-dimensional *SIFT* descriptors s_i^k extracted from face k. Matching is performed between each pair $(S_k^\epsilon, S_l^\lambda)$ related to *SIFT* descriptors extracted from faces k and l retained from V^λ and V^ϵ respectively. In this case, C_{ij} and R_{ij} elements are computed between $s_i^{k,\epsilon}$ and $s_j^{l,\lambda}$ descriptors. An authentication score (i.e: the number of matchings between descriptors) is obtained for each pair $(S_k^\epsilon, S_l^\lambda)$. These scores are firstly normalized according to the number of *SIFT* descriptors and their mean then produces a single score:

$$S(V^\epsilon, V^\lambda) = \frac{1}{(N_f^{\text{SIFT}})^2} \sum_{k=1}^{N_f^{\text{SIFT}}} \sum_{l=1}^{N_f^{\text{SIFT}}} \frac{M(S_k^\epsilon, S_l^\lambda)}{\min(N_{\text{desc}}^k, N_{\text{desc}}^l)} \, . \tag{7}$$

where $M(S_k^\epsilon, S_l^\lambda)$ is the number of matchings between $S_k^\epsilon = \{s_i^{\epsilon,k}\}_{i\in[1...N_{desc}^k]}$ and $S_l^\lambda = \{s_i^{\lambda,l}\}_{i\in[1...N_{desc}^l]}$.

Let us consider the same $\{\epsilon - \lambda\}$ authentication test to set out the matching process for global representations. The same number N_f^{PCA} of detected faces is kept in each video. Their eigenface features will be denoted afterwards as $\{E_k^\epsilon\}_{k \in [1...N_f^{\text{PCA}}]}$ and $\{E_k^\lambda\}_{k \in [1...N_f^{\text{PCA}}]}$ respectively.

Pairwise matching is performed between each E_k^ϵ and E_k^λ, that is between faces directly. As these features treat faces as a whole, location information is lost and the G matrix is reduced to its description part: $G_{ij} = f(C_{ij})$. These C_{ij} elements are computed between E_i^ϵ and E_j^λ. This differs with $SIFT$ matching since a single authentication score will be obtained for each test:

$$S(V^\epsilon, V^\lambda) = M(E^\epsilon, E^\lambda) . \tag{8}$$

where $M(E^\epsilon, E^\lambda)$ is the number of matchings between $E^\epsilon = \{E_k^\epsilon\}_{k \in [1...N_f^{PCA}]}$ and $E^\lambda = \{E_l^\lambda\}_{l \in [1...N_f^{PCA}]}$.

Parameters have been set in the following manner during our experiments: $N_f^{\text{SIFT}} = 5$, $N_f^{\text{SIFT}} = 100$, $E_i \in \mathbb{R}^{97}$ (i.e we chose to keep the 97 most influent directions to compute global representations), $\text{Corr}_{th} = 0.4$. The f function is linear for global matching and exponential for local matching. The form of f function has been chosen by cross-validation between groups G1 and G2 of the BANCA database.

Speaker verification. Speaker verification is based on GMM modeling (cf section 3.1) of each speaker included in the BANCA database. To overcome the lack of training data dedicated to each speaker, adaptation of a world (or universal) model is performed using the MAP algorithm. The verification score is computed as the following likelihood ratio :

$$S(V^\epsilon, V^\lambda) = \frac{1}{N_x} \sum_x \log \left(\frac{P(\mathbf{x}_\epsilon | \lambda)}{P(\mathbf{x}_\epsilon | \Omega)} \right)$$

where $\mathbf{x}_\epsilon$ denotes an observation vector in the audio stream of V^ϵ, Ω the world model and N_x the number of observation vectors considered in the whole speech sequence.

Synchrony modality

Speaker conversion and face animation can be considered as high-effort forgeries, which – if they are performed correctly – are very difficult to detect. But, most of the current talking-face biometrics verification systems can be fooled by much simpler attacks, e.g. replay attacks [43]. In this scenario, the impostor previously acquired a biometric sample of his/her target. For instance, he could have recorded his/her voice during a phone call and taken a picture of his/her face without being noticed. Then, a basic idea would be to play the recording of the voice through speakers while displaying the picture in front of the camera. An example of the resulting acquired picture is shown in figure 12.

Therefore we introduced a new biometric modality based on a client-dependent measure of the synchrony between acoustic and visual speech features.

Fig. 12. Example of a simple replay attack

Audio and visual speech features are respectively MFCC and DCT coefficients extracted as explained in sections 2.5 and 2.6. In order to equalize the sample rates of acoustic and visual features (initially 100 Hz and 25 Hz respectively), visual features are linearly interpolated.

Using the acoustic and visual features X and Y extracted from the enrollment sequence, CoIA (cf section 2.8) is applied in order to compute the client-dependent synchrony model $(\mathbf{A}, \mathbf{B})$.

At test time, acoustic and visual feature vectors X^ϵ and Y^ϵ of the test sequence ϵ are extracted and a measure S_C of their synchrony is computed using the synchrony model $(\mathbf{A}^\lambda, \mathbf{B}^\lambda)$ of the claimed identity λ:

$$S_C(V^\epsilon, V^\lambda) = \frac{1}{D} \sum_{k=1}^{D} \mathrm{corr}\left(\mathbf{a}_k^{\lambda t} X^\epsilon, \mathbf{b}_k^{\lambda t} Y^\epsilon \right) \tag{9}$$

where D is the number of dimensions actually used to compute the correlation. In our case we chose $D = 3$.

Scores fusion. The scores provided by each modality are finally fused in a late fusion framework involving SVM (cf section 2.7). Results obtained on groups G1 and G2 of the BANCA database are depicted in figure 13 which validates the initial idea of taking benefit from different modalities to improve performances.

It has already been explained that the synchrony modality is appropriate whenever robustness to high-effort attacks is required. In order to test synchrony modality superiority, some work has then been dedicated to generate forgeries which would defeat traditional modalities. Speech conversion is one of the possible high effort attack and will be adressed in the next section.

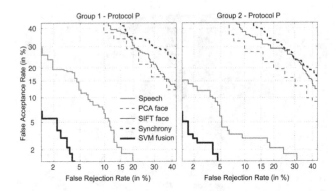

Fig. 13. Performances of mono-modal and multimodal verification systems

Speaker conversion. Automatic voice conversion may be defined as the process of transforming the characteristics of speech uttered by a source speaker, such that a listener would believe the speech was pronounced by a target speaker.

Different kinds of information are included in the speech signal: environmental noise, speech message, speaker identity. The question of voice conversion is firstly, to establish the most characteristic features of a source individual to transform them to their target counterpart. The analysis part of a voice conversion algorithm focuses on the extraction of speaker identity. Secondly, it will calculate the transformation function to apply. Both operations must be performed independently of the environment and of the message. At last, a synthesis step will be achieved to replace the source speaker characteristics by the target speaker characteristics.

Consider a sequence $X_s = [x_1, x2, \ldots xn]$ of spectral vectors pronounced by the source speaker and a sequence pronounced by the target speaker composed by the same words $Y_t = [y_1, y_2, \ldots y_n]$.

Voice conversion is based on the calculation of a conversion function F that minimizes the mean square error:

$$\epsilon_{mse} = E(\|y - F(x)\|^2)$$

where E is the expectation.

Two steps are useful to build a conversion system: a training step and a conversion step. In the training phase speech samples from the source and the target speaker are analysed to extract the main features. Then these features are time aligned and a conversion function is estimated to map the source and the target features.

The aim of the conversion step is then to apply the estimated conversion function rule to the source speech signal so that the new utterance sounds like the speech of the target speaker. The last step is the re-synthesis of the signal in order to reconstruct the speech segment of the source voice after the conversion.

The most representative techniques of voice conversion are based on vector quantization [44], on Gaussian Mixture Models and derived [45,46,47,48], on

Multiple Linear Regression [49] and on an indexation in a client memory [50].
Two of these conversion methods will be developed afterwards and their influence
on an automatic speaker recognition system will be evaluated.

The first one is based on ALISP (cf section 2.1) [50]. One hour of speech
pronounced by the target speaker is available. This speech signal is segmented
and vector quantization allows to extract 64 classes which will constitute the
target codebook. As this speech signal is now annotated regarding these 64
recognition units (or classes), a HMM may be trained and applied on the source
signal.

Once the source signal has been segmented, the synthesis stage is applied:
each segment is replaced by one of its closest counterpart in the same class (i.e
the one with the same index) among target classes. This counterpart is selected
comparing prosodic parameters (Harmonic plus Noise [48]) between the source
segment and all the segment contained in the target class (cf figure 14) thanks
to the Dynamic Time Warping (DTW).

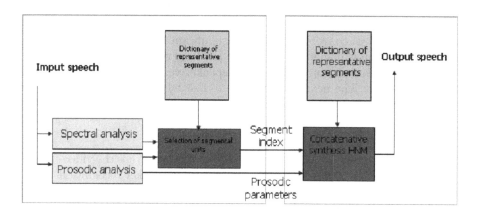

Fig. 14. Conversion step

This technique of conversion provided interesting results on the NIST 2004
corpus [50], as the recognition rate effectively decreased when applying speech
conversion.

The second technique we experimented consists in modifying all the shape
of the source spectrum to correspond to the target spectrum [49]. The different
stages of this techniques are depicted in the figure 15. In the first time, the
source segment and the target segment (they contain the same utterance) are
aligned using DTW. Vector Quantization is then applied on each segment to
extract 64 classes. Mappings between source and target classes is then estimated
using DTW (mapping codebook). After a normalization stage over each class,
conversion matrices (from source class i to target class j, ...) are then estimated
using Multiple Linear Regression. These matrices finally allow to transform a
new source segment so that it corresponds to target speech in the feature space.

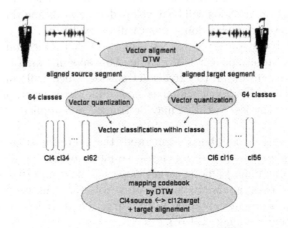

Fig. 15. Obtaining the Mapping Codebook

As in the previous conversion method a significant decrease of the automatic speaker recognition is demonstrated on the DET curve (cf figure 16).

The impact of speech conversion over a speaker verification system has been clearly established. The next stage will be to test whether a modality like the synchrony could help to deal with such attacks.

4.4   OUISPER

The audio-visual speech based applications discussed before use the video stream in addition to the audio stream to improve speech or speaker recognition. However, for some applications, the audio stream cannot be used at all: whenever audio is too much corrupted by noise, or, at the opposite, in the context of speech communication in situations where silence and privacy must be maintained. These applications address the issue of speech recognition and/or speech reconstruction from silent-speech, that is normal speech without glottal activity. Speech recognition from silent-speech using electromyographic sensors to monitor the articulatory muscles has been introduced in [51]. In [52], an isolated word recognition task from whispered speech is investigated using a special acoustic sensor called non-audible microphone (NAM). In [53], Denby proposes to use ultrasound acquisition of the tongue and video sequences of the lips as visual inputs of an artificial neural network and predict a relative robust LSF (Line Spectral Frequency) representation of voiced parts of speech. This envisioned ultrasound-based speech synthetiser could be helpful for patient having undergone a laryngectomy because it could provide an alternative to the tracheooesophageal speech. In [54], an approach based on visual speech recognition and concatenative synthesis driven by ultrasound and optical images of the voice organ is introduced. This system is based on the building of a one-hour audio-visual corpus of phonetic units, which associates visual features extracted from

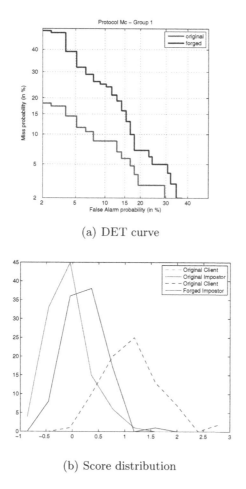

(a) DET curve

(b) Score distribution

Fig. 16. Results obtained using the Multiple Linear Regression approach

video to acoustic observations. Ultrasound and optical images are coded using a PCA-based approach similar to the EigenFaces approach described previously. As the visual and audio streams are synchronized, the initial phonetic segmentation of the video sequences can be obtained from the temporal boundaries of the phonemes in the audio signal. These labels are generated using speech forced alignment techniques. Then, HMM-based stochastic models trained on these visual features sequences are used to predict phonetic targets from video-only data. Finally, a Viterbi unit selection algorithm is used to find the optimal sequence of acoustic units given this phonetic prediction. The system is already able to perform phonetic transcription from visual speech data with over 50% correct recognition. Figure 17 presents an overview of this system and figure 18 shows a typical image of the database in which a lip profile image is embedded into the

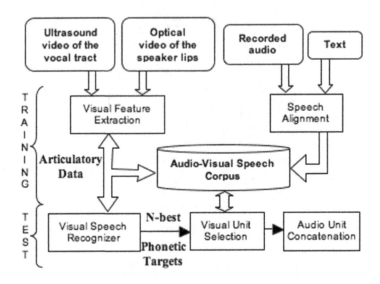

Fig. 17. Ouisper corpus-based synthesis system overview

ultrasound image. The use of a large word dictionary and the introduction of a Language Model will help improving the rendered signal.

4.5   Speaker Indexing

One of the most promising on-going experiments concerns speaker indexing. The goal of this application is to answer automatically the question: *Who is speaking in a video sequence ?*, taking benefit from information extracted from the audio channel and from the video stream. This application is clearly audiovisual and is based on many of the tools detailed in the previous sections.

First, faces are located within each frame of the considered video. Given a sliding temporal window, audio energy is computed. A visual feature vector is then attached to each pixel within the image (its values over time). The audio feature vectors are sampled to match with the frame rate and both vectors are $\sigma - \mu$ normalized. Correlations between all these vectors (the single audio vector and visual feature vectors attached to each pixel) are computed. The mean correlation is then computed for each detected face and the one with the greatest value is defined as locating the 'current speaker'. First results are depicted in figure 19.

While very simple, this first method has proven to perform quite well. Further experiments are under way, focusing especially on the choice of appropriate visual features. The idea would then be to fuse the obtained segmentation with face tracking/recognition and the speaker segmentation to obtain better results and to be able to extract voice-over speech segments.

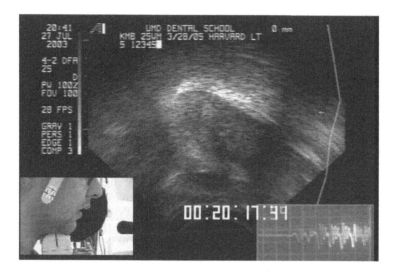

Fig. 18. Example of an ultrasound vocal tract image with embedded lip profile

Fig. 19. Some good localizations of the current speaker (green rectangles)

5   Conclusion and Perspectives

Speech is not only an acoustic signal. It is produced by a speaker moving his articulators. The observation of these movements helps in all aspects of speech processing: coding, recognition, synthesis, ... This chapter described a few ongoing experiments exploiting the correlation between acoustic and visual features of speech. It is demonstrated that the correlation of audio and visual information can be exploited usefully in many applications.

Aknowledgments

The research leading to this chapter was supported by the European Commission (K-SPACE, BioSecure, SecurePhone), by regional fundings (InfoM@gic), and by the Franco-Lebanese program CEDRE.

References

1. Chollet, G., Cernocky, J., Constantinescu, A., Deligne, S., Bimbot, F.: Towards ALISP: a Proposal for Automatic Language Independent Speech Processing. In: Computational Models of Speech Pattern Processing. NATO ASI Series, Series F: Computer and System Sciences, vol. 169, pp. 375–387. Springer, Heidelberg (1999)
2. Bimbot, F., Chollet, G., Deleglise, P., Montacié, C.: Temporal Decomposition and Acoustic-Phonetic Decoding of Speech. In: IEEE International Conference on Acoustics, Speech and Signal Processing, pp. 445–448 (1988)
3. Gersho, A., Gray, R.: Vector Quantization and Signal Compression. Kluwer, Boston (1992)
4. Petrovska-Delacretaz, D., Chollet, G.: Searching Through a Speech Memory for Efficient Coding, Recognition and Synthesis. In: Braun, A., Masthoff, H. (eds.) Phonetics and its Applications. Festschrift for Jens-Peter Köster on the occasion of his 60th birthday, pp. 453–464. Franz Steiner Verlag (2002)
5. Yang, M.H., Kriegman, D., Ahuja, N.: Detecting Faces in Images: a Survey. IEEE Transactions on Pattern Analysis and Machine Intelligence 24(1), 34–58 (2002)
6. Viola, P.A., Jones, M.J.: Robust Real-Time Object Detection. International Journal of Computer Vision 57(2), 137–154 (2002)
7. Fasel, I., Fortenberry, B., Movellan, J.: A Generative Framework for Real-Time Object Detection and Classification. Computer Vision and Image Understanding 98(1), 182–210 (2004)
8. Santana, M.C., Navarro, J.L., Suárez, O.D., Martel, A.F.: Multiple Face Detection at Different Resolutions for Perceptual User Interfaces. In: 2nd Iberian Conference on Pattern Recognition and Image Analysis, Estoril, Portugal (June 2005)
9. Kass, M., Witkin, A., Terzopoulos, D.: Snakes: Active contour models. International Journal of Computer Vision 1(4), 321–331 (1988)
10. Davis, S., Mermelstein, P.: Comparaison of Parametric Representations of Monosyllabic Word Recognition in Continuously Spoken Sentences. In: IEEE International Conference on Acoustics, Speech ans Signal Processing, pp. 357–366 (April 1980)
11. Hermansky, H.: Perceptual Linear Predictive (plp) Analysis of Speech. J. Acoust. Soc. America 87, 1738–1752 (1990)
12. Lowe, D.: Distinctive Image Features from Scale-Invariant Keypoints. Int. Journal of Computer Vision 60(2), 91–110 (2004)
13. Mikolajczyk, K., Schmid, C.: A Performance Evaluation of Local Descriptors. IEEE trans on Pattern Analysis and Machine Intelligence 27(10) (2005)
14. Witkin, A.: Scale-Space Filtering. In: Proceedings of the 8th International Joint Conference on Artificial Intelligence, pp. 1019–1022 (1983)
15. Koenderink, J.: The Structure of Images. Biological Cybernetics 50, 363–370 (1984)
16. Turk, M., Pentland, A.: Eigenfaces for Recognition. Journal of Cognitive Neuroscience 3(1), 71–86 (1991)
17. Kittler, J., Hatef, M., Duin, R., Matas, J.: On combining classifiers. IEEE Trans. Pattern Anal. Mach. Intell. 20(3), 226–239 (1998)
18. Dolédec, S., Chessel, D.: Co-Inertia Analysis: an Alternative Method for Studying Species-Environment Relationships. Freshwater Biology 31, 277–294 (1994)
19. Reynolds, D., Quatieri, T., Dunn, R.: Speaker Verification Using Adapted Gaussian Mixture Models. Digital Signal Processing (10), 19–41 (2000)
20. Mokbel, C.: Online Adaptation of HMMs to Real-Life Conditions: A Unified Framework. IEEE Trans. On Speech and Audio Processing 9(4), 342–357 (2001)

21. Rabiner, L.: A Tutorial on Hidden Markov Models and Selected Applications in Speech Recognition. Proceedings of the IEEE 77(2), 257–286 (1989)
22. Potamianos, G., Neti, C., Luettin, J., Matthews, I.: Audio-Visual Automatic Speech Recognition: An Overview. In: Bailly, G., Vatikiotis-Bateson, E., Perrier, P. (eds.) Issues in Visual and Audio-Visual Speech Processing, MIT Press, Cambridge (2004)
23. Argones-Rúa, E., García-Mateo, C., Bredin, H., Chollet, G.: Aliveness Detection using Coupled Hidden Markov Models. In: SWB 2007. First Spanish Workshop on Biometrics, Girona, Spain (June 2007)
24. Brand, M., Oliver, N., Pentland, A.: Coupled hidden markov models for complex action recognition (1996)
25. Misra, H.: Multi-stream processing for noise robust speech recognition. PhD thesis, Lausanne (2006)
26. Bailly-Baillière, E., Bengio, S., Bimbot, F., Hamouz, M., Kittler, J., Mariéthoz, J., Matas, J., Messer, K., Popovici, V., Porée, F., Ruiz, B., Thiran, J.P.: The BANCA and Evaluation Protocol. In: Kittler, J., Nixon, M.S. (eds.) AVBPA 2003. LNCS, vol. 2688, pp. 625–638. Springer, Heidelberg (2003)
27. Hazen, T.: Visual Model Structures and Synchrony Constraints for Audio-Visual Speech Recognition. IEEE Transactions on Audio, Speech and Language Processing 14(3) (2006)
28. Dupont, S., Luettin, J.: Audio-Visual Speech Modeling for Continuous Speech Recognition. IEEE Transcations on Multimedia 2(3) (2000)
29. Potamianos, G., Neti, C., Gravier, G., Garg, A., Senior, A.: Recent Advances in the Automatic Recognition of Audiovisual Speech. IEEE 91(9) (2003)
30. Chu, S., Huang, T.: Audio Visual Speech Modelling using Coupled Hidden Markov Models. In: IEEE International Conference on Acoustics, Speech and Signal Processing, pp. 2009–2012 (2002)
31. Nakamura, S.: Statistical Multimodal Integration for Audio-Visual Speech Processing. IEEE Transactions on Neural Networks 13(4), 854–866 (2002)
32. Brugger, F., Zouari, L., Bredin, H., Amehraye, A., Chollet, G., Pastor, D., Ni, Y.: Reconnaissance Audio-Visuelle de la Parole par VMike. In: JEP 2006. XXVIème Journés d'Étude sur la Parole, Dinard, France, pp. 417–420 (June 2006)
33. The NoiseX Database: http://spib.rice.edu/spib
34. Young, S., Evermann, G., Kershaw, D., Moore, G., Odell, J., Ollason, D., Povey, D., Valtchev, V., Woodland, P.: The HTK Book (for HTK Version 3.2). Cambridge University Engineering Department (December 2002)
35. Ross, A.A., Nandakumar, K., Jain, A.K.: Handbook of Multibiometrics. Springer, Heidelberg (2006)
36. Scott, G., Longuet-Higgins, H.: An Algorithm for Associating the Features of Two Images. Proc. of the Royal Society of London. Series B. Biological Sciences 244(1309), 21–26 (1991)
37. Pilu, M.: Uncalibrated Stereo Correspondence by Singular Value Decomposition. Technical Report HPL-97-96, Digital Media Department HP Laboratories (1997)
38. Delponte, E., Isgr, F., Odone, F., Verri, A.: SVD-Matching using SIFT Features. In: Proc. of the Int. Conf. on Vision, Video and Graphics, pp. 125–132 (2005)
39. Bicego, M., Lagorio, A., Grosso, E., Tistarelli, M.: On the Use of SIFT Features for Face Authentication. In: CVPRW. Conf. on Computer Vision and Pattern Recognition Workshop (2006)
40. Ullman, S.: The Interpretation of Visual Motion. MIT Press, Cambridge, MA (1979)

41. Golub, G., Loan, C.V.: Matrix Computations, 3rd edn. The Johns Hopkins University Press, Baltimore, MD (1996)
42. Pilu, M.: A Direct Method for Stereo Correspondence based on Singular Value Decomposition. In: Proceedings of CVPR, pp. 261–266 (1997)
43. Bredin, H., Miguel, A., Witten, I.H., Chollet, G.: Detecting Replay Attacks in Audiovisual Identity Verification. In: ICASSP 2006. 31st IEEE International Conference on Acoustics, Speech, and Signal Processing, Toulouse, France, vol. 1, pp. 621–624 (May 2006)
44. Abe, M., Nakamura, S., Shikano, K., Kuwabara, H.: Voice Conversion through Vector Quantization. In: International Conference on Acoustics, Speech and Signal Processing (1988)
45. Cappé, O., Stylianou, Y., Moulines, E.: Statistical Methods for Voice Quality Transformation. In: EUROSPEECH (1995)
46. Sundermann, D., Hge, H., Bonafonte, A., Ney, H., Black, A., Narayanan, S.: Text-Independent Voice Conversion Based on Unit Selection. In: International Conference on Acoustics, Speech and Signal Processing, Toulouse, France (2006)
47. Genoud, D., Chollet, G.: Voice Transformations: Some Tools for the Imposture of Speaker Verification Systems, pp. 375–387 Franz Steiner Verlag (1999)
48. Stylianou, Y., Cappé, O.: A System for Voice Conversion Based on Probabilistic Classification and a Harmonic Plus Noise Model. In: International Conference on Acoustics, Speech and Signal Processing (1998)
49. Valbret, H., Moulines, E., Tubach, J.: Voice Transformation Using TDPSOLA Technique. In: International Conference on Acoustics, Speech and Signal Processing (1992)
50. Perrot, P., Aversano, G., Blouet, R., Charbit, M., Chollet, G.: Voice Forgery using ALISP. In: International Conference on Acoustics, Speech and Signal Processing (2005)
51. Jou, S.C.S., Schultz, T., Waibel, A.: Continuous Electromyographic Speech Recognition with a Multi-Stream Decoding Architecture. In: International Conference on Communication Audio and Speech Processing, Honolulu, Hawaii (April 2007)
52. Heracleous, P., Nakajima, Y., Saruwatari, H., Shikano, K.: A Tissue-Conductive Acoustic Sensor Applied in Speech Recognition for Privacy. In: sOc-EUSAI 2005. Proceedings of the 2005 joint conference on Smart objects and ambient intelligence, pp. 93–97. ACM Press, New York (2005)
53. Denby, B., Oussar, Y., Dreyfus, G., Stone, M.: Prospect for a Silent Speech Interface Using Ultrasound Imaging. In: International Conference on Acoustics, Speech and Signal Processing, Toulouse, France (2006)
54. Hueber, T., Chollet, C., Denby, B., Stone, M., Zouari, L.: Ouisper: Corpus Based Synthesis Driven by Articulatory Data. In: International Conference on Phonetic Science (to appear, 2007)

Exploiting Nonlinearity in Adaptive Signal Processing

Phebe Vayanos, Mo Chen, Beth Jelfs, and Danilo P. Mandic

Department of Electrical and Electronic Engineering, Imperial College London,
London SW7 2AZ, UK
{foivi.vayanos,mo.chen,beth.jelfs,d.mandic}@ic.ac.uk

Abstract. *Quantitative* performance criteria for the analysis of machine learning architectures and algorithms have been long established. However, the *qualitative* performance criteria, *e.g.*, nonlinearity assessment, are still emerging. To that end, we employ some recent developments in signal characterisation and derive criteria for the assessment of the changes in the nature of the processed signal. In addition, we also propose a novel online method for tracking the system nonlinearity. A comprehensive set of simulations in both the linear and nonlinear settings and their combination supports the analysis.

1 Introduction

Real–world processes are typically mixtures of linear and nonlinear signal components (which can be either deterministic or stochastic) and noise, yet it is a common practice to process them using linear, mathematically tractable, models. To illustrate the need to asses the *nature of a real world signal* prior to choosing the actual computational model, Figure 1 (modified from [1]), shows the range spanned by the fundamental signal properties of "nonlinear" and "stochastic". Despite the fact that real-world processes, due to nonlinearity, uncertainty and noise, are located in areas such as those denoted by (a), (b), (c) and '?', in terms of computational models, only the very specialised cases such as the linear-stochastic autoregressive moving average (ARMA), and chaotic (nonlinear-deterministic) models are well understood. It is therefore necessary to verify the presence of an underlying linear or nonlinear signal generation system, *before* the actual filters or models are constructed. Indeed, in the absence of nonlinearity within a signal in hand, it is not advantageous to use nonlinear models since these are more difficult to train than their linear counterparts, due to issues such as overfitting and computational complexity.

Research on "signal modality characterisation" started in physics in the mid 1990s and its applications in machine learning and signal processing application are just beginning to emerge. It is essential that during processing of such signals we not only optimise for the "best" performance in terms of a certain quantitative performance criterion, but also that the processing preserves the desired fundamental properties of the signal, for instance, the nonlinear and deterministic nature (qualitative performance). If the desired signal property has

M. Chetouani et al. (Eds.): NOLISP 2007, LNAI 4885, pp. 57–77, 2007.

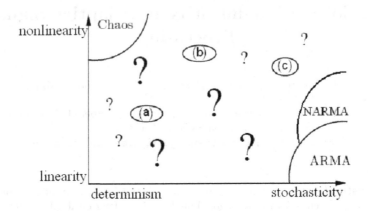

Fig. 1. Sketch of the variety of signals spanned by the properties "nonlinearity" and "stochasticity". Areas where theoretical knowledge and technology for the analysis of time series are available are outlined, such as "Chaos" and "ARMA". (Modified from (Schreiber, 1999)).

significantly changed after processing (*e.g.* prediction within compression algorithms and denoising), the application of such filters will be greatly limited. As a consequence, such architectures and algorithms will not be suitable in situations where the signal nature is of critical importance, for instance, in speech processing.

Notice that the very core of adaptive learning is the change in the shapes of signal spectrum, this reflects only the performance in terms of second order statistics, and no account of other signal characteristics is provided. To that cause, we propose a new framework for the assessment of *qualitative performance* in machine learning, and set out to investigate whether an improvement in the quantitative performance is necessarily followed by the improvement in the qualitative performance. For generality and to illustrate this trade-off, this is achieved for both the linear and nonlinear filters.

On the other hand, the existing signal modality characterisation algorithms in this area are typically based on hypothesis testing [2,3,4] and describe the signal changes in a statistical manner. However, there are very few online algorithms which are suitable for this purpose. Therefore, in this chapter, we will also propose to demonstrate the possibility of online algorithms which can be used not only to identify the nature of the signal, but also to track changes in the nature of the signal (signal modality detection).

2   Background Theory

Before introducing new criteria for the analysis of qualitative performance in machine learning and the online algorithm for tracking system nonlinearity, we set out to provide some necessary background focusing on some recent results on signal characterisation.

2.1 "Nature" of a Signal

By the signal 'nature' [5][6], we adhere to a number of signal properties such as:-

i) Linear (strict definition) – A linear signal is generated by a linear time-invariant system, driven by white Gaussian noise;

ii) Linear (commonly adopted) – Definition i) is relaxed somewhat by allowing the distribution of the signal to deviate from the Gaussian one, which can be interpreted as a linear signal from i), measured by a static (possibly nonlinear) observation function;

iii) Nonlinear – A signal that cannot be generated in the above way is considered nonlinear;

iv) Deterministic (predictable) – A signal is considered deterministic if it can be precisely described by a set of equations;

v) Stochastic – A signal that is not deterministic.

2.2 Method of Surrogate Data and the Concept of "Phase Space"

Research on signal nonlinearity detection started in physics in the 1990s, and out of the several proposed methods, the so-called 'surrogate data' method, introduced by Theiler et $al.$ [7], has been extensively used in the context of statistical nonlinearity testing. A surrogate time series, or 'surrogate' for short, is a realisation of a 'composite' null hypothesis. In our case this null hypothesis is that the original signal is linear, $i.e.$, generated by a linear stochastic system driven by white Gaussian noise, measured by a static, monotonic and possibly nonlinear observation function. Then, a discriminating statistic is calculated for both the original time series and a set of surrogate data. If the statistics for the original time series do not lie in the range of those for the surrogate data, the null hypothesis is rejected, and the original data is judged to be nonlinear, otherwise, it is judged to be linear. There exist many discriminating statistics, the commonly used ones include the so-called third-order auto-covariance (C3) [4] and the asymmetry due to time reversal (REV) [4]. In order to increase the power of the surrogate test and decrease the spurious rejections of the null hypothesis, several modified methods for the generation of surrogate data have been proposed. In this chapter, we adopt the iterative amplitude adjusted Fourier Transform (iAAFT) surrogate method [8]. The iAAFT surrogate data have their amplitude spectra similar and their amplitude distribution identical to those of the original time series.

Techniques described in this chapter rest upon the method of time delay embedding for representing a time series in so-called 'phase space', $i.e.$, by a set of delay vectors (DVs) $\mathbf{x}(k)$ of a given embedding dimension m, that is $\mathbf{x}(k) = [x_{k-m\tau}, \ldots, x_{k-\tau}]^T$, where τ is a time lag, which for simplicity is set to unity in all simulations. In other words, $\mathbf{x}(k)$ is a vector containing m consecutive time samples.

From Figure 2(a), although the wave form and the power spectrum of the two signals are similar to one another, distinct difference can be observed in two

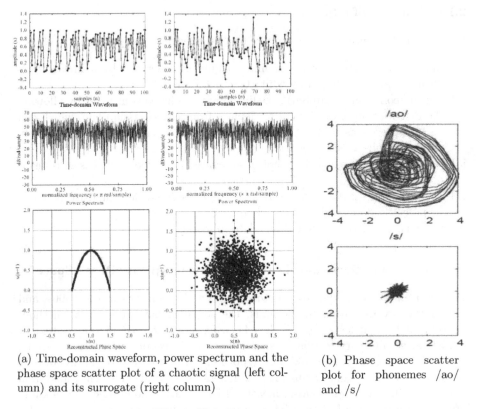

(a) Time-domain waveform, power spectrum and the phase space scatter plot of a chaotic signal (left column) and its surrogate (right column)

(b) Phase space scatter plot for phonemes /ao/ and /s/

Fig. 2. Phase space scatter plot

phase space scatter plots. There is some sort of structure in the scatter plot for the chaotic signal, whereas the surrogate displays randomness in the scatter plot. The reason for this is that during the surrogate-generation process the temporal and spatial correlations were completely destroyed due to the randomisation scheme. Figure 2(b) illustrates the attractors for vowel /ao/ and consonant /s/ in phase space scatter plot. From the Figure, it is clear that these two phonemes differ from one another in nature.

2.3   Signal Characterisation Tool: "Delay Vector Variance" (DVV) Method

Many methods for detecting the nonlinear structure within a signal have been proposed, such as the above mentioned surrogate data with different choices of discriminating statistics, *"Deterministic versus Stochastic"* (DVS) plot [9], δ-ε Method [10]. For our purpose, it is desirable to have a method which is straightforward to visualise, and which makes use of some notions from nonlinear dynamics and chaos theory, *e.g.*, embedding dimension and phase space. One such method is our recently proposed "Delay Vector Variance" (DVV) method

[2], which is based upon examining the predictability of a signal in the phase space, and examines simultaneously the determinism and nonlinearity within a signal.

The DVV algorithm can be summarised in the following way:- For a given optimal embedding dimension[1] m:

- Map the original time series from time domain to a set of delay vectors (DVs) in phase space, $\mathbf{x}(k) = [x_{k-\tau m}, \ldots, x_{k-\tau}]^T$, where τ is the time lag which for convenience is set to unity in all the simulations and the corresponding target x_k;
- The mean μ_d and standard deviation σ_d are computed over all pairwise Euclidean distances between DVs, $\|\mathbf{x}(i) - \mathbf{x}(j)\| (i \neq j)$;
- The sets $\Omega_k(r_d)$ are generated such that $\Omega_k(r_d) = \{\mathbf{x}(i) | \|\mathbf{x}(k) - \mathbf{x}(i)\| \leq r_d\}$, i.e., sets which consist of all DVs that lie closer to $\mathbf{x}(k)$ than a certain distance

$$r_d(n) = \mu_d - n_d \sigma_d + (n-1)\frac{2 n_d \sigma_d}{N_{tv} - 1}, \quad n = 1, \ldots, N_{tv} \tag{1}$$

where N_{tv} denotes how fine the standardised distance is uniformly spaced, and n_d is a parameter controlling the span over which to perform the DVV analysis;

- For every set $\Omega_k(r_d)$, the variance of the corresponding targets, $\sigma_k^2(r_d)$, is computed. The average over all sets $\Omega_k(r_d)$, normalised by the variance of the time series, σ_x^2, yields the 'target variance', $\sigma^{*2}(r_d)$:

$$\sigma^{*2}(r_d) = \frac{\frac{1}{N}\sum_{k=1}^{N} \sigma_k^2(r_d)}{\sigma_x^2} \tag{2}$$

We only consider a variance measurement *valid*, if the set $\Omega_k(r_d)$ contains at least $N_0 = 30$ DVs, since too few points for computing a sample variance yields unreliable estimates of the true variance. For more details, please refer to [2] [5].

For a predictable signal, the idea behind the DVV method is:- if two DVs lie close to one another in terms of their Euclidean distance, they should also have similar targets. The smaller the Euclidean distance between them, the more similar targets they have. Therefore, the presence of a strong deterministic component within a signal will lead to small target variances for small spans r_d. The minimal target variance, $\sigma_{min}^{*2} = min_{r_d}[\sigma^{*2}(r_d)]$, is a measure for the amount of noise present within the time series. Besides, the target variance σ_{min}^{*2} has an upper bound which is unity. This is because, when r_d becomes large enough, all the DVs belong to the same set $\Omega_k(r_d)$. Thus, the variance of the corresponding target of those DVs will be almost identical to that of the original time series.

In the following step, the linear or nonlinear nature of the time series is examined by performing the DVV test on both the original and a number of

---

[1] In this chapter, the optimal embedding dimension is calculated by Cao's method [11], since this method is demonstrated to yield robust results on various signals.

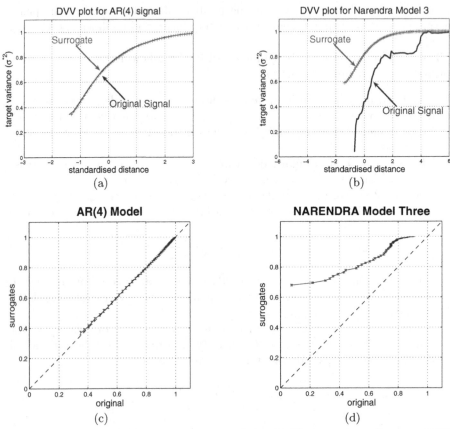

Fig. 3. Nonlinear and deterministic nature of signals. The upper two diagrams (DVV plot) are obtained by plotting the target variance as a function of standardised distance. The lower two diagrams (DVV scatter diagram) are obtained by plotting the target variance of the original data against the mean of the target variances of the surrogate data.

surrogate time series[2] [7], using the optimal embedding dimension of the original time series. Due to the standardisation of the distances, the DVV plots can be conveniently combined[3] within a *scatter diagram*, where the horizontal axis corresponds to the DVV plot of the original time series, and the vertical axis to that of the surrogate time series. If the surrogate time series yield DVV plots similar to that of the original time series, the 'DVV scatter diagram' coincides with the bisector line, and the original time series is *judged to be linear*, as shown

---

[2] In this chapter, all the DVV tests are performed using 19 surrogate data realisations. The reason for that is that with the increase in the number of surrogate data, DVV test does not yield a much better result whereas the computational complexity is much increased.

[3] In fact, target variance (σ^{*2}) of the original data is plotted against the mean of the target variance of 19 surrogate data, for all corresponding distances ($\frac{r_d - \mu_d}{\sigma_d}$).

in Figure 3(c). If not, the original time series is *judged to be nonlinear*, as depicted in Figure 3(d). Since the minimal target variance indicates a strong deterministic component within the signal, we conclude that in DVV scatter diagrams, the more the curve approaches the vertical axis, the more deterministic the nature of the signal. This can be employed as a convenient criterion for estimating the level of noise within a signal.

3   Qualitative and Quantitative Performance Analysis

To assess the *quantitative* performance of learning algorithms, it is convenient to use the standard one-step forward prediction gain [12]:-

$$R_p = 10 \log_{10} \left(\frac{\hat{\sigma}_s^2}{\hat{\sigma}_e^2} \right) [dB] \tag{3}$$

which is a logarithmic ratio between the estimated signal variance $\hat{\sigma}_s^2$ and estimated prediction error variance $\hat{\sigma}_e^2$. On the other hand, to assess the *qualitative* performance, that is, *a possible change in the signal nature introduced by a filter*, we proposed to compare DVV scatter diagrams of the output signals with those of the original signal. In the prediction setting, the target variances Eq. (2) for the predicted signal and its surrogates are obtained by performing the DVV test on the predicted signal. For robustness, these steps are repeated 100 times.

If the considered filters yield high prediction gain (R_p), the quantitative performance of the filters is judged to be "good". As for the qualitative performance, the more similar the DVV scatter diagram for the filtered signal is to that for the original signal, the better the qualitative performance of the considered prediction architecture.

For generality, we illustrate the usefulness of the proposed methodology for both linear and nonlinear (neural networks) adaptive filters and their combinations.

4   Experimental Settings

To illustrate the effect of the chosen mode of processing (linear, nonlinear, etc.), we have chosen a general hybrid architecture, which is shown to be able to improve the overall quantitative performance, as compared to the performance of single modules. In particular, it has been suggested that a cascaded combination of a recurrent neural network (RNN) and finite infinitive response (FIR) filter can simultaneously model the nonlinear and linear component of a signal [12]. The nonlinear neural filter can model the nonlinearity and a portion of the linearity within a signal, while the subsequent linear FIR filter models the remaining linear part of the signal.

The nonlinear neural filters used in simulations were the dynamical perceptron (nonlinear FIR filter) trained by the nonlinear gradient descent algorithm (NGD) and a recurrent perceptron, trained by the real time recursive learning (RTRL)

[13] algorithm. The linear filters considered were standard FIR filters trained by least mean square (LMS) and recursive least squares (RLS) algorithms.

The inputs were a benchmark linear AR(4) signal, given by

$$x(k) = 1.79x(k-1) - 1.85x(k-2) + 1.27x(k-3)$$
$$- 0.41x(k-4) + n(k) \tag{4}$$

where $n(k) \sim \mathcal{N}(0,1)$ and a benchmark nonlinear signal, the Narendra Model Three, given by [14]

$$z(k) = \frac{z(k-1)}{1+z^2(k-1)} + r^3(k)$$
$$r(k) = 1.79\,r(k-1) - 1.85\,r(k-2) + 1.27\,r(k-3)$$
$$- 0.41\,r(k-4) + n(k) \tag{5}$$

where $n(k) \sim \mathcal{N}(0,1)$. For these signals their DVV scatter diagrams are shown as Figure 3(c) and 3(d), clearly indicating the linear nature of (4) (DVV scatter diagram on the bisector line), and nonlinear nature of (5) (DVV scatter diagram deviating from the bisector line).

4.1 Simulations

The first experiment was conducted for prediction of the linear benchmark signal (4). The DVV scatter diagrams show the nonlinearity information about the output of such filters. From Figure 4, in terms of preserving the nature of the signal (linear in this case), both the nonlinear filters and hybrid filters performed well on a linear AR(4) signal, indicated by the fact that all the DVV scatter diagrams in Figure 4 lie on the bisector line. In terms of the prediction gain R_p, the NGD and RTRL performed similarly, and as expected, the hybrid filters performed better than single nonlinear filters. The hybrid filter realised as a cascaded combination of a dynamical perceptron trained by RTRL and FIR filter trained by RLS gave the best performance, as illustrated in bottom right diagram of Figure 4.

Figure 5 illustrates a similar experiment performed on prediction of a much more complex benchmark nonlinear signal (5). From Figure 5, both nonlinear filters trained by NGD and RTRL performed poorly on their own in terms of the prediction gain. However, from the change of the nature of the original signal, seen in Figure 3(d), they preserved the nature of the benchmark nonlinear signal better than the hybrid filters, even though the quantitative gain R_p for hybrid filters was higher. For instance, the recurrent perceptron trained by the RTRL exhibited worse quantitative performance but better qualitative performance. A hybrid filter consisting of a combination of a dynamical perceptron trained by NGD and an FIR filter trained by LMS, showed a considerable increase in gain, however, the signal was considerably linearised as illustrated by the DVV scatter diagram approaching the bisector line. The bottom right diagram in Figure 5 shows the performance of a hybrid filter consisting of a recurrent perceptron

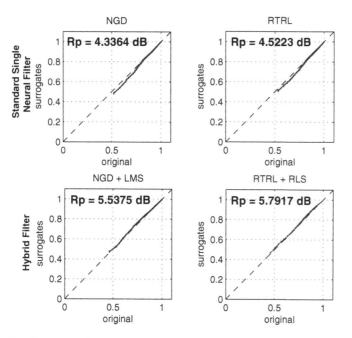

Fig. 4. Qualitative and quantitative comparison of the performance between nonlinear neural and hybrid filters for a linear benchmark signal (4). The top panels denote the DVV scatter diagrams for single neural filters (feedforward and feedback), trained by NGD and RTRL algorithm respectively. The bottom panel diagrams relate to hybrid filters.

trained by RTRL followed by a FIR filter trained by the RLS algorithm. This case gave best balance between the quantitative and qualitative performance out of all the combinations of hybrid filters considered. The quantitative performance gain for this combination was the second best of all the combinations, whereas the nature of the signal was preserved reasonably well.

We now investigate whether exchanging the order of filters within a hybrid filter will affect the overall performance. Given the highly nonlinear nature of the problem, it is expected that the performances will be significantly different. To this end we re-ran the experiments for the nonlinear benchmark signal. The results of the experiments are shown in Figure 6.

Figure 6 confirms that exchanging the order of the modules within a hybrid architecture does not provide the same performance, both quantitatively and qualitatively. Indeed, the quantitative performance are considerably worse and also the nature of the predicted signal changed significantly towards a linear one. This can be explained in the following way. When a linear filter is placed at the first stage of the hybrid filter, it linearise the input signal significantly and the subsequent nonlinear filter will not be able to recover the lost information as the system is not aware of presence of a nonlinear signal. However, if a nonlinear

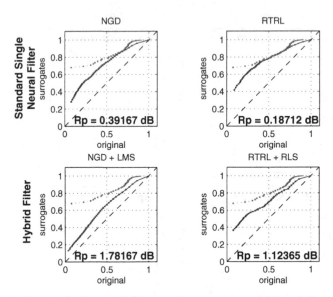

Fig. 5. Qualitative and quantitative performance comparison of the performance between nonlinear neural and linear filters for a nonlinear benchmark signal (5). The dotted line denotes the DVV scatter diagram for the original nonlinear benchmark signal Eq.(5), whereas the solid line denotes that for the output of the filters.

filter is placed as the first module, it will capture the input signal nonlinearity and inform the system that the upcoming signal is nonlinear in nature so that the subsequent linear filter is able to refine the output.

5   Online Nonlinearity Tracking Using Hybrid Filters

We have shown a novel framework of evaluating the qualitative performance of adaptive filters. This is achieved based upon examining the change in signal nature in terms of nonlinearity and determinism, which is considered an offline method. It is natural to ask whether it is possible to track the system nonlinearity online.

In [15] one such 'online' approach is considered which relies on parametric modeling to effectively "identify" the signal in hand. Figure 7 shows an implementation of this method which uses a third order Volterra filter (nonlinear subfilter) and a linear subfilter trained by the normalised LMS (NLMS) algorithm with a step size $\mu = 0.008$ to update the system parameters. The system was fed with the signal $y[k]$ obtained from

$$u[k] = \sum_{i=0}^{I} a_i x[k-i] \text{ where } I = 2 \text{ and } a_0 = 0.5, a_1 = 0.25, a_2 = 0.125 \quad (6)$$

$$y[k] = F(u[k]; k) + \eta[k] \quad (7)$$

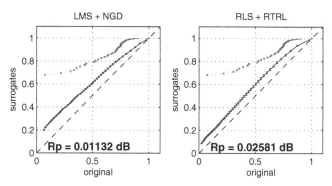

Fig. 6. Qualitative and quantitative comparison of the performance between "inverse order" hybrid filters for a nonlinear benchmark signal (5). The filter order is interchanged from the one in previous experiments. The dotted line denotes the DVV scatter diagram for the original nonlinear benchmark signal (5), whereas the solid line denotes that for the output of the filters.

where $x[k]$ are independent identically distributed and uniformly distributed over the range $[-0.5, 0.5]$ and $\eta[k] \sim \mathcal{N}(0, 0.0026)$. The function $F(u[k]; k)$ varies with the range of k as follows

$$F(u[k]; k) = \begin{cases} u^3[k], \text{ for } 10000 < k \leq 20000 \\ u^2[k], \text{ for } 30000 < k \leq 40000 \\ u[k], \text{ elsewhere} \end{cases} \qquad (8)$$

The signal $y[k]$ can be seen in the first trace of Figure 7. The second and third traces show the residual estimation errors of the optimal linear system and Volterra system respectively. The final trace is the estimated degree of system nonlinearity. Whilst these results show that this approach can detect changes in nonlinearity and is not affected by the presence of noise, this may be largely due to nature of the input signal being particularly suited to the Volterra model.

In this chapter, we propose to overcome this problem be making use of the concept of convexity. A convex combination can be described as [16]

$$\lambda x + (1 - \lambda)y \text{ where } \lambda \in [0, 1] \qquad (9)$$

as illustrated on Figure 8. The point resulting from the convex combination of x and y will lie somewhere on the line defined by x and y, between the two. The benefits of using convex optimisation are threefold:

– The existence of the solution is guaranteed;
– The solution is unique;
– This facilitates the collaborative adaptive filtering approach

Intuitively, a convex combination of the output of two adaptive filters with different dynamical characteristics ought to be able to "follow" the subfilter with better performance, provided a suitable adaptation of λ. Indeed, such a

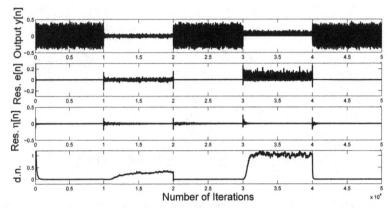

Fig. 7. NLMS with Volterra series

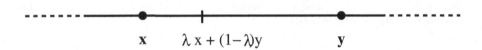

$$x \qquad \lambda x + (1-\lambda)y \qquad y$$

Fig. 8. Convexity

hybrid filter has been proposed in [17,18] in a form that adaptively combines the outputs of the subfilters based on their instantaneous output error. In [19], this approach has demonstrated to yield considerable improvement in the steady state and convergence capabilities of the resultant filter.

While previous applications of hybrid filters have focused on the improved performance they can offer over the individual constituent filters, our approach relies on the observation of the evolution of the so-called mixing parameter λ over time. For example, in the standard setting, λ would vary so as to initially favour the faster subfilter (learning) and finally, the filter with the best steady state properties[4].

In this section, we consider hybrid combinations of filters. The analysis of λ then provides insight into the nature of the signal under consideration. In particular, we focus on quantifying the degree of "nonlinearity" in a signal. As a subset of nonlinearity we also consider the degree of "sparsity", as sparse signals occur naturally in many real world applications. The benchmark signals considered are linear $(AR(4))$ or nonlinear by design, whereas the real world signals considered in this case are speech data.

5.1 Hybrid Adaptive Filter for Signal Modality Characterisation

Figure 9 shows a block diagram of a hybrid adaptive filter aimed at signal modality characterisation. In this Chapter, we focus on tracking the degree of

---

[4] This differs from the traditional "search then converge" approach, since it caters for potentially nonstationary data.

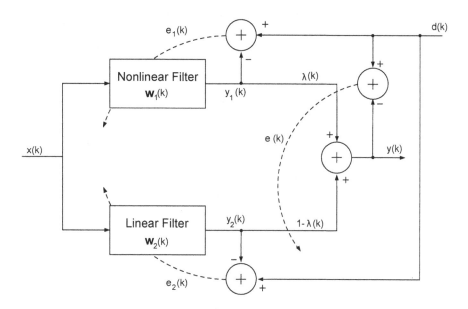

Fig. 9. Block-diagram of a hybrid adaptive filter for nonlinearity tracking

nonlinearity in a signal by combining the outputs of a linear and a nonlinear subfilter in a hybrid fashion. Following the approach from [17,19], the output of such a structure was obtained as

$$y(k) = \lambda(k)y_1(k) + [1 - \lambda(k)]\, y_2(k) \qquad (10)$$

where $y_1(k) = \mathbf{x}^T(k)\mathbf{w}_1(k)$ and $y_2(k) = \mathbf{x}^T(k)\mathbf{w}_2(k)$ are the outputs of the two subfilters, with respective weight vectors $\mathbf{w}_1^T(k)$ and $\mathbf{w}_2^T(k)$ and where $\mathbf{x}(k)$ is the common input vector. For simplicity, $\mathbf{w}_1(k)$ and $\mathbf{w}_2(k)$ are assumed to be of equal length $L = 10$ and are adapted independently, using their own design rules and depending on the property we aim at tracking. Parameter $\lambda(k)$ is a mixing scalar parameter, which is adapted using a stochastic gradient rule that minimises the quadratic cost function $J(k) = e^2(k)$ of the overall filter, where $e(k)$ is the output error given by $e(k) = d(k) - y(k)$. Using LMS type adaptation to minimise the error of the overall filter, the generic form the the λ update can be written as

$$\lambda(k + 1) = \lambda(k) - \mu_\lambda\, \nabla_\lambda J(k)|_{\lambda = \lambda(k)} \qquad (11)$$

where μ_λ is the adaptation step-size of the hybrid filter. Using (10) and the expression for the output error, the partial derivative of the cost function with respect to $\lambda(k)$ can be written as

$$\nabla_\lambda J(k)|_{\lambda = \lambda(k)} = -e(k)[y_1(k) - y_2(k)] \qquad (12)$$

Then equation (11) can be rewritten as

$$\lambda(k + 1) = \lambda(k) + \mu_\lambda e(k)[y_1(k) - y_2(k)] \qquad (13)$$

To ensure the combination of adaptive filters remains a convex function, λ was kept in the range $0 \leq \lambda(k) \leq 1$. For this purpose, in [17] the authors used a sigmoid function to bound $\lambda(k)$ in the range $[0, 1]$. Since, in order to determine the changes in the modality of a signal, we are not interested in the overall performance of the filter but in the variable λ, the use of a sigmoid function would interfere with the true values of $\lambda(k)$ and was therefore not used. Instead, a hard limit on the set of allowed values for λ was implemented.

5.2   Performance of the Combination on Benchmark Signals

In order to illustrate the operation of the convex combination aimed at signal modality tracking, simulations were initially performed on a set of synthetic signals made by alternating between blocks of linear and nonlinear data. 100 runs of independent trials were performed and averaged, in the one-step ahead prediction setting. The linear signal used was a stable $AR(4)$ process given by

$$x(k) = 1.79x(k-1) - 1.85x(k-2) + 1.27x(k-3) - 0.41x(k-4) + n(k) \quad (14)$$

where $n(k) \sim \mathcal{N}(0, 1)$ is white Gaussian noise (WGN). The benchmark nonlinear input signal was [14]

$$x(k) = \frac{x^2(k-1)(x(k-1)+2.5)}{1 + x(k-1)^2 + x(k-2)^2} + n(k-1) \quad (15)$$

For the experiments, the linear adaptive filter was the ϵ-NLMS (Normalised Least Mean Square) while the nonlinear filter was the Normalised Nonlinear Gradient Descent (NNGD) [20]. NNGD and NLMS were used as opposed to the standard NGD and LMS algorithms in order to overcome the issue of high dependence of the convergence of the individual subfilters and hence of the combination on input signal statistics. Furthermore, since these subfilters exhibit a rate of convergence that is potentially faster, this alternative also increased the speed of adaptation of λ.

The nonlinearity at the output of the nonlinear filter was the logistic sigmoid function, given by

$$\Phi(z) = \frac{1}{1 + e^{-\beta z}} \ , \ z \in \mathbb{R} \quad (16)$$

with a slope of $\beta = 1$. Intuitively, we expect the linear filter to take over (i.e. $\lambda \to 0$) when the modality of the input signal is more linear while the output is expected to follow the more nonlinear filter (i.e. $\lambda \to 1$) when the input is nonlinear [see Fig. 9].

Figure 10 shows the evolution of λ at the output of the hybrid combination from Figure 9 for a signal alternating between linear and nonlinear every 200 and 100 samples respectively. The combination proved robust to changes in step-sizes within the combination and was always capable of tracking the degree of nonlinearity in the input signal, provided $\mu_{NLMS} = \mu_{NNGD}$ and provided the step-size values were such that both subfilters converged.

Having demonstrated the ability of the combination at tracking the degree of nonlinearity in synthetically generated data, we next perform simulations on real-world speech data.

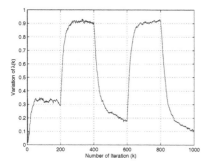
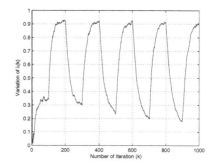

(a) Input signal nature alternating every 200 samples

(b) Input signal nature alternating every 100 samples

Fig. 10. Mixing parameter λ at the output of the hybrid combination from Figure 9, with $\mu_\lambda = 20$, for input signal nature alternating between linear (14) and nonlinear (15)

5.3 Tracking the Degree of Nonlinearity in Speech Data

In this section, we aim at giving a flavour of the potential of the hybrid adaptive filtering approach on speech data. The area of speech modality characterisation is only emerging and in fact, only little is known about the nature of speech. Recently, much effort has been devised in developing accurate models for the speech production system and for characterising the modality of speech. It is believed that the accurate knowledge of speech characteristics will lead significant advances in several areas of speech processing, including speech coding and speech synthesis.

Typically, the vocal tract[5] is modeled as an all-pole filter, i.e. using a linear difference equation. This is mainly due to the solid theory underlying linear systems and to the corresponding decrease in computational complexity. However, the physical nature of the vocal tract is itself an indication of the potentially nonlinear nature of the radiated speech. In fact, several studies have suggested that linear models do not sufficiently model the human vocal tract [21,22].

Due to its nonstationary nature, the characterisation of speech is a complex task and much research has been done recently to study the nonlinear properties of speech and to find an efficient model for the speech signal. These studies have typically been based on a classification between vowels and consonants or between voiced and unvoiced sounds[6]. It is known that all vowels and certain consonants are voiced, i.e. highly periodic in nature with a periodic excitation source. In the case of unvoiced consonants, the folds may be completely open (e.g. for the /s/, /sh/ and /f/ sounds) or partially open (e.g. for /h/ sound), resulting in a noise like waveform [23,24,25].

---

[5] The vocal tract is the cavity where sound that is produced at the sound source is filtered. It consist of the laryngeal cavity, the pharynx, the oral and nasal cavities; it starts at the vocal folds (vocal cords).

[6] A sound is referred to as being voiced when the vocal folds are vibrating, whereas it is voiceless (or unvoiced) in a contrary case.

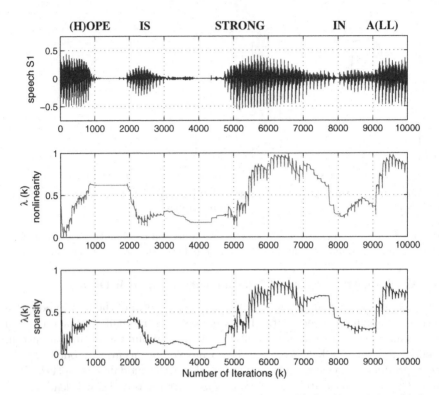

Fig. 11. Speech signal S1 and corresponding variation of λ for determining the degree of "nonlinearity" and "sparsity"

In [26], Kubin shows that there are several nonlinearities in the human vocal tract, whereas he demonstrates that linear autoregressive models are fully adequate for unvoiced speech. In [27,28,29] chaotic behaviour is found in voiced sounds such as vowels and nasals like /n/ and /m/. In [30], the speech signal is modeled as a chaotic process. Finally, hybrid methods combining linear and nonlinear structures have previously been applied to speech processing [31,32,33].

While the majority of the studies so far have suggested a nonlinear nature of voiced speech, the form of fundamental nonlinearity is still unknown. In [34], it is suggested that speech may contain different types of linear/nonlinear characteristics, and that for example, vowels may be modeled by either chaotic features or types of higher order nonlinear features, while consonants may be modeled by random processes.

For the simulations, speech signals S1 and S3 from [35] were first analysed. Finally, a randomly selected recording from the APLAWD database [36] was considered, together with the corresponding laryngograph[7] signal. All amplitude

---

[7] A laryngograph monitors vocal fold closure by measuring variations in the conductance between a transmitting electrode delivering a high frequency signal to the neck on one side of the larynx and a receiving electrode on the other side of the larynx.

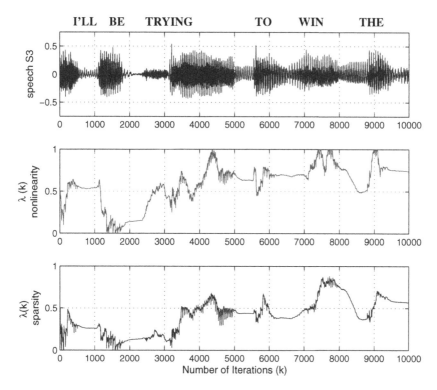

Fig. 12. Speech signal S3 and corresponding variation of λ for "nonlinearity" and "sparsity" tracking

signals were standardised so that the amplitude range was between $[-0.5, 0.5]$. For generality, the values of step-sizes were kept as in the simulations on stationary data, namely $\mu_{NLMS} = \mu_{NNGD} = 0.4$ and μ_λ was varied according to the aim of the experiment (larger μ_λ used for demonstrating the correlation between the laryngograph signal and the evolution of λ). The nonlinearity used in the complex NNGD (CNNGD) algorithm was the hyperbolic tanh function given by

$$\Phi(x) = \tanh(x) = \frac{\sinh x}{\cosh x} = \frac{\exp^x - \exp^{-x}}{\exp^x + \exp^{-x}} \, , \, x \in \mathbb{R} \qquad (17)$$

Prediction was performed in the one-step ahead setting (short-term prediction). One may in the future perform simulations using long-term prediction, i.e. using a prediction delay of one pitch period, as in [37].

In order to investigate the potential of using hybrid filters for the purpose of determining the degree of nonlinearity and sparsity in a speech waveform, the combination of CNLMS and CNNGD (complex linear and nonlinear subfilters) and NLMS and SSLMS (signed sparse LMS) (following the approach from [38]) were both fed with the speech waveforms S1 and S3 in turn. The first trace from Figures 11 and 12 shows the speech waveform while the second and third traces respectively show the corresponding variations of λ for tracking the degree of

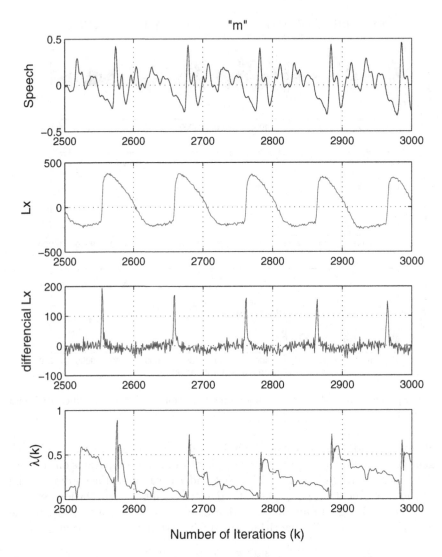

Fig. 13. Speech waveform for letter "m"; corresponding Lx waveform and differential Lx; variation of λ

nonlinearity and sparsity in the waveform. In the second trace, and as above, a value of λ close to 1 indicated the predominantly nonlinear nature of speech and vice versa for $\lambda \to 0$. Finally, in the third trace, and for consistency, a $\lambda \to 1$ showed the predominantly sparse nature of the waveform.

From the figures, the expected correlation between nonlinearity and sparsity is confirmed. We note that certain parts of a speech signal are better modeled using nonlinear structures ($\lambda \to 1$), while for others, linear structures are sufficient ($\lambda \to 0$). Furthermore, voiced speech appears to be indicated by regions where λ exhibits a "spiky" behaviour. From Figure 11, it can be noticed that the noise like sounds /z/ (around samples 2800-3200) and /s/ (around samples 4100-4200) are linear which agree with previous findings in the field. From Figure 12, it can be inferred that highly voiced sounds such as /a/ in "trying" is more nonlinear.

5.4   Correlation Between Laryngograph Signal and the Variation of λ

In this section, we aim at exploring the relationship between the variation of λ and the laryngograph waveform (Lx). For this purpose, simulations are performed on the randomly selected speech waveform from the APLAWD database [36]: the letter "m" read by a male speaker. Figure 13 shows the speech and corresponding laryngograph waveforms and the evolution of λ at the output of the hybrid combination of CNLMS and CNNGD. From this figure, it is clear that there is some correlation between the two waveforms during certain periods of voiced speech. In particular, it appears that sharp transitions in λ and in the derivative of the Lx waveform (indicating glottal opening instant) occur simultaneously (the delay between the two waveforms is due to the larynx-to-microphone delay and estimated in [39] to be of approximately 0.95ms, i.e. $20 \text{ kHz} \times 0.95ms = 19$ samples). This does not necessarily imply that the hybrid filter is capable of detecting glottal opening instants, but that there is a clear relationship between the two signals which requires further investigation.

References

1. Schreiber, T.: Interdisciplinary application of nonlinear time series methods. Phys. Rep. 308(1), 1–64 (1999)
2. Gautama, T., Mandic, D.P., Van Hulle, M.M.: The delay vector variance method for detecting determinism and nonlinearity in time series. Physica D 190(3–4), 167–176 (2004)
3. Gautama, T., Mandic, D., Van Hulle, M.: Signal nonlinearity in fMRI: A comparison between BOLD and MION. IEEE Trans. Med. Imaging 22(5), 636–644 (2003)
4. Schreiber, T., Schmitz, A.: On the discrimination power of measures for nonlinearity in a time series. Phys. Rev. E 55(5), 5443–5447 (1997)
5. Gautama, T., Mandic, D.P., Van Hulle, M.M.: On the characterisaion of the deterministic/stochastic and linear/nonlinear nature of time series. Technical Report DPM-04-5, Imperial College London (2004)
6. Schreiber, T., Schmitz, A.: Surrogate time series. Physica D 142, 346–382 (2000)
7. Theiler, J., Eubank, S., Longtin, A., Galdrikian, B., Farmer, J.: Testing for nonlinearity in time series: The method of surrogate data. Physica D 58, 77–94 (1992)
8. Schreiber, T., Schmitz, A.: Improved surrogate data for nonlinearity tests. Phys. Rev. Lett., 635–638 (1996)
9. Weigend, A.S., Gershenfeld, N.A.: Time Series Prediction: Forecasting the Future and Understanding the Past. Addison-Wesley, Reading, MA (1993)

10. Kaplan, D.: Exceptional events as evidence for determinism. Physica D 73(1), 38–48 (1994)
11. Cao, L.: Practical method for determining the minimum embedding dimension of a scalar time series. Physica D: Nonlinear Phenomena 110(1-2), 43–50 (1997)
12. Haykin, S., Li, L.: Nonlinear adaptive prediction of nonstationary signals. IEEE Transactions on Signal Processing 43(2), 526–535 (1995)
13. Mandic, D.P., Chambers, J.A.: Recurrent Neural Networks for Prediction: Learning Algorithms, Architectures and Stability. John Wiley & Sons, Chichester (2001)
14. Narendra, K.S., Parthasarathy, K.: Identification and control of dynamical systems using neural networks. IEEE Transactions on Neural Networks 1(1), 4–27 (1990)
15. Mizuta, H., Jibu, M., Yana, K.: Adaptive estimation of the degree of system nonlinearity. In: IEEE Adaptive Systems for Signal Processing and Control Symposium (AS-SPCC), pp. 352–356 (2000)
16. Cichocki, A., Unbehauen, R.: Neural networks for optimization and signal processing. Wiley, Chichester (1993)
17. Figueras-Vidal, A.R., Arenas-Garcia, J., Sayed, A.H.: Steady state performance of convex combinations of adaptive filters. In: ICASSP 2005. Proceedings of the International Conference on Acoustis, Speech and Signal Processing, pp. 33–36 (2005)
18. Kozat, S.S., Singer, A.C.: Multi-stage adaptive signal processing algorithms. In: Proceedings of the 2000 IEEE Sensor Array and Multichannel Signal Processing Workshop, pp. 380–384 (2000)
19. Mandic, D.P., Vayanos, P., Boukis, C., Goh, S.L., Jelfs, B., Gautama, T., Rutkowski, T.: Collaborative adaptive learning using hybrid filters. In: Proceedings of ICASSP 2007, vol. III, pp. 921–924 (2007)
20. Mandic, D.P.: NNGD algorithm for neural adaptive filters. Electronics Letters 36(9), 845–846 (2000)
21. Schroeter, J., Sondhi, M.: Speech coding based on physiological models of speech production. In: Furui, S., Sondhi, M. (eds.) Advances in speech Signal Processing, pp. 231–268. Marcel Dekker, New York, NY, USA (1992)
22. Thyssen, J., Nielsen, H., Hansen, S.: Non-linear short-term prediction in speech coding. In: ICASSP 1994. Proceedings of the International Conference on Acoustics, Speech and Signal Processing, vol. 1, pp. 185–188 (1994)
23. Deller, J.R., Proakis, J.G., Hansen, H.L.: Discrete Time Processing of speech Signals. Prentice-Hall, Englewood Cliffs (1987)
24. Rabiner, L., Juang, B.H.: Fundamentals of speech recognition. Prentice-Hall, Englewood Cliffs (1993)
25. Rabiner, L., Schafer, R.W.: Digital Processing of Speech Signals. Prentice-Hall, Englewood Cliffs (1978)
26. Kubin, G.: Nonlinear processing of speech. In: Kleijn, W., Paliwal, K. (eds.) Speech coding and synthesis, pp. 557–610. Elsevier Science B.V., Amsterdam (1995)
27. Banbrook, M., McLaughlin, S., Mann, I.: Speech characterisation and synthesis by nonlinear methods. In: Proceedings of the International Conference on Speech and Audio Processing, vol. 7, pp. 1–17 (1999)
28. Martinez, F., Guillamon, A., Alcaraz, J., Alcaraz, M.: Detection of chaotic behaviour in speech signals using the largest lyapunov exponent. In: DSP 2002. IEEE International Conference on Digital Signal Processing, pp. 317–320 (2002)
29. Miyano, T., Nagami, A., Tokuda, I., Aihara, K.: Detecting nonlinear determinism in voiced sounds of japanese vowel /a/. International Journal of Bifurcation and Chaos 10(8), 1973–1979 (2000)

30. Townshend, B.: Nonlinear prediction of speech. In: ICASSP 1991. Proceedings of the International Conference on Acoustics, Speech and Signal Processing, pp. 425–428 (1991)
31. Hansen, J., Gavidia-Ceballos, L., Kaiser, J.: A nonlinear operator-based speech feature analysis method with applications to vocal fold pathology assessment. IEEE Transactions on Biomedical Engineering 45(3), 300–313 (1998)
32. Maragos, P., Quatieri, T., Kaiser, J.: Speech nonlinearities, modulations, and energy operators. In: ICASSP 1991. Proceedings of the International Conference on Acoustics, Speech and Signal Processing, pp. 421–424 (1991)
33. Wokurek, W.: Time-frequency analysis of the glottal opening. In: ICASSP 1997. Proceedings of the International Conference on Acoustics, Speech and Signal Processing, pp. 1435–1438 (1997)
34. Turunen, J., Tanttu, J.T., Loula, P.: Hammerstein model for speech coding. EURASIP Journal on Applied Signal Processing 2003(12), 1238–1249 (2003)
35. Mandic, D.P., Baltersee, J., Chambers, J.A.: Nonlinear prediction of speech with a pipelined recurrent neural network and advanced learning algorithms. In: Prochazka, A., Uhlir, J., Rayner, P.J.W., Kingsbury, N.G. (eds.) Signal Analysis and Prediction, pp. 291–309. Birkhauser, Boston (1998)
36. Lindsey, G., Breen, A., Nevard, S.: Spar's archivable actual-word databases (1987)
37. Birgmeier, M., Bernhard, H.P., Kubin, G.: Nonlinear long-term prediction of speech signals. In: ICASSP 1997. IEEE International Conference on Acoustics, Speech, and Signal Processing, vol. 2, pp. 1283–1286 (1997)
38. Jelfs, B., Mandic, D.P.: Toward online monitoring of the changes in signal modality: The degree of sparsity. In: Proceedings of the 7th IMA International Conference on Mathematics for Signal Processing, pp. 29–32 (2006)
39. Brookes, M., Gudnasonand, J., Kounoudes, A., Naylor, P.: Estimation of glottal closure instants in voiced speech using the DYPSA algorithm. IEEE Transactions on Audio, Speech and Language Processing 15(1), 34–43 (2007)

Mixing HMM-Based Spanish Speech Synthesis with a CBR for Prosody Estimation*

Xavi Gonzalvo, Ignasi Iriondo, Joan Claudi Socoró,
Francesc Alías, and Carlos Monzo

GPMM - Grup de Recerca en Processament Multimodal
Enginyeria i Arquitectura La Salle, Universitat Ramon Llull
Quatre Camins 2, 08022 Barcelona (Spain)
{gonzalvo,iriondo,jclaudi,falias,cmonzo}@salle.url.edu
http://www.salle.url.edu/tsenyal

Abstract. Hidden Markov Models based text-to-speech (HMM-TTS) synthesis is a technique for generating speech from trained statistical models where spectrum, pitch and durations of basic speech units are modelled altogether. The aim of this work is to describe a Spanish HMM-TTS system using an external machine learning technique to help improving the expressiveness. System performance is analysed objectively and subjectively. The experiments were conducted on a reliably labelled speech corpus, whose units were clustered using contextual factors based on the Spanish language. The results show that the CBR-based F0 estimation is capable of improving the HMM-based baseline performance when synthesizing non-declarative short sentences while the durations accuracy is similar with the CBR or the HMM system.

1 Introduction

One of the main interests in TTS synthesis is to improve quality and naturalness in general purpose applications. Concatenative speech synthesis for a limited domains (e.g. Virtual Weather man [1]) presents drawbacks when used in a different domain and new recordings become time consuming and expensive. In contrast, the main benefit of HMM-TTS is the capability of modelling voices in order to synthesize different speaker features, styles and emotions. In that sense, voice transformation with concatenative speech synthesis still requires large databases in contrast to HMM which can obtain better results with smaller databases [2] (e.g. speaker interpolation [3] or eigenvoices [4]). Furthermore, language is a key topic during the design of a TTS and HMM synthesis has also been used to design polyglot systems [5]. The HMM-TTS scheme based on contextual factors for clustering can be used for any language (e.g. English [6], Portuguese [7] or Japanese-Spanish for the polyglot system [5]). Basic synthesis units

---

* Thanks to Prof. Dr. Eric Keller, University of Lausanne, for kindly spending a time on verifying this paper. This work has been partially supported by the European Commission, project SALERO FP6 IST-4-027122-IP.

M. Chetouani et al. (Eds.): NOLISP 2007, LNAI 4885, pp. 78–85, 2007.

(i.e. phonemes) and their context attributes-values pairs are the main language dependent information. As a result, HMM-TTS systems provide a stable synthesis performance though it sometimes presents a lower quality and a plain expressiveness in comparison with concatenative systems. For the former drawback, some techniques have been shown to improve the quality (i.e. Global Variance or GV [8]) and for the latter, this work presents a mixed F0 approach (HMM+CBR) for improving the expressiveness for delivering different types of sentences with the original speaker style.

The HMM-TTS system presented in this work is based on a source-filter model approach to generate speech directly from HMM itself in contrast to other approaches that unified concatenative and HMM approaches [9]. It uses a decision tree based on context clustering in order to improve model training and to characterize phoneme units introducing a counterpart approach with respect to English [6]. As the HMM-TTS system is a complete technique to generate speech, this research presents objective results to measure its performance as a prosody estimator and subjective measures to test the synthesized speech. It is compared with a tested Machine Learning strategy based on case based reasoning (CBR) for prosody estimation [10].

This paper is organized as follows: Section 2 describes the HMM system workflow, parameter training and synthesis. Section 3 concerns CBR for prosody estimation. Section 4 describes the mixed F0. Section 5 presents measures and discusses the results and section 6 presents the concluding remarks and future planned research.

2   HMM-TTS System

2.1   Training and Synthesis

As in any HMM-TTS system, two stages are distinguished: training and synthesis. Figure 1 depicts the classical training and synthesis workflow (dotted lines stand for the optional F0 generation from the CBR module). First, HMM for isolated phonemes (each HMM represents a contextual phoneme) are estimated and each of these models are used as an initialization of the contextual phonemes. Then, similar phonemes are clustered by means of a decision tree using contextual information and specific questions. Unseen units during the training stage can be synthesized using these decision trees. Each contextual phoneme HMM definition includes spectrum, F0 and state durations. Topology used is a 5 states left-to-right with no-skips. Each state is represented with 2 independent streams, one for spectrum and another for pitch. Both types of information are completed with their delta and delta-delta coefficients. Spectrum is modelled by 13th order mel-cepstral coefficients which can generate speech with the MLSA (Mel Log Spectrum Approximation) filter [11]. The spectrum model is a multivariate Gaussian distribution [2]. The Spanish corpus was pitch marked using the approach described in [12]. This algorithm refines mark-up to get a smoothed F0 contour in order to reduce discontinuities in the generated curve for synthesis. The model is a multi-space probability distribution [2] that may be used in order to store continuous logarithmic values of the F0 contour and a discrete indicator for voiced/unvoiced. State durations of each HMM are modelled by a Multivariate Gaussian distribution [13]. Its dimensionality is equal to the number of states in the corresponding HMM.

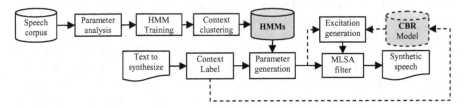

Fig. 1. Training and synthesis workflow

Once the system has been trained, it provides a set of phonemes represented by a contextual factor. The first step in the synthesis stage produces a complete contextualized list of phonemes from a text to be synthesized. Chosen units are converted into a sequence of HMMs. Durations are estimated to maximize the probability of state durations and then, using the algorithm proposed by Fukada in [11], spectrum and F0 parameters are generated from HMM models using dynamic features. The excitation signal is generated from the F0 curve and the voiced and unvoiced information. Finally, in order to reconstruct speech, the system uses spectrum parameters as the MLSA filter coefficients and excitation as the input signal.

2.2   Context Based Clustering

The decision trees used to perform the clustering are based on information refer-ring to spectrum, F0 and state durations and are designed independently because they are affected by different contextual factors. As the number of contextual fac-tors increases, there is less data to train the models. To deal with this problem, the clustering scheme presented in [2] will be used to provide the HMMs with enough samples as some states can be shared by similar units. Text analysis for HMM-TTS based decision tree clustering was carried out by Festival [15] updating an existing Spanish voice for linguistic analysis. Spanish HMM-TTS required the de-sign of specific questions to use in the tree. Table 2.2 enumerates the main features and contextual factors taken into account. Correct questions will determine clus-ters to reproduce a fine F0 contour in relation with the real intonation.

3   CBR System Description

As shown in figure 1, CBR system for prosody estimator can be included as a module in any TTS system (i.e. excitation signal can be created using either

Table 1. Spanish phonetic features and contextual factors

Unit		Features	Contextual factor
Phoneme	Vowel	Frontal, Back, Half open, Open, Closed	{Preceding, next} Position in syllable
	Consonant	Dental, velar, bilabial, alveolar lateral, Rhotic, palatal, labio-dental, Interdental, Prepalatal, plosive, nasal, fricative	
Syllable		Stress, position in word, vowel	{Preceding, next} stress, #phonemes, #stressed syllables
Word		POS, #syllables	Preceding, next POS, #syllables
Phrase		End Tone	Preceding, next #syllables

HMM, CBR or the mixed system proposed in this work). It was shown in [10] that a CBR approach is appropriate to create prosody even with expressive speech. The CBR strategy was originally designed for retrieving mean phoneme information related to F0, energy and duration, but this research compares the F0 and the duration with the HMM based estimator.

This CBR system is a corpus oriented method for the quantitative modelling of prosody. Analysis of texts is carried out by the SinLib library [14], an engine developed to Spanish text analysis. Prosody cases are built from features extracted from texts (i.e. a set of attribute-value pair). These are based on the accentual group (AG) that incorporates syllable influence and is related to speech rhythm, and the intonational group (IG). Structure at IG level is reached by concatenating AGs. Main features to characterize each intonational unit are: position of AG in IG, number of syllables, accent type, IG phrase position, IG as interrogative, declarative or exclamative, stressed syllable position, duration values or polynomial coefficients for the F0 estimation.

The system training can be divided in two stages: selection and adaptation. Each sentence is analysed in order to convert it into a new case (i.e. a set of attribute-value pairs). In order to optimize the system, case reduction is carried out by grouping similar attributes. Once the memory of cases is created, the goal is to obtain a solution that best matches the new problem (i.e. the most similar case). Mean F0 per phoneme is retrieved by first estimating phoneme durations, normalizing temporal axis and computing the mean pitch for each phoneme using the retrieved polynomial.

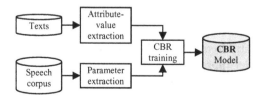

Fig. 2. CBR Training workflow

4   Mixed F0

The aim of using an external F0 estimation is to build a better excitation signal able to produce an improved expressiveness. The standard HMM F0 estimation is over-smoothed due to the statistical processing during the training stage and the CBR approach produces a F0 that can be too high to be synthesized by the HMM-TTS. Moreover, in the work presented in [8] it was not clearly shown that the GV technique was able to improve the quality when applied only to F0. In this work, the final F0 contour is produced as the mean value of both approaches, hence it fuses the advantages of stability (HMM) and high expressiveness (CBR). Notice that the CBR estimation can be viewed as the global variance for a specific sentence.

5   Experiments

Experiments were conducted on the corpus to evaluate objective and subjective measures. On the one hand, objective measures compare real prosody (F0 and duration) with HMM-TTS and CBR system estimations. On the other hand, subjective results validate the Spanish synthesis[1]. Results are presented for various phrase types and lengths (number of phonemes). Phrase lengths classification is referenced to the corpus average length. Thus, a short (S) and a long (L) sentence are below and above the standard deviation ($\mu \pm \sigma$), while very short (VS) and very long (VL) exceed double the standard deviation above and below ($\mu \pm 2\sigma$).

The Spanish female voice was created from a corpus developed together with LAICOM [10]. Speech was recorded by a professional speaker in neutral emotion and segmented and revised by speech processing researchers. The corpus features contains 8.3% of examples for exclamative (EXC), 70.7% for the declarative (DEC) and 21% for the interrogative (INT). The system was trained with HTS [16] using 620 phrases of a total of 833 (25% of the corpus is used for testing purposes). The training part was build using closed percentages (8.1% EXC, 70.8% DEC and 21.9% INT).

First, texts were labelled using contextual factors described in table 2.2. Then, HMMs were trained and clustered with different decision trees for spectrum, F0 and state durations. Spectrum states are basically clustered according to phoneme features while F0 questions show the influence of syllable, word and phrase contextual factors [2].

5.1   Objective Measures

Since both fundamental frequency and duration accuracy estimations are crucial in a source-filter model approach and are important factors for the expressiveness modelling, the evaluation of these parameters becomes a key step [17]. Objectives

---

[1] See http://www.salle.url.edu/~gonzalvo/hmm, for some synthesis examples

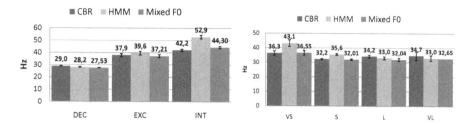

Fig. 3. RMSE for F0 contour: (a) phrase type, (b) phrase length for interrogative type

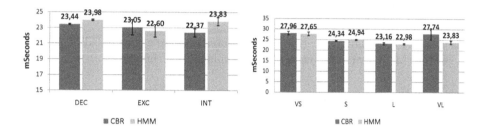

Fig. 4. RMSE for duration: (a) phrase type, (b) phrase length

measures evaluate the RMSE (i.e. estimated vs. real) of the F0 contour (figure 3) and the mean duration of each phoneme (figure 4).

In the one hand, figure 3 (a) shows that both systems (CBR and HMM) present a similar performance except for the case of interrogative sentences. For this kind of sentence, short ones are worse (see figure 3 (b)). On the other hand, the HMM and the CBR system have a similar RMSE for duration (figure 4) though interrogative are worse with HMM and VL worse with CBR.

A real example is presented in figure 5 (b). For the short declarative part (frames < 350) both HMM and CBR estimate a similar F0 contour. However, for the short and interrogative part (frames > 350), the CBR approach becomes a better approach because it reproduces fast changes better. The mixed F0 contour presents variations when the expressiveness must be improved thanks to the CBR system, hence the final excitation signal produces a better intonation.

5.2   Subjective Evaluation

The aim of the subjective measures (see figure 5 (a)) is to assess synthesized speech from HMM-TTS using HMM-based F0 estimators and a mixed F0 system using HMM and CBR. The preference of the users is biased towards the mixed system with INT or EXC sentences. In the case of EXC sentences, the preference for the mixed system decreases and the non-distinction option is bigger than for the INT case. Although the expressiveness is also improved in this case, some of the synthesized sentences were harder to be distinguished and even the mixed system intonation was subjectively considered not appropriate in some cases, though it

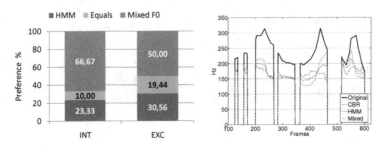

Fig. 5. (a) Preference for phrase type, (b) Example of F0 estimation for HMM-TTS "Su sistema de comunicación, podrá adaptarse?" translated as "Your communication system, can it be adapted?"

was closer to the original recording. DEC sentences were not included in the test due to the similarity of the synthesis (i.e. similar RMSE in figure 3 (a)).

6   Conclusions and Future Work

A Spanish HMM-TTS was presented here and its performance was compared with CBR for F0 and duration estimation. The HMM system performance has been analysed by objective and subjective measures. Objective measures showed that HMM prosody reproduction depends on the phrase type and length. For declarative sentences, HMM and CBR has a similar RMSE performance. Exclamative and interrogative sentences (i.e. intonational variations) are better reproduced by the F0 CBR estimator. This can be explained, since the CBR approach uses AG and IG attributes in a polynomial interpolation to retrieve a changing F0 contour that becomes a better solution in non-declarative phrases and low contextual information cases. Moreover, HMM and CBR are similar estimators for durations, so the CBR estimation contributes little though more research will be carried out in this respect. The final mixed F0 contour improved the expressiveness when we used HMM as the stable information as well as CBR for the desirable variance. Subjective measures validated the HMM-TTS synthesis using the mixed F0. In addition, notice that the CBR approach involves a low computational cost and that HMM training process is able to model all parameters together in a HMM taking advantage of voice analysis and transformation.

Future HMM-TTS system could include AG and IG in its features to improve F0 estimation. Furthermore, vocoded speech produced by the HMM-TTS system will be improved when a mixed excitation technique is applied using well defined models of the parametrized residual excitation that will be implemented using a multi-band mixing structure. Also, the main power of HMM-TTS is the statistical modelling of information. Regarding this, the prosody study shown in this work serves as the starting point for future systems using voice modification. Furthermore, the HMM-TTS systems are also able to model a voice with a reduced corpus, so it would be interesting to set the minimum number of sentences needed to produce a good synthesis in terms of naturalness and expressiveness [17].

References

1. Alías, F., Iriondo, I.: Formiga, Ll., Gonzalvo, X., Monzo, C., Sevillano, X.: High quality Spanish restricted-domain TTS oriented to a weather forecast application. In: INTERSPEECH (2005)
2. Yoshimura, T., Tokuda, K., Masuko, T., Kobayashi, T., Kitamura, T.: Simultaneous modeling of spectrum, pitch and duration in hmm-based speech synthesis. In: Eurospeech (1999)
3. Yoshimura, T., Tokuda, K., Masuko, T., Kobayashi, T., Kitamura, T.: Speaker interpolation in HMM-based speech synthesis. In: EUROSPEECH (1997)
4. Shichiri, K., Sawabe, A., Yoshimura, T., Tokuda, K., Masuko, T., Kobayashi, T., Kitamura, T.: Eigenvoices for HMM-based speech synthesis. In: ICSLP (2002)
5. Latorre, J., Iwano, K., Furui, S.: Cross-language synthesis with a polyglot synthesizer. In: INTERSPEECH, pp. 1477–1480 (2005)
6. Tokuda, K., Zen, H., Black, A.W.: An HMM-based speech synthesis system applied to English, IEEE SSW (2002)
7. Maia, R., Zen, H., Tokuda, K., Kitamura, T., Resende, J.F.G.: Towards the development of a Brazilian Portuguese text-to-speech system based on HMM. In: Eurospeech (2003)
8. Toda, T., Tokuda, K.: A Speech Parameter Generation Algorithm Considering Global Variance for HMM-Based Speech Synthesis. IEICE Transactions E90-D(5), 816–824 (2007)
9. Donovan, R.E., Woodland, P.C.: A hidden Markov-model-based trainable speech synthesizer. Computer Speech and Language 13, 223–241 (1999)
10. Iriondo, I., Socoró, J.C., Formiga, L., Gonzalvo, X., Alías, F., Miralles, P.: Modeling and estimating of prosody through CBR. In: JTH 2006 (in Spanish)
11. Fukada, T., Tokuda, K., Kobayashi, T., Imai, S.: An adaptive algorithm for mel-cepstral analysis of speech. In: ICASSP 1992 (1992)
12. Alías, F., Monzo, C., Socoró, J.C.: A Pitch Marks Filtering Algorithm based on Restricted Dynamic Programming. In: InterSpeech - ICSLP 2006 (2006)
13. Yoshimura, T., Tokuda, K., Masuko, T., Kobayashi, T., Kitamura, T.: Duration modeling in HMM-based speech synthesis system. In: ICSP 1998 (1998)
14. Section software in http://www.salle.url.edu/tsenyal
15. Black, A.W., Taylor, P., Caley, R.: The Festival Speech Synthesis System, http://www.festvox.org/festival
16. HTS, http://hts.ics.nitech.ac.jp
17. Keller, E., Zellner Keller, B.: How Much Prosody Can You Learn from Twenty Utterances? Linguistik online 17(5/03), 57–78 (2003), http://www.linguistik-online.de/

Objective and Subjective Evaluation of an Expressive Speech Corpus*

Ignasi Iriondo, Santiago Planet, Joan-Claudi Socoró, and Francesc Alías

GPMM - Grup de Recerca en Processament Multimodal
Enginyeria i Arquitectura La Salle, Universitat Ramon Llull
C/ Quatre Camins 2, 08022 Barcelona, (Spain)
{iriondo,splanet,jclaudi,falias}@salle.url.edu

Abstract. This paper presents the validation of the expressiveness of an acted oral corpus produced to be used in speech synthesis. Firstly, an objective validation has been conducted by means of automatic emotion identification techniques using statistical features extracted from the prosodic parameters of speech. Secondly, a listening test has been performed with a subset of utterances. The relationship between both objective and subjective evaluations is analyzed and the obtained conclusions can be useful to improve the following steps related to expressive speech synthesis.

1 Introduction

There is a growing tendency toward the use of speech in human-machine interaction by incorporating automatic speech recognition and speech synthesis. The recognition of emotional states or the synthesis of emotional speech can improve the communication by doing it more natural [1]. Therefore, one of the most important challenges in the study of the expressive speech is the development of oral corpora with authentic emotional content that enable robust analysis according to the task for which they are developed. It is not the objective of the present work to carry out an exhaustive summary of the available databases for the study of emotional speech, since recently, complete studies have appeared in the literature. In [2], a new compilation of 48 databases is presented showing a notable increase of multimodal databases. In [3], the databases used in 14 experiments of automatic detection of the emotion are summarized. Finally, in [4] a revision of 64 databases of emotional speech is done, providing a basic description of each one and its application.

Section 2 introduces different aspects about expressive speech. Section 3 explains the production of our corpus. Section 4 details the process of the objective validation carried out using techniques of automatic emotion identification. Section 5 concerns subjective evaluation by means of a listening test, and finally, the conclusions are presented in Section 6.

---

* This work has been partially supported by the European Commission, project SALERO FP6 IST-4-027122-IP.

M. Chetouani et al. (Eds.): NOLISP 2007, LNAI 4885, pp. 86–94, 2007.
© Springer-Verlag Berlin Heidelberg 2007

2   Building Emotional Speech Corpora

According to [5], four aspects have to be considered for building emotional speech corpora: *i)* the **scope** (number, genre and age of speakers, language, dialects, and emotional states); *ii)* the **context** where an utterance takes place (emotional significance related to semantics, prosody, facial expression and gestures); *iii)* the **descriptors** that represent the linguistic, emotional and acoustic content of the speech; and *iv)* the **naturalness**, which will depend on the strategy followed to obtain the emotional speech. With respect to the latter, the main debate is centered on the compromise between authenticity and audio quality. Campbell [1] and Schröder [6] propose 4 emotional speech sources:

Natural occurrences. Human interaction presents the most natural emotional speech but there are some drawbacks: lack of control on its content, poor sound quality, difficulty of labeling, and legal or ethical aspects (e.g. *The Reading-Leeds*, *The Belfast Naturalistic* and *The CREST* databases [5]).

Elicitation. The provocation of authentic emotions in people in the laboratory is a way of compensating some of the problems described previously, although the fullblown emotions would remain out of place [1].

Stimulated emotional speech. This method consists of the reading of texts with a verbal content adapted for the emotion to be expressed. The difficulty of comparing utterances with different texts should be counteracted with an increase of the corpus size so that statistical methods allow to generalize models [1] (e.g. the *Belfast Structured Emotion Database* [5]).

Acted emotional speech. The great advantage of this method is the control of the verbal and phonetic content of speech since all the emotional states are produced using the same sentences, allowing direct comparisons between them. The great objection is the lack of authenticity of the expressed emotion [1].

Another important aspect to keep in mind is the purpose of the speech and emotion research. It is necessary to distinguish between processes of perception (*centered on the speaker*) and expression (*centered on the listener*) [6]. The objective of the former is to establish the relation between the speaker emotional state and quantifiable parameters of speech. Usually, they deal with the recognition of emotions from the speech signal. According to [3], one of the challenges is the identification of oral indicators (prosodic, spectral and vocal quality) attributable to the emotional behavior and that are not simply own characteristics of conversational speech. The latter model the parameters of the speech with the goal to transmit a certain emotional state. The description of emotional states and the choice of speech parameters are key in the final result. There is a high consensus in the scientific community for obtaining emotional speech by means of stimulated/acted speech for synthesis purposes [2,5], although other authors argue in favor of constructing an enormous corpus gathered from recordings of the daily life of a number of voluntary speakers [7].

This work combines methods of both types of studies. On the one hand, the production of the corpus follows the guidelines of the studies *centered on the listener* since it is oriented to speech synthesis. On the other hand, we apply techniques of emotion recognition in order to validate its expressive content.

3 Our Expressive Speech Corpus

We considered the development of a new expressive oral corpus for Spanish due to lack of availability of a corpus with the suitable characteristics within the framework of our research in expressive speech synthesis. This corpus had a twofold purpose: to learn the acoustic models of emotional speech and to be used as the speech unit database for the synthesizer. This section describes the steps followed in the production of the corpus.

For the recording, a female professional speaker was chosen to read texts from different categories with the suitable style (stimulated/acted speech). For the design of texts semantically related to different expressive styles, an existing textual database of advertisements was used. Based on a study of the voice in the audio-visual publicity [8], five categories of the text corpus were chosen and the most suitable emotion/style was assigned to each one: new technologies (neutral-mature), education (joy-elation), cosmetic (style sensual-sweet), automobiles (aggressive-hard) and trips (sad-melancholic).

A set of phrases was selected from each category by means of a *greedy* algorithm [9] allowing phonetic balance for each style. This type of algorithms take the locally optimum choice at each stage with the hope to find an adequate global solution. Therefore, the application of this algorithm to the raised problem will obtain a valid solution, although may be not the optimum one. In addition, sentences that contain exceptions (e.g. foreign words, abbreviations) were avoided to make easy the automatic phonetic transcription and labeling.

The recording of the oral corpus was carried out in a professional recording studio. Speech signals were sampled at 48 KHz and quantized using 24 bits per sample and stored in WAV files. A forced time alignment using Hidden Markov Models from the phonetic transcription was conducted for the corpus segmentation in phrases, and later, there was a manual review. The result of this alignment also was used to segment the phrases in phonemes. The recorded database has 4638 sentences and it is 5 h 12 min long.

4 Objective Validation

The goal of this experiment was to validate the expressiveness of the corpus by means of automatic emotion identification using different data mining techniques applied to statistical features computed from prosodic parameters of speech. An exhaustive subjective evaluation of the full corpus (more than 5 hours of speech) would be unfeasible.

4.1 Acoustic Analysis

Prosodic features of speech (fundamental frequency, energy, duration of phones and frequency of pauses) are related to vocal expression of emotion [10]. In this work, an automatic acoustic analysis of the utterances is performed using information from the previous phonetic segmentation.

F0 related parameters. The analysis of the fundamental frequency (F0) is based on the result of the pitch marker described in [11]. This system assigns marks over the whole signal. The unvoiced segments and silences are marked using interpolated values from the neighboring voiced segments. For each phrase, three sequences of local F0 values are computed (complete, excluding silences and unvoiced sounds, and only the stressed vowels). The information about the boundaries of voiced/unvoiced (V/UV) segments and silences is obtained from the corpus labeling. Notice that if the phonetic segmentation was not available, an automatic voice-activity detector (VAD) and a V/UV detector would be required [12]. Moreover, F0 is calculated in linear and logarithmic scales.

Energy related parameters. For energy, speech is processed with 20-ms rectangular windows and 50% of overlap, calculating the energy (linear and dBs) every 10ms. Following the same idea that for F0, three sequences per utterance are generated (complete, excluding silences, and only in the stressed vowels).

Rhythm related parameters. The duration of phones is an important cue for vocal expression of emotion. However, some studies omit this parameter due to the difficulty to obtain it automatically [12]. In the present work we have incorporated this information to generate datasets with and without this information in order to contrast its relevance. Usually, z-score has been employed for duration modeling in text-to-speech synthesis to predict individual segment duration and to control the speed of the delivery. Therefore, we incorporate rhythm information using the z-score duration of each phoneme as a means to analyze the temporal structure of the speech [13]. Also, a sequence with only the values for the stressed vowels is computed. Moreover, two pausing related parameters are added for each utterance: the frequency and duration of pauses.

4.2 Statistical Analysis and Datasets

The prosody of an utterance is represented by 5 sequences of values by phoneme: F0 (linear and logarithmic), energy (linear and dB) and normalized durations (z-score). For each sequence, the first and the second derivative are calculated. For all these sequences, the following statistics are obtained: mean, variance, maximum, minimum, range, skew, kurtosis, quartiles, and interquartilic range. As a result, 464 parameters by utterance are calculated, considering both parameters related to the pausing.

This set of parameters was divided into different subsets according to different strategies to reduce the dimensionality (see figure 1). The first criterion was to omit the second derivative (from Data1 to Data2) in order to assess the

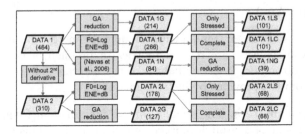

Fig. 1. Generation of different datasets

Table 1. Learning Algorithms used for the automatic recognition experiment

Name	Description	mean(95%CI)	max(Data)
J48	Decision tree based on C4.5	93.4 ± 2.0	96.4 (2G)
B.J48	Adaboosted version of J48	96.4 ± 1.4	98.3 (1L)
Part	Decision Rules (PART)	94.2 ± 2.0	96.9 (2L)
B.Part	Adaboosted version of PART	96.7 ± 1.3	98.4 (1G)
DT	Decision Table	88.7 ± 2.6	92.3 (1L)
B.T	Adaboosted version of D. T.	93.4 ± 1.6	96.1 (1L)
IB1	Instance-based (1 solution)	93.3 ± 2.8	97.5 (2G)
IBk	Instance-based (k solutions)	94.0 ± 2.3	97.9 (2G)
NB	Naive Bayes with discretization	94.6 ± 1.9	97.8 (1L)
SMO1	SVM with 2nd degree pol. Kernel	97.3 ± 1.2	99.0 (1G)
SMO2	SVM with 3rd degree pol. Kernel	97.1 ± 1.5	98.9 (1G)

significance of this function. Secondly, two new datasets were generated without the linear versions of both F0 and energy due to preliminary experiments showed better results for the logarithmic versions. Also, both Data1L and Data2L were divided in two new sets considering all the phonemes or only the stressed vowels. Moreover, an automatic reduction of both initial datasets was carried out by means of the simple genetic algorithm (GA) implemented in Weka [14] (Data1G and Data2G). Finally, two similar datasets to [12] were generated to test the significance of omitting the timing parameters (Data1N and Data1NG).

4.3   Experiments and Results

Numerous schemes of automatic learning can be used in a task such as classifying the emotion from the speech analysis. The objective evaluation of expressiveness in our speech corpus is based on [15], where a large-scale data mining experiment about the automatic recognition of basic emotions in short utterances was conducted. After different preliminary experiments, the set of machine learning algorithms shown in table 1 was selected in order to be tested with the different datasets. Some algorithms were completed with their *boosted* versions that achieve better results although they present a greater computational cost. All the experiments were carried out using Weka software [14] by means of ten-fold cross-validation. Both tried versions of SMO (Support Vector Machine of Weka) obtain the best results so much on average as in maximum value (see table 1). SMO algorithms achieve the highest results with Data1G, showing

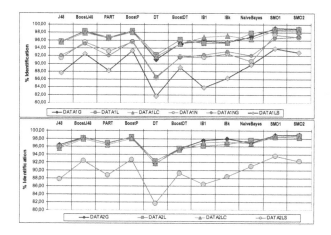

Fig. 2. Identification percentage for the ten tested datasets

that the dimensionality reduction based in GA helps to these systems, although differences with Data1L and Data1LC are minimum. However, other algorithms (i.e. J48, IB1 and IBk) work better with datasets generated by two consecutive reductions (without 2nd derivative and latter GA reduction). And finally, we can observe that there is a third group of algorithms that work better if the linear/logarithmic redundancy of F0 and energy is removed. Also we can observe that the boosted versions improve significantly the results respect to their corresponding algorithms. Figure 2 shows a comparison between different datasets depending on the algorithm. Notice that Data1LC obtains almost the same results than Data1G and Data1L, but with less than the half of parameters. The same effect is presented in the datasets without the 2nd derivative. Results experiment a slight loss when timing parameters are removed (Data1N and Data 1NG). However, results worsen significantly when parameters are calculated only in the stressed vowels (Data1LS and Data2LS). Table 2 shows the confusion matrix with the average results for the eleven classifiers with Data2G, that has achieved the best mean percentage of identification (97.02 % ± 1.23).

5   Subjective Evaluation

Subjective evaluation allows to validate the expressiveness of acted speech from the user viewpoint. An exhaustive evaluation of corpus would be excessively tedious (the corpus has 4638 utterances). For each style, 96 utterances were chosen, having done a total of 480. This test set was divided in 4 subsets, having 120 utterances each one. An ordered pair of subsets was assigned to each subject. Therefore, 12 different tests were generated. The allocation of ordered pairs tries to compensate the fact that the second test could be easier to evaluate due to the previous training.

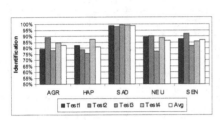 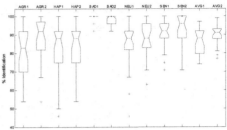

Fig. 3. Percentage of identification depending on the test and average

Fig. 4. Boxplots for first-second round depending on the style and the average

Table 2. Average confusion matrix for the automatic identification (Data2G)

Table 3. Average confusion matrix for the subjective test

	Agr	Hap	Sad	Neu	Sen
AGR	**99.1%**	0.8%	0.1%	0.0%	0.0%
HAP	1.6%	**97.1%**	0.0%	1.2%	0.2%
SAD	0.2%	0.1%	**99.3%**	0.4%	0.1%
NEU	0.2%	0.9%	0.4%	**93.9%**	4.5%
SEN	0.0%	0.1%	0.2%	4.9%	**94.8%**

	Agr	Hap	Sad	Neu	Sen	Dk/A
AGR	**82.7%**	14.2%	0.1%	1.8%	0.1%	1.1%
HAP	15.6%	**81.0%**	0.1%	1.9%	0.2%	1.2%
SAD	0.0%	0.0%	**98.8%**	0.5%	0.6%	0.1%
NEU	5.3%	1.3%	0.7%	**86.4%**	3.6%	2.7%
SEN	0.0%	0.1%	5.7%	4.7%	**86.8%**	2.6%

A forced answer test was designed with the question ¿*What emotional state do you recognize from the voice of the speaker in this phrase?*. The possible answers were the 5 styles of the corpus plus one more option *Don't know / Another*, with the objective of avoid insecure answers for the confusing cases. Adding this option has the risk that some evaluators use excessively this answer to accelerate the end of the test [12]. However, this effect was not considerable in this test. The listening test was carried out on a web platform developed for this type of tests, that permits to leave the test and to resume it subsequently. The evaluators belong mainly to the staff of *Enginyeria i Arquitectura La Salle* with a quite heterogeneous profile. Only the results of the 26 volunteers who finished the two tests have been reported.

The results of the subjective test show that all the styles achieve a high percentage of identification. The figure 3 shows the percentage of identification by style and test, being the sad style the best rated (98.8% of average), followed by sensual (86.8%) and neutral (86.4%) styles, and finally the aggressive (82.7%) and happy (81%) ones.

The confusion matrix (table 3), shows that the main errors are in the aggressive style (14.2% identified as happy) and the happy one (15.6% identified as aggressive). Moreover, neutral style is confused slightly with all and there is certain confusion of sensual with sad (5.7%). If we compare these results with the confusion matrix for the best average rated dataset (table 2), we can conclude that the algorithms confuse mainly sensual with neutral, however subjects show confusions between happy and aggressive. This difference is due to the lack of voice quality parameters because sadness and neutral have similar prosody, but sensual voice is most whispered than neutral, a difference which is clearly noticed by the subjects. Also, the influence of order has been studied. In average, the second round obtains better results than the first, especially for neutral, sensual, and aggressive styles (see figure 4).

6 Conclusion and Future Work

In this paper, the production of an oral corpus oriented to expressive speech synthesis has been presented. We performed subjective (listening test) and objective (automatic emotion identification) evaluation in order to validate its expressive content showing good results. The advantage of the automatic experiments is that they are performed over the whole corpus, while the listening test comprises a subset of utterances.

In future, we will introduce voice quality parameterization in addition to prosody to minimize the confusion between sensual and neutral styles. Moreover, this work should serve to analyze the bad classified utterances in order to eliminate them and to improve the latter modeling and synthesis processes.

References

1. Campbell, N.: Databases of emotional speech. In: Proceedings of the ISCA Workshop on Speech and Emotion, pp. 34–38 (September 2000)
2. Cowie, R., Douglas-Cowie, E., Cox, C.: Beyond emotion archetypes: databases for emotion modelling using neural networks. Neural Networks 18, 371–388 (2005)
3. Devillers, L., Vidrascu, L., Lamel, L.: Challenges in real-life emotion annotation and machine learning based detection. Neural Networks 18, 407–422 (2005)
4. Ververidis, D., Kotropoulos, C.: Emotional speech recognition: Resources, features, and methods. Speech Communication 48(9), 1162–1181 (2006)
5. Douglas-Cowie, E., Campbell, N., Cowie, R., Roach, P.: Emotional speech: towards a new generation of databases. Speech Communication 40, 33–60 (2003)
6. Schröder, M.: Speech and emotion research: An overview of research frameworks and a dimensional approach to emotional speech synthesis. Ph.D. dissertation, PHONUS 7, Saarland University, Germany (2004)
7. Campbell, N.: Developments in corpus-based speech synthesis: Approaching natural conversational speech. IEICE - Trans. Inf. Syst. E88-D(3), 376–383 (2005)
8. Montoya, N.: El papel de la voz en la publicidad audiovisual dirigida a los niños. Zer. Revista de estudios de comunicación 4, 161–177 (1998)
9. François, H., Boëffard, O.: The greedy algorithm and its application to the construction of a continuous speech database. In: Proc. of LREC, Las Palmas de Gran Canaria (Spain), May 2002, vol. 5, pp. 1420–1426 (2002)
10. Cowie, R., Douglas-Cowie, E., Tsapatsoulis, N., Votsis, G., Kollias, S., Fellenz, W., Taylor, J.G.: Emotion recognition in human computer interaction. IEEE Signal Processing 18(1), 33–80 (2001)
11. Alías, F., Monzo, C., Socoró, J.C.: A pitch marks filtering algorithm based on restricted dynamic programming. In: Proc. of ICSLP, Pittsburgh (USA), September 2006, pp. 1698–1701 (2006)

12. Navas, E., Hernáez, I., Luengo, I.: An Objective and Subjective Study of the Role of Semantics and Prosodic Features in Building Corpora for Emotional TTS. IEEE Trans. on Audio, Speech and Language Processing 14(4), 1117–1127 (2006)
13. Schweitzer, A., Möbius, B.: On the structure of internal prosodic models. In: Proc. of the 15th ICPhS, Barcelona (Spain), pp. 1301–1304 (2003)
14. Witten, I.H., Frank, E.: Data Mining: Practical Machine Learning Tools and Techniques, 2nd edn. Morgan Kaufmann, San Francisco (2005)
15. Oudeyer, P.-Y.: The production and recognition of emotions in speech: features and algorithms. Int. Journal of Human Computer Interaction (special issue on Affective Computing) 59(1-2), 157–183 (2003)

On the Usefulness of Linear and Nonlinear Prediction Residual Signals for Speaker Recognition

Marcos Faundez-Zanuy

Escola Universitària Politècnica de Mataró, UPC (Spain)
faundez@eupmt.es

Abstract. This paper compares the identification rates of a speaker recognition system using several parameterizations, with special emphasis on the residual signal obtained from linear and nonlinear predictive analysis. It is found that the residual signal is still useful even when using a high dimensional linear predictive analysis. On the other hand, it is shown that the residual signal of a nonlinear analysis contains less useful information, even for a prediction order of 10, than the linear residual signal. This shows the inability of the linear models to cope with nonlinear dependences present in speech signals, which are useful for recognition purposes.

1 Introduction

Several parameterization techniques exist for speech [17] and speaker [15] recognition, cepstral analysis and its related parameterizations such as Delta-Cepstral features, Cepstral Mean Subtraction, etc. being the most popular. There are two main ways to compute the cepstral coefficients and one important drawback in both cases: relevant information is discarded, as follows:

1. LP-derived cepstral coefficients. The linear prediction analysis produces two main components, the prediction coefficients (synthesis filter) and the residue of the predictive analysis. This latter signal is usually discarded. However, experiments exist [9] where it is shown that human beings are able to recognize the identity of the speaker listening to residual signals of LP analysis. Based on this fact several authors have evaluated the usefulness of the LPC-residue and have found that although the identification rates using this kind of information alone does not perform as well as the LP-derived cepstral coefficients, a combination of both can improve the results [20,12,14,22,11].
2. Fourier Transform derived cepstral coefficients. Instead of working out a set of Linear prediction coefficients, are based on the power spectrum information, where phase information has been discarded. [19] proposed the use of new acoustic features based on the short-term Fourier phase spectrum. The results are similar to the LP-derived cepstral coefficients. Although these (phase spectrum) features cannot outperform the classical cepstral parameterization, the results are improved using a combination of both features.

In this paper we will focus on the first kind of parameterization, because they are a clear alternative to the nonlinear predictive models, which have shown an improvement

M. Chetouani et al. (Eds.): NOLISP 2007, LNAI 4885, pp. 95–104, 2007.

over the classical linear techniques in several fields (for a recent overview about these techniques [7]).

In [4,6] we proposed a new set of features and models based on these types of nonlinear models and an improvement was also found when this information was combined with the traditional cepstral analysis, but so far, the relevance of the residual signals from linear and nonlinear predictive analysis has not been studied and compared.

In this paper we will study if the relevance of the residual signal is due to an insufficient linear predictive analysis order or because of the incapability of the linear analysis to model nonlinearities present in speech and demonstrate is usefulness for speaker recognition purposes. This important question has not been solved in previous papers that focus on a typical 8 to 16 prediction order.

2 Experiment Setup

2.1 Database

For our experiments we have used the Gaudi database [16]. We have used one subcorpora of 49 speakers acquired with a simultaneous stereo recording with two different microphones. The speech is in wav format with a sampling frequency (fs) = 16 kHz, 16 bit/sample and the bandwidth is 8 kHz. From this database we have generated narrow-band signals using the potsband routine that can be downloaded from [21]. This function meets the specifications of G.151 for any sampling frequency. Thus, our study has been performed on telephone bandwidth.

2.2 Identification Algorithm

In this study, we are only interested in the relative performance between linear and nonlinear analyses. Thus, we have chosen a simple algorithm for speaker recognition.

In the training phase, we compute, for each speaker, empirical covariance matrices based on feature vectors extracted from overlapped short time segments of the speech signals. As features representing short time spectra we use both linear prediction cepstral coefficients (LPCC) and mel-frequency cepstral coefficients melceps [3]. In the speaker-recognition system, the trained covariance matrices for each speaker are compared with an estimate of the covariance matrix obtained from a test sequence from a speaker. An arithmetic-harmonic sphericity measure is used in order to compare the matrices [1]: $d = \log\left(\text{tr}(C_{test}C_j^{-1})\,\text{tr}(C_jC_{test}^{-1})\right) - 2\log(l)$, where tr($\cdot$) denotes the trace operator, l is the dimension of the feature vector, C_{test} and C_j is the covariance estimate from the test speaker and speaker model j, respectively.

2.3 Parameterizations

We have used the following parameterizations

1. LP-derived cepstral coefficients (LPCC)
2. Fourier transform derived cepstral coefficients (melceps)
3. LP- residue coefficients

The first two first parameterizations can be found, for instance, in [17,15,3], while the third is proposed in [11] and will be described in more detail next.

Feature extraction from the LP-residual signal

We will use the Power Difference of Spectrum in Subband (PDSS) obtained as follows [11]:

1. Calculate the LP-residual signal using the Pth-order linear prediction coefficients.
2. Calculate the Fast Fourier Transform (fft) of the LP-residual signal using zero padding in order to increase the frequency resolution: $S = \left| fft\left(residue \right) \right|^2$
3. Group power spectrum into P subbands.
4. Calculate the ratio of the geometric to the arithmetic mean of the power spectrum in the ith subband, and subtract it from 1: $PDSS(i) = 1 - \dfrac{\left(\prod_{k=L_i}^{H_i} S(k) \right)^{\frac{1}{N_i}}}{\frac{1}{N_i} \sum_{k=L_i}^{H_i} S(k)}$, where

$N_i = H_i - L_i + 1$ is the sample number of frequency points in the ith subband and L_i, H_i is the lower and upper limit of frequency in i^{th} subband respectively. We have used the same bandwidth for all the bands.

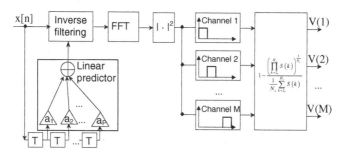

Fig. 1. LP residual signal parameterization

PDSS can be interpreted as the subband version of spectral flatness measure for quantifying the flatness of the signal spectrum. Figure 1 summarizes the procedure.

3 New Possibilities Using Non-linear Predictive Analysis

Although the relevance of residual NL-predictive analysis for speaker recognition has not been studied previously, nonlinear predictive analysis has been widely studied in the context of speech coding. For instance, [5] revealed that a forward ADPCM scheme with nonlinear prediction can achieve the same Segmental Signal to Noise Ratio (SEGSNR) as the equivalent linear predictive system (same prediction order) with one less quantization bit. We propose an analogous scheme replacing the linear predictor with a nonlinear predictor. Figure 2 shows the scheme.

We have used a Multi-Layer Perceptron (MLP). The structure of the neural net has 10 inputs, 2 neurons in the hidden layer, and one output. The selected training algorithm was the Levenberg-Marquardt [10]. The number of epochs has been set up to 6. First layer and hidden layer transfer functions are tansig, while the output layer is linear.

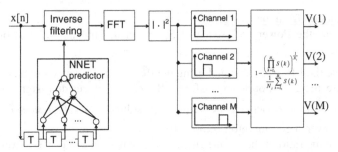

Fig. 2. Block diagram used to calculate PDSS parameters from NL-prediction residual signal

4 Experimental Results

Obviously one important question when dealing with residual LP signals is: Is the information contained in this residual signal coming from an insufficient predictive analysis order? That is, what happens when the prediction analysis order is so high that it is not possible to extract more relevant information using a linear analysis?

The experimental approach used to solve this question is to use a number of LP coefficients higher than usual. Two possible results can be obtained:

1. When the analysis order is increased, the discriminative power of the residual signal is reduced to simple chance results. This means that there is potential for speaker recognition rate improvements through extraction of the LP coefficients in a more efficient manner, probably by increasing the number of coefficients.
2. When the analysis order is increased, the residual signal still contains useful information. This means that a linear analysis is unable to extract this information, and there is room for improvement combining parameterizations defined on the LP coefficients and the residual signal. In order to obtain the optimal results, both signals should be extracted and optimized jointly.

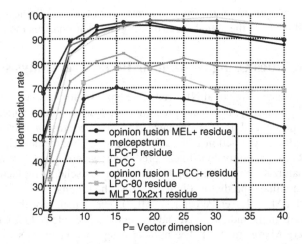

Fig. 3. Identification for several parameterization algorithms

Figure 3 shows the results obtained with the following parameterizations: Melcepstrum, LPC –P residue, LPCC, LPC-80 residue, MLP 10x2x1 and several combinations between them.LPC-P residue is the parameterization obtained from the residual P-analysis order. It is interesting to observe the following:

- The residual signal of an LPC-80 analysis can produce a recognition rate higher than 80% for a 15 dimensional vector extraction. Thus, it was found that the residual signal of a LP analysis contains relevant information, and this is due to the inability to extract this information using a linear analysis (80th order analysis is enough to model short term and long term dependencies between samples, but if the analysis is linear, it is limited to linear dependencies).
- The residual signal of a nonlinear predictive analysis, as expected, produces the lower recognition rates, because the relevant information has been retained in the predictor coefficients. However, a maximum of 70% recognition rate is possible.

4.1 Opinion Fusion

One way to improve the results is by means of a combination of different classifiers opinion [13]. In our case, we will use the same classifier scheme, but different parameterizations. In order to study the complementarity of the parameterizations studied, we have computed the correlation coefficient and scatter diagrams.

Table 1 shows the correlation coefficients between distances of several parameterizations. The higher the correlation, the smaller the complementarity of both measures. Figure 2 shows a scatter diagram, which represents points on a two-dimensional space. The coordinates correspond to the obtained distance measures, which correspond to each parameterization (one in each axis). Looking at the diagram we observe that the points diverge from a strip. Thus, they have complementary information and can be combined in order to improve the results.

Table 1. Correlation coefficients between obtained distance values for P=20

	LPCC	Mel-ceps	LP-20 resid	LP-80 resid	MLP 10x2x1
LPCC		0,79	0,68	0,52	0,55
melceps	0,79		0,69	0,56	0,62
LP-20 resid	0,68	0,69		0,78	0,64
LP-80 resid	0,52	0,56	0,78		0,60
MLP 10x2x1	0,55	0,62	0,64	0,60	

When combining different measures, special care must be taken for the range of the values. If they are not commensurate, some kind of normalization must be applied. We have tested the following, based on a sigmoid function [18], $o_i' = \dfrac{1}{1+e^{-k_i}}$

where: $k_i = \dfrac{o_i - (m_i - 2\sigma_i)}{2\sigma_i}$, $o_i' \in [0,1]$, and o_i is the initial opinion of the ith classifier.

m_i, σ_i are the mean and standard deviation of the opinions of the i classifier, obtained with data from the authentic speakers (intra-model distances).

Table 2. Identification rates (combinations with sum rule)

P \ Param.	5	10	15	20	25	30	40
LPCC	46.9	90.6	93.5	97.1	98.0	98.8	94.7
Melceps	65.7	89.8	92.7	95.5	93.5	91.8	87.4
LP-P resid	44.1	75.9	84.1	78.4	82.0	78.8	77.1
LP-80 resid	32.7	72.2	78.0	78.0	73.5	68.6	68.6
MLP resid	20.0	65.3	70.2	66.1	65.3	62.9	53.5
LPCC+LP-P	64.9	89.8	94.7	97.6	97.1	97.1	95.1
LPCC+MLP	51.0	91.4	95.1	97.1	97.96	98.4	95.1

We have limited the combinations to the outputs of two different classifiers, and the sum and product combination rules [13].

We have experimentally observed that slightly better results are obtained without normalization. Looking at figure 4 it can be seen that the distance values obtained with the residual signal parameterization have less amplitude (about 2 to 3 times). Thus, if the normalization is not done, it is equivalent to a weighted combination where the LPCC distances have more influence over the combined result than the residual signal.

Figure 3 and table 2 summarize the identification rates for several vector dimensions (P) and different combined parameters.

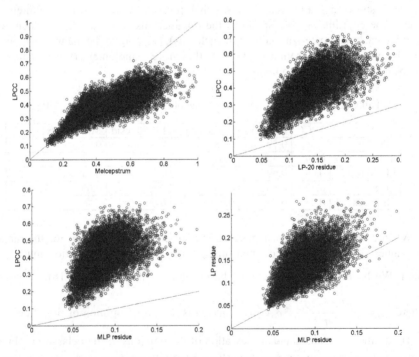

Fig. 4. Scatter diagram of distances for observing the correlation between parameters

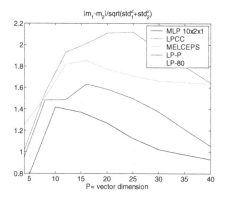

Fig. 5. Discrimination measure for several feature extractors

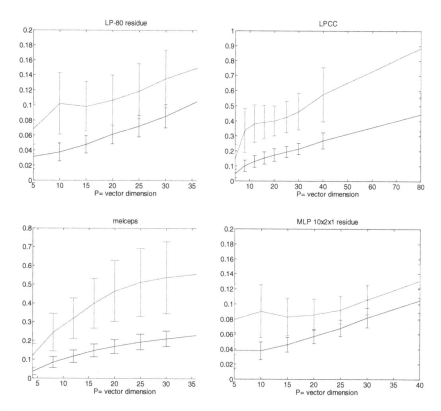

Fig. 6. Mean and variance for inter and intra distances, for several parameterization orders and feature extractors

We have experimentally observed that slightly better results are obtained without normalization. Looking at figure 4 it can be seen that the distance values obtained with the residual signal parameterization have less amplitude (about 2 to 3 times).

Thus, if the normalization is not done, it is equivalent to a weighted combination where the LPCC distances have more influence over the combined result than the residual signal.

Figure 3 and table 2 summarize the identification rates for several vector dimensions (P) and different combined parameters. Figure 5 shows a discrimination capability measure based on the ratio $\dfrac{|m_1 - m_2|}{\sqrt{\sigma_1^2 - \sigma_2^2}}$ for several feature extractors. The higher this ratio is, the better the recognition rates are. Figure 6 shows the mean (solid line) and standard deviation (vertical bar) for several feature extractors and vector dimensions. For a good biometric recognition, we are looking for no overlap between intra and interdistances, and as much separation as possible. We can see that there is much more overlap for nonlinear residual signal than for the linear one. Thus, nonlinear residual signal has lesser potential for speaker recognition.

5 Conclusions

So far several papers have established that a combination between classical parameters (LPCC, melceps) with some kind of parameterization computed over the residual analysis signal can yield improvements in recognition rates. In our experiments we have found that this is only true when the analysis order ranges from 8 to 16. These values have been selected mainly because a spectral envelope can be sufficiently fitted with this amount of data, so there was no reason to increase the number of parameters. Although we consider that this is true for speech analysis, synthesis and coding, it is interesting to observe that the parameterization step for a speaker recognition system is twofold:

1. We make a dimensionality reduction, so it is easier to compute models, distances between vectors, etc.
2. We make a transformation from one space to another one. In this new domain, it can be easier to discriminate between speakers, and some parameterizations are better than others.

Thus, we are not looking for good quality representation of the speech signal (or a compromise between good representation with the smallest number of parameters). We are just looking for good discrimination capability.

In our experiments we have found that for parameter vectors of high order, although the residual signal has a significant discriminative power among speakers, this signal seems to be redundant with LPCC or melceps, and it is not useful.

If instead of using the residual signal of a linear analysis a nonlinear analysis is used, both combined signals are more uncorrelated and although the discriminative power of the NL residual signal is lower, the combined scheme outperforms the linear one for several analysis orders.

The results show that there is just a marginal improvement on the results when increasing the number of parameters (the identification rate plot saturates), but the residual signal is whiter when increasing the prediction order, especially for the nonlinear analysis. This is a promising result, because although a good parameterization based on nonlinear analysis has not yet been established, this paper reveals that the NL analysis can extract more relevant information with the same prediction order as a linear analysis. Thus, it opens a new way for investigation that has started to provide successful results [2] and is a promising approach for improving biometric systems [23,8]. We think that the flow chart in order to evaluate the relevance of residual signals is the one depicted in figure 7. It is not enough to achieve a reasonable recognition rate. We must check that this information is complementary to the classical one. Otherwise, it is worthless because it cannot help to improve recognition rates. It is fundamental to take into account the second question.

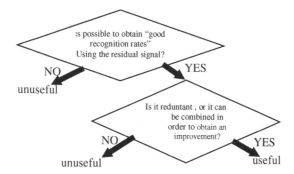

Fig. 7. Flow chart of deciding if a residual signal is suitable for improving speaker recognition rates

Acknowledgements

This work has been supported by FEDER and MEC TEC2006-13141-C03-02/TCM.

References

1. Bimbot, F., Mathan, L.: Text-free speaker recognition using an arithmetic-harmonic sphericity measure. In: Eurospeech 1993, pp. 169–172 (1993)
2. Chetouani, M., Faundez, M., Gas, B., Zarader, J.L.: A New Nonlinear speaker parameterization algorithm for speaker identification. In: ISCA Speaker Odyssey Workshop (2004)
3. Deller, J., et al.: Discrete-Time Processing of Speech Signals. Prentice-Hall, Englewood Cliffs (1993)
4. Faundez-Zanuy, M., Rodriguez, D.: Speaker recognition using residual signal of linear and nonlinear prediction models. In: ICSLP 1998, Sidney, vol. 2, pp. 121–124 (1998)
5. Faundez-Zanuy, M., Vallverdú, F., Monte, E.: Nonlinear prediction with neural nets in adpcm. In: ICASSP 1998. IEEE International Conference on Acoustics, Speech, and Signal Processing, Seattle, vol. I, pp. 345–348 (1998)
6. Faundez-Zanuy, M.: Speaker recognition by means of a combination of linear and nonlinear predictive models. In: EUROSPEECH 1999, Budapest, vol. 2, pp. 763–766 (1999)
7. Faundez-Zanuy, M., et al.: Nonlinear speech processing: overview and applications. Control and intelligent systems 30(1), 1–10 (2002)
8. Faundez-Zanuy, M.: Biometric recognition: why not massively adopted yet? IEEE Aerosp. Electron. Syst. Mag. 20(8), 25–28 (2005)

9. Feustel, T.C., Velius, G.A.: Human and machine performance on speaker identity verification. In: Speech Tech 1989, pp. 169–170 (1989)
10. Foresee, F.D., Hagan, M.T.: Gauss-Newton approximation to Bayesian regularization. In: Proceedings of the 1997 International Joint Conference on Neural Networks, pp. 1930–1935 (1997)
11. Hayakawa, S., Takeda, K., Itakura, F.: Speaker identification using harmonic structure of LP-Residual spectrum. In: Bigün, J., Borgefors, G., Chollet, G. (eds.) AVBPA 1997. LNCS, vol. 1206, pp. 253–260. Springer, Heidelberg (1997)
12. He, J., Liu, L., Palm, G.: On the use of features from prediction residual signals in speaker identification. In: EUROSPEECH 1995, pp. 313–316 (1995)
13. Faundez-Zanuy, M.: Data fusion in Biometrics. IEEE Aerosp. Electron. Syst. Mag. 20(1), 34–38 (2005)
14. Liu, L., et al.: Signal modelling for speaker identification. In: Proceedings of the IEEE ICASSP 1996, vol. 2, pp. 665–668 (1996)
15. Faundez-Zanuy, M., Monte-Moreno, E.: State-of-the-art in speaker recognition. IEEE Aerosp. Electron. Syst. Mag. 20(5), 7–12 (2005)
16. Ortega, J., et al.: Ahumada: a large speech corpus in Spanish for speaker identification and verification. In: ICASSP 1998, Seattle, vol. 2, pp. 773–776 (1998)
17. Picone, J.W.: Signal Modeling techniques in speech recognition. Proceedings of the IEEE 79(4), 1215–1247 (1991)
18. Sanderson, C.: Information fusion and person verification using speech & face information. IDIAP Research Report 02-33, pp. 1–37 (September 2002)
19. Schlüter, R., Ney, H.: Using phase spectrum information for improved speech recognition performance. In: Proceedings of the IEEE ICASSP, vol. 1, pp. 133–136 (2001)
20. Thévenaz, P., Hügli, H.: Usefulness of the LPC-residue in text-independent speaker verification. Speech Communication 17, 145–157 (1995)
21. http://www.ee.ic.ac.uk/hp/staff/dmb/voicebox/voicebox.html
22. Yegnanarayana, B., et al.: Source and system features for speaker recognition using AANN models. In: IEEE ICASSP, vol. 1, pp. 409–412 (2001)
23. Faundez-Zanuy, M.: Biometric security technology. IEEE Aerospace and Electron. Syst. Mag. 21(6), 15–26 (2006)

Multi Filter Bank Approach for Speaker Verification Based on Genetic Algorithm

Christophe Charbuillet, Bruno Gas, Mohamed Chetouani,
and Jean Luc Zarader

Université Pierre et Marie Curie-Paris6, FRE2507
Institut des Systèmes Intelligents et Robotique (ISIR), Ivry sur Seine, F-94200 France

Abstract. Speaker recognition systems usually need a feature extraction stage which aims at obtaining the best signal representation. State of the art speaker verification systems are based on cepstral features like MFCC, LFCC or LPCC. In this article, we propose a feature extraction system based on the combination of three feature extractors adapted to the speaker verification task. A genetic algorithm is used to optimise the features complementarity. This optimisation consists in designing a set of three non linear scaled filter banks. Experiments are carried out using a state of the art speaker verification system. Results show that the proposed method improves significantly the system performances on the 2005 Nist SRE Database. Furthermore, the obtained feature extractors show the importance of some specific spectral information for speaker verification.

1 Introduction

Speech feature extraction plays a major role in speaker verification systems. State of the art speaker verification systems front end are based on the estimation of the spectral envelope of the short term signal, e.g., Mel-scale Filterbank Cepstrum Coefficients (MFCCs), Linear-scale Filter bank Cepstrum Coefficients (LFCCs), or Linear Predictive Cepstrum Coefficients (LPCCs). Even if these extraction methods achieve good performances on speaker verification, they do not take into account specific information about the task to achieve. To avoid this draw back, several approaches have been proposed to optimize the feature extractor to a specific task. These methods consist to simultaneously learn the parameters of both the feature extractor and the classifier [1]. This procedure consists in the optimisation of a criterion, which can be the Maximisation of the Mutual Information (MMI) [2] or the Minimisation of the Classification Error (MCE) [3]. In this paper we propose to use a genetic algorithm for the design of feature extraction system adapted to the speaker verification task.

Genetic algorithms (GA) were first proposed by Holland in 1975 [4] and became widely used in various domains as a new mean of complex systems optimization. Recently their have been successfully applied to speech processing. Chin-Teng Lin and al. [5] proposed to apply a GA to the feature transformation problem for speech recognition and M. Zamalloa and al. [6] worked on a GA

M. Chetouani et al. (Eds.): NOLISP 2007, LNAI 4885, pp. 105–113, 2007.

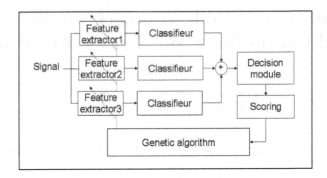

Fig. 1. Feature extraction optimisation

based feature selection algorithm for speaker recognition. The most attractive quality of GAs is certainly their aptitude to avoid local minima. However, our study relies on another quality which is the fact that GAs are unsupervised optimisation methods. So they can be used as an exploration tool, free to find the best solution without any constraint. In a previous work [7] we used this approach to show the importance of specific spectral information for the speaker diarization task.

State of the art speaker verification systems are based on a cepstral feature extraction front end (LFCC, MFCC, LPCC) follow by a GMM [8] or an hybrid GMM/SVM classifier [9]. Nowadays, an alternative an increasingly used approach consists in fusing different systems. This technique can be divided in two main categories depending on the source of this difference. The systems based on a classifier's variety [10] and the systems based on different features. Our study deals with the second principle. We can quote the work of M. Zhiyou and al. [11] which consist of combining the LFCC and MFCC features, or the study of Poh Hoon Thian & al. [12] who proposed to complete the LFCC's with spectral centroids sub-bands features.

In this paper we proposed to fuse three systems based on different feature extractors. A genetic algorithm is used to optimise the feature extractor's complementarity. Figure 1 describes this approach. In the second section, a description of the feature extraction method is given. Afterwards, we describe the genetic algorithm we used, followed by its application to complementary feature extraction. Then, the experiments we made and the obtained results are presented.

2   Filter Bank Based Feature Extractors

The conventional MFCC and LFCC feature extractor process mainly consists of modifying the short-term spectrum by a filter bank. This process has four steps:

- Compute the power spectrum of the analysed frame;
- Sum the power spectrum for each triangular filter of the bank;
- Apply the log operator to the obtained coefficients;
- Compute the Discrete Cosine Transform (DCT).

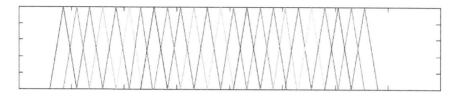

Fig. 2. Linear scaled filter bank

Fig. 2. presents the linear scaled filter bank used for the LFCC's computation. This feature extractor is known to be the most robust for telephone signals representation. The purpose of our study is to find a set of three cepstrum based feature extractors design for high level fusion. To this end, we propose to use a genetic algorithm to optimise, the number of filters on the bank, the scaled of the filter bank and the number of cepstral output coefficients.

3   Genetic Algorithm

A genetic algorithm is an optimisation method. Its aim is to find the best values of the system's parameters in order to maximise its performance. The basic idea is that of "natural selection", i.e. the principle of "the survival of the fittest". A GA operates on a population of systems. In our application, each individual of the population is a feature extractor defined by its genes. Genes consists in a condensed an adapted representation of the feature extractor's parameters.

3.1   Gene Encoding

Parameter's encoding plays a major role in genetic algorithms. By an adapted parameter representation, this method can strongly increase the speed convergence of the algorithm. Moreover it reduces the over fitting effect by reducing the parameters dimension. The parameters we chose to optimise are the followin ones:

- Nf: Number of filters in the bank;
- Nc: Number of cepstral coefficients;
- C_i: Center frequency of the ith filter in the bank;
- B_i: Band width of the ith filter in the bank.

Parameters C and B are encoded with two polynomial functions described by the equations (1) and (2). This encoding method reduces the parameter's dimension from 50 to 12 (average case) and guaranties the filter bank's regularity. The parameter Nf and Nc are not encoded and will be directly muted.

$$C_i = gc_0 + gc_1 \cdot \frac{i}{Nf} + gc_2 \cdot (\frac{i}{Nf})^2 + ... + gc_N \cdot (\frac{i}{Nf})^N \qquad (1)$$

$$B_i = gb_0 + gb_1 \cdot \frac{i}{Nf} + gb_2 \cdot (\frac{i}{Nf})^2 + ... + gb_N \cdot (\frac{i}{Nf})^N \qquad (2)$$

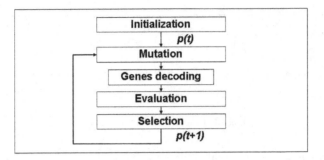

Fig. 3. Genetic algorithm

Where $\{gc_0,...,gc_N\}$ and $\{gb_0,...,gb_N\}$ are the genes relative to the parameters $\{C_0,...,C_{Nf}\}$ and $\{B_0,...,B_{Nf}\}$; N is the polynomial order; Nf represents the number of filter.

3.2   Genetic Algorithm Description

The algorithm we used is made of four operators: **M**utation, **D**ecoding, **E**valuation and **S**election (M, D, E, S). These operators are applied to the current population $p(t)$ to produce a new generation $p(t+1)$ by the relation:

$$p(t+1) = S \circ E \circ D \circ M(p(t)) \tag{3}$$

Fig. 3. represents this algorithm. The first step consists on a random initialisation of the feature extractor's genes. Then, the operators are iteratively applied.

The *Mutation* operator consists in a short random variation of the genes.

The *Decoding* operator aims at decoding the genes to obtain the operational feature extractor's parameters.

The *Evaluation* operator's goal is to evaluate each feature extractor performances. The evaluation criterion we used is defined on the next section.

The *Selection* operator selects the Ns better feature extractors of the current population. These individuals are then cloned according to the evaluation results to produce the new generation $p(t+1)$ of Np feature extractors. As a consequence of this selection process, the average of the performance of the population tends to increase and in our application adapted feature extractors tend to emerge.

3.3   Application to Complementary Feature Extraction

The objective is to obtain a set of three complementary feature extractors. The main idea is to evolve three isolated populations of feature extractors and to select the best combination. At each generation, the fusion is done for all combination of feature extractors and the resulting Equal Error Rate (EER) is memorised. At the end of this process, the fitness of an individual is defined as the lower

EER obtained (e.i. the EER corresponding to the best combination including this feature extractor). As a consequence of this process, each population tends to specialise on specific feature, complementary with the others.

4   Experiments and Results

4.1   Databases

The databases used are extracted from the 2005 Nist SRE corpus [13]. This corpus is composed of conversational telephone speech signals passed through different channels, (land-line, cordless or cellular) and sampled to 8 kHz. We used 10 males and 10 females with one utterance of 2 min 30s per speaker for the evolution phase. 30 males and 30 females for the cross validation base and 50 males and 50 females for the test. This three sets are speaker independent.

4.2   Speaker Verification System

All experiments we made are based on a state of the art GMM-UBM speaker verification system. This system, called LIA SpkDet [14] was provided by the University of Avignon, France. We used a system with 16 Gaussian per mixture, with diagonal covariance matrix.

4.3   Genetic Algorithm Parameters

The genes $\{gc_0,...,gc_N\}$ and $\{gb_0,...,gb_N\}$ are initialised with a Gaussian normalised random variable. The parameter Nf are initialised to 24, and Nc to 16. The parameter we used for the feature extractor's evolution are:

- Population size Np : 20;
- Number of selected individuals Ns : 5;
- Polynomial order for the genes encoding N : 5;
- Mutation method for the polynomials coefficients: Gaussian random variation of $\pm$ 0.1;
- Mutation method for Nf : uniform random variation of $\pm$ 5;
- Mutation method for Nc : uniform random variation of $\pm$ 3;

4.4   Minimisation of the over Fitting Effect

The over fitting effect is a common problem in machine learning. A formal definition was given by T. M. Mitchell [15]:

Given a hypothesis space H, a hypothesis h $\in$ H is said to overfit the training data if there exists some alternative hypothesis h' $\in$ H such that h has smaller error than h' over the training examples, but h' has a smaller error than h over the entire distribution of instances.

To avoid this effect, several approaches were proposed for evoltionary computation such as cross validation (CV), early stopping (ES), complexity reduction
(CR), noise addition (NA) or random sampling technic (RST) [16], [17], [18].
In our application we used a combination of the cross validation and random
sampling technic.

RST consists of using a random selected subset of trainning data to evaluate
the individual performance. A new sub-set of data is used for each generation.
We selected a subset of 10 males and 10 females from a global train set of 30
speakers of each gender.

CV technic consists of evaluating the generalisation capacity of an individuals
by the use of unseen data. For each generation we evaluate and memorise the
perfomaces of the best individual of the population on a cross validation base.
The speakers involved on this set are independent of both the train and test set.
The algorithm is stopped when a stagnation of the performances is observed.
Then, the best individual of the best generation on the cross validation base is
evaluated on the test database.

4.5   Results

In this section, obtained feature extractors are presented and analysed. Fig. 4.b
presents the obtained filter banks. In order to interpret the obtained solution,
a statistical analysis of the fundamental frequency and formants was done on a
database composed of 20 males and 20 females. Fig. 4.a presents the probability
distributions of these measures. Table 1 details both the feature extractor's characteristics and the results obtained on the test base. The combination method
used is an arithmetic fusion, as illustrated by the Fig. 1. Table 2 presents the
correlation coefficients between the compared system and the EER obtained by
fusion. The correlation is based on the log-likelihood outputs of the compared
systems for the whole tests of the test database. A test consists to measure
the log-likelihood between a speaker model and test signal. The r correlation
coefficient is defined by:

$$r = \frac{\sum_{i=1}^{Nt}(S1_i - \bar{S}1) \cdot (S2_i - \bar{S}2)}{\sqrt{\sum_{i=1}^{Nt}(S1_i - \bar{S}1)^2} \cdot \sqrt{\sum_{i=1}^{Nt}(S2_i - \bar{S}2)^2}} \quad (4)$$

Where $S1_i$ represents the log-likelihood obtained by the system 1 on i^{th} test; Nt
is the number of test.

The correlation coefficient, which takes value in [-1;1], is a measure of the
system's decision similarity. In our application, the classifiers are identical. As
a consequence, this measure can be interpreted as the similarity between the
information provided by the feature extractors. A correlation of 1 means that
the information supplied by the feature extractors are equivalent (i.e. they lead
to the same decision). A correlation of 0 means that the information supplied

are independent. Taking into account these different information, we can high light some key points:

- Information relative to the fundamental frequencies is not used;
- C2 covers a large spectral zone and obtained results similar are to the LFCC or MFCC feature extractors;
- C1 seems to focus exclusively on the first formant;
- C3 presents a high filter density centred on the first formant, while keeping the whole spectre information;
- The decorrelation of the obtained systems is significant.
- The final combination of the three feature extractors improve the system performance of 12% compare to the baseline system.

These results show that the proposed method is reliable. The correlation between the different systems and the improvement supplied by the fusion show that the obtained feature extractors are complementary. This improvement seems to be related to the information provided by the first formant.

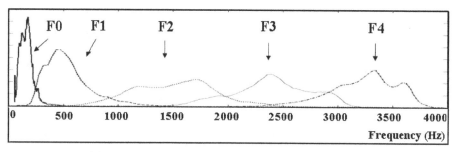

(a) Formant and fundamental frequency distributions

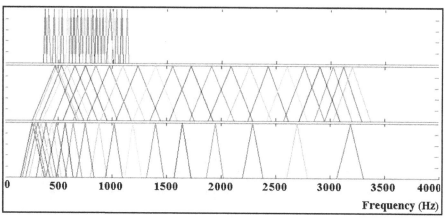

(b) Obtained filter banks for C1 (top) C2 (midle) and C3 (bottom)

Fig. 4. Spectral analyse and obtained solutions

Table 1. Comparative results

Feature extractor	Nf	Nc	Freq. min (Hz)	Freq. max (Hz)	EER%
LFCC	24	16	300	3400	**14.44**
MFCC	24	16	300	3400	**14.88**
C1	23	15	360	1145	22.90
C2	25	20	266	3372	14.79
C3	19	19	156	3309	16.07
C1+C2+C3	- -	- -	- -	- -	**12.69**

Table 2. Fusion analysis

Feature extractor	Correlation	EER obtained by fusion
C1+C2	0.51	13.21%
C2 + C3	0.83	13.45%
C1 + C3	0.64	15.39%

5   Conclusion

In this paper, we proposed to use a genetic algorithm in order to optimise a feature extraction system adapted to the speaker verification task. The proposed system is based on a combination of three complementary feature extractors. Obtained results show that the proposed method improves significantly the system performance. Furthermore, the obtained feature extractors reveal the importance of specific spectral information relatives to the first formant.

Our future work will consist in study the robustness of the obtained solutions according to both the initial conditions and the corpus used for the evolution phase.

References

1. Chetouani, M., Faundez-Zanuy, M., Gas, B., Zarader, J.L.: Non-linear Speech Feature Extraction for Phoneme Classification and Speaker Recognition. In: Chollet, G., Esposito, A., Faúndez-Zanuy, M., Marinaro, M. (eds.) Nonlinear Speech Modeling and Applications. LNCS (LNAI), vol. 3445, pp. 344–350. Springer, Heidelberg (2005)
2. Torkkola, K.: Feature extraction by non parametric mutual information maximization. The Journal of Machine Learning Research 3, 1415–1438 (2003)
3. Miyajima, C., Watanabe, H., Tokuda, K., Kitamura, T., Katagiri, S.: A new approach to designing a feature extractor in speaker identification based on discriminative feature extraction. Speech Communication 35(3-4), 203–218 (2001)
4. Holland, J.H.: Adaptation in natural and artificial systems. University of Michigan Press (1975)
5. Chin-Teng, L., Hsi-Wen, N., Jiing-Yuan, H.: Ga-based noisy speech recognition using two-dimensional cepstrum. IEEE Transactions on Speech and Audio Processing 8, 664–675 (2000)

6. Zamalloa, M., Bordel, G., Rodriguez, J.L., Penagarikano, M.: Feature selection based on genetic algorithms for speaker recognition. In: IEEE Odyssey, vol. 1, pp. 1–8 (2006)
7. Charbuillet, C., Gas, B., Chetouani, M., Zarader, J.L.: Filter bank design for speaker diarization based on genetic algorithms. In: ICASSP 2006. IEEE International Conference on Acoustics, Speech, and Signal Processing, 2006. Proceedings, vol. 1, pp. 673–676 (2006)
8. Reynolds, D., Rose, R.: Robust text-independent speaker identification using gaussian mixture speaker models. IEEE Transactions on Speech and Audio Processing 3(1), 72–83 (1995)
9. Fine, S., Navratil, J., Gopinath, R.: A hybrid gmm/svm approach to speaker identification. In: ICASSP 2001. 2001 IEEE International Conference on Acoustics, Speech, and Signal Processing, 2001. Proceedings, vol. 1, pp. 417–420 (2001)
10. Farrell, K., Ramachandran, R., Mammone, R.: An analysis of data fusion methods for speaker verification. In: ICASSP 1998. Proceedings of the 1998 IEEE International Conference on Acoustics, Speech, and Signal Processing, 1998, vol. 2, pp. 1129–1132 (1998)
11. Zhiyou, M., Yingchun, Y., Zhaohui, W.: Further feature extraction for speaker recognition. IEEE International Conference on Systems, Man and Cybernetics 5, 4153–4158 (2003)
12. Poh Hoon Thian, N., Sanderson, C., Bengio, S., Zhang, D., Jain Anil, K.: Spectral subband centroids as complementary features for speaker authentication. In: Zhang, D., Jain, A.K. (eds.) ICBA 2004. LNCS, vol. 3072, pp. 631–639. Springer, Heidelberg (2004)
13. 2005 Nist SRE web site, http://www.nist.gov/speech/tests/spk/2005/
14. Lia spkdet web site, http://www.lia.univ-avignon.fr/heberges/ALIZE/LIA_RAL
15. Mitchell, T.: Machine learning. McGraw-Hill Higher Education (1997)
16. Paris, G., Robilliard, D., Fonlupt, C.: Exploring Overfitting in Genetic Programming. In: Liardet, P., Collet, P., Fonlupt, C., Lutton, E., Schoenauer, M. (eds.) EA 2003. LNCS, vol. 2936, pp. 267–277. Springer, Heidelberg (2004)
17. Yi, L., Khoshgoftaar, T.: Reducing overfitting in genetic programming models for software quality classification. In: Eighth IEEE International Symposium on High Assurance Systems Engineering, 2004. Proceedings (2004)
18. Ross, B.: The effects of randomly sampled training data on program evolution. In: GECCO, pp. 443–450 (2000)

Speaker Recognition Via Nonlinear Phonetic- and Speaker-Discriminative Features

Lara Stoll[1,2], Joe Frankel[1,3], and Nikki Mirghafori[1]

[1] International Computer Science Institute, Berkeley, CA, USA
[2] University of California at Berkeley, CA, USA
[3] Centre for Speech Technology Research, Edinburgh, UK
{lstoll,nikki}@icsi.berkeley.edu, joe@cstr.ed.ac.uk

Abstract. We use a multi-layer perceptron (MLP) to transform cepstral features into features better suited for speaker recognition. Two types of MLP output targets are considered: phones (Tandem/HATS-MLP) and speakers (Speaker-MLP). In the former case, output activations are used as features in a GMM speaker recognition system, while for the latter, hidden activations are used as features in an SVM system. Using a smaller set of MLP training speakers, chosen through clustering, yields system performance similar to that of a Speaker-MLP trained with many more speakers. For the NIST Speaker Recognition Evaluation 2004, both Tandem/HATS-GMM and Speaker-SVM systems improve upon a basic GMM baseline, but are unable to contribute in a score-level combination with a state-of-the-art GMM system. It may be that the application of normalizations and channel compensation techniques to the current state-of-the-art GMM has reduced channel mismatch errors to the point that contributions of the MLP systems are no longer additive.

1 Introduction

The speaker recognition task is that of deciding whether or not a (previously unseen) test utterance belongs to a given target speaker, for whom there is only a limited amount of training data available. The traditionally successful approach to speaker recognition uses low-level cepstral features extracted from speech in a Gaussian mixture model (GMM) system. Although cepstral features have proven to be the most successful choice of low-level features for speech processing, discriminatively trained features may be better suited to the speaker recognition problem. We utilize multi-layer perceptrons (MLPs), which are trained to distinguish between either phones or speakers, as a means of performing a feature transformation of acoustic features.

There are two types of previous work directly related to our research, both involving the development of discriminative features. In the phonetically discriminative case, the use of features generated by one or more MLPs trained to distinguish between phones has been shown to improve performance for automatic speech recognition (ASR). At ICSI, Zhu and Chen, et al. developed what they termed Tandem/HATS-MLP features, which incorporate longer term temporal information through the use of MLPs whose outputs are phone posteriors [1,2].

M. Chetouani et al. (Eds.): NOLISP 2007, LNAI 4885, pp. 114–123, 2007.
© Springer-Verlag Berlin Heidelberg 2007

In the area of speaker recognition, Heck and Konig, et al. focused on extracting speaker discriminative features from MFCCs using an MLP [3,4]. They used the outputs from the middle layer of a 5-layer MLP, which was trained to discriminate between speakers, as features in a GMM speaker recognition system. The MLP features, when combined on the score-level with a cepstral GMM system, yielded consistent improvement when the training data and testing data were collected from mismatched telephone handsets [3]. A similar approach was followed by Morris and Wu, et al.[5]. They found that speaker identification performance improved as more speakers were used to train the MLP, up to a certain limit [6].

In the phonetic space, we use the Tandem/HATS-MLP features in a GMM speaker recognition system. The idea is that we can use the phonetic information of a speaker in order to distinguish that speaker from others. More specifically, a person's speech contains more information than just vocal quality; the speech also encapsulates variations on a phonetic level, in terms of the phonetic articulation tendencies of a speaker. Examples of speaker recognition systems that successfully utilize the phonetic information of a speaker include the MLLR [7] and phone n-gram [8] systems.

In the speaker space, we train 3-layer Speaker-MLPs of varying sizes to discriminate between a set of speakers, and then use the hidden activations as features for a support vector machine (SVM) speaker recognition system. The intuition behind this method is that the hidden activations from the Speaker-MLP represent a nonlinear mapping of the input cepstral features into a general set of speaker patterns. Our Speaker-MLPs are on a larger scale than any previous work: we use more training speakers, training data, and input frames of cepstral features, and larger networks.

To begin, Section 2 outlines the experimental setup. The results of our experiments are reported in Section 3. Finally, we end with discussion and conclusions in Section 4.

2   Experiments

2.1   Overall Setup

The basic setups of the Tandem/HATS-GMM and Speaker-SVM systems are shown in Figures 1 and 2, respectively. Frames of perceptual linear prediction (PLP) coefficients, as well as frames of critical band energies in the former case, are the inputs to the MLPs. A log is applied to either the output or hidden activations, and after either dimensionality reduction or calculation of mean, standard deviation, histograms, and percentiles, the final features are used in a speaker recognition system (GMM or SVM).

2.2   Baseline GMM Systems

We make use of two types of GMM baselines for purposes of comparison. The first is a state-of-the-art GMM system, which was developed by our colleagues

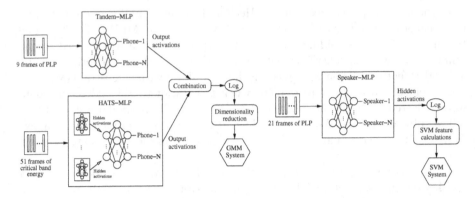

Fig. 1. Tandem/HATS-GMM System   **Fig. 2.** Speaker-SVM System

at SRI, and which we will refer to as SRI-GMM [9]. It utilizes 2048 Gaussians, CMS, T-norm, H-norm, and channel mapping to improve its results. We use this system for score-level combinations, in which the scores from SRI's GMM system are combined with the scores from our MLP features systems. For more details, see Section 2.6.

The second system, on the other hand, is a very basic GMM system, with 256 Gaussians, and which includes only CMS, without any other normalizations. This system, which we will refer to as Basic-GMM, is useful for the purpose of feature-level combination (where we use MFCC features augmented with MLP features as features in the GMM system), as well as for score-level combination.

2.3   Tandem/HATS-MLP Features

There are two components to the Tandem/HATS-MLP features, namely the Tandem-MLP and the HATS-MLP. The Tandem-MLP is a single 3-layer MLP, which takes as input 9 frames of PLPs (12th order plus energy) with deltas and double-deltas, contains 20,800 units in its hidden layer, and has 46 outputs, corresponding to phone posteriors. The hidden layer applies the sigmoid function, while the output uses softmax.

The HATS-MLP is actually two stages of MLPs that perform phonetic classification with long-term (500-1000 ms) information. The first stage MLPs take as input 51 frames of log critical band energies (LCBE), with one MLP for each of the 15 critical bands; each MLP has 60 hidden units (with sigmoid applied), and the output layer has 46 units (with softmax) corresponding to phones. For the HATS (Hidden Activation TRAPS) features, the hidden layer outputs are taken from each first-stage critical band MLP, and then input to the second-stage merger MLP, which contains 750 hidden units, and 46 output units.

The Tandem-MLP and HATS-MLP features are then combined using a weighted sum, where the weights are a normalized version of inverse entropy (for the Tandem/HATS-GMM). The log is applied to the output, and a Karhunen-Loeve Transform (KLT) dimensionality reduction is applied to reduce the output feature vector to an experimentally determined optimal length of 25. This process is illustrated in Figure 1.

The Tandem/HATS-MLP system is trained on roughly 1800 hours of conversational speech from the Fisher [10] and Switchboard [11] corpora.

2.4   Speaker-MLP Features

Speaker Target Selection Through Clustering. As a contrast to using all speakers with enough training data available (with the idea that including more training speakers will yield better results), we also implemented MLPs trained using only subsets of specifically chosen speakers. These speakers were chosen through clustering in the following way. First, a background GMM model was trained using 286 speakers from the Fisher corpus. Then, a GMM was adapted from the background model with the data from each MLP-training speaker. These GMMs used 32 Gaussians, with input features of 12th order MFCCs plus energy and their first order derivatives. The length-26 mean vectors of each Gaussian were concatenated to form a length-832 feature vector for each speaker. Principal component analysis was performed, keeping the top 16 dimensions of each feature vector (accounting for 68% of the total variance). In this reduced-dimensionality speaker space, k-means clustering was done, using the Euclidean distance between speakers, for $k = 64$ and $k = 128$. Finally, the sets of 64 and 128 speakers were chosen by selecting the speaker closest to each of the (64 or 128) cluster centroids.

MLP Training. A set of 64, 128, or 836 speakers was used to train each Speaker-MLP, with 6 conversation sides per speaker used for training, and 2 for cross-validation (CV). The training speaker data came from the Switchboard-2 corpus [11]. The set of 836 speakers included all speakers in the Switchboard2 corpus with at least 8 conversations available. The smaller sets of speakers, selected through clustering, used training and CV data that was balanced in terms of handsets.

ICSI's QuickNet MLP training tool [12] was used to train the Speaker-MLPs. The input to each Speaker-MLP is 21 frames of PLPs (12th order plus energy) with first and second order derivatives appended. The hidden layer applies a sigmoid, while the output uses softmax.

Table 2 shows the sizes of MLPs (varying in the number of hidden units) trained for each set of speakers.

2.5   SVM Speaker Recognition System

The GMM system is well suited to modeling features with fewer than 100 dimensions. However, problems of data sparsity and singular covariance matrices soon arise in trying to estimate high dimensional Gaussians. Previous work in speech recognition (HATS) has shown that there is a great deal of information in the hidden structure of the MLP. Preliminary experiments also showed that reducing the dimensionality of the hidden activations using principal component analysis (PCA) or linear discriminant analysis (LDA), so that the features could be used in a GMM system, yielded poor results. In order to take advantage of the speaker discriminative information in the hidden activations of the Speaker-MLPs, we use an SVM speaker recognition system, which is better suited to handle the high dimensional sparse features, is naturally discriminative in the way it is posed, and has proven useful in other approaches to speaker verification.

Since the SVM speaker recognition system requires the same length feature vector for each speaker (whether a target, an impostor, or a test speaker), we produce a set of statistics to summarize the information along each dimension of the hidden activations. These statistics (mean, standard deviation, histograms of varying numbers of bins, and percentiles) are then used as the SVM features for each speaker. For our experiments, the set of impostor speakers used in the SVM system is a set of 286 speakers from the Fisher corpus designed to be balanced in terms of gender, channel, and other conditions.

2.6   System Combinations Using LNKnet

In order to improve upon the baseline of the SRI-GMM system, we choose to combine our various systems on the score-level with the SRI-GMM, using LNKnet software [13]. We use a neural network with no hidden layer and sigmoid output non-linearity, which takes two or more sets of likelihood scores as input. We use a round-robin approach and divide our test data into two subsets for development and evaluation.

3   Results

3.1   Testing Database

In order to compare the performance of our systems, we use the database released by NIST for the 2004 Speaker Recognition Evaluation (SRE) [14]. This database consists of conversational speech collected in the Mixer project, and includes various languages and various channel types. We use only telephone data, containing a variety of handsets and microphones.

One conversation side (roughly 2.5 minutes) is used for both the training of each target speaker model and the testing of each test speaker. As performance measures, we use the detection cost function (DCF) of the NIST evaluation and the equal error rate (EER). The DCF is defined to be a weighted sum of the miss and false alarm error probabilities, while the EER is the rate at which these error probabilites are equal.

3.2   Tandem/HATS-GMM

For NIST's SRE2004, the DCF and EER results are given in Table 1 for the Basic-GMM system, the Tandem/HATS-GMM system, and their score- and feature-level combinations, as well as for the SRI-GMM system and its combination with the Tandem/HATS-GMM. Changes relative to each baseline (where a positive value indicates improvement) are shown in parentheses.

Table 1. Tandem/HATS-GMM system improves upon Basic-GMM system, especially in combination, but there is no improvement for SRI-GMM system

	DCF×10	EER (%)
Basic-GMM	0.724	18.48
Tandem/HATS-GMM	0.713 (2%)	18.48 (0%)
Score-level fusion	0.618 (15%)	16.26 (12%)
Feature-level fusion	0.601 (17%)	16.35 (12%)
SRI-GMM	0.374	9.01
Tandem/HATS-GMM	0.713	18.48
Score-level fusion	0.378 (-1%)	9.09 (-1%)

Alone, the Tandem/HATS-GMM system perform slightly better than the Basic-GMM system. Feature-level combination of MFCC and Tandem/HATS features in a GMM system, as well as score-level combination of the Tandem/HATS-GMM system with the Basic-GMM, both yield significant improvements. When the Tandem/HATS-GMM system is combined on the score-level with the SRI-GMM system, there is no gain in performance over the SRI-GMM alone.

In order to consider phonetic features comparable to those produced by the Speaker-MLP, we also tested the Tandem-MLP features individually, i.e., without combination with the HATS-MLP features. The Tandem-GMM system actually yields better results than the Tandem/HATS-GMM, although in combinations with the Basic-GMM and SRI-GMM there is no improvement. Thus, we may conclude that the added complexity of the HATS-MLP component does not lead to any significant difference in speaker recognition results for the Tandem/HATS-GMM system. For more detailed results, see [15].

3.3   Speaker-SVM

Both the cross-validation and SRE2004 results for the Speaker-MLPs are shown in Table 2 for each size MLP. It is clear that the CV accuracy increases with respect to the number of hidden units, for each training speaker set. The accuracy increase on adding further hidden units does not appear to have reached a plateau at 2500 hidden units for the 836 speaker net, though for the purposes of the current study the training times became prohibitive. With the computation shared between 4 CPUs, it took over 4 weeks to train the MLP with 2500 hidden units.

Similar to the CV accuracy, the speaker recognition results improve with an increase in the size of the hidden layer when considering a given number of training speakers.

In Table 3, the results are given for the score-level combination of the 64 speaker, 1000 hidden unit, Speaker-SVM system with the Basic-GMM and SRI-GMM systems. For the SRI-GMM, the best combination is yielded when the Speaker-MLP is trained with 64 speakers and 1000 hidden units (although the 128 speakers with 2000 hidden units does somewhat better in combination with

Table 2. Speaker-SVM results improve as the number of hidden units, as well as the CV accuracy, increase

# spkrs	Hid. units	CV acc.	DCF×10	EER (%)
64	400	37.8%	0.753	21.04
64	1000	47.8%	0.715	20.41
128	1000	39.4%	0.702	20.45
128	2000	44.5%	0.691	19.70
836	400	20.5%	0.756	22.88
836	800	25.5%	0.734	21.37
836	1500	32.0%	0.711	20.45
836	2500	35.5%	0.689	19.91

Table 3. System combination with 64 speaker, 1000 hidden unit, Speaker-SVM improves Basic-GMM results, but not the SRI-GMM

	DCF×10	EER (%)
Basic-GMM	0.724	18.48
Speaker-SVM	0.715	20.41
Score-level fusion	0.671 (7%)	17.52 (5%)
SRI-GMM	0.374	9.01
Speaker-SVM	0.715	20.41
Score-level fusion	0.373 (0%)	9.01 (0%)

Table 4. Breakdown of results for matched and mismatched conditions for the MLP-based systems and their score-level fusions with the Basic-GMM

	System Alone		Fusion with Basic-GMM	
	Matched EER (%)	Mismatched EER (%)	Matched EER (%)	Mismatched EER (%)
Basic-GMM	9.13	22.65	–	–
Tandem/HATS-GMM	12.53	21.54	8.67 (5%)	19.84 (12%)
Speaker-SVM (1000hu, 64ou)	13.93	23.56	8.78 (4%)	20.95 (7%)

Table 5. Breakdown of results for matched and mismatched conditions for the MLP-based systems and their score-level fusions with the SRI-GMM

	System Alone		Fusion with SRI-GMM	
	Matched EER (%)	Mismatched EER (%)	Matched EER (%)	Misatched EER (%)
SRI-GMM	5.74	10.71	–	–
Tandem/HATS-GMM	12.53	21.54	5.74 (0%)	10.77 (-1%)
Speaker-SVM (1000hu, 64ou)	13.93	23.56	5.74 (0%)	10.64 (1%)

the Basic-GMM). There is a reasonable gain made when combining the Speaker-SVM system with the Basic-GMM, but there is no significant improvement for the combination of the Speaker-SVM and SRI-GMM systems.

3.4   Mismatched Train and Test Conditions

We now consider matched (same gender and handset) and mismatched (different gender or handset) conditions between the training and test data. Such a breakdown is given for the Tandem/HATS-GMM and Speaker-SVM systems and their score-level combinations with the Basic-GMM and SRI-GMM in Tables 4 and 5, respectively. For each combination, changes relative to the appropriate baseline system are given in parentheses.

When considering a score-level fusion with the Basic-GMM system, gains are made in the matched and especially the mismatched conditions for both the Tandem/HATS-GMM and Speaker-SVM. For the SRI-GMM baseline, combination with the Tandem/HATS-GMM and Speaker-SVM systems has marginal impact in either the matched or mismatched case.

4   Discussion and Conclusions

For the first time, phonetic Tandem/HATS-MLP features were tested in a speaker recognition application. Although developed for ASR, the Tandem/HATS-MLP features still yield good results when used in a GMM for a speaker recognition task. In fact, the Tandem/HATS-GMM performs slightly better than a basic cepstral GMM system, with even more improvement coming from score- and feature-level combinations of the two.

Prior related work used discriminative features from MLPs trained to distinguish between speakers. Motivated by having a well-established infrastructure for neural network training at ICSI, we felt that there was potential for making greater gains by using more speakers, more hidden units, and a larger contextual window of cepstral features at the input. Even though preliminary experiments confirmed this, ultimately, however, a smaller subset of speakers chosen through clustering proved similar in performance and could be trained in less time.

Although the MLP-based systems do not improve upon the SRI-GMM baseline in combination, this result could be explained by considering the difference in the performance between the two types of systems: standalone, each MLP-based system performs much more poorly than the SRI-GMM. The addition of channel compensating normalizations, like T-norm [16], to an MLP-based system should help reduce the performance gap between the MLP-based system and the SRI-GMM. It may then be possible for the MLP-based system to improve upon the state-of-the-art cepstral GMM system in combination, in the event that the performance gap is narrowed sufficiently.

Similar to results observed in prior work, the Speaker-SVM system improved speaker recognition performance for a cepstral GMM system lacking sophisticated normalizations (such as feature mapping [17], speaker model synthesis

(SMS) [18], and T-norm); such a result was also true for the Tandem/HATS-GMM system. However, no gains were visible in addition with the SRI-GMM, which is significantly improved from the Basic-GMM (as well as the GMM systems of Wu and Morris, et al. and Heck and Konig, et al.) by the addition of feature mapping, T-norm, as well as increasing the number of Gaussians to 2048.

As shown in Table 4, combinations of the Basic-GMM with the phonetic- and speaker-discriminant MLP-based systems of this paper do yield larger improvements for the mismatched condition (which refers to the training data and test data being different genders or different handset types). However, as seen in Table 5, such a result does not hold for combinations of the MLP-based systems with the SRI-GMM. The previous work of Heck and Konig, et al., completed prior to the year 2000, showed that the greatest strength of an MLP-based approach was for the case when there is a handset mismatch between the training and test data, however, the state-of-the-art has since advanced significantly in normalization and channel compensation techniques. As a result, the contributions of the MLP-based systems, without any normalizations applied, to a state-of-the-art cepstral GMM system are no longer significant for the mismatched condition.

Acknowledgements

This material is based upon work supported under a National Science Foundation Graduate Research Fellowship and upon work supported by the National Science Foundation under grant number 0329258. This work was also made possible by funding from the EPSRC Grant GR/S21281/01 and the AMI Training Programme. We would also like to thank our colleagues at ICSI and SRI.

References

1. Chen, B., Zhu, Q., Morgan, N.: Learning long-term temporal features in LVCSR using neural networks. In: ICSLP (2004)
2. Zhu, Q., Chen, B., Morgan, N., Stolcke, A.: On using MLP features in LVCSR. In: ICSLP (2004)
3. Heck, L.P., Konig, Y., Sönmez, M.K., Weintraub, M.: Robustness to telephone handset distortion in speaker recognition by discriminative feature design. Speech Communications 31(2-3), 181–192 (2000)
4. Konig, Y., Heck, L., Weintraub, M., Sönmez, K.: Nonlinear discriminant feature extraction for robust text-independent speaker recognition. In: Proceedings of RLA2C - Speaker Recognition and Its Commercial and Forensic Applications, Avignon, France (1998)
5. Morris, A.C., Wu, D., Koreman, J.: MLP trained to separate problem speakers provides improved features for speaker identification. In: IEEE Int. Carnahan Conf. on Security Technology (2005)
6. Wu, D., Morris, A., Koreman, J.: MLP internal representation as discriminative features for improved speaker recognition. In: Faundez-Zanuy, M., Janer, L., Esposito, A., Satue-Villar, A., Roure, J., Espinosa-Duro, V. (eds.) NOLISP 2005. LNCS (LNAI), vol. 3817, pp. 25–33. Springer, Heidelberg (2006)

7. Stolcke, A., Ferrer, L., Kajarekar, S., Shriberg, E., Venkataraman, A.: MLLR transforms as features in speaker recognition. In: EUROSPEECH 2005, pp. 2425–2428 (2005)
8. Andrews, W., Kohler, M., Campbell, J.: Phonetic speaker recognition. In: Eurospeech, pp. 149–153 (2001)
9. Kajarekar, S., Ferrer, L., Shriberg, E., Sönmez, K., Stolcke, A., Venkataraman, A., Zheng, J.: SRI's 2004 NIST speaker recognition evaluation system. In: ICASSP, vol. 1, pp. 173–176 (2005)
10. Cieri, C., Miller, D., Walker, K.: The Fisher corpus: a resource for the next generations of speech to text. In: LREC, pp. 69–71 (2004)
11. Linguistic Data Consortium, Switchboard-2 corpora, http://www.ldc.upenn.edu
12. Johnson, D.: QuickNet3 (2004), http://www.icsi.berkeley.edu/Speech/qn.html
13. MIT Lincoln Labs, LNKNet (2005), http://www.ll.mit.edu/IST/lnknet
14. National Institute of Standards and Technology, The NIST year 2004 speaker recognition evaluation plan (2004), http://www.nist.gov/speech/tests/spk/2004/SRE-04_evalplan-v1a.pdf
15. Stoll, L.: Phonetic- and speaker-discriminant features for speaker recognition, Master's thesis, University of California at Berkeley (December 2006), http://www.icsi.berkeley.edu/ lstoll/publications/stoll_masters_dec20 06.pdf
16. Auckenthaler, R., Carey, M., Lloyd-Thomas, H.: Score normalization for text-independent speaker verification systems. Digital Signal Processing 10, 42–54 (2000)
17. Reynolds, D.: Channel robust speaker verification via feature mapping. In: ICASSP (2003)
18. Teunen, R., Shahshahani, B., Heck, L.: A model-based transformational approach to robust speaker recognition. In: ICSLP (2000)

Perceptron-Based Class Verification

Michael Gerber, Tobias Kaufmann, and Beat Pfister

Speech Processing Group
Computer Engineering and Networks Laboratory
ETH Zurich, Switzerland
gerber@tik.ee.ethz.ch

Abstract. We present a method to use multilayer perceptrons (MLPs) for a verification task, i.e. to verify whether two vectors are from the same class or not. In tests with synthetic data we could show that the verification MLPs are almost optimal from a Bayesian point of view. With speech data we have shown that verification MLPs generalize well such that they can be deployed as well for classes which were not seen during the training.

1 Introduction

Multilayer perceptrons (MLPs) are successfully used in speech processing. For example they are used to calculate the phoneme posterior probabilities in hybrid MLP/HMM speech recognizers (see for example [1]). In this case their task is to output for every phoneme the posterior probability that a given input feature vector is from this phoneme. They are thus used to *identify* a feature vector with a given phoneme. Expressed in more general terms the MLPs are used for the *identification* of input vectors with a class from within a closed set of classes.

There are applications however, where the identification of input vectors is not necessary but it has to be *verified* whether two given input vectors x and y are from the same class or not. In Section 2 we present two verification tasks in the domain of speech processing. In this work we show that MLPs have the capability to optimally solve verification problems. Furthermore we have observed in a task with real-world data that the verification MLPs can even be used to discriminate between classes which were not present in the training set. This is an especially useful property for two reasons:

- The verification MLP is usable for an open set of classes.
- Since we do not need training data from the classes present in the application but can collect training data from other classes which have the same classification objective (e.g. classifying speakers). Therefore we can build a training set of a virtually unlimited size.

In Section 2 we present the motivation for our approach to class verification and outline how MLPs can be used for that purpose. The structure and training of our verification MLPs is described in Section 3. Our evaluation methods are described in Section 4. In order to test whether verification MLPs are capable

M. Chetouani et al. (Eds.): NOLISP 2007, LNAI 4885, pp. 124–131, 2007.

of performing the verification task in an optimal way from a Bayesian point of view we made experiments with synthetic data. These experiments and their results are described in Section 5. The results of experiments with speech data are shown in Section 6. Finally, our conclusions are summarized in Section 7.

2   Motivation

Our method to decide whether two speech signals are spoken by the same speaker or not includes the following 3 steps: First equally worded segments are sought in the two speech signals. This results in a series of frame pairs where both frames of a pair are from the same phoneme. In a second step for each frame pair the probability that the two phonetically matching frames come from the same speaker is computed. Finally, the global indicator that the two speech signals were spoken by the same speaker can be calculated from these frame-level probabilities. See e.g. [2] for a more detailed description of the speaker-verification approach. We used the verification MLPs for the following two tasks:

- For seeking phonetically matching segments in two speech signals we use a phonetic probability matrix. This matrix is spanned by the two signals and every element $P_{ij}(x_{1i}, x_{2j})$ gives the probability that frame i of signal 1 given as feature vector x_{1i} and frame j of signal 2 given as feature vector x_{2j} are from the same phoneme. The probabilities $P_{ij}(x_{1i}, x_{2j})$ are calculated by an appropriately trained verification MLP.
- For every pair of phonetically matching frames we use a verification MLP to calculate a score which stands for the probability that the two frames are from the same speaker. In this case we use a MLP which was trained with data from speakers which are not present in the test. Therefore we make use of the generalization capability of the verification MLP.

3   Verification MLP

Since the MLP has to decide whether two given input vectors x and y are from the same class the MLP has to process vector pairs rather than single vectors. The target output of the MLP is o_s if the two vectors of the pair are from the same class and o_d if they are from different classes. The vectors are decided to belong to the same class if the output is closer to o_s and to different classes otherwise.

The sizes of the 3-layer perceptrons used for the experiments described in Sections 5 and 6 are as follows:

	input size	1st hidden layer	2nd hidden layer	output layer
synthetic data	$2 \cdot 2...5$	20 (tanh)	10 (tanh)	1 (tanh)
phoneme verification	$2 \cdot 26$	80 (tanh)	35 (tanh)	1 (tanh)
speaker verification	$2 \cdot 16$	70 (tanh)	18 (tanh)	1 (tanh)

The verification MLPs were trained by means of the backpropagation algorithm. The weights were randomly initialized and a momentum term was used during the training. For a hyperbolic tangent output neuron a good choice for the output targets is $o_s = 0.75$ and $o_d = -0.75$ such that the weights are not driven towards infinity (see for example [3]). With these settings we experienced that at the beginning of the training the difference between desired and effective output decreased quite slowly but that the training was never stuck in a local minimum.

4   Performance Evaluation

In order to evaluate a verification MLP, we measure its verification error rate for a given dataset and compare it to a reference error rate which is optimal in a certain sense. By formulating our verification task as a classification problem, we can use the Bayes error as a reference. The Bayes error is known to be optimal for classification problems given the distribution of the data.

To reformulate a verification task as a classification problem, each pair of vectors is assigned one of the following two groups:

G_S group of all vector pairs where the two vectors are from the same class
G_D group of all vector pairs where both vectors are from different classes

Provided that the same classes which are present in the tests are used to estimate the distributions of G_S and G_D, the Bayes error is optimal, since the two distributions are modeled properly. Otherwise there is a mismatch which leads to ill-modeled G_S and G_D and thus the Bayes classifier is not necessarily optimal any more.

In the case of synthetic data it is possible to calculate the Bayes verification error since the data distributions are given in a parametric form. For real-world problems the data distributions are not given in a parametric form and hence the Bayes verification error can't be computed directly. In this case we can use a k nearest neighbor (KNN) classifier to asymptotically approach the Bayes error as described below.

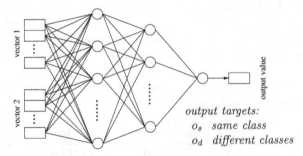

Fig. 1. Structure of the verification MLPs

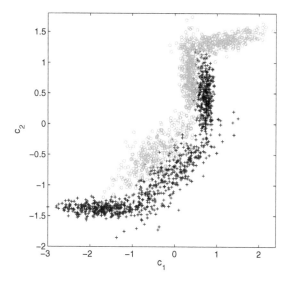

Fig. 2. Synthetic data: 2 classes with 2-dimensional non-Gaussian distributions

The KNN approach is a straightforward means of classification. The training set for the KNN algorithm consists of training vectors with known classification $(a_{tr,i}, b_{tr,i})$ where $a_{tr,i}$ is the training vector and $b_{tr,i}$ is its associated class. A test vector $a_{tst,j}$ is classified by seeking the k nearest training vectors $a_{tr,i}$ and it is assigned to the class which is most often present among the k nearest neighbors. The KNN classifier is known to reach the Bayes error when an infinite number of training vectors is available (see e.g. [4]) and is therefore a means to approximate the Bayes error if the data distributions are not known in a parametric form.

5   Experiments with Synthetic Data

The aim of the experiments with synthetic datasets, i.e. datasets with known data distributions, was to test if the verification MLP achieves the lowest possible verification error from a Bayesian point of view. The data sets had 2 to 4 classes and were 2- to 5-dimensional. We illustrate these investigations by means of an experiment with a 2-dimensional dataset with 2 classes that are distributed as shown in Figure 2.

The number of training epochs which were necessary to train the verification MLP depended largely on the type of the dataset. We observed the following dependencies:

– If only a few features carried discriminating information and all other features were just random values the verification MLP learned quickly which features were useful and which ones could be neglected.
– The shape of the distributions strongly influenced the number of epochs that were necessary for the training. For example, two classes distributed in two

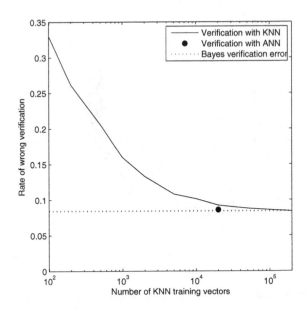

Fig. 3. Class verification error for the test set as shown in Figure 2: the KNN verification error is shown in function of the training set size. As expected, with increasing size it approximates the Bayes limit which is indicated by the dotted line. The error rate of the verification MLP is close to the Bayes error.

parallel stripes or classes that had a non-linear Bayes decision boundary, such as those shown in Figure 2, required many epochs.

Figure 3 shows the error rates of different verification methods for data distributed as shown in Figure 2. It can be seen that the error of the verification MLP is almost as low as the Bayes error. Note that the MLP was trained with a fixed number of 20'000 vector pairs. We are only interested in the best possible verification error for a given task and not in the verification error in function of the number of training vectors (see Section 1). Therefore the MLP training set was chosen as large as necessary.

For all investigated datasets the verification error achieved with the verification MLP was not significantly higher than the Bayes verification error.

6   Experiments with Speech Data

6.1   Data Description and Feature Extraction

For a speaker verification task with single speech frames we used speech signals from 48 male speakers recorded from different telephones. From short speech segments (32 ms frames) the 13 first Mel frequency cepstral coefficients (MFCCs) were extracted and used as feature vectors for our experiments. For the phoneme

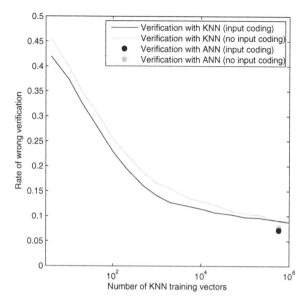

Fig. 4. Phoneme verification task: The KNN error rates decrease with increasing number of KNN training vectors. The error rates of the verification MLPs are shown as dots. The error rates for both, KNN and MLP are given for coded and uncoded input vectors.

verification task the first derivatives of the MFCCs were used in addition to the static MFCCs. The data from all speakers was divided into 3 disjoint sets (i.e. no speaker was present in more than one set). The MLP and KNN training vector pairs were extracted from the *training set* (26 speakers). The *validation set* (10 speakers) was used to stop the MLP training at the optimal point and to find the optimal value of k for the KNN classifier. The test vector pairs were taken from the *test set* (12 speakers). Note that all vector pairs were formed in a way that the two vectors of a pair were always from the same phoneme. In every set the number of pairs with vectors of the same speaker and the number of pairs with vectors from different speakers were equal.

6.2   Phoneme Verification

In this task the objective was to decide whether two speech feature vectors originate from the same phoneme. In this task the same classes (phonemes) are present in all 3 datasets since all signals have similar phonetic content. Yet all sets are extracted from different speakers as is described in Section 6.1.

Because of the large number of KNN training vectors which were necessary that the KNN algorithm converged, we used two types of input, namely pairs of concatenated vectors $\boldsymbol{p}_{in} = (\boldsymbol{x}, \boldsymbol{y})$ as mentioned above and coded vector pairs $\boldsymbol{p}_{in} = (|\boldsymbol{x} - \boldsymbol{y}|, \boldsymbol{x} + \boldsymbol{y})$ (see [5] for details about the input coding). This input coding sped up the training of the MLPs and led to a steeper descent of the KNN verification error in function of the number of training vectors.

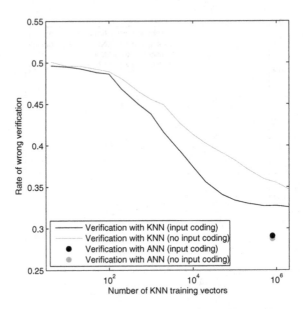

Fig. 5. Speaker verification: The KNN error rates decrease with increasing number of KNN training vectors. The error rates of the verification MLPs are shown as dots. The error rates for both, KNN and MLP are given for coded and uncoded input vectors.

The verification error of an MLP trained with 580000 vector pairs is shown in Figure 4. For comparison also the KNN error rate in function of the training set size is drawn. It can be seen that with this data the verification KNN converges only with a large number training vectors. This was expected because of the more complex nature of the problem. It can only be guessed where the asymptote and therefore the Bayes error will be. It seems that the verification error of the MLP is close to the Bayes verification error however. Since we did not have enough training data we could not prove this assumption. Furthermore it does not seem that the input coding had a big effect on the optimal verification result.

6.3   Speaker Verification

In this task the objective was to decide whether two speech frames are from speech signals of the same speaker or not. In this case all 3 sets of classes (speakers) were disjoint. Therefore a good generalization of the verification MLP is required.

The experiment results are shown in Figure 5. It can be seen that the KNN verification error in function of the training set size decreases much less steeply than in the experiments done with synthetic data and does not even get as low as the verification error of the MLP. This is possible since the training and test set have some mismatch because the speaker sets are disjoint (see Section 4). Here it can be seen very well that the KNN which is based on coded vector pairs converged with much less training vectors. In this case the verification MLP which used coded vector pairs was a bit worse however.

The verification error of the MLP is quite low if it is considered that the feature vectors x and y were extracted from single speech frames only. If all phonetically matching frame pairs of two equally worded speech segments of about 1 s length are fed separately into the MLP and the output values of the MLP are averaged, the verification error rate is about 6 %. More detailed results can be found in [5], [6] and [2].

7   Conclusions

By means of experiments we have shown that the error rate of an appropriately configured and trained verification MLP is close to the Bayes error rate. Depending on the class distributions, the training can be fairly time-consuming, however. This is not critical in our application since the MLP is class independent and does not need to be retrained whenever new classes are added to the application.

For speech data with a virtually unlimited set of classes, as it is for example the case in speaker verification, MLP-based class verification has shown to be very efficient not only in terms of verification error but also with respect to computational complexity. For a speaker-verification task the good generalization property of the verification MLP could be shown. Thus the verification MLPs are able to learn a general rule to distinguish between classes rather than class-specific features.

Acknowledgements

This work was partly funded by the Swiss National Center of Competence in Research IM2.

References

1. Hermansky, H., Ellis, D.P.W., Sharma, S.: Tandem connectionist feature extraction for conventional HMM systems. In: Proceedings of the ICASSP 2000, vol. 3, pp. 1635–1638 (2000)
2. Gerber, M., Beutler, R., Pfister, B.: Quasi text-independent speaker verification based on pattern matching. In: ISCA. Proceedings of Interspeech 2007, pp. 1993–1996 (2007)
3. Haykin, S.: Neural Networks: A Comprehensive Foundation, 2nd edn. Prentice-Hall, Englewood Cliffs (1999)
4. Duda, R.O., Hart, P.E., Stork, D.G.: Pattern Classification. Wiley Interscience, Chichester (2001)
5. Niesen, U., Pfister, B.: Speaker verification by means of ANNs. In: Proceedings of ESANN 2004, Bruges (Belgium), pp. 145–150 (2004)
6. Gerber, M., Pfister, B.: Quasi text-independent speaker verification with neural networks. MLMI 2005, Edinburgh (United Kingdom) (July 2005)

Manifold Learning-Based Feature Transformation for Phone Classification

Andrew Errity, John McKenna, and Barry Kirkpatrick

School of Computing
Dublin City University
Dublin 9, Ireland
{andrew.errity,john.mckenna,barry.kirkpatrick}@computing.dcu.ie

Abstract. This study aims to investigate approaches for low dimensional speech feature transformation using manifold learning. It has recently been shown that speech sounds may exist on a low dimensional manifold nonlinearly embedded in high dimensional space. A number of manifold learning techniques have been developed in recent years that attempt to discover this type of underlying geometric structure. The manifold learning techniques locally linear embedding and Isomap are considered in this study. The low dimensional representations produced by applying these techniques to MFCC feature vectors are evaluated in several phone classification tasks on the TIMIT corpus. Classification accuracy is analysed and compared to conventional MFCC features and those transformed with PCA, a linear dimensionality reduction method. It is shown that features resulting from manifold learning are capable of yielding higher classification accuracy than these baseline features. The best phone classification accuracy in general is demonstrated by feature transformation with Isomap.

1 Introduction

Feature transformation is an important part of the speech recognition process and can be viewed as a two step procedure. Firstly, relevant information is extracted from short-time segments of the acoustic speech signal using a procedure such as Fourier analysis, cepstral analysis, or some other perceptually motivated analysis. The resulting D-dimensional parameter vectors are then transformed to a feature vector of lower dimensionality d $(d \leq D)$. The aim of this dimensionality reduction is to produce features which are concise low dimensional representations that retain the most discriminating information for the intended application and are thus more suitable for pattern classification. Dimensionality reduction also decreases the computational cost associated with subsequent processing.

Physiological constraints on the articulators limit the degrees of freedom of the speech production apparatus. As a result humans are only capable of producing sounds occupying a subspace of the entire acoustic space. Thus, speech data can be viewed as lying on or near a low dimensional manifold embedded in the

M. Chetouani et al. (Eds.): NOLISP 2007, LNAI 4885, pp. 132–141, 2007.

original acoustic space. The underlying dimensionality of speech has been the subject of much previous research using many different approaches including classical dimensionality reduction analysis [1], [2], nonlinear dynamical analysis [3], and manifold learning [4]. The consensus of this work is that some speech sounds, particularly voiced speech, are inherently low dimensional.

Dimensionality reduction methods aim to discover such underlying low dimensional structure. These methods can be categorised as linear or nonlinear. Linear methods are limited to discovering the structure of data lying on or near a linear subspace of the high dimensional input space. Two of the most widely used linear dimensionality reduction methods are principal component analysis (PCA) [5] and linear discriminant analysis (LDA) [6]. These methods have been successfully applied to feature transformation in speech processing applications in the past [7], [8].

However if speech data occupies a low dimensional submanifold nonlinearly embedded in the original space, as proposed previously [2], [4], linear methods will fail to discover the low dimensional structure. A number of manifold learning, also referred to as nonlinear dimensionality reduction, algorithms have been developed [9], [10], [11] which overcome the limitations of linear methods. Manifold learning algorithms have recently been shown to be useful in a number of speech processing applications including low dimensional visualization of speech [11], [12], [13], [4], [14] and limited phone classification tasks [15], [14].

In this study, we build upon previous work and apply two manifold learning algorithms, locally linear embedding (LLE) [9] and isometric feature mapping (Isomap) [10], to extract features from speech data. These features are evaluated in phone classification experiments using a support vector machine (SVM) [16] classifier. The classification performance of these features is compared to baseline Mel-frequency cepstral coefficients (MFCC) and those resulting from the classical linear method, PCA. These classification experiments are primarily used as a means of evaluating how much meaningful discriminatory information is contained in the low dimensional representations produced by each method. These experiments also serve to display the potential value of these methods in speech processing applications.

The remainder of this paper is structured as follows. In Section 2, the manifold learning algorithms LLE and Isomap are briefly described. Section 3 details the experimental procedure, data set, parameter extraction, feature transformation, and classification technique used. Results are examined and discussed in Section 4, with conclusions presented in Section 5.

2   Manifold Learning Algorithms

2.1   Locally Linear Embedding

LLE [9] is an unsupervised learning algorithm that computes low dimensional embeddings of high dimensional data. The principle of LLE is to compute a low dimensional embedding with the property that nearby points in the high dimensional space remain nearby and similarly co-located with respect to one another in the low dimensional space. In other words, the embedding is optimised to preserve local neighbourhoods.

The LLE algorithm can be summarised in three steps:

1. For each data point X_i, compute its k nearest neighbours (based on Euclidean distance or some other appropriate definition of 'nearness').
2. Compute weights W_{ij} that best reconstruct each data point X_i from its neighbours, minimising the reconstruction error E:

$$E(W) = \sum_i \left| X_i - \sum_j W_{ij} X_j \right|^2 . \tag{1}$$

3. Compute the low dimensional embeddings Y_i, best reconstructed by the weights W_{ij}, minimising the cost function Ω:

$$\Omega(Y) = \sum_i \left| Y_i - \sum_j W_{ij} Y_j \right|^2 . \tag{2}$$

In step 2, the reconstruction error is minimised subject to two constraints: first, that each input is reconstructed only from its nearest neighbours, or $W_{ij} = 0$ if X_i is not a neighbour of X_j; second, that the reconstruction weights for each data point sum to one, or $\sum_j W_{ij} = 1 \ \forall \ i$. The optimum weights for each input can be computed efficiently by solving a constrained least squares problem.

The cost function in step 3 is also based on locally linear reconstruction errors, but here the weights W_{ij} are kept fixed while optimising the outputs Y_i. The embedding cost function in (2) is a quadratic function in Y_i. The minimisation is performed subject to constraints that the outputs are centered and have unit covariance. The cost function has a unique global minimum solution for the outputs Y_i. This is the result returned by LLE as the low dimensional embedding of the high dimensional data points X_i.

2.2   Isomap

The Isomap algorithm [10] offers a differently motivated approach to manifold learning. Isomap is a nonlinear generalisation of multidimensional scaling (MDS) [6] that seeks a mapping from a high dimensional dataset to a low dimensional dataset that preserves geodesic distances between pairs of data points— that is, distances on the manifold from which the data is sampled.

While Isomap and LLE have similar aims, Isomap is based on a different principle than LLE. In particular, Isomap attempts to preserve the global geometric properties of the manifold while LLE attempts to preserve the local geometric properties of the manifold.

As with LLE, the Isomap algorithm consists of three steps:

1. Construct a neighbourhood graph: Determine which points are neighbours on the manifold based on distances, $\text{dist}(X_i, X_j)$, between pairs of points X_i, X_j in the input space (as in step 1 of LLE). These neighbourhood relations are then represented as a weighted graph over the data points with edges of weight $\text{dist}(X_i, X_j)$ between neighbouring points.

2. Compute the shortest path between all pairs of points among only those paths that connect nearest neighbours using a technique such as Dijkstra's algorithm.
3. Use classical MDS to embed the data in a d-dimensional Euclidean space so as to preserve these geodesic distances.

3 Experiments

The objective of these experiments is to evaluate how much meaningful discriminatory information is contained in the low dimensional representations produced by the manifold learning and linear dimensionality reduction methods.

3.1 Classification Tasks

Phone classification experiments were performed using four different feature types: baseline MFCC vectors and features produced by applying PCA, Isomap, and LLE to the baseline MFCC vectors. Two types of baseline MFCC vectors were used: standard static MFCCs only and static MFCCs concatenated with dynamic information, in the form of delta coefficients. The experimental procedure detailed below was repeated separately for the static and dynamic baseline MFCCs.

Each of the four feature types were evaluated in three phone classification experiments. The first experiment involves distinguishing between a set of five vowels ('aa', 'iy', 'uw', 'eh', and 'ae'). Phones are labeled using TIMIT symbols [17]. In the second test, a further five vowels ('ah', 'ax', 'ao', 'ih', and 'ow') were added to the previous vowel set, forming a more complex ten class vowel classification problem. The final test involves classifying a set of 19 phones into their associated phone classes. The phone classes and phones used were: vowels (listed above), fricatives ('s', 'sh'), stops ('p', 't', and 'k'), nasals ('m', 'n') and, semivowels and glides ('l', 'y').

3.2 Data

The speech data used in this study was taken from the TIMIT corpus [17]. This corpus contains 6300 utterances, 10 spoken by each of 630 American English speakers. The speech recordings are provided at a sampling frequency of 16 kHz.

3.3 Parameter Extraction

Based on the phonetic transcriptions and associated phone boundaries provided in TIMIT all units of a subset of phones, listed in Section 3.1, were extracted from the corpus. For each phone unit, frames of length 40 ms were extracted with a frame shift of 20 ms. Units of duration less than 100 ms were discarded. The raw speech frames were preemphasized with the filter $H(z) = 1 - 0.98z^{-1}$ and Hamming windowed. Following this preprocessing 13-dimensional MFCC vectors, including the zeroth cepstral coefficients, were computed for each frame. Standard delta coefficients, Δ, were also computed. These MFCC vectors and those concatenated with their deltas, MFCC+Δ, serve as both baseline features and high dimensional inputs for PCA, Isomap, and LLE.

3.4 Feature Transformation

For each of the three phone classification experiments, 250 units representing each of the required phones were chosen at random from those extracted above to make up the data set. PCA, Isomap, and LLE were individually applied to the equivalent sets of MFCC and MFCC+Δ vectors.

In order to examine the ability of the feature transformation methods to compute concise representations of the input vectors retaining discriminating information, the dimensionality of the resulting feature vectors was varied from 1 to 13 for static MFCC features and from 1 to 26 for MFCC+Δ features. A separate classifier was subsequently trained and tested using feature vectors with each of the different dimensionalities. Thus the ability of these feature transformation methods to produce useful low dimensional features could be evaluated and changes in performance with varying dimension analysed. As a baseline the original MFCC and MFCC+Δ vectors were used, also varying in dimensionality as detailed above.

The number of nearest neighbours, k, used in Isomap and LLE was set equal to 14 and 6 respectively. These values were chosen empirically by varying k and examining classification performance.

3.5 Support Vector Machine Classification

Initially, a number of classifiers—including K-nearest neighbours, Gaussian mixture models, and support vector machines (SVMs)—were tested in phone classification tasks. SVMs [16] yielded the best performance and thus were used in the following experiments. SVM is a binary pattern classification algorithm. For our experiments it is necessary to construct a multiclass classifier. This was achieved using a one-against-one training scheme, training one classifier for every possible pair of classes. The final classification result was determined by majority voting.

It is also necessary to choose an appropriate kernel function to be used in the SVM. In order to select an effective kernel, different SVM models using linear, polynomial, and radial basis function (RBF) kernels were evaluated in a number of phone classification tasks. SVM with RBF kernel demonstrated the best classification accuracy and was used throughout this work.

In all classification experiments 80% of the data was assigned as training data with the remaining 20% withheld and used as testing data. The data was partitioned such that the training and test sets had no speakers in common, thus ensuring speaker independence.

4 Results

4.1 Static Features

Firstly, the results of experiments conducted using 13-dimensional MFCCs as baseline feature vectors and inputs to the dimensionality reduction methods are presented. In each experiment the classifier was evaluated on each of the four

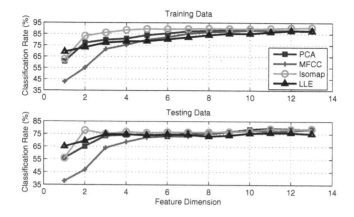

Fig. 1. Five vowel classification results for baseline MFCC, PCA, Isomap, and LLE features on the TIMIT database

feature types: baseline MFCC vectors and PCA, LLE, and Isomap embeddings of these baseline vectors. The dimensionality of the feature vectors used in the experiment vary from 1 to 13—the original, full dimension. Results are presented for evaluation on both the training data and testing data.

Figure 1 shows the results of the five vowel classification task using the baseline MFCC, PCA, Isomap, and LLE features. The percentage of phones correctly classified is given on the vertical axis. The horizontal axis represents the dimensionality of the feature vector. The results in Fig. 1 can be summarized as follows:

– The performance of the baseline MFCC vectors improves with increasing dimensionality, until reaching a performance plateau.
– PCA features offer improvements over baseline MFCC for low dimensions, one to seven.
– For the training data, maximum classification accuracy in dimensions 2–13 is demonstrated with Isomap features, outperforming all other features including the original 13-dimensional MFCC vectors.
– Isomap features also offer performance comparable to, and in some dimensions better than, other features on the testing data. In fact, Isomap yields 78% accuracy with only two dimensions; the other feature types require a much greater number of dimensions, $d > 10$, to reach this level of classification accuracy.
– LLE features can be seen to offer improved performance over other features in low dimensions, $d < 3$. However in higher dimensions LLE features do not offer a performance increase over other methods.

Results for ten vowel classification are shown in Fig. 2. The results are similar to those of the task above, with reduced classification accuracy due to increased complexity and possibility of phone confusion. The important findings are as follows:

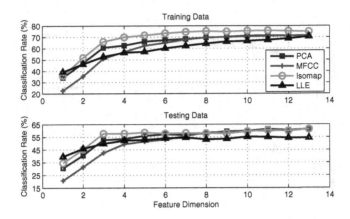

Fig. 2. Ten vowel classification results for baseline MFCC, PCA, Isomap, and LLE features on the TIMIT database

- Again, for the training data Isomap features outperform the other features in all dimensions, apart from the one-dimensional case were LLE performs best. Isomap also gives the best performance for the testing data in low dimensions ($d < 8$).
- A classification accuracy of 58.6% is achieved on the testing data with 5-dimensional Isomap features. This performance is only reached by higher dimensional, $d \geq 9$, MFCC and PCA features.

The mean classification accuracy results for each feature type in the ten vowel classification task are presented in Table 1. The mean accuracy scores were computed for the testing data evaluation. Averages are computed for three dimensionality ranges. It can be seen that Isomap gives the highest average accuracy overall, followed by PCA, LLE, and finally MFCC. LLE and Isomap are both shown to perform better than PCA and MFCC in low dimensions.

Phone class classification results are presented in Fig. 3. The following is evident:

- LLE features perform well in very low dimensions, $d < 3$, but yield the lowest classification rates in higher dimensions.
- The best accuracy is achieved in all other dimensions with Isomap features.
- PCA and MFCC features yield similar performance, with PCA features offering improved accuracy for low dimensional features.

Table 1. Mean classification accuracy in the ten vowel classification task for MFCC, PCA, Isomap, and LLE features

Dimensions	MFCC	PCA	Isomap	LLE
1–4	36.050	44.400	48.850	46.900
5–13	57.689	58.867	59.022	54.133
1–13	51.031	54.415	55.892	51.908

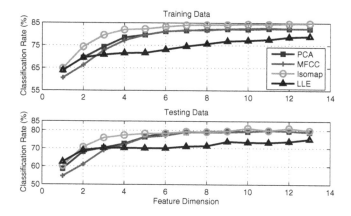

Fig. 3. Phone class classification results for baseline MFCC, PCA, Isomap, and LLE features on the TIMIT database

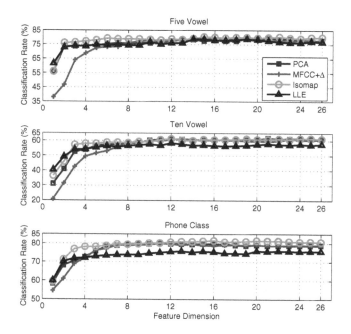

Fig. 4. Classification results for baseline MFCC+Δ, PCA, Isomap, and LLE features used in three different phone classification tasks

4.2 Dynamic Features

As detailed in Section 3, experiments were also performed using 26-dimensional MFCC+Δ vectors as high-dimensional inputs to the three dimensionality reduction methods. The results of performing phone classification using the features output by each of these methods and the original MFCC+Δ vectors are shown in Fig. 4. These results are based on tests carried out on the testing data. It can be seen that these results are very similar to those using the static features, as detailed in Section 4.1. The manifold learning methods offer improved performance over both MFCC+Δ and PCA-derived features in low dimensions. In general, features output by Isomap offer the best performance, outperforming all other feature types in 74.36% of the classification tests shown in Fig. 4. Classification performance on the training set was also found to be consistent with the static feature results.

5   Conclusions

In this study a phone classification approach using nonlinear manifold learning-based feature transformation was proposed and evaluated against a baseline linear dimensionality reduction method, PCA, and conventional MFCC features. All of the dimensionality reduction methods presented outperform the baseline MFCC features for low dimensions. This illustrates the capability of these methods to extract discriminating information from the original MFCC features.

Higher classification accuracy is shown for manifold learning-derived features compared to baseline MFCC and PCA-transformed features for low dimensions. This indicates that manifold learning algorithms are more capable of retaining information required to discriminate between phones, especially in low dimensional space. This may be due to the ability of these methods to exploit nonlinear structure in the speech space. In general, Isomap was found to yield superior performance to both MFCC and PCA features.

Comparing the two manifold learning methods, Isomap generally demonstrates better classification accuracy than LLE. This indicates that preserving global structure rather than local relationships may be more important for speech feature transformation.

Acknowledgments

Andrew Errity would like to acknowledge the support of the Irish Research Council for Science, Engineering and Technology; grant number RS/2003/114.

References

1. Klein, W., Plomp, R., Pols, L.C.W.: Vowel spectra, vowel spaces, and vowel identification. J. Acoust. Soc. Amer. 48(4), 999–1009 (1970)
2. Togneri, R., Alder, M., Attikiouzel, J.: Dimension and structure of the speech space. IEE Proceedings-I 139(2), 123–127 (1992)
3. Banbrook, M., McLaughlin, S., Mann, I.: Speech characterization and synthesis by nonlinear methods. Speech and Audio Processing 7(1), 1–17 (1999)
4. Jansen, A., Niyogi, P.: Intrinsic Fourier analysis on the manifold of speech sounds. In: Proc. of the IEEE Int. Conf. on Acoustics, Speech and Signal Processing (ICASSP), vol. 1, pp. 241–244 (2006)

5. Jolliffe, I.: Principal Component Analysis. Springer Series in Statistics. Springer-Verlag, New York (1986)
6. Duda, R.O., Hart, P.E.: Pattern Classification and Scene Analysis. Wiley, New York (1973)
7. Wang, X., Paliwal, K.K.: Feature extraction and dimensionality reduction algorithms and their applications in vowel recognition. Pattern Recognition 36(10), 2429–2439 (2003)
8. Somervuo, P.: Experiments with linear and nonlinear feature transformations in HMM based phone recognition. In: Proc. of the IEEE Int. Conf. on Acoustics, Speech and Signal Processing (ICASSP), vol. 1, pp. 52–55 (April 2003)
9. Roweis, S.T., Saul, L.K.: Nonlinear dimensionality reduction by locally linear embedding. Science 290(5500), 2323–2326 (2000)
10. Tenenbaum, J.B., de Silva, V., Langford, J.C.: A global geometric framework for nonlinear dimensionality reduction. Science 290(5500), 2319–2323 (2000)
11. Belkin, M., Niyogi, P.: Laplacian eigenmaps and spectral techniques for embedding and clustering. In: Dietterich, T.G., Becker, S., Ghahramani, Z. (eds.) Advances in Neural Information Processing Systems, vol. 14, pp. 585–591. MIT Press, Cambridge, MA (2002)
12. Hegde, R.M., Murthy, H.A.: Cluster and intrinsic dimensionality analysis of the modified group delay feature for speaker classification. In: Pal, N.R., Kasabov, N., Mudi, R.K., Pal, S., Parui, S.K. (eds.) ICONIP 2004. LNCS, vol. 3316, pp. 1172–1178. Springer, Heidelberg (2004)
13. Jain, V., Saul, L.K.: Exploratory analysis and visualization of speech and music by locally linear embedding. In: Proc. of the IEEE Int. Conf. on Acoustics, Speech and Signal Processing (ICASSP), vol. 3, pp. 984–987 (2004)
14. Errity, A., McKenna, J.: An investigation of manifold learning for speech analysis. In: Proc. of the Int. Conf. on Spoken Language Processing (Interspeech 2006 - ICSLP), Pittsburgh PA, USA, pp. 2506–2509 (September 2006)
15. Belkin, M., Niyogi, P.: Semi-supervised learning on Riemannian manifolds. Machine Learning 56(1-3), 209–239 (2004)
16. Vapnik, V.: The Nature of Statistical Learning Theory. Springer, N.Y (1995)
17. Garofalo, J.S., Lamel, L.F., Fisher, W.M., Fiscus, J.G., Pallett, D.S., Dahlgren, N.L.: The DARPA TIMIT Acoustic-Phonetic Continuous Speech Corpus CDROM. NIST (1990)

Word Recognition with a Hierarchical Neural Network

Xavier Domont[1,2], Martin Heckmann[1], Heiko Wersing[1], Frank Joublin[1], Stefan Menzel[1], Bernhard Sendhoff[1], and Christian Goerick[1]

[1] Honda Research Institute Europe GmbH,
D-63073 Offenbach am Main, Germany
martin.heckmann@honda-ri.de
[2] Technische Universität Darmstadt, Control Theory and Robotics Lab,
D-64283 Darmstadt, Germany
xavier.domont@rtr.tu-darmstadt.de

Abstract. In this paper we propose a feedforward neural network for syllable recognition. The core of the recognition system is based on a hierarchical architecture initially developed for visual object recognition. We show that, given the similarities between the primary auditory and visual cortexes, such a system can successfully be used for speech recognition. Syllables are used as basic units for the recognition. Their spectrograms, computed using a Gammatone filterbank, are interpreted as images and subsequently feed into the neural network after a preprocessing step that enhances the formant frequencies and normalizes the length of the syllables. The performance of our system has been analyzed on the recognition of 25 different monosyllabic words. The parameters of the architecture have been optimized using an evolutionary strategy. Compared to the Sphinx-4 speech recognition system, our system achieves better robustness and generalization capabilities in noisy conditions.

Keywords: speech recognition, robust features, feed-forward architecture.

1   Introduction

Conventional speech recognition systems perform very well in clean scenarios but their performance drastically decreases in noisy environments. This poor performance in adverse conditions prohibits the application of such systems for many scenarios, especially our target scenario, the control of a humanoid robot. In contrast to this, human speech perception is far less susceptible to such distortions [1].

In this article we present a speech recognition system with a higher robustness towards noise and reverberation. This system is based on a feedforward neural network inspired from an object recognition system.

Several studies have shown that auditory and visual primary cortices show substantial similarities. In 1988 Sur et al. have shown that the primary auditory cortex of young ferrets is plastic enough to allow the ferrets to attain visual

M. Chetouani et al. (Eds.): NOLISP 2007, LNAI 4885, pp. 142–151, 2007.

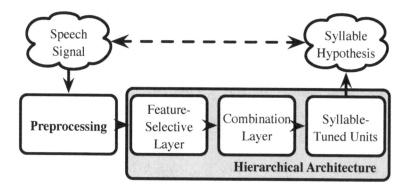

Fig. 1. Overview of the word recognition system

perception via the auditory cortex [2]. More recently Shamma determined the shape of the time-frequency receptive fields in the primary auditory cortex of newborn ferrets [3]. They are selective to modulations in the time-frequency domain and, as in the visual cortex, have Gabor-like shapes. These receptive fields have been modeled by Chin [4] and used for source separation [5] and speech detection [6].

As Gabor-like filters are extensively used in object recognition systems [7,8], we decided to develop a system for speech recognition by adapting the feed-forward neural network initially developed by Wersing and Körner for object recognition [8]. This approach is similar to the spectro-temporal features and the direct recognition on spectrograms proposed by Kleinschmidt in [9].

Syllables are the basic units for speech production and show less coarticulatory effects across their boundaries. Therefore, we believe that they are the adequate speech units for our biologically-inspired system. Moreover, the syllable segmentation required for the training of the system seems biologically plausible for speech acquisition.

The building blocks of the system (Fig. 1) are detailed in the following sections. After explaining how we optimized the parameters of the architecture using an evolutionary strategy, we will compare our results to a state of the art speech recognition system and conclude with a discussion of the obtained results.

2   Preprocessing of the Spectrogram

The preprocessing mainly aims at transforming a previously segmented speech signal, corresponding to one syllable, into an "image" that is fed into the hierarchical recognition architecture. A two-dimensional representation of a signal is obtained by computing its spectrogram. In addition to the phonetic information, the speech signal also contains many speaker and recording specific information. As the phonetic information is chiefly conveyed by the formant trajectories, we enhance them in the spectrograms prior to recognition.

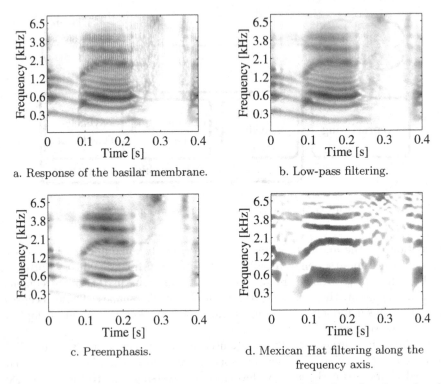

a. Response of the basilar membrane.

b. Low-pass filtering.

c. Preemphasis.

d. Mexican Hat filtering along the frequency axis.

Fig. 2. Overview of the preprocessing step for the word "list" spoken by a female American speaker. The 128 channels logarithmically span the frequency range from 80 Hz to 8 kHz. The harmonic structure has been removed using a filtering along the frequency axis.

We used a Gammatone filterbank to compute the spectrogram of the signal. It models the response of the basilar membrane in the human inner ear and is, therefore, adapted to a biology-inspired system. The signal's sampling frequency is 16 kHz. The filterbank has 128 channels ranging from 80 Hz to 8 kHz and follows the implementation given in [10]. Figure 2 shows the response of the Gammatone filterbank after rectification (a.) and low-pass filtering (b.). To compensate for the influence of the speech excitation signal, the high frequencies are emphasized by +6 dB per octave resulting in a flattened spectrogram (Fig. 2 c.). Next, the formant frequencies are enhanced by filtering along the channel axis using mexican-hat filters (Fig. 2 d.), only the positive values are kept. For the filtering the size of the kernel is channel-dependent, varying from 90 Hz for low frequencies to 120 Hz for high frequencies. This takes the logarithmic arrangement of the center frequencies in the Gammatone filterbank into account.

Finally, the length of the spectrogram is scaled using linear interpolation so that all the spectrograms feeding the recognition hierarchy have the same size. The sampling rate is then reduced to 100 Hz. By doing so syllables of different lengths are scaled to the same length. This relies on the assumption that a linear scaling can handle variations in the length of the same syllable uttered at different speaking rates. However, these are known to be non-linear. In particular, some parts of the signal, like vowels, are more affected by variation in the speech rate than other parts, e.g. plosives. The generalization over these variations is a main challenge in the recognition task. In order to also assess the performance of the recognition hierarchy independent of this non-linear scaling, we applied the Dynamic Time Warping (DTW) method to the spectrograms. For each syllable, we selected one single repetition as reference template and aligned the other by DTW.

Afterwards the syllables were again scaled to the same length and downsampled. At the output of the preprocessing stage the spectrograms feeding the recognition hierarchy have all the size of 128×128, i.e. 128 time frames over 128 frequency channels. Note, however, that the application of DTW requires that a hypothesis for the syllable is available. Thus, it cannot easily be applied to a real recognition test.

3   The Recognition Hierarchy

The preprocessed two-dimensional spectrogram is from now on considered to be an image and feeds into a feedforward architecture initially aimed at visual object recognition. However, the structure of spectrograms differs from the structure of images taken from objects and, while keeping the overall layout of the network described in [8], the receptive fields and the parameters of the neurons were retrained for the task of syllable recognition. The recognition hierarchy is illustrated in Fig. 3.

3.1   Feature-Selective Layer

The first feature-matching stage consists of a linear receptive field summation, a Winner-Take-Most (WTM) and a pooling mechanism. The preprocessed spectrogram is first filtered by eight different Gabor-like filters. The purpose of these filters is to extract local features from the spectrogram. In [8] the receptive fields were chosen as four first-order even Gabor filters. For syllable recognition, 8 receptive fields were learned using independent component analysis on 3500 randomly selected local patches of preprocessed spectrograms.

The WTM competition mechanism between features at the same position introduces nonlinearity into the system. The value $r_l(t,f)$ of the spectrogram in the lth neuron of the feature-selective layer after the WTM competition is given at the position (t,f) by the following equation:

$$r_l(t,f) = \begin{cases} 0, & \text{if } \frac{q_l(t,f)}{M(t,f)} < \gamma_1 \text{ or } M(t,f) = 0 \\ \frac{q_l(t,f) - \gamma_1 M(t,f)}{1 - \gamma_1}, & \text{else} \end{cases} \tag{1}$$

where $q_l(t,f)$ is the value of the spectrogram before the WTM competition, $M(t,f) = \max_k q_k(t,f)$ the maximal value at position (t,f) over the eight neurons and $0 \leq \gamma_1 \leq 1$ is a parameter controlling the strength of the competition.

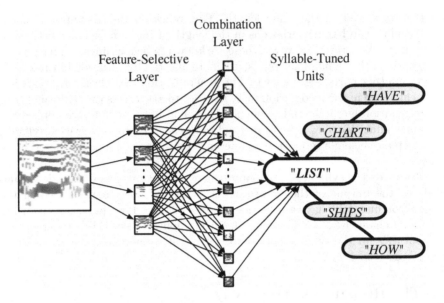

Fig. 3. The system is based on a feedforward architecture with weight-sharing and a succession of feature sensitive matching and pooling stages. It comprises three stages arranged in a processing hierarchy.

A threshold θ_1 is applied to the activity $r_l(t, f)$. This threshold is common for all the neurons in the layer. The pooling performs a downsampling of the spectrogram by four in both time and frequency direction. It is done by a Gaussian receptive field with width σ_1. The feature-selective layer transforms the 128×128 original spectrogram to eight 32×32 spectrogram feature maps.

3.2   Combination Layer

The goal of the combination layer is to detect relevant local feature combinations in the first layer. Similar to the previous layer it consists of a linear receptive field summation, a Winner-Take-Most and a pooling mechanism. These combination cells are learned using the non-negative sparse coding method (NNSC) as in [8], however no invariance transformations have been implemented at this stage. Similarly to Non-Negative Matrix Factorization (NMF), the NNSC method decomposes data vectors $\mathbf{I}^p$ into linear combinations (with non-negative weights s_i^p) of non-negative features $\mathbf{w}_i$ by minimizing the following cost function:

$$E = \sum_p \|\mathbf{I}^p - \sum_i s_i^p \mathbf{w}_i\|^2 + \beta \sum_p \sum_i |s_i^p| \,.$$

NNSC differs from NMF by the presence of a sparsity enforcing term in the cost function, controlled by the parameter β, which aims at limiting the number of non-zero coefficients required for the reconstruction. Consequently, if a feature appears often in the data, it will be learned, even if it can be obtained by a combination of two or more other features. Therefore, the NNSC is expected to learn complex and global features appearing in the data. An comprehensive description of this method can be found in [11].

For the proposed syllable recognition system 50 complex features $\mathbf{w}_i$ have been learned from image patches extracted from the output of the feature-selective layer. At last, a WTM competition (γ_2, θ_2) and pooling (σ_2) are applied to the 50 neurons and their size is reduced to 16×16.

3.3 Syllable-Tuned Units

In the last stage of the architecture, linear discriminant classifiers are learned based on the output of the combination layer. A classical gradient descent is used for this supervised learning including an early stopping mechanism to avoid overfitting. The obtained classifiers are called Syllable-Tuned Units (STUs) in reference to the View-Tuned Units used in [7] and [8].

Due to the high dimensionality (640) and sparseness of the features after the combination layer learning the STUs is unproblematic.

4 Optimization of the Architecture

The performance of the recognition highly depends on the choice of the non-linearities present in the hidden layers of the architecture, i.e. the coefficients and the thresholds of the WTM competitions (Eq. 1) and the width of the poolings. The six parameters ($\gamma_{1,2}$, $\theta_{1,2}$ and $\sigma_{1,2}$) have to be tuned simultaneously and the receptive field of the combination layer as well as the Syllable-Tuned Units have to be learned at each iteration, similarly to the method used in [12].

Practically, this tuning of the model parameter set has been realized within an evolutionary optimization aiming at maximizing the recognition performance in a clean speech scenario. Due to the stochastic components and the use of a population of solutions evolutionary algorithms need more quality evaluations than other algorithms, but on the other hand they allow for a global search and are able to overcome local optima. In the present context, an evolutionary strategy with global step size adaptation (GSA-ES) has been applied relying on similar ranges of the object variables. Initially, standard values, see [13,14], have been used and then tuned in some test experiments to this specific task. Based on these experiments we have chosen a population size of 32 individuals. Each generation, the two individuals with the best performance have been chosen as parents for the next generation. The optimization parameters have been scaled and the initial global step size was set to 0.003.

Although the evolutionary optimization used a clean scenario for the performance evaluation of each individual we will show that the optimized parameters are robust with respect to noisy signals.

5 Recognition Performance

In order to evaluate the performance of the system, a database was built using 25 very frequent monosyllabic words extracted from the DARPA Resource

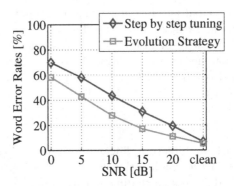

Fig. 4. Improvement of the recognition performance using an evolutionary algorithm to tune the parameters, compared to manual tuning one layer after the other. The spectrograms are scaled using a linear interpolation.

Management (RM) database. Isolated monosyllabic words have been chosen in lack of a syllable segmented database with sufficient size. The words were segmented using forced-alignment. For each of the monosyllabic words we selected 140 occurrences from 12 different speakers (6 males and 6 females) from the speaker dependent part of the database. For training 70 repetitions of each word were used, 20 for the early stopping validation of the Syllable-Tuned Units and 50 for testing.

The performance of our system has been compared to the Sphinx-4 speech recognition system, an open source speech recognition system that performs well on the whole RM corpus [15]. MFCC features were used as front-end for the HMMs. 13 cepstral coefficients plus delta and double delta were computed using the default parameters of Sphinx. Cepstral Mean Normalization [16] has been used in order to improve the robustness of the MFCC features. SphinxTrain was employed to train triphones HMMs. Each model had 3 states without skip over states and each state used a mixture of 8 Gaussians. The Hidden Markov Models were trained on the segmented monosyllabic words.

The robustness towards noise has been investigated by adding babble noise, white noise, and factory noise from the NOISEX database to the test database at different signal to noise ratios (SNR) while training was still performed on clean data.

Figure 4 illustrates the gain in performance on babble noise obtained using the evolutionary algorithm, compared to a manual tuning of the parameters one layer after the other. Following the notation introduced in [8], the optimal parameters given by the evolution strategy are $\gamma_1 = 0.82$, $\theta_1 = 2.66$, $\sigma_1 = 3.16$ for the first layer and $\gamma_2 = 0.84$, $\theta_2 = 2.78$, $\sigma_2 = 1.87$ for the second layer, when linear interpolation is used to scale the signals. Using a DTW, the optimal set of parameters is $\gamma_1 = 0.99$, $\theta_1 = 0.32$, $\sigma_1 = 4$ for the first layer and $\gamma_2 = 0.89$, $\theta_2 = 0.99$, $\sigma_2 = 1.93$. As can be seen, the performance increased due to the optimization at all SNR levels. With clean speech we observe an improvement

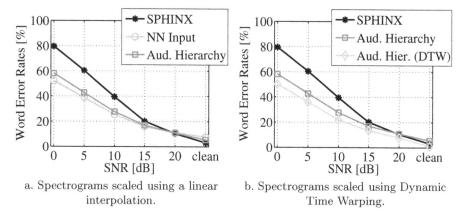

a. Spectrograms scaled using a linear   b. Spectrograms scaled using Dynamic
            interpolation.   Time Warping.

Fig. 5. Comparison of the Word Error Rates (WER) between the proposed system and
Sphinx-4 in the presence of babble noise

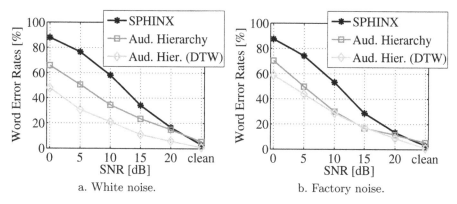

a. White noise.   b. Factory noise.

Fig. 6. Comparison of the Word Error Rates (WER) between the proposed system and
Sphinx-4 in the presence of white and factory noise

from 6.72% to 5.44% (19% relative). The largest improvement was achieved at
15 dB SNR from 30.72% to 17.04% (44.5% relative).

Figure 5 summarizes the performance of both Sphinx-4 and the proposed
system in presence of a babble noise. To measure the baseline similarities of
the image ensemble, we also give the performance of a nearest neighbor classifier (NN) that matches the test data against all available training "views". An
exhaustive storage of examples is, however, not a viable model for auditory classification. With clean signals, the STUs show better generalization capabilities
and perform better than a nearest neighbor on the input layer (Fig. 5 a.). For
noisy signals, the STUs are slightly worse, however, at a strong reduction of
representational complexity.

With a simple linear time scaling our system only outperforms Sphinx-4 in noisy conditions but shows inferior performance on clean data. When Dynamic Time Warping is used to properly scale the signals, the STUs improve the already good performance obtained directly after the preprocessing in all the cases and our system outperforms Sphinx-4 even for clean signals (Fig. 5 b.). With clean data Sphinx obtains a 3.1% Word Error Rate (WER), our system achieves 0.9% WER with the DTW and 5.4% without the DTW. Figure 6 shows that the performance is very similar when adding white or factory noise.

6   Discussion and Summary

In this paper, we presented a novel approach to speech recognition interpreting spectrograms as images and deploying a hierarchical object recognition system. To optimize the main free parameters of the system, we used an evolutionary algorithm which allows us to quickly change the system without the need for manual parameter tuning.

We could show that our system performs better than a state of the art system in noisy conditions even when we applied a simplistic linear scaling of the input for time alignment. When we aligned the current utterance with the DTW to a known representation in an optimal non-linear way, we obtained better than state of the art results for all cases tested. However, in its current form the DTW makes use of information not available in real situations.

From this we conclude that our architecture and the underlying features are more robust against noise than the commonly used mel frequency cepstral coefficients (MFCCs). This robustness against noise is very important for real world scenarios which are usually characterized by significant background noise and variations in the recording conditions. A similar robustness was also observed for visual recognition in clutter scenes [8].

Our comparison between the linear scaling and the DTW shows that the performance of the model could be significantly improved by better temporal alignment. We therefore consider methods for improving this alignment as interesting future research directions.

The complexity of our recognition task is very low. Therefore, it remains an open question how our system will scale to more complex tasks. We can expect that our system generalizes well to larger vocabulary. In fact, the high dimensionality and the sparseness of the vector space at the output of the combination layer should allow to train STUs for a large number of syllables.

In order to process continuous speech, syllable segmentation is required. One way to obtain this segmentation is to implement a syllable segmentation system prior to the recognition. This would allow to keep the advantages of the recognition hierarchy: its fast implementation and the capacity to train or update STUs on the fly. Another possibility is to use the architecture as a front-end for Hidden Markov Models similarly to [17].

References

1. Lippmann, R.: Speech recognition by machines and humans. Speech Communication 22(1), 1–15 (1997)
2. Sur, M., Garraghty, P., Roe, A.: Experimentally induced visual projections into auditory thalamus and cortex. Science 242(4884), 1437–1441 (1988)
3. Shamma, S.: On the role of space and time in auditory processing. Trends in Cognitive Sciences 5(8), 340–348 (2001)
4. Chih, T., Ru, P., Shamma, S.: Multiresolution spectrotemporal analysis of complex sounds. Journal of the Acoustical Society of America 118, 887–906 (2005)
5. Elhilali, M., Shamma, S.: A bilogically-inspired approach to the cocktail party problem. In: Proc. ICASSP, vol. 5, pp. 637–640 (2006)
6. Mesgarani, N., Slaney, M., Shamma, S.: Discrimination of speech from non-speech based on multiscale spectro-temporal modulations. IEEE Transactions on Speech and Audio Processing, 920–930 (2006)
7. Riesenhuber, M., Poggio, T.: Hierachical models of object recognition in cortex. Nature Neuroscience 2, 1019–1025 (1999)
8. Wersing, H., Körner, E.: Learning optimized features for hierarchical models of invariant recognition. Neural Computation 15(7), 1559–1588 (2003)
9. Kleinschmidt, M., Gelbart, D.: Improving word accuracy with gabor feature extraction. In: ICSLP, Denver (2002)
10. Slaney, M.: An efficient implementation of the Patterson-Holdsworth auditory filterbank. Technical report, Apple Computer Co, Technical report #35 (1993)
11. Hoyer, P.O.: Non-negative matrix factorization with sparseness constraints. Journal of Machine Learning Research 5, 1457–1469 (2004)
12. Schneider, G., Wersing, H., Sendhoff, B., Körner, E.: Evolutionary optimization of a hierarchical object recognition model. IEEE Transaction on Systems, Man and Cybernetics. Part B: Cybernetics 35(3), 426–437 (2005)
13. Schwefel, H.P.: Evolution and Optimum Seeking. John Wiley and sons, New York (1995)
14. Bäck, T.: Evolutionary Algorithms in Theory and Practice. Oxford University Press, Oxford (1996)
15. Walker, W., Lamere, P., Kwok, P.: Sphinx-4: A flexible open source framework for speech recognition. Technical report, Sun Microsystems Inc. (2004)
16. Liu, F.H., Stern, R.M., Huang, X., Acero, A.: Efficient cepstral normalization for robust speech recognition. In: HLT 1993: Proceedings of the workshop on Human Language Technology, Morristown, NJ, USA, Association for Computational Linguistics, pp. 69–74 (1993)
17. Meyer, B., Kleinschmidt, M.: Robust speech recognition based on localized, spectro-temporal features. In: Elektronische Sprachsignalverarbeitung (ESSV) (2003)

Hybrid Models for Automatic Speech Recognition: A Comparison of Classical ANN and Kernel Based Methods

Ana I. García-Moral, Rubén Solera-Ureña, Carmen Peláez-Moreno,
and Fernando Díaz-de-María

Department of Signal Theory and Communications
EPS-Universidad Carlos III de Madrid
Avda. de la Universidad, 30, 28911-Leganés (Madrid), Spain
{aisabel,rsolera,carmen,fdiaz}@tsc.uc3m.es

Abstract. Support Vector Machines (SVMs) are state-of-the-art methods for machine learning but share with more classical Artificial Neural Networks (ANNs) the difficulty of their application to input patterns of non-fixed dimension. This is the case in Automatic Speech Recognition (ASR), in which the duration of the speech utterances is variable. In this paper we have recalled the hybrid (ANN/HMM) solutions provided in the past for ANNs and applied them to SVMs performing a comparison between them. We have experimentally assessed both hybrid systems with respect to the standard HMM-based ASR system, for several noisy environments. On the one hand, the ANN/HMM system provides better results than the HMM-based system. On the other, the results achieved by the SVM/HMM system are slightly lower than those of the HMM system. Nevertheless, such a results are encouraging due to the current limitations of the SVM/HMM system.

Keywords: Robust ASR, Additive noise, Machine Learning, Hybrid systems, Artificial Neural Networks, Support Vector Machines, Hidden Markov Models.

1 Introduction

Hidden Markov Models (HMMs) have become the most employed core technique for Automatic Speech Recognition (ASR). After several decades of intense research work in the field, it seems that HMM-based ASR systems are very close to reach their limit of performance. Some alternative approaches, most of them based on Artificial Neural Networks (ANNs), were proposed during the late eighties and early nineties. Among them, it is worth to mention hybrid ANN/HMM systems (see [1] for an overview), since the reported results were comparable or even slightly superior to those achieved by HMMs.

On the other hand, during the last decade, a new tool appeared in the field of machine learning that has proved to be able to cope with hard classification problems in several fields of application: the Support Vector Machines (SVMs) [2]. The

M. Chetouani et al. (Eds.): NOLISP 2007, LNAI 4885, pp. 152–160, 2007.

SVMs are effective discriminative classifiers with several outstanding characteristics, namely: their solution is that with maximum margin; they are capable to deal with samples of a very high dimensionality; and their convergence to the minimum of the associated cost function is guaranteed.

Nevertheless, it seems clear that the application of these kernel-based machines to the ASR problem is not straightforward. In our opinion, there are three main difficulties to overcome: 1) SVMs are originally static classifiers and have to be adapted to deal with the variability of duration of speech utterances; 2) the SVMs were originally formulated as binary classifiers while the ASR problem is multiclass; and 3) current SVM training algorithms are not able to manage the huge databases typically used in ASR. In order to cope with these difficulties, some researchers have suggested hybrid SVM/HMM systems [3,4], that notably resemble the previous hybrid ANN/HMM systems ([5]). In this paper we comparatively describe both types of hybrid systems (SVM/ and ANN/HMM), highlighting both their common fundamentals and their special characteristics, and conduct an experimental performance comparison for both clean and noisy speech recognition tasks.

2 Hybrid Systems for ASR

As a result of the difficulties found in the application of ANNs to speech recognition, mostly motivated by the duration variability of the speech instances corresponding to the same class, a variety of different architectures and novel training algorithms that combined both HMMs with ANNs were proposed in the late eighties and early nineties. For a comprehensive survey of these techniques see [1]. In this paper, we have focused on those that employ ANNs (and SVMs) to estimate the HMM state posterior probabilities proposed by Bourlard and Morgan ([5,6]).

The starting point for this approach is the well-know property of using feed-forward networks such as multi-layer perceptrons (MLPs) for estimating *a-posteriori* probabilities given two conditions: 1) there must be high enough number of input samples to train a good approximation between the input and output layers; and 2) a global minimum error criterion must be used to train the network (for example, mean square error or relative entropy).

The fundamental advantage of this approach is that it introduces a discriminative technique (ANN) into a generative system (HMM) while retaining their ability to handle the temporal variability of the speech signal.

However, this original formulation had to be modified to estimate the true emission (likelihood) probabilities by applying the Bayes' rule. Therefore, the *a-posteriori* probabilities should be normalized by the class priors to obtain what is called *scaled likelihoods*. This fact was further reinforced by posterior theoretical developments in the search of a global ANN optimization procedure (see [7]).

Thus, systems of this type keep being locally discriminant given that the ANN was trained to estimate *a-posteriori* probabilities. However, it can also be shown that, in theory, HMMs can be trained using local posterior probabilities as emission probabilities, resulting in models that are both locally and globally discriminant. The problem is that there are generally mismatches between the prior class probabilities implicit to the training data and the priors that are implicit to the lexical and syntactic models that are used in recognition. In fact, some experimental results show that for certain cases the division by the priors is not necessary [7].

Among the advantages of using hybrid approaches we highlight the following (from [7]):

- Model accuracy: both MLPs and SVMs have more flexibility to provide more accurate acoustic models including the possibility of using different combinations of features as well as different sizes of context.
- Local discrimination ability (at a frame level) provided by MLPs.
- Parsimonious use of parameters: all the classes share the same ANN parameters.
- HMMs and MLPs exhibit complementary abilities for ASR tasks, which lead to higher recognition rates.

3   Experimental Setup

3.1   Database

We have used the well-known SpeechDat Spanish database for the fixed telephone network [8]. This database comprises recordings from 4000 Spanish speakers recorded at 8 KHz over the fixed PSTN using an E-1 interface, in a noiseless office environment.

In our experiments we have used a large vocabulary (more than 24000 words) continuous speech recognition database. The training set contains approximately 50 hours of voice from 3146 speakers (71000 utterances). The callers spoke 40 items whose contents are varied, comprising isolated and connected digits, natural numbers, spellings, city and company names, common applications words, phonetically rich sentences, etc. Most items are read and some of them are spontaneously spoken. The test set, corresponding to a connected digits task, contains approximately 2122 utterances and 19855 digits (5 hours of voice) from 499 different speakers.

3.2   Parameterization

In our experiments we have used the classical parameterization based on 12 MFCCs (Mel-Frequency Cepstral Coefficients) plus energy, and the first and second derivatives. These MFCCs are computed every 10 ms using a time window of 25 ms. Thus, the resulting feature vectors have 39 components. In this work, we have considered a per-utterance normalization, that is, every parameter is normalized in mean and variance according to the following expression:

$$\hat{x}_i\,[n] = \frac{x_i\,[n] - \mu_f}{\sigma_f}, \tag{1}$$

where $x_i[n]$ represents the ith component of the feature vector corresponding to frame n, μ_f is the estimated mean from the whole utterance, and σ_f is the estimated standard deviation. As a result, per-utterance normalization will be more appropriate in the case of noisy environments where training and testing conditions do not match.

3.3   Database Contamination

We have tested our systems in clean conditions and in presence of additive noise. For that purpose, we have used two different kinds of noises (white and babble) extracted from the NOISEX database [9]. These noises have been added to the clean speech signals at four different signal-to-noise ratios (SNRs), namely: 12 dB, 9 dB, 6 dB and 3 dB. Only the testing subset has been corrupted in the way previously stated, whereas the acoustic models (GMMs (Gaussian Mixture Models) in the case of the baseline HMM system and the MLPs and the SVMs in the case of the hybrid systems) have been estimated or trained using only clean speech.

3.4   Baseline Experiment with HMMs

The recognition rates achieved by a left-to-right HMM-based recognition system based in the COST-249 SpeechDat Reference Recognizer will be our reference results. We use 18 context-dependent phones (this is the number of phones usually used for digits recognition tasks in Spanish) with 3 states per phone. Emission probabilities for each state were modeled by a mixture of 32 Gaussians.

3.5   Experiments with Hybrid Recognition Systems

In this work we consider two different hybrid recognition systems, an ANN/HMM system and a SVM/HMM one. Both of them use a Viterbi decoder with *a-posteriori* probabilities as local scores as discussed in section 2.

The whole hybrid recognition system is composed of two stages. The first one estimates initial evidences for phones in the form of *a-posteriori* probabilities using an MLP or an SVM. The second stage consists of a classical Viterbi decoder where we replace the likelihoods estimates provided by the reference HMM-based recognition system by the posteriors obtained in the first stage.

For the hybrid systems presented in this paper, we have partitioned every phone into three segments. For this purpose, we have obtained a segmentation of the training database by performing a forced alignment with the HMM baseline system, considering each segment delimited by the state transitions. Experimental results with both ANN/HMM and SVM/HMM hybrid systems show significant improvements in the word recognition rate due to the use of three classes per phone, especially for the case of the SVM-based system (see [4]).

Whereas the reference HMM-based recognition system uses the whole training data set (71000 utterances), the hybrid SVM-based recognition system only uses a small portion of the available training data, due to a practical limitation regarding the number of training samples that the SVM software can consider.

Thus, in order to compare the two hybrid systems, we decided to use the same small quantity of training data in the ANN/HMM hybrid system, although we also obtained some results using the whole training data set. Therefore, we have considered useful to evaluate the evolution of the accuracy of each system performing incremental tests using balanced subsets of the available training data set (equal number of frames per class -three classes per phone-, randomly selected from the whole training set), between 250 and 20000 frames per class.

Experiments with ANNs. A *posteriori* probabilities used by the Viterbi decoder are obtained using a MLP trained on either a smaller version of the training data set or the whole training data set, as we mentioned before. The MLP has one hidden layer with 1800 units. There are 39 input units corresponding to the feature vector dimension described in section 3.2, and 54 output units, each of them corresponding to one of the three parts of the 18 phones considered, as we described in section 3.5. The MLP is trained using the relative entropy criterion and the back-propagation factor μ was experimentally fixed at 0.02 by using a separate tuning set.

Experiments with SVMs. In this case, a multiclass SVM (using the *1-vs-1* approach) is used to estimate posteriors for each frame using Platt's approximation ([10]). The SVM uses a RBF (Radial Basis Function) kernel whose parameter, γ, must be tuned by means of a cross-validation process, as well as a parameter C, which establishes a compromise between error minimization and generalization capability in the SVM. The values we have used in our experiments are $C = 2$ and $\gamma = 0.03125$ also obtained empirically using the tuning set we already mentioned in 3.5. For more details about the hybrid SVM/HMM system, please refer to [4].

4   Results and Discussion

This section is devoted to the presentation and discussion of the results obtained by the systems described in the previous section.

Preliminary experiments show a similar behaviour of both SVMs and ANNs at a frame classification level. We can also see in figure 1 that better results are achieved when more samples are added to the training database, up to a final frame recognition rate around 72% obtained for the maximum number of input samples that our SVM-based system can handle (1080000, 20000 frames per class). Nevertheless, when we use our MLP-based system, that can handle the whole (and not balanced) set of input samples (16378624 frames), we manage to improve this frame recognition rate up to 78.47%. Similar behaviour is expected for the SVM/HMM hybrid system if the employed software could process such an amount of input samples.

We compare our hybrid systems to the standard HMM-based speech recognition system at word and sentence levels, in the different noise environments described in section 3.3. We can see in figures 2 and 3 the Word Recognition Rate (WRR) and the Sentence Recognition Rate (SRR), respectively, of the

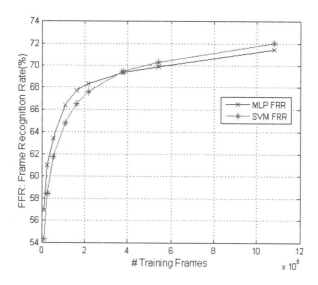

Fig. 1. Frame recognition rate of ANNs and SVMs

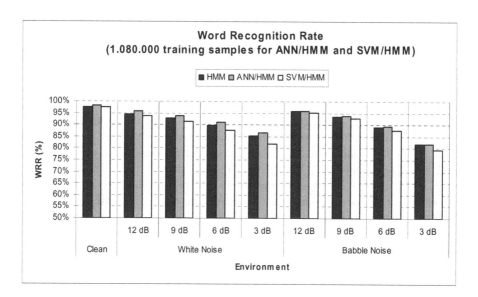

Fig. 2. Word recognition rate of HMMs and Hybrid ANN- and SVM-based systems

three systems. Thus, we can notice that, using only a 6.6% of the available data samples, our hybrid systems get results which are comparable or even better (in the case of the ANN/HMM system) than the standard HMM-based system trained using the entire database.

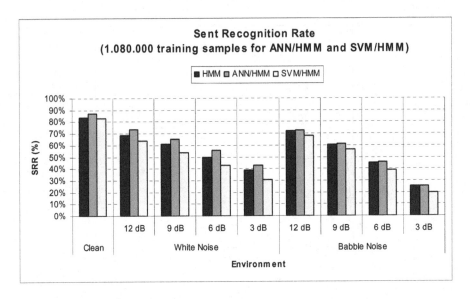

Fig. 3. Sentence recognition rate of HMMs and Hybrid ANN- and SVM-based systems

The SVM software used in the experiments [11], which requires to keep the kernel matrix in memory, is the responsible for the limit in the SVM/HMM training data set. However, without this restriction, we have observed in the ANN/HMM system that the more samples we add to the training database, the higher is the improvement in WRR and SRR with regard to the baseline HMM-based system, as we could see at the frame classification level.

In addition, as we have stated in Section 2, both SVMs and ANNs provide a-posteriori probabilities to the Viterbi decoder, whereas what we really need (and HMMs compute) are likelihoods [5]. We tried to use likelihoods in the ANN/HMM system, but we achieved worse results than that of posterior probabilities in all the cases except for the case we train the ANN/HMM hybrid using the entire database. If we analyze these results, we can see that, in fact, when we train the MLP using a balanced set of samples, the a-priori probability is the same for all the classes and posteriors provided by the MLP are actually scaled likelihoods.

5   Conclusions

The clear success of SVMs classifiers in several fields of application has called the attention of researchers in the field of ASR. The first attempts to use SVMs for connected-digit recognition have resulted in hybrid SVM/HMM systems [4] that resemble the hybrid systems based on ANN proposed during the last decade. Consequently, it becomes relevant to compare the performance achieved by both types of systems. Furthermore, since the robustness of the ASR systems is one of the current open problems, the comparative assessment of hybrid systems should be carried out in a noisy environment. The ANN/HMM and SVM/HMM hybrid systems presented in this work are inspired in the work due to Bourlard and Morgan [5]. Our more significant contribution with respect to this reference consists of using sub-phone units. Specifically, three classes (parts) per phone are considered instead of one.

Some limitations regarding the publicly available software implementation of the SVMs have prevented us to train our hybrid SVM/HMM ASR system using the whole training set. Therefore, in order to carry out a fair comparison, the hybrid ANN/HMM has been trained using the same small subset of the training set. In this conditions, the achieved results can be summarized as follows:

- The hybrid ANN/HMM system provides slightly better results than the HMM-based system used as reference, for all the noise types and SNR values considered.
- The performance of the hybrid SVM/HMM system is slightly lower than that of the HMM-based system.

In our opinion these results are encouraging. On the one hand, the hybrid ANN/HMM system using sub-phone units turns out to be competitive. On the other hand, though the design of the hybrid SVM/HMM system is still preliminar, it has reached a reasonable level of performance. In particular, as can be expected from previous results in an isolated-digit recognition task [12], the maximum margin principle used for its training can make an important difference in noisy environment. For that purpose, several issues should be addressed; for example: the possibility to incorporate more training samples, the addition of a wider temporal context in the feature vectors and the selection of appropriate feature sets. Besides, hybrid systems are more amenable for its use with different types of parameterizations that do not comply with the restrictions of independence imposed by HMMs. This could result advantageous in the search of robustness.

Acknowledgments. This work is partially supported by the regional grant (Comunidad Autónoma de Madrid - UC3M) CCG06-UC3M/TIC-0812

References

1. Trentin, E., Gori, M.: A Survey of Hybrid ANN/HMM Models for Automatic Speech Recognition. Neurocomputing 37, 91–126 (2001)
2. Boser, B.E., Guyon, I., Vapnik, V.: A Training Algorithm for Optimal Margin Classifiers. In: Computational Learning Theory, pp. 144–152 (1992)
3. Ganapathiraju, A., Hamaker, J., Picone, J.: Hybrid SVM/HMM Architectures for Speech Recognition. In: Proceedings of the 2000 Speech Transcription Workshop, Maryland (USA), vol. 4, pp. 504–507 (2000)
4. Padrell-Sendra, J., Martín-Iglesias, D., Díaz-de-María, F.: Support Vector Machines for Continuous Speech Recognition. In: Proceedings of the 14th European Signal Processing Conference, Florence, Italy (2006)

5. Bourlard, H., Morgan, N.: Connectionist Speech Recognition: a Hybrid Approach, Boston. Kluwer Academic, Norwell, MA (USA) (1994)
6. Morgan, N., Bourlard, H.: Continuous Speech Recognition: An Introduction to the Hybrid HMM/Connectionist Approach. IEEE Signal Processing Magazine, 25–42 (1995)
7. Bourlard, H., Morgan, N., Giles, C.L., Gori, M.: Hybrid HMM/ANN Systems for Speech Recognition: Overview and New Research Directions. In: Adaptive Processing of Sequences and Data Structures. International Summer School on Neural Networks 'E. R. Caianiello'. Tutorial Lectures, pp. 389–417. Springer-Verlag, Germany; Berlin (1998)
8. Moreno, A.: SpeechDat Spanish Database for Fixed Telephone Network. Technical report, Technical University of Catalonia (1997)
9. Varga, A.P., Steenneken, J.M., Tolimson, M., Jones, D.: The NOISEX-92 Study on the Effect of Additive Noise on Automatic Speech Recognition. Technical report, DRA Speech Research Unit (1992)
10. Platt, J.C.: Probabilities for SV Machines. In: Advances in Large Margin Classifiers, pp. 61–74. MIT Press, Cambridge (1999)
11. Chang, C.C., Lin, C.J.: LIBSVM: a library for support vector machines (2001), Software available at http://www.csie.ntu.edu.tw/cjlin/~libsvm
12. Solera-Ureña, R., Martín-Iglesias, D., Gallardo-Antolín, A., Peláez-Moreno, C., Díaz-de-María, F.: Robust ASR Using Support Vector Machines. Speech Communication 49(4), 253–267 (2007)

Towards Phonetically-Driven Hidden Markov Models: Can We Incorporate Phonetic Landmarks in HMM-Based ASR?

Guillaume Gravier and Daniel Moraru

Institut de Recherche en Informatique et Systèmes Aléatoires
IRISA – CNRS, Rennes, France
`guillaume.gravier@irisa.fr`

Abstract. Automatic speech recognition mainly relies on hidden Markov models (HMM) which make little use of phonetic knowledge. As an alternative, landmark based recognizers rely mainly on precise phonetic knowledge and exploit distinctive features. We propose a theoretical framework to combine both approaches by introducing phonetic knowledge in a non stationary HMM decoder. To demonstrate the potential of the method, we investigate how broad phonetic landmarks can be used to improve a HMM decoder by focusing the best path search. We show that, assuming error free landmark detection, every broad phonetic class brings a small improvement. The use of all the classes reduces the error rate from 22 % to 14 % on a broadcast news transcription task. We also experimentally validate that landmarks boundaries does not need to be detected precisely and that the algorithm is robust to non detection errors.

1 Data-Driven *vs.* Knowledge-Based Speech Recognition

In hidden Markov models (HMM) based speech recognition systems, the decoding process consists in compiling a graph which includes all the available sources of knowledge (language model, pronunciations, acoustic models) before finding out the best path in the graph in order to obtain the best word sequence

$$\hat{w} = \arg\max_{w} p(y|w)p(w) \ . \tag{1}$$

At the acoustic level, this approach relies on data-driven methods that learn from examples. Therefore, integrating explicit phonetic knowledge in such systems is difficult.

Alternately, various studies aim at explicitly relying on phonetic knowledge to represent the speech signal for automatic speech recognition [1,2,3]. These approaches are most of the time based on the extraction of a set phonetic features, a.k.a. landmarks, on top of which a model, either rule based or statistical based, is build for the purpose of recognition. Phonetically-driven ASR relies on fine grain phonetic features such as onset and offset times [2] and distinctive features [1,3]. However, in practice, automatically detecting such features might be

M. Chetouani et al. (Eds.): NOLISP 2007, LNAI 4885, pp. 161–168, 2007.

difficult and error prone, in particular in the case of noisy signals or spontaneous speech.

This work presents a preliminary study which aims at bridging these two paradigms in order to make use of explicit phonetic knowledge in the framework of HMM. While landmark-based systems use phonetic landmarks as a feature describing the signal, the idea of our approach is to use landmarks in order to guide the search for the best path during Viterbi decoding in an HMM-based system. Hence, prior knowledge on the nature of the signal is used as *anchor points* during decoding. We will use indistinctly the two terms landmark and anchor to designate constraints on the search.

The aim of this study is twofold. The first aim is to define a theoretical framework to incorporate phonetic knowledge in HMM based systems using anchor points and to experimentally validate this approach. This framework allows for uncertainty in the landmark detection step, though this is not validated in the study as of now. The second aim is to study which landmarks effectively complements the data-driven knowledge embedded in HMM systems. We believe that detecting fine grain phonetic features is a particularly challenging problem – in spite of recent promising results on the detection of distinctive features, see *e.g.* [4,5,3] – while detecting broad phonetic features can be achieved with reasonably good performance [6,7,8]. Hence, to avoid problems related to the detection of fine grain features, we investigate if, and to what extent, broad phonetic landmarks can help.

In this paper, we first extend the Viterbi algorithm in order to incorporate prior knowledge carried out by landmarks. We then study the impact of broad phonetic landmarks in an ideal setting where landmarks are manually detected, with an emphasis on the temporal precision of the landmarks. Finally, we discuss actual landmark detection.

2   Landmark-Driven Viterbi Decoding

Most HMM-based systems rely on the Viterbi algorithm in order to solve (1), along with pruning techniques to keep the search tractable for large vocabularies. We briefly recall the basics of the Viterbi algorithm before extending this algorithm for the integration of phonetic anchors.

2.1   Beam-Search Viterbi Decoding

The Viterbi algorithm aims at finding out the best alignment path in a graph using dynamic programming (DP) on a trellis. The DP algorithm proceeds incrementally by searching for the best hypothesis reaching the state (j, t) of the trellis according to

$$S(j, t) = \max_i S(i, t - 1) + \alpha_{ij} + \ln(p(y_t|j)) \ , \tag{2}$$

where j is the state in the decoding graph and t the frame index in the observation sequence. In (2), α_{ij} denotes the weight for the transition from state i to j in the graph while $p(y_t|j)$ denotes the likelihood of the feature vector y_t conditional to state j. Hence, $S(i,t)$ represents the score of the best partial path ending in state i at time t.

In practice, not all paths are explored in order to keep the algorithm tractable on large decoding graphs. Unlikely partial hypotheses are pruned according to the score of the best path ending at time t.

2.2   Introducing Landmarks

Landmarks can be considered as hints on the best path. For example, if a landmark indicates that a portion of an utterance corresponds to a vowel, then we can constrain the best path to be consistent with this piece of information since nodes in the decoding graph are linked to phonemes. One easy way to do this is to penalize, or even prune, all the paths of the trellis which are inconsistent with the knowledge brought by the landmark. Assuming confidence measures are associated with the landmarks, the penalty should be proportional to the confidence.

Formally, the above principle can be expressed using non-stationary graphs, *i.e.* graphs whose transition weights are dependent on time. The idea is that if a transition leading to state (i,t) of the trellis is inconsistent with the landmark knowledge, then the transition cost increases. In order to do this, we replace in (2) the transition weights α_{ij} by

$$\alpha_{ij}(t) = \alpha_{ij} - \lambda(t) \, I_j(t) \ . \tag{3}$$

$I_j(t)$ is an indicator function whose value is 0 if node j is compatible with the available anchor information and 1 otherwise. The penalization term $\lambda(t) > 0$ reflects the confidence in the anchor available at time t, if any. Hence, if no anchor is available or if a node is consistent with the anchor, no penalty is applied. In the opposite case, we apply a penalty where the higher the confidence in the landmark, the higher the penalty. In the ideal case where landmark detection is perfect, setting $\lambda(t) = \infty$, enables to actually prune paths inconsistent with the landmarks. In (3), one can notice that the penalty term only depends on the target state j and hence the proposed scheme is equivalent to modifying the state-conditional probability $p(y_t|j)$ to include a penalty. However, introducing the penalty at the transition level might be useful in the future to introduce phonological constraints or word-level constraints.

A by product of the proposed method is that decoding should be much faster with landmarks as adding a penalty will most likely result in inconsistent paths being pruned.

In this preliminary study, we use manually detected landmarks in order to investigate whether or not broad phonetic landmarks can help and to what extent in an ideal case. We will therefore set $\lambda(t) = \infty, \forall t$ in all the experiments described in section 4.

3   Baseline System

Before describing the experiments, we briefly present the data and baseline system used.

Experiments are carried out on a radio broadcast news corpus in the French language. The data used is a 4 hour subset of the development data for the ESTER broadcast news rich transcription evaluation campaign [9]. The corpus mostly contains high-fidelity planned speech from professional radio speakers. Interviews, however, contain more spontaneous speech from non professional speakers, sometimes in degraded acoustic conditions.

The entire data set was labeled phonetically based on the reference orthographic transcription, using our ASR system to select pronunciation variants.

Two reference systems were used in this study. Both systems are two-pass systems where a first pass aims at generating a word graph which is then rescored in a second pass with more sophisticated acoustic models. The two systems differ in the complexity of the acoustic models used for the word graph generation: context-independent models are used in the first system while word-internal context-dependent ones are used in the second one. Clearly, using landmarks to guide the decoding is more interesting when generating the word graph as it should enable better and smaller word graphs which already take into account the landmark knowledge. Therefore, the reason for comparing two systems for word graph generation is to determine to what extent phone models capture broad phonetic information.

Both transcription passes are carried out with a trigram language model. Monophone acoustic models have 114 states with 128 Gaussians per state while the word-internal triphone models have 4,019 distinct states with 32 Gaussians each. Cross-word triphones models are used for word graph rescoring, with about 6,000 distinct states and 32 Gaussians per state.

4   Broad Phonetic Landmarks

The experiments described in this section are performed using manually detected broad phonetic landmarks, the goal being to measure the best expected gain from the use of such landmarks. The main motivation for using this type of landmarks, as opposed to distinctive features, is that we believe that reliable and robust automatic broad phonetic landmark detectors can be build. For example, in [6,7,8] (to cite a few), good results are reported on the detection of nasals and vowels. Fricatives also seems relatively easy to detect using energy and zero crossing rate information. Moreover, we observed that, most of the time, the heap of active hypotheses in the ASR system contains hypotheses corresponding to different broad phonetic classes. Though this is normal since hypotheses correspond to complete partial paths rather than to local decisions, this observation indicates that a better selection of the active hypotheses based on (locally detected) landmarks is bound to improve the results.

Table 1. Word error rate (in %) as a function of the landmarks used. The landmark ratio indicates the amount of signal (in %) for which a landmark is available.

landmarks		none	all	VSF	vow.	stop	fri.	nas.	gli.
landmark ratio			43.6	34.6	18.3	9.0	7.3	2.8	6.2
monophones	passe 1	29.2	15.3	21.7	26.6	26.5	27.5	27.8	25.1
	passe 2	22.3	13.9	17.6	21.2	20.7	21.0	21.5	20.1
triphones	passe 1	27.3	19.6	23.9	27.0	26.3	26.0	26.4	24.9
	passe 2	21.3	15.0	18.2	20.7	20.4	20.3	20.7	19.6

4.1   Landmark Generation

Five broad phonetic classes are considered in this study, namely vowels, fricatives, stops, nasal consonants and glides. Landmarks are generated from the available phonetic alignments obtained from the orthographic transcription. For each phone, a landmark corresponding to the broad phonetic class to which the phone belongs is generated, centered on the phone segment. The landmark duration is proportional to the phone segment length. In the first set of experiments, the landmark length is set to 50 % of the phone segment length. We study in section 4.3 the impact of the landmark duration.

4.2   Which Landmarks?

The first question to answer is what is the optimal improvement that can be obtained using each broad phonetic class separately. Results are given in table 1 for the monophone and triphone systems after the first and second pass, with each landmark type taken separately. Results using all the landmarks or only vowel, stop and fricative landmarks are also reported.

Results show a small improvement for each type of landmarks, thus clearly indicating that the transcription system is not misled by phones from a particular broad phonetic class. The best improvement is obtained with landmarks for glides, that correspond to highly transitory phones which are difficult to model, in particular because of co-articulation effects. More surprisingly, vowel landmarks yield a small but significant improvement, in spite of the fact that the phone models used in the ASR system do little confusions between vowels and other phones. This result is due to the fact that the DP maximization not only depends on the local state-conditional probabilities but also on the score of the entire path resulting in an hypothesis. In other words, even if the local probabilities $p(y_t|i)$ are much better for states corresponding to a vowel than for states corresponding to some other class, some paths, incompatible with the knowledge of a vowel landmark, might get a good cumulated score and are therefore kept in the heap of active hypotheses. Using the landmark-driven version of the Viterbi algorithm actually removes such paths from the search space, thus explaining the gain obtained with vowel landmarks.

Clearly, using all the available landmarks strongly improves the WER for both systems, the improvement being unsurprisingly better for the monophone-based system. One interesting point to note is that, when using all the landmarks, the two systems exhibit comparable levels of performance, with a slight advantage for the monophone system. This advantage is due to the fact that the word graph generated with the monophone system contains more sentence hypotheses than the one generated with the triphone system, though both graphs have roughly the same density. A last point worth noting is the rather good performance obtained after the first pass using the monophone system. This result suggest that combining landmark-driven decoding with fairly simple acoustic models can provide good transcriptions with a limited amount of computation. Indeed, the average number of active hypotheses, and hence the decoding time, is divided by a factor of four when using landmarks.

In a practical setting, the reliable detection and segmentation of a signal into broad phonetic classes is somewhat unrealistic, the detection of nasals and glides being a rather difficult problem. However, detecting vowels, stops and fricatives seems feasible with a great accuracy. We therefore report results using only landmarks from those three classes (VSF results in table 1). Using such landmarks, a nice performance gain can still be expected, in particular with a monophone-based word graph generation.

These results show the optimal gain that can be obtained using broad phonetic landmarks as anchors in a Viterbi decoding, thus justifying further work on landmark detection.

4.3   Landmark Precision

Two questions arise regarding the precision of the landmark detection step. The first question is to determine whether a precise detection of the landmark boundaries is necessary or not. The second question concerns the robustness to detection errors of the proposed algorithm.

Temporal Precision. Table 2 shows the word error rate for the two systems as a function of the landmark extent, where the extent is defined as the relative duration with respect to the phone used to generate the landmark. An extent of 10 therefore means that the duration of a landmark is 0.1 times that of the corresponding phone. All the landmarks are considered in these experiments. Unsurprisingly, the longer the landmarks, the better the transcription. It was also observed that longer landmarks reduce the search space and yield smaller, yet better, word graphs. In spite of this, most of the improvement comes from the fact that landmarks are introduced, no matter their extent. Indeed, with a landmark extent of only 5 %, the word error rate decreases from 22.3 % to 14.3 % with the monophone system. When increasing the landmark extent to 50 %, the gain is marginal, with a word error rate of 13.9 %. Note that with an extent of 5 %, the total duration of landmarks corresponds to 4.4 % of the total

Table 2. WER (in %) as a function of the landmark duration

extent (in %)	0	5	10	20	30	40	50	60
monophones	22.3	14.3	14.4	14.3	–	14.2	13.8	13.5
triphones	20.7	–	15.2	15.1	15.0	14.8	14.4	14.3

duration of the signal, and therefore landmark-based pruning of the hypotheses heap happens only for 4.4 % of the frames. Similar conclusions were obtained using only the vowel landmarks. This is a particularly interesting result as it demonstrates that landmark boundaries do not need to be detected precisely. Reliably detecting landmarks on some very short portion of the signal (one or two frames) is sufficient to drive a Viterbi decoder with those landmarks.

Robustness to non-detection errors. In the absence of confidence measures, landmark-driven Viterbi is highly sensitive to detection errors. Clearly, false alarms, *i.e.* insertion and confusion errors, have detrimental effects on the system. However, miss detection errors are less disastrous. Therefore, automatic broad phonetic landmark detection systems should be designed to have as low as possible a false alarm rate. However, lower false alarm rates unfortunately imply higher miss detection rates. We tested the robustness of our landmark-driven decoder by simulating miss detection errors at various rates, assuming a uniform distribution of the errors across the five broad phonetic classes. Results show that the word error rate is a linear function of the miss detection rate. For example, with the monophone system, the word error rate is 17.9 % (resp. 15.8 %) for a miss detection error rate of 50 % (resp. 25 %).

5   Discussion

The preliminary experiments reported in this paper are encouraging and prove that integrating broad phonetic landmarks in a HMM-based system can drastically improve the performance, assuming landmarks can be detected reliably. These results also validate the proposed paradigm for the integration of various sources of knowledge: phonetic knowledge via landmarks and data-driven knowledge acquired by the HMM. However, results are reported in an ideal laboratory setting where landmark detection is perfect. The first step is therefore to work on robust detectors of broad phonetic landmarks, at least for vowels, stops and fricatives, in order to validate the proposed paradigm in practical conditions.

Experiments carried out with broad phonetic segmentation using HMM on top of cepstral coefficients, along with a trigram model, resulted in an accuracy of 76.6 which did not prove sufficient to provide reliable landmarks. Indeed, landmarks extracted from this segmentation with a landmark extent of 20 % are incorrectly labeled for 10.8 % of the time, which resulted in a small increase of the WER from 22.3 to 23.2 % with vowels, stops and fricative landmarks.

However, the segmentation system is naive in the sense that it relies on the same features and techniques than the ASR system and therefore does not bring any new information. Still, HMM based broad phonetic segmentation used as is does not seem reliable enough for landmark detection. Promising results were obtained with support vector machines applied to the classification of isolated frames into broad phonetic classes with miss rates between 2 and 5 % for a false alarm rate of 0.5 %. These results still need to be improved – for example using additional features on top of cepstral coefficients, context frames, boosting strategies, etc. – in order to use SVM scores either to directly detect landmarks or to validate landmarks from an existing segmentation.

Finally, let us conclude this discussion with two remarks. First, we believe that mixing the landmark paradigm with data-driven methods offers a great potential to tackle the problem of robustness. In this sense, broad phonetic landmarks seem a reasonable choice to achieve robustness. Second, the proposed framework is not limited to ASR. The framework offers a way to integrate knowledge in a DP algorithm in a general way and has many application fields such as multimodal fusion or audiovisual speech recognition.

Acknowledgments. This work was partially financed in the framework of the Action Concertée Incitative Masses de Données Demi-Ton – Multimodal Description for the Automatic Structuring of TV Streams.

References

1. Liu, S.A.: Landmark detection for distinctive feature-based speech recognition. PhD thesis, Massachusetts Institute of Technology (1995)
2. Juneja, A.: Speech recognition based on phonetic features and acoustic landmarks. PhD thesis, University of Maryland (2004)
3. John Hopkins University, Center for Language and Speech Processing: Landmark-based speech recognition: report of the 2004 John Hopkins Summer Workshop, John Hopkins University, Center for Language and Speech Processing (2005)
4. McDermott, E., Hazen, T.: Minimum classification error training of landmark models for real-time continuous speech recognition. In: Proc. IEEE Intl. Conf. Acoust. Speech, Signal Processing, vol. 1 (2004)
5. Schutte, K., J.G.: Robust detection of sonorant landmarks. In: European Conf. on Speech Communication and Technology – Interspeech (2005)
6. Chen, M.: Nasal landmark detection. In: Intl. Conf. Speech and Language Processing (2000)
7. Howitt, A.: Vowel landmark detection. In: Intl. Conf. Speech and Language Processing (2000)
8. Li, J., Lee, C.H.: On designing and evaluating speech event detectors. In: European Conference on Speech Communication and Technology – Interspeech (2006)
9. Galliano, S., Geoffrois, E., Bonastre, J.F., Gravier, G., Mostefa, D., Choukri, K.: Corpus description of the Ester evaluation campaign for the rich transcription of french broadcast news. In: Language Resources and Evaluation Conference (2006)

A Hybrid Genetic-Neural Front-End Extension for Robust Speech Recognition over Telephone Lines

Sid-Ahmed Selouani[1], Habib Hamam[2], and Douglas O'Shaughnessy[3]

[1] Université de Moncton, campus of Shippagan NB, E8S1P6, Canada
selouani@umcs.ca
[2] Université de Moncton, campus of Moncton NB, E1A 3E9, Canada
hamamh@umoncton.ca
[3] INRS-Énergie-Matériaux-télécommunications, 800, de la Gauchetiere Ouest,
Montréal, Canada
dougo@emt.inrs.ca

Abstract. This paper presents a hybrid technique combining the Karhonen-Loeve Transform (KLT), the Multilayer Perceptron (MLP) and Genetic Algorithms (GAs) to obtain less-variant Mel-frequency parameters. The advantages of such an approach are that the robustness can be reached without modifying the recognition system, and that neither assumption nor estimation of the noise are required. To evaluate the effectiveness of the proposed approach, an extensive set of continuous speech recognition experiments are carried out by using the NTIMIT telephone speech database. The results show that the proposed approach outperforms the baseline and conventional systems.

1 Introduction

Adaptation to the environment changes and artifacts remains one of the most challenging problems for the Continuous Speech Recognition (CSR) systems. The principle of CSR methods consists of building speech sound models based on large speech corpora that attempt to include common sources of variability that may occur in practice. Nevertheless, not all situations and contexts can be exhaustively covered. As speech and language technologies are being transferred to real applications, the need for greater robustness in recognition technology becomes more apparent when speech is transmitted over telephone lines, when the signal-to-noise ratio (SNR) is extremely low, and more generally, when adverse conditions and/or unseen situations are encountered. To cope with these adverse conditions and to achieve noise robustness, different approaches have been studied. Two major approaches have emerged. The first approach consists of preprocessing the corrupted speech input signal prior to the pattern matching in an attempt to enhance the SNR. The second approach attempts to establish a compensation method that modifies the pattern matching itself to account for the effects of noise. Methods in this approach include noise masking, the use of robust distance measures, and HMM decomposition. For more details see [5].

M. Chetouani et al. (Eds.): NOLISP 2007, LNAI 4885, pp. 169–178, 2007.
© Springer-Verlag Berlin Heidelberg 2007

As an alternative approach, we propose a new enhancement scheme based on the combination of subspace filtering, the Multilayer Perceptron (MLP) and Genetic Algorithms (GAs) to obtain less-variant Mel-frequency parameters. The enhanced parameters are expected to be insensitive to the degradation of speech signals due to telephone-channel degradation. The main advantages of such an approach over the compensation method are that the robustness can be reached without modifying the recognition system, and without requiring assumption or estimation of the noise.

This paper is organized as follows. In section 2, we describe the basis of the signal subspace approach, namely the Karhonen-Loeve Transform (KLT) and the extension we proposed to enable the use of the technique in the Mel-frequency space. In section 3, we briefly describe the principle of MLP-based enhacement method. Then, we proceed in section 4 with the description of the evolutionary-based paradigm that we introduced to perform noise reduction. In section 5, we evaluate the hybrid MLP-KLT-GA-based front-end technique in the context of telephone speech. Finally, in section 6, we conclude and discuss our results.

2 Signal and Mel-frequency Subspace Filtering

The principle of the signal subspace techniques is based on the construction of an orthonormal set of axes. These axes point in the directions of maximum variance, thus forming a representational basis that projects on the direction of maximum variability. Applied in the context of noise reduction, these axes enable decomposing the space of the noisy signal into a signal-plus-noise subspace and a noise subspace. The enhancement is performed by removing the noise subspace and estimating the clean signal from the remaining signal space. The decomposition of the space into two subspaces can be performed by using KLT (eigendecomposition). Let $\mathbf{x} = [\mathbf{x_1}, \mathbf{x_2}, ..., \mathbf{x_N}]^{\mathbf{T}}$ be an N-dimensional noisy observation vector which can be written as the sum of an additive noise distortion vector $\mathbf{w}$ and the vector of clean speech samples $\mathbf{s}$. The noise is assumed to be uncorrelated with the clean speech. Further, let $\mathbf{R_x}$, $\mathbf{R_s}$, and $\mathbf{R_w}$ be the covariance matrices from $\mathbf{x}$, $\mathbf{s}$, and $\mathbf{w}$ respectively. The eigendecomposition of $\mathbf{R_s}$ is given by $\mathbf{R_s} = \mathbf{Q}\mathbf{\Lambda_s}\mathbf{Q^T}$ where $\mathbf{\Lambda_s} = \text{diag}(\lambda_{s1}, \lambda_{s2}, ..., \lambda_{sN})$ is the diagonal matrix of eigenvalues given in a decreasing order. The eigenvector matrix $\mathbf{Q}$ of the clean speech covariance matrix is identical to that of the noise. Major signal subspace techniques assume the noise to be white with $\mathbf{R_w} = \sigma_w^2 \mathbf{I}$ where σ_w^2 is the noise variance and $\mathbf{I}$ the identity matrix. Thus, the eigendecomposition of $\mathbf{R_x}$ is given by: $\mathbf{R_s} = \mathbf{Q}(\mathbf{\Lambda_s} + \sigma_w^2 \mathbf{I})\mathbf{Q^T}$. The enhancement is performed by assuming that the clean speech is concentrated in an $r < N$ dimensional subspace, the so-called signal subspace, whereas the noise occupies the $N - r$ dimensional observation space. Then the noise reduction is obtained by considering only the signal subspace in the reconstruction of the enhanced signal. Mathematically it consists of finding a linear estimate of $\mathbf{s}$ given by $\hat{\mathbf{s}} = \mathbf{Fx} = \mathbf{Fs} + \mathbf{Fw}$ where $\mathbf{F}$ is the enhancement filter. This filter matrix $\mathbf{F}$ can be written as follows: $\mathbf{F} = \mathbf{Q_r}\mathbf{G_r}\mathbf{Q_r^T}$ in which the diagonal matrix $\mathbf{G_r}$ contains the weighting factors

g_i with $i = 1, ..., r$, for the eigenvalues of the noisy speech. Perceptually mean-ingful weighting functions exist to generate g_i. These functions are empirically guided in order to constitute an alternative choice for g_i, which results in a more or less aggressive noise suppression, depending on the SNR. In [1], the linear estimation of the clean vector is performed using two perceptually meaningful weighting functions. The first function is given by :

$$g_i = \left[\frac{\lambda_{xi}}{\lambda_{xi} + \sigma_w^2} \right]^{\gamma}, \quad i = 1, ..., r, \tag{1}$$

where $\gamma \geq 1$.

The second function constitutes an alternative choice for g_i which results in a more aggressive noise suppression:

$$g_i = \exp \left\{ \frac{-\nu \sigma_w^2}{\lambda_{xi}} \right\}. \quad i = 1, ..., r, \tag{2}$$

The value of the parameter ν is to be fixed experimentally.

Instead of dealing with the speech signal, we chose to use the noisy Mel-Frequency Cepstral Coefficients (MFCC) vector $\mathbf{C}'$ as well. The reason is that these parameters are suited to speech recognition due to the advantage that one can derive from them a set of parameters which are invariant to any fixed frequency-response distortion introduced by either the adverse environments or the transmission channels [6]. The main advantage of the approach proposed here is that we do not need to define weighting functions. In this approach, the filter matrix $\mathbf{F}$ can be written as follows: $\mathbf{F_{gen}} = \mathbf{Q} \mathbf{G_{gen}} \mathbf{Q^T}$ in which the diagonal matrix $\mathbf{G_{gen}}$ contains now weighting factors optimized using genetic operators. Optimization is reached when the Euclidian distance between the noisy and clean MFCCs is minimized. To improve the enhancement of noisy MFFCs, we introduce a preprocessing level which uses the MLP. As depicted in Figure 1, the noisy (MFCC) vectors $\mathbf{C}'$ are first enhanced by MLP. Then, a KLT is performed on the output of MLP, denoted by $\hat{\mathbf{C}}$. Finally, the space of feature representation is reconstructed by using the eigenvectors weighted by the optimal factors of the $\mathbf{G_{gen}}$ matrix.

3   MLP-Based Enhancement Preprocessing of the KLT

Numerous approaches were proposed in the literature to incorporate acoustic features estimated by the MLP under noisy conditions [6] [13]. The connectionist approaches offer inherent nonlinear capabilities as well as easy training from pairs of corresponding noisy and noise-free signal frames. Because the front end is very modular, the MLP estimator can be introduced at different stages in the feature processing stream. For instance, the MLP can estimate robust filterbank log-energies that will then be processed with the traditional Distrete Cosine Transform to get the unnormalized cepstral coefficients. Alternatively, we can estimate the cepstral features directly with an MLP. Yet another possibility

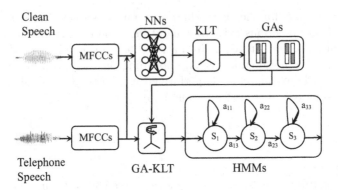

Fig. 1. The proposed MLP-KLT-GA-based CSR system

is to estimate filterbank log-energies but to measure the feature distortion at the cepstrum level and optimize the filterbank log-energy estimator accordingly [13]. The fact that the noise and the speech signal are combined in a nonlinear way in the cepstral domain led us to choose the second alternative described above. MLP can approximate the required nonlinear function to some extent [6]. Hence, the input of the MLP is the noisy MFCC vector $\mathbf{C}'$, while the actual response of the network $\hat{\mathbf{C}}$ is computed during a training phase by using a convergence algorithm to update the weight vector in a manner to minimize the error between the output $\hat{\mathbf{C}}$ and the desired clean cepstrum value $\mathbf{C}$. The weights of this network are calculated during a training phase with a back-propagation training algorithm using a mean square error criterion.

The noisy 13-dimensional vector (12 MFCCs + energy) is fed to an MLP network in order to reduce the noise effects on this vector. Once the enhanced vector is obtained, it is fed to the KLT-GA module. This latter module refines the enhanced vector by projecting its components in the subspace generated by a genetically weighted version of the eigenvectors of the clean signal. The motivation behind the use of a second level of enhancement after using the MLP network is to compensate for the limited power of the MLP network for enhancement outside the training space [6].

4   Hybrid MLP-KLT-GA Speech Front-end

The KLT processing on the MLP-enhanced noisy vectors $\hat{\mathbf{C}}$ gives the diagonal matrix $\mathbf{G_r}$ containing the weighting factors g_i with $i = 1, ..., r$. In the classical subspace filtering approaches, a key issue is to determine the rank r from which the high order components (those who are supposed to contain the noise are removed). In the evolutionary-based method we propose, all components are used in the optimization process. Only the performance criterion will determine the final components that are retained to perform the reconstruction of the space of enhanced features.

The evolution process starts with the creation of a population of the weight factors, g_i with $i = 1, ..., N$, which represent the individuals. The individuals evolve through many generations in a pool where genetic operators are applied [4]. Some of these individuals are selected to reproduce according to their performance. The individuals' evaluation is performed through the use of an objective function. When the fittest individual (best set of weights) is obtained, it is then use in the test phase to project the noisy data. Genetically modified MFCCs, their first and second derivatives, are finally used as enhanced features for the recognition process. As mentioned earlier, the problem of determining optimal r is not needed, since the GA considers the complete space dimension N.

4.1   Initialization, Termination and Solution Representation

A solution representation is needed to describe each individual in the population. For our application, the useful representation of an individual for function optimization involves genes or variables from an alphabet of floating point numbers with values within the variables' upper and lower bounds, noted (a_i, b_i) respectively. Concerning the initialization of the pool, the ideal zero-knowledge assumption is to start with a population of completely random values of weights. These values follow an uniform distribution within the upper and lower boundaries. The evolution process is terminated when a certain number of maximum generations is reached. This number corresponds to a convergence of the objective function.

4.2   Selection Function

A common selection method assigns a probability of selection, P_j, to each individual, j, based on its objective function value. Various methods exist to assign probabilities to individuals. In our application, the normalized geometric ranking is used [7]. This method defines P_j for each individual by:

$$P_j = \frac{q(1-q)^{s-1}}{1-(1-q)^P},$$

(3)

where q is the probability of selecting the best individual, s is the rank of the individual (1 is the rank of the best), and P is the population size.

4.3   Crossover

In order to avoid the extension of the exploration domain of the best solution, a simple crossover operator can be used [7]. It generates a random number l from a uniform distribution and does an exchange of the genes of the parents (X and Y) on the offspring genes (X' and Y'). It can be expressed by the following equations:

$$\begin{cases} X' = lX + (1-l)Y \\ Y' = (1-l)X + lY. \end{cases}$$

(4)

4.4   Mutation

The principle of the non-uniform mutation consists of randomly selecting one component, x_k, of an individual X, and setting it equal to a non-uniform random number, x'_k:

$$x'_k = \begin{cases} x_k + (b_k - x_k)f(Gen) & \text{if } u_1 < 0.5 \\ x_k - (a_k + x_k)f(Gen) & \text{if } u_1 \geq 0.5, \end{cases} \qquad (5)$$

where the function $f(Gen)$ is given by:

$$f(Gen) = (u_2(1 - \frac{Gen}{Gen_{max}}))^t , \qquad (6)$$

where u_1, u_2 are uniform random numbers in the range $(0,1)$, t is a shape parameter, Gen is the current generation and Gen_{max} is the maximum number of generations. The multi-non-uniform mutation generalizes the application of the non-uniform mutation operator to all the components of the parent X.

4.5   Objective Function

The GA must search all the axes generated by the KLT of the MEL-frequency space to find the closest to the clean MFCCs. Thus, evolution is driven by a fitness function defined in terms of a distance measure between noisy MFCCs pre-processed by MLP and projected on a given individual (axis), and the clean MFCCs. The fittest individual is the axis which corresponds to the minimum of that distance. The distance function applied to cepstral (or other voice representations) refers to *spectral distortion measures* and represents the cost in a classification system of speech frames. For two vectors $\mathbf{C}$ and $\hat{\mathbf{C}}$ representing two frames, each with N components, the geometric distance is defined as:

$$d(\mathbf{C}, \hat{\mathbf{C}}) = (\sum_{k=1}^{N}(\mathbf{C_k} - \hat{\mathbf{C}_k})^l)^{1/l} . \qquad (7)$$

For simplicity, the Euclidian distance is considered ($l = 2$), which turned out to be a valuable measure for both clean and noisy speech. Note that $-d(\mathbf{C}, \hat{\mathbf{C}})$ is used as a distance measure because the evaluation function must be maximized.

5   Experiments and Results

Extensive experimental studies were carried out to characterize the impairment induced by telephone networks [3]. When speech is recorded through telephone lines, a reduction in the analysis bandwidth yields a higher recognition error, particularly when the system is trained with high-quality speech and tested using simulated telephone speech [9].

Table 1. Percentages of word recognition rate ($\%C_{Wrd}$), insertion rate ($\%\epsilon_{Ins}$), deletion rate ($\%\epsilon_{Del}$), and substitution rate ($\%\epsilon_{Sub}$) of Mean-normalized MFCCs their first and second derivatives denoted (CMN), KLT, MLP, MLP-KLT, KLT-GA, and MLP-KLT-GA CSR systems using (a) 1-mixture, (b) 2-mixture, (c) 4-mixture and (d) 8-mixture tri-phone models. (Best rates are highlighted in boldface.)

	$\%\epsilon_{Sub}$	$\%\epsilon_{Del}$	$\%\epsilon_{Ins}$	$\%C_{Wrd}$
No processing	82.71	4.27	33.44	13.02
CMN	79.35	4.24	29.15	17.14
KLT	77.05	5.11	30.04	17.84
MLP	77.03	5.02	28.74	18.18
MLP-KLT	76.84	5.06	28.89	20.17
KLT-GA	58.11	5.28	24.48	39.50
MLP-KLT-GA	52.15	5.07	21.36	**43.22**

[a] Results using 1-mixture triphone models.

	$\%\epsilon_{Sub}$	$\%\epsilon_{Del}$	$\%\epsilon_{Ins}$	$\%C_{Wrd}$
No processing	81.25	3.44	38.44	15.31
CMN	79.36	3.12	37.92	17.81
KLT	78.11	3.81	38.89	18.08
MLP	78.47	3.56	40.78	17.94
MLP-KLT	70.71	3.09	43.02	21.86
KLT-GA	54.01	3.96	49.85	45.03
MLP-KLT-GA	49.78	3.68	49.40	**46.48**

[b] Results using 2-mixture triphone models.

	$\%\epsilon_{Sub}$	$\%\epsilon_{Del}$	$\%\epsilon_{Ins}$	$\%C_{Wrd}$
No processing	78.85	3.75	38.23	17.40
CMN	77.50	3.96	39.87	19.12
KLT	76.27	4.88	39.54	18.85
MLP	75.42	4.05	38.44	19.97
MLP-KLT	70.43	3.98	36.65	22.18
KLT-GA	54.88	3.79	35.46	48.42
MLP-KLT-GA	50.95	3.58	22.98	**49.10**

[c] Results using 4-mixture triphone models.

	$\%\epsilon_{Sub}$	$\%\epsilon_{Del}$	$\%\epsilon_{Ins}$	$\%C_{Wrd}$
No processing	78.02	3.96	40.83	18.02
CMN	77.48	4.95	34.75	19.46
KLT	77.36	5.37	34.62	17.32
MLP	77.13	5.04	32.32	21.58
MLP-KLT	75.29	5.13	33.88	21.72
KLT-GA	55.66	5.46	27.12	47.01
MLP-KLT-GA	47.85	5.86	25.39	**50.48**

[d] Results using 8-mixture triphone models.

In our experiments, the training set composed of the $dr1$ and $dr2$ subdirectories of the TIMIT database, described in [2], was used to train a set of clean speech models. The speech recognition system used the $dr1$ subdirectory of NTIMIT as test set [2]. HTK, the HMM-based speech recognition system described in [12], has been used throughout all experiments. We compared seven systems: a baseline system where no enhancement processing is done, a system which performs the Cepstral Mean Normalization (CMN)in order to attenuate the effect of inserting a transmission channel on the input speech, a KLT-based system as detailed in [10], a system based on a MLP preprocessing, a hybrid MLP-KLT system, a hybrid KLT-GA system, and finally, the MLP-KLT-GA-based CSR system. All the systems use the MFCCs, first and second derivatives front-end. Note that in our KLT process the mean is globally normalized and the standard deviation is equal to one.

The architecture of the MLP network consists of three layers. The input layer consists of 13 neurons, while the hidden layer and the output layer consists of 26 and 13 neurons, respectively. The input to the network is the noisy 12-dimensional MFCC vector in addition to the energy. The weights of this network are calculated during a training phase with a back-propagation algorithm with a learning rate equal to 0.25 and a momentum coefficient equal to 0.09. The obtained weight values are then used during the recognition process to reduce the noise in the enhanced obtained vector that is incorporated into the KLT-GA module.

To control the run behaviour of a genetic algorithm, a number of parameter values must be defined. The initial population is composed of 250 individuals and was created by duplicating the elements of the weighting matrix. The genetic algorithm was halted after 500 generations. The percentages of crossover rate and mutation rate are fixed respectively at 28% and 4%. The number of total runs was fixed at 70. After the GA processing, the MFCCs static vectors are then expanded to produce a 39-dimensional (static+dynamic) vector upon which the hidden Markov models (HMMs), which model the speech subword units, were trained.

We found through experiments that using the MLP-KLT-GA as an approach to enhance the MFCCs that were used for recognition with N-mixture Gaussian HMMs for $N=1$, 2, 4 and 8, using tri-phone models, leads to an important improvement in the accuracy of the word recognition rate. A correct rate of 50.48% is reached by the MLP-KLT-GA-based CSR system when the second best result, 48.42%, is achieved by the KLT-GA. These two systems outperform significantly the systems that use either MLP or KLT solely or combined together. As found in [10] [11] in the context of additive car noise, this result confirms that the use of GAs to optimize the space representation of noisy data leads to more robustness of the CSR process. Note that an important improvement of more than 31% is achieved comparatively to the CMN-based system when the 8-mixture tri-phone model is used. Expanding to more than 8 mixtures did not improve the performance. The results in Table 1 show also that substitution and insertion errors are considerably reduced when the hybrid neural-evolutionary approach is included, leading to more effectiveness for the CSR system.

6 Conclusion

In this paper, a hybrid genetic-neural front-end was proposed to improve speech recognition over telephone lines. It is based on an MLP-KLT-GA hybrid enhancement scheme which aims to obtain less-variant MFCC parameters under telephone-channel degradation. Experiments show that use of the proposed robust front-end processing greatly increases the recognition rate when *dr1* and *dr2* TIMIT directories are used for the training and *dr1* directory of NTIMIT for the test. The MLP-KLT-GA system outperforms significantly the systems that use either MLP or KLT solely or combined together. This indicates that both neural preprocessing, subspace filtering and GA-based optimization gained from their combination as front-end for speech recognition over telephone lines. It is worthy to note that the neural-evolutionary-based technique is less complex than many other enhancement techniques, which need to either model or compensate for the noise. For further work, many other directions remain open. Present goals include the improvement of the objective function in order to perform the online adaptation of the HMM-based CSR system when it faces new and unseen contexts and environments.

References

1. Ephraim, Y., Van Trees, H.L.: A signal subspace approach for Speech Enhancement. IEEE Transactions on Speech and Audio Processing 3(4), 251–266 (1995)
2. Fisher, W.M., Dodington, G.R., Goudie-Marshall, K.M.: The DARPA Speech Recognition Research Database: Specification and Status. In: Proc. DARPA Workshop on Speech Recognition, pp. 93–99 (1986)
3. Gaylor, W.D.: Telephone voice transmission. standards and measurements. Prentice Hall, Englewood Cliffs (1989)
4. Goldberg, D.E.: Genetic algorithms in search, optimization and machine learning. Addison-Wesley Publishing, Reading (1989)
5. Gong, Y.: Speech Recognition in Noisy Environments: A survey. Speech Communication 16, 261–291 (1995)
6. Haverinen, H., Salmela, P., Hakkinen, J., Lehtokangas, M., Saarinen, J.: MLP Network for Enhancement of Noisy MFCC Vectors. In: Proc. Eurospeech, pp. 2371–2374 (1999)
7. Houk, C.R., Joines, J.A., Kay, M.G.: A Genetic Algorithm for function optimization: a matlab implementation, North Carolina University-NCSU-IE, TR 95-09 (1995)
8. Jankowski, C., Kalyanswamy, A., Basson, S., Spitz, J.: NTIMIT: A phonetically balanced continuous speech, telephone bandwidth speech database. In: Proc. IEEE-ICASSP, vol. 1, pp. 109–112 (1990)
9. Moreno, P.J., Stern, R.: Sources of degradation of speech recognition in the telephone network. In: Proc. IEEE-ICASSP, vol. 1, pp. 109–112 (1994)

10. Selouani, S.-A., O'Shaughnessy, D.: Robustness of speech recognition using genetic algorithms and a Mel-cepstral subspace approach. Proc. IEEE-ICASSP I, 201–204 (2004)
11. Selouani, S.-A., O'Shaughnessy, D.: Investigation into a Mel Subspace Based Front-End Processing for Robust Speech Recognition. In: Proc. IEEE-International symposium in signal processing and Information Technology, Roma, pp. 187–190 (2004)
12. Speech Group, Cambridge University, The HTK Book (Version 3.4), Cambridge University Group (2006)
13. Weintraub, M., Beaufays, F.: Increased Robustness of Noisy Speech Features Using Neural Networks. In: Workshop on Robust Methods for Speech Recognition in Adverse Conditions, Tampere, Finland (May 1999)

Efficient Viterbi Algorithms for Lexical Tree Based Models*

S. España-Boquera, M.J. Castro-Bleda, F. Zamora-Martínez, and J. Gorbe-Moya

Departamento de Sistemas Informáticos y Computación
Universidad Politécnica de Valencia, Valencia, Spain
{sespana,mcastro,fzamora,jgorbe}@dsic.upv.es

Abstract. In this paper we propose a family of Viterbi algorithms specialized for lexical tree based FSA and HMM acoustic models. Two algorithms to decode a tree lexicon with left-to-right models with or without skips and other algorithm which takes a directed acyclic graph as input and performs error correcting decoding are presented. They store the set of active states topologically sorted in contiguous memory queues. The number of basic operations needed to update each hypothesis is reduced and also more locality in memory is obtained reducing the expected number of cache misses and achieving a speed-up over other implementations.

1 Introduction

Most of large vocabulary Viterbi based recognizers (for speech, handwritten or other recognition tasks, although speech terminology is used in this work with no loss of generality) make use of a lexicon tree organization which has many advantages over a linear lexicon representation [1,2]. As it is shown in the literature, more compact representations are possible (using a *lexicon network* [3], which is a minimized Finite State Automaton –FSA–) but the gain in space is accompanied with a more complex Viterbi decoder. Therefore, lexical tree organization is a very good tradeoff between compact space representation and adequacy for decoding.

The search space in a recognizer can be huge and the key to achieve practical performance is to consider only the set of active hypothesis (those with non trivial zero probability) and to apply pruning techniques such as beam search which only maintain active the best hypothesis. Large vocabulary one-step decoders [4] usually keep a set of lexical tree based Viterbi parsers in parallel. Two common approaches are the *time-start copies* and *language model history copies* [5,6]. In the time-start approach, all hypothesis competing in a tree parsing share the same word start time. When a trigram language model is used, the language model history copies approach maintains a tree parsing for every bigram history $(w1, w2)$. This second approach has a loss of optimality which is known as *word-pair approximation* [6]. In both cases, it is straightforward to use a specialized Viterbi algorithm for the lexical tree model and, as the core of an automatic speech recognizer lies in the search process, every little improvement in performing

---

* This work has been partially supported by the Spanish Government (TIN2006-12767) and by the Generalitat Valenciana (GVA06/302).

M. Chetouani et al. (Eds.): NOLISP 2007, LNAI 4885, pp. 179–187, 2007.

specialized decoding of lexical tree models has a great impact in the overall performance. Therefore, it is not strange to find specialized algorithms which take advantage of the properties of tree based Hidden Markov Models (HMM) which integrate the tree lexicon and the acoustic HMM models.

In this work, three specialized Viterbi algorithms based on contiguous memory queues (FIFO data structures) are proposed. When performing a Viterbi step, a new result queue is created with the help of one or several auxiliary queues. The basic algorithm uses left-to-right HMM acoustic models with no skips. This algorithm can be applied whenever acoustic left-to-right models without skips are used: it can be used for isolated word or continuous speech recognition, either with a one-step or a two-step approach, with time-start or language model history copies, and also within-word or across-word context dependent units (triphones, quinphones, etc.). A simple extension is presented to show how to use it with across-word context dependent models [7]. A second version of the algorithm extends the first one to allow the use of skips in the acoustic units with a negligible additional cost.

The last proposed algorithm performs an error correcting Viterbi decoding and is capable of analyzing a DAG instead of a sequence. This algorithm can be used, for instance, to obtain a word-graph from a phone-graph.

2   Left-to-Right without Skips Algorithm

When the acoustic models are strict left-to-right without skips, the resulting expanded tree based HMM model is acyclic if loops are ignored, and every node has only zero or one preceding state to take into account in the dynamic programming equation. If a lexicon tree is expanded with left-to-right acoustic HMM models without skips, the following observations about the expanded tree models are straightforward:

- Every state has at most two predecessors: itself and possibly his parent.
- If we ignore the loops, the expanded model is acyclic. Therefore, a topological order is possible in general.
- A level traversal of the tree provides a topological order with additional features:
  - The children of a given node occupy contiguous positions. The grandchildren also occupy contiguous positions.
  - If a subset of states is stored in topological order and we generate the children of every active state following that order, the resulting list also is ordered with respect to the topological order.

2.1   Model Representation

A tree model T of n states is represented with three vectors of size n and one of size $n + 1$ as follows:

- *loop_prob* stores the loop transition probabilities.
- *from_prob* stores the parent incoming transition probabilities.
- *e_index* stores the index of the associated emission probability class associated to the acoustic frame to be observed. The vector of emission probabilities can be obtained with a multilayer perceptron in a hybrid model [8] or with a set of mixture of Gaussian distributions in a conventional continuous density HMM.

– *first_child* stores the index of the first child. The last child is deduced by looking the first child of the next state thanks to the topological sorting. This representation allows specifying an empty set of children. A sentinel in position $n + 1$ is needed for the last state.

2.2   Viterbi-Merge Algorithm

The Viterbi-M algorithm takes a sequence of acoustic frames as input and updates a set of active states after observing every frame (a Viterbi step). An active state is composed by an index state and a score (i, s). A queue $\alpha(t)$ (a FIFO data structure) is used to store the set of active states at time t. The purpose of a Viterbi step consists of creating another queue $\alpha(t + 1)$ given the model T, the current queue $\alpha(t)$ and the vector of emission probabilities *emission* associated to the observed acoustic frame.

An auxiliary queue *aux_child* is used to store temporally the scores of states produced by the transitions from parent to child. The algorithm proceeds as follows (see Figure 1):

1. $best\_prob \leftarrow 0$.
2. For every active state (i, s) of the queue $\alpha(t)$ whose score s is above the beam threshold:
   (a) $s\_next \leftarrow s \cdot loop\_prob[i]$.
   (b) While the first active state (i', s') of the queue *aux_child* satisfies $i' < i$, extract it, update $s' \leftarrow s' \cdot emission[e\_index[i']]$ and place (i', s') in $\alpha(t+1)$. Update $best\_prob \leftarrow \max(best\_prob, s')$.
   (c) If the first active state (i', s') of the queue *aux_child* satisfies $i' = i$, drop it and update the score $s\_next \leftarrow \max(s\_next, s')$.
   (d) $s\_next \leftarrow s\_next \cdot emission[e\_index[i]]$, insert (i, s_next) in queue $\alpha(t + 1)$. Update $best\_prob \leftarrow \max(best\_prob, s\_next)$.
   (e) For every state j from $first\_child[i]$ to $first\_child[i + 1] - 1$, add the active state $(j, s \cdot from\_prob[j])$ to the queue *aux_child*.

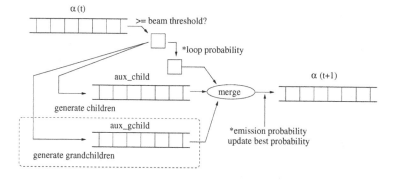

Fig. 1. Viterbi-M and Viterbi-MS algorithms. The queue *aux_gchild* (dotted part) is only used in Viterbi-MS.

3. For every active state (i', s') of the queue *aux_child*, extract it, update the score $s' \leftarrow s' \cdot emission[e\_index[i']]$ and place (i', s') in the queue $\alpha(t + 1)$. Update $best\_prob \leftarrow \max(best\_prob, s')$.

The active states of $\alpha(t)$ whose score is below the beam threshold are discarded. Whenever an active state is placed in the queue $\alpha(t + 1)$, the emission probability associated to it is applied, and the best probability is updated. This value is used to obtain the beam threshold for the following Viterbi step.

This algorithm is linear with the number of active states and the number of children of active states which is an upper bound to the number of active states in the resulting queue. In total, the global cost is linear with the number of active states, which is the same as any reasonable implementation of a conventional Viterbi implementation. The main advantage of this algorithm is the use of contiguous memory FIFO queues to store the active states. Therefore, a better cache performance and an internal loop with less overhead is obtained compared to other algorithms that use linked lists or use hash tables to store and look up the set of active states. Therefore, the asymptotic cost is the same but a practical speed-up is obtained.

2.3 Extension to Across-Word Context Dependent Units

Since this algorithm is used on lexical tree models with expanded acoustic HMM models, the use of context dependent units is straightforward for within-word context modeling. Across-word models [7] consider a different context dependent unit at the beginning of a word to take into account the last phones of the preceding word during continuous speech recognition. It would be very inefficient to use a different tree model for every possible context since they only differ in the first context dependent acoustic models. Therefore, a model which resembles a tree lexicon excepting the root is used. This model can be composed of two models: a general HMM connecting a set of tree lexicon models. A set of trees can be traversed by levels as if they were just one tree and the resulting model can be used with the same algorithm with no modification. Therefore, a conventional Viterbi algorithm can be used to update the scores of the states of the general topology HMM part of the model, and the rest of the model (a forest) can be computed with the Viterbi-M algorithm.

3 Left-to-Right with Skips Algorithm

This algorithm generalizes the previous one by allowing the use of Bakis HMM acoustic models. Left-to-right units with skips are known as Bakis topology and have a widespread use as acoustic models in most recognizers. When those models are used in conjunction with a tree lexicon, the number of predecessors given an active state can be zero, one or two.

3.1 Model Representation

The model representation is similar to the previous section. The only difference is another vector *skip_prob* which stores, for every state, the incoming skip transition probabilities. In order to iterate over the set of grandchildren of a given state i, the algorithm loops from $first\_child[first\_child[i]]$ to $first\_child[first\_child[i + 1]] - 1$.

3.2   Viterbi-Merge Algorithm with Skips

The Viterbi-MS algorithm is the same of previous section but another auxiliary queue *aux_gchild* is used to store the active states with scores computed by means of the skip transitions. Every time an active state is extracted from $\alpha(t)$, the set of grandchildren is used to add items to the queue *aux_gchild* just as the set of children is used to add items to the other auxiliary queue. Now, the resulting queue $\alpha(t+1)$ is obtained by merging the loop transition score of the processed active state with the states from the two auxiliary queues (see Figure 1).

This algorithm is linear with the number of active states and the number of children and grandchildren of active states. The resulting cost is thus linear with the number of active states.

3.3   Extension to Across-Word Context Dependent Units

The same observations of previous algorithm are also applicable here.

4   Error-Correcting Viterbi for DAGs

Not expanding the acoustic models in the tree lexicon and maintaining a pure tree structure which matches a phone-graph is another possibility. In this case, the input is no longer a sequence of acoustic frames but a phone-graph (a directed acyclic graph –DAG– labelled with phones and acoustic scores). Besides the capability of using a directed acyclic input, the possibility of insertions, deletions and substitutions of phones is needed to tolerate the errors in the phone-graph generation. The last proposed algorithm performs an error correcting Viterbi decoding and is capable of analyzing a DAG instead of a sequence.

4.1   Model Representation

A tree model T of n states where symbols are placed at the transitions is represented with two vectors of size n and other of size $n+1$ as follows:

– *symbol* stores the incoming transition label.
– *from_prob* stores the incoming transition probability.
– *first_child* stores the index of the first child as in the previous algorithms.

A table with the costs of insertions, deletions and substitution of every symbol is also required.

4.2   Error-Correcting Viterbi-Merge Algorithm for DAGs

The Viterbi-MEC-DAG algorithm takes a DAG as input. A set of active states is associated to every vertex of the input DAG. The root of the tree model is added to the active state set of initial DAG vertices. The algorithm applies two different procedures associated to the input DAG following a topological order: the vertex-step and the edge-step,

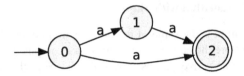

Fig. 2. An example of phone-graph. A possible sequence of calls for this example is vertex-step(0), edge-step(0,1,a), vertex-step(1), edge-step(1,2,a), edge-step(0,2,a), vertex-step(2). Another sequence is vertex-step(0), edge-step(0,2,a), edge-step(0,1,a), vertex-step(1), edge-step(1,2,a), vertex-step(2).

which are explained in detail below. The vertex-step must be applied to a given vertex once all edges arriving to it have been processed using the edge-step procedure. On the other hand, the edge-step must be aplied after the origin vertex has been processed with the vertex-step procedure. An example of a phone-graph together with possible sequences of edge-step and vertex-step calls is shown in Figure 2.

Edge-Step. For every edge, a Viterbi step takes the set of active states of the origin vertex and use them to update the active states of the destination vertex. This procedure only considers the cost of deletions and substitutions. As can be observed in Figure 3 (top), this algorithm is similar to the Viterbi-M algorithm where loop probability updating is replaced by the deletion operation, the generation of children states corresponds to the substitution operation (including a symbol by itself). Another difference, which

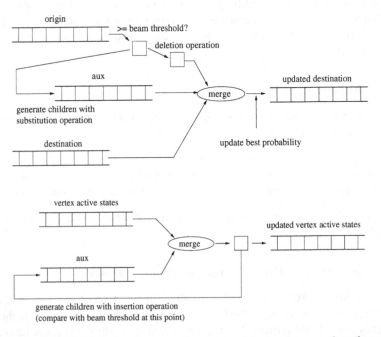

Fig. 3. Viterbi-MEC-DAG edge-step procedure (*top*) and vertex-step procedure (*bottom*)

can be also used in Viterbi-M and Viterbi-MS to process a DAG as input data, is the presence of second input queue which stores the active states already updated at the destination vertex by means of other edges of the DAG. The cost of this procedure is linear with the number of active states in both input queues because the number of generated successor states grows linearly with the number of active states.

Vertex-Step. Once all edges arriving at a given vertex have been processed, the insertion operation is considered. This operation updates a set of active states without consuming any symbol. As can be observed in Figure 3 (bottom), the output of the auxiliary queue is used to insert more active states in the same queue to take into account the possibility of several insertion operations. The cost is not linear with the number of active states: a sole active state at the root could, in principle, activate all the states of the model, but most of them are expected to be pruned by the beam search depending on the cost of insertions and the beam width. The cost of this operation is linear with the number of active states before applying the procedure plus the number of active states after the procedure, which is bounded by the number of states in the model.

5   Experimental Results

A previous work related to lexical tree Viterbi decoding we were aware of after our algorithms were developed is the *active envelope* algorithm [9]. This algorithm also uses a total order which subsumes the partial order of the states of the model and places siblings contiguously. This algorithm is specified for left-to-right models without skips, so it is only comparable to our first algorithm Viterbi-M. The active envelope algorithm uses a single linked list to perform a Viterbi step, which is an advantage in memory usage. Since this algorithm modifies the original set of active states, it is restricted to sequential input data and cannot be used when the input data is a DAG. In order to use only a list, the active hypothesis in active envelope algorithm are traversed in *reverse* topological order. The "price to pay" for this advantage is the need of linked lists instead of contiguous memory arrays. Since the use of linked lists cannot assure memory locality and the cost of traversing them is greater than traversing memory arrays, it is expected to perform worse than Viterbi-M algorithm. The memory occupied by an active hypothesis is an index state and a score; if linked lists are used, a pointer is also needed: so a linked list needs approximately 50% or 100% more memory per active state depending on the computer architecture. On the other hand, the use of memory arrays needs an estimation of the number of active states.

In order to compare the performance of our Viterbi-M and Viterbi-MS algorithms, three more algorithms have been implemented: a conventional Viterbi algorithm based on hash tables with chaining to store and to look up the active states (for HMM without and with skips) and the active envelope algorithm. All algorithms have been implemented in C++ and use the same data structures to represent the tree based HMM models as described in sections 2.1 and 3.1.

The experiments were done on a Pentium D machine at 3GHz with 2 Gbytes of RAM using a Linux with kernel `2.6.18` and the `gcc` compiler version `4.1.2` with `-O3` optimization. The lexical trees used in the experiments were obtained by expanding 3-state left-to-right without and with skips hybrid neural/HMM acoustic models in

Table 1. Experimental results (in millions of active states or hypothesis updated per second)

States	Viterbi-M			Viterbi-MS	
	Hash	AEnvelope	Viterbi-M	Hash	Viterbi-MS
9 571	3.00	16.08	28.54	2.06	27.60
76 189	2.76	12.92	28.50	1.41	27.78
310 894	1.92	6.44	26.57	0.90	25.99

the tree lexicon. The size of these trees varies from 9 571 to 310 888 states. Only the Viterbi decoding time has been measured (the emission scores calculation and other preprocessing steps were not taken into account). The results are shown in Table 1. The speed is measured in millions of active states updated per second.

6 Conclusions

In this paper, three Viterbi algorithms specialized for lexical tree based FSA and HMM acoustic models have been described. Two of these algorithms are useful to decode a set of words given a sequence of acoustic frames and the third one is useful to parse a phone-graph with error-correcting edition operations. These algorithms are based on contiguous memory queues which contain the set of active states topologically sorted.

Although the asymptotic cost of these algorithms is the same as any reasonable implementation of the Viterbi algorithm, the experimental comparison between the Viterbi-M algorithm, a conventional Hash-table swapping algorithm and the active envelope algorithm, shows that our algorithm is approximately 10 times faster than the hash-table swapping implementation and from 2 to 4 times faster than the active envelope algorithm. A decrease in speed with the size of the models is observed in the three algorithms, which is possibly related with the main memory and the cache relative speeds. Analogous conclusions can be drawn for the Viterbi-MS algorithm. For this reason, more experimentation is needed in order to better understand this behaviour and also to study the effect of other parameters such as the beam width of the pruning during the search.

References

1. Klovstad, J., Mondshein, L.: The CASPERS linguistic analysis system. IEEE Trans. on ASSP 23(1), 118–123 (1975)
2. Klatt, D.: Scriber and Lafs: Two New Approaches to Speech Analysis. In: Trends in Speech Recognition, pp. 525–529. Prentice-Hall, Englewood Cliffs (1980)
3. Demuynck, K., Duchateau, J., Compernolle, D.V.: A Static Lexicon Network Representation for Cross-word Context Dependent Phones. In: Proc. Eurospeech, vol. I, pp. 143–146 (1997)
4. Aubert, X.L.: An overview of decoding techniques for large vocabulary continuous speech recognition. In: Computer Speech and Language, vol. 16, pp. 89–114 (2002)
5. Ortmanns, S., et al.: A comparison of time conditioned and word conditioned search techniques for large vocabulary speech recognition. In: Proc. ICSLP, vol. 4, pp. 2091–2094 (1996)
6. Ney, H., Ortmanns, S.: Dynamic programming search for continuous speech recognition. IEEE Signal Proc. Mag. 16(5), 64–83 (1999)

7. Kanthak, S., et al.: Within-word vs. across-word decoding for online speech recognition (2000)
8. Konig, Y., Bourlard, H., Morgan, N.: REMAP: Recursive estimation and maximization of A posteriori probabilities. In: Advances in NIPS, vol. 8, pp. 388–394. The MIT Press, Cambridge (1996)
9. Nguyen, P., Rigazio, L., Junqua, J.C.: EWAVES: An efficient decoding algorithm for lexical tree based speech recognition. In: Proc. ICSLP, vol. 4, pp. 286–289 (2000)

Non-stationary Self-consistent Acoustic Objects as Atoms of Voiced Speech

Friedhelm R. Drepper

Zentralinstitut für Elektronik, Forschungszentrum Jülich, 52425 Jülich, Germany
f.drepper@fz-juelich.de

Abstract. To account for the strong non-stationarity of voiced speech and its nonlinear aero-acoustic origin, the classical source-filter model is extended to a cascaded drive-response model with a conventional linear secondary response, a synchronized and/or synchronously modulated primary response and a non-stationary fundamental drive which plays the role of the long time-scale part of the basic time-scale separation of acoustic perception. The transmission protocol of voiced speech is assumed to be based on non-stationary acoustic objects which can be synthesized as the described secondary response and which are analysed by introducing a self-consistent (filter stable) part-tone decomposition, suited to reconstruct the hidden fundamental drive and to confirm its topological equivalence to a glottal master oscillator. The filter-stable part-tone decomposition opens the option of a phase modulation transmission protocol of voiced speech. Aiming at communication channel invariant acoustic features of voiced speech, the phase modulation cues are expected to be particularly suited to extend and/or replace the classical feature vectors of phoneme and speaker recognition.

Keywords: signal analysis, instantaneous part-tone frequencies, fundamental drive, cascaded response, generalized synchronization, voiced continuants.

1 Introduction

In spite of the undisputedly high degree of non-stationarity of speech signals, the present day determination of its acoustic features is based on the assumption that *speech production* can be described as a linear time invariant (LTI) system on the time scale of about 20 ms [1]. As an evolutionarily plausible supplement, *speech perception* is also assumed to be focussed on acoustic features which can be analyzed by psycho-acoustic experiments with LTI signals [2]. The wide sense stationarity of an LTI–system is typically used either as prerequisite for the consistent estimation of Fourier spectra or of autoregressive (all pole) models [1, 3]. In the latter case it is common practice to introduce a drive-response (input-output or source-filter) model, which restricts the stationary autoregressive description to the resonance properties of the vocal tract [1, 3]. Linear autoregressive models are suited to describe transients with varying decay rates in different frequency ranges including relatively long (resonant formant) transients. The average decay rates of such transients are known to

M. Chetouani et al. (Eds.): NOLISP 2007, LNAI 4885, pp. 188–203, 2007.

represent topological invariants [4] which are (largely invariant with respect to changes of the geometry of the acoustic transmission and) important cues for the distinction of vowels [1, 3]. However, the conventional LTI system assumption turns out to be problematic in the case of voiced phones. The vocal tract filter should not be assumed to be time invariant [1, 3] and the source not to be generated by an *autonomous linear* dynamical system [5-7].

The physiologically more plausible assumption of a *nonlinear* dynamical system [5-7] as underlying voice source does not exclude that *near periodic* motion in the basin of attraction of a stable limit cycle can successfully be approximated by transients of a stable or nearly stable LTI system [3]. However, there is empirical evidence that the complex neural control of the vocal fold dynamics leading to shimmer, jitter and vocal tremor [8] impedes or excludes a low dimensional *autonomous* deterministic description of the phonation process. Being hopelessly irregular from the point of view of acoustics, the time evolution of pitch and loudness (intonation and stress) can partially be given phonological and paralinguistic (emotion related) interpretation [9]. Pitch and loudness of human speech show relevant frequency components up to the range of at least 15 Hz [8]. This invalidates or challenges the *stationary* (stochastic) process description of the voice source.

A physiologically and phonologically more consistent phenomenological description of the aero-acoustics of voiced speech can be achieved by introducing an additional drive-response step, which describes the highly complex wideband acoustic source as *stationary* (primary) response of a *non-stationary*, band-limited fundamental drive process in the frequency range of the pitch [10-13]. The importance, generality and precision of the acoustic percept of pitch can be taken as a first hint that the hidden fundamental drive (FD) can directly be extracted from the speech signal. This leads to a two-level cascaded drive-response model (DR model) of voiced speech production which describes non-stationary acoustic objects of 30-40 ms as stationarily coupled response of a non-stationary hidden FD.

Following common practice the potentially *long transients* of the *secondary* response are simplified by assuming time invariant stable linear response dynamics (resulting from an all pole filter) with a fixed point attractor [1, 3]. (An attractor is an invariant set of states which homes the asymptotic long time behaviour of stationary dynamics [4].) As complementary simplification the *primary* response is assumed to result from a *strongly dissipative* nonlinear response dynamics [4], which generates predominantly *short transients* [5]. The resulting two response levels cannot only be interpreted (more or less erroneously) as source and vocal tract filter output but (more consistently) as two complementarily simplified steps of a cascaded response dynamics [13].

The dissipative primary response dynamics can be simplified drastically by restricting the dynamics to the asymptotic invariant set (which neglects the transient behaviour). Stationary (unidirectionally coupled) DR systems with dissipative responses are known to have invariant sets which represent continuous *synchronization manifolds* (lines or surfaces) in the combined state space of drive and response [14, 15]. Being constrained to a continuous synchronization manifold, the (primary) response can be expressed by a continuous coupling function which describes the momentary state of the response by a unique coupling function of a *response related* state of the (fundamental) drive [10-13]. As a slightly more general synchronization concept, the algebraic relation may be limited to the phases of drive and response. Synchronization of phases or *phase locking* is known to be a generic property of *nonlinearly* coupled DR dynamics [4]. Due to the broader frequency range of the primary response, the coupling function represents a noninvertible (multimodal) function. As an important special case of generalized synchronization an invertible coupling function describes a coupling between two oscillators which are topologically equivalent (behave like a single oscillator). [4, 14]

1.1 History and Role of the Fundamental Drive (FD)

The idea that the higher frequency acoustic modes of voiced speech, song and music as well as the perception of their pitch are causally connected to a single (acoustic) mode in the frequency range of the pitch (*son fundamentale* or fundamental bass), can be traced back to Rameau [16]. However, Seebeck [17] could show that (virtual) pitch perception does not rely on a fundamental acoustic mode which is part of the heard signal. Based on *stationary* voiced signals it has been shown in numerous studies that virtual pitch perception relies on a subband decomposition with harmonically related frequencies of several subbands or part-tones [18, 19]. The present study replaces Rameau's *son fundamentale* by an abstract "order parameter" termed FD which is obtained by using harmonically related part-tones, which can be confirmed as topologically equivalent image of a glottal master oscillator of the voice source [10-13] and which is closely related to an acoustic correlate of *non-stationary* virtual pitch perception.

In preliminary studies the principle feasibility of the receiver side reconstruction of the FD from a voiced speech signal as well as from a simultaneously recorded electro-glottogramme has been demonstrated and compared [10-11]. Inspired by the prevailing interpretation of the function of the cochlea, the extraction of the FD had been based on part-tones with time independent centre filter frequencies (within the current window of analysis). Similar part-tones or sinusoids have also been used in several other studies [18-23]. As will be explained below, the restriction on time invariant filter frequencies leads to part-tones of non-stationary voiced speech, which cannot be expected to be precisely related to respective acoustic modes in the vocal tract of the transmitter.

The introduction of self-consistent filter frequency contours of the part-tone filters opens the option to reconstruct topologically equivalent images of formant specific acoustic modes. The higher frequency formant images are particularly suited to reconstruct the instantaneous frequency of the fundamental drive. Whereas the confirmation of the topological equivalence of the images of formant oscillators is limited to analysis windows of about 30-40 ms, the reconstruction of a coherent FD can be achieved for uninterrupted voiced segments of speech, i.e. for time spans of more than 100 ms [11-13]. The self-consistent FD represents the long time scale part of the basic time scale separation of human acoustic perception which separates the phone or timbre specific fast dynamics from intonation and prosody. Due to the hypothetically unique definition of their centre filter frequencies, filter-stable part-tones of voiced phones are suited for a phase-modulation transmission protocol. The transmission of filter-stable phases gives rise to additional topologically invariant cues of voiced speech which can be expected to be robust under variation of the acoustic communication channel. In contrast to conventional approaches [1, 3], the self-consistent time scale separation does not rely on the assumption of stationary excitation of the vocal tract or a related gap in the relevant time scales (or frequencies) of speech production. It cannot be excluded that the conventional assumption of a frequency gap suppresses important acoustic correlates of emotions being expressed during affective speech.

2 Voice Adapted Part-Tones

It is well known that virtual pitch (and loudness) perception are based on a (subband or) part-tone decomposition [2] and that the band-pass filters of the peripheral auditory pathway can roughly be approximated by Γ-tone filters [24] or more simply by cascaded complex first order autoregressive filters [25].

Cascaded first order filters have the nice property that they can be implemented efficiently as low dimensional linear dynamical systems [25] and can be described analytically by matrix recursion [12-13]. By introducing the autoregressive order Γ and the bandwidth parameters λ_j which are simply related to the part-tone specific equivalent rectangular bandwidths ERB_j ($\lambda_j = \exp(-a_\Gamma ERB_j)$) [25], the output of the (non-normalized) complex bandpass filter of part-tone j is obtained as [12-13].

$$z_{j,t} = \sum_{t'=0}^{t} \exp\left(i \sum_{k=t'+1}^{t} \omega_{j,k}\right) \lambda_j^{t-t'} \frac{(t-t'+\Gamma-1)!}{(\Gamma-1)!(t-t')!} s_{t'} \tag{1}$$

from which the part-tone (carrier) phase is determined as $\varphi_{j,t} = \arctan(im(z_{j,t})/re(z_{j,t}))$. For $j=1,...,N$ the set of (normalized) part-tones can be interpreted as an over-critically sampled time-frequency decomposition of the speech signal s_t, into elementary impulse responses each being separated into complex phase factor and real amplitude. To exclude an *a priori* correlation between neighboring part-tones, the set of centre filter frequency contours $\{\omega_{j,k} | k=0,1,...,t\}$ is chosen in such a way that an oversampling with respect to frequency is avoided. As a rather unconventional assumption, the centre filter frequencies are assumed to be time variant even on the intrinsic time scale of the current window of analysis.

2.1 *A Priori* Knowledge about the Centre Filter Frequencies

The receiver side decomposition of voiced speech can be based on the *a priori* knowledge that the common origin of the transmitter side acoustic modes (the pulsed airflow through the glottis and the nonlinearity of the aero-acoustic dynamics in the vocal tract) leads to a characteristic phase locking of some of these acoustic modes [13]. Since at least the lower frequency transmitter side acoustic modes are well separated in frequency it can be expected that there exists a range of part-tones for which an appropriate adaptation of the centre filter frequencies of their bandpass filters leads to part-tones which are topologically equivalent to the corresponding transmitter side acoustic modes.

The (roughly) audiological choice of the bandwidths of the part-tone filters has the effect that we can distinguish a lower range of part-tone indices $1 \leq j \leq 6$ characterized by guaranteed single harmonic (resolved) part-tones and a range of potentially multiple harmonic (unresolved) part-tones [2]. As a remarkable feature of speech segments, which correspond to nasals or vowels, it is typical that some of the (optimally adapted) part-tones in the (a priori) unresolved frequency range are also dominated by a single harmonic acoustic mode. The instantaneous frequency contours of at least a subset of the part-tones of a voiced speech signal can thus be expected to be centered around rational multiples of the frequency contour of the glottal oscillator. Other a posteriori resolved part-tones can be expected to have minor phase shifts which are consistent with formant specific resonance properties of a stationarily coupled secondary response. Excluding for a moment the so called diplophonic voice type [8], it is typical for voiced signals that there exists a fundamental phase velocity $\dot{\varphi}_0$ for which the winding number ratios of some of the part-tone phase velocities to $\dot{\varphi}_0$ simplify to an integer harmonic number h_j. For stationary voiced signals the latter feature can be detected by using the harmonic frequency template introduced by Goldstein [19] or the subharmonic coincidence cluster of Terhardt [18].

For non-stationary voiced signals the detection of a strict $(n : n')$ synchronization of the phases of *a priori* independent part-tone pairs (with non-overlapping spectral bands) represents a phenomenon, which has a low probability to happen by chance. For such part-tone pairs it can therefore be assumed that there exists an uninterrupted causal link between those part-tones, including the only plausible case of two uninterrupted causal links to a common drive, which can be identified as a formant specific acoustic mode and/or as the glottal master oscillator. Since the $(n : n')$ phase-locking with $n \neq n'$ is generated by the *nonlinear* coupling to the glottal oscillator, a stable synchronization of *a priori* independent part-tone phases can be taken as a confirmation of topological equivalence between these part-tones and respective acoustic modes in the vocal tract of the transmitter. The topologically equivalent part-tones with higher frequency (in particular the ones of the 3. formant) are particularly suited to reconstruct the FD which is interpreted as topologically equivalent image of the glottal master oscillator.

2.2 Time-Frequency Atoms with Time Variant Frequency

The impulse responses of equation (1) can be simplified by introducing a logarithmic expansion around the maximum of the amplitude of the impulse response at $t = t' - \tau_j$.

For higher Γ-orders a second order expansion of the exponent (Gaussian approximation) is well suited to approximate the impulse response. To be consistent with the second order expansion of the real part, the imaginary part of the exponent should also include in general a second order term. Following ideas of Gabor [26] such Gaussian wave packets

$$S_G(t) = \frac{1}{\sqrt{2\pi\sigma^2}}\exp(i\omega_0 t\,(1+c/2t) - \frac{1}{2\sigma^2}(t-t'+\tau_j)^2) \qquad (2a)$$

represent time-frequency atoms (TFA) which are optimally suited to describe simultaneously event (particle) and wave type properties of non-stationary wave processes. Contrary to the conventional one [26], this parametric set of non-stationary time-frequency atoms is characterized by a linear trend of the phase velocity with a non-zero relative chirp c

$$\omega_{0,t} \;=\; \omega_0\,(1+c\,t) \tag{2b}$$

Numerous subband or part-tone decompositions of speech signals, like the ones introduced by McAuley and Quatieri [22], Terhardt [18, 23] and all wavelet decompositions [3], are based on the additional assumption that the phase velocities (instantaneous frequencies) of the impulse responses (time-frequency atoms) are constant within the extent of the time-frequency atom or of the current window of analysis.

The zero chirp assumption is conventionally used to obtain orthogonal time-frequency atoms, which have the advantage that their squared amplitude can be interpreted in terms of a time-frequency energy distribution [3]. The time variable centre filter frequencies of the present approach, however, have the alternative advantage that the part-tones can be generated as topologically equivalent images of physically interpretable underlying (non-stationary) acoustic modes. The choice of a high Γ order ($\Gamma = 5$ in the present study) guarantees a maximal time resolution which is compatible with a frequency resolution which is necessary to isolate a sufficient number of part-tones to confirm their topological equivalence to the underlying acoustic modes.

In view of the important phonological (and paralinguistic) role of non-stationary pitch fluctuations of voiced speech within human speech communication (and in view of the well known efferent enervation of the outer hear cells of the cochlea), it is plausible to assume that speech perception is based on a decomposition into (near optimal) time-frequency atoms with a *non-stationary* (time variant) instantaneous frequency as described in equation (1). As indicated in equations (2a, 2b) a near optimal (perception equivalent) analysis of non-stationary speech signals can only be achieved with centre filter frequency contours with an at least linear trend of the phase velocity within the current window of analysis.

2.3 Self-consistent Centre Filter Frequencies

For a constant amplitude input $S_t \;=\; A\exp(i\sum_{k=0}^{t}\omega_k')$ with arbitrary instantaneous frequency $\omega_k'/2\pi$ and a centre filter frequency $\omega_k/2\pi$ chosen as identical to the instantaneous frequency, the application of bandpass filter (1) generates the output

$$Z_t \;=\; A\,\exp(i\sum_{k=0}^{t}\omega_k')\;\sum_{t'=0}^{t}\lambda^{t-t'}\,\frac{(t-t'+\Gamma-1)!}{(\Gamma-1)!\,(t-t')!} \tag{3}$$

with a phase velocity which is identical to the one of the input signal. In the limit $t \to \infty$ the sum in equation (3) represents an asymptotic gain factor $g_{j,\Gamma}$. Being exclusively dependent on the bandwidth parameter λ_j and the Γ order, the gain factors can be used to obtain the (normalized) part-tone amplitudes $a_{j,t} = |z_{j,t}| / g_{j,\Gamma}$.

For a given filter frequency contour $\{\omega_k | k = 0,1,...,t\}$, input signals with $\omega'_k \neq \omega_k$ experience a damping due to interference of the phase factors. For a given input frequency contour, other filter frequency contours generate a phase distortion of the filter output. For sufficiently small distortions of the filter frequency contour, the corresponding instantaneous frequency distortions are smaller than the (preliminary) deviation of the filter frequency contour. The latter (contractive) feature represents a characteristic feature of voiced phones. It motivates an iterative approach to determine optimally adapted (self-consistent) centre filter frequencies.

With the help of a simple example it will be demonstrated that the iterative replacement of the filter frequency contour by a smoothed instantaneous frequency contour of the part-tone outputs can be used to obtain stable bandpass filters whose centre filter frequency contour is identical to the instantaneous frequency contour of the respective filter output and thus also to obtain an instantaneous output frequency which is identical to the one of the respective (dominant) input. Due to this *self-consistency* such filter-stable part-tones are suited to transmit phase-modulation cues to the receiver of a speech signal.

It is well known that human auditive perception is not limited to the frequency range of separable part-tones and that the amplitudes (envelopes) of the higher frequency subbands show a modulation in the frequency range of the pitch [2, 18, 20, 24]. It is therefore plausible to extend the analysis of part-tone phases to phases, which can be derived from the envelopes of the part-tones. Being used preferentially for part-tones in the unresolved frequency range, the envelope phases are determined e.g. as Hilbert phases of appropriately highpass filtered, scaled and smoothed [18-21, 24] modulation amplitudes $a_{j,t}$ of the part-tones. The relative importance of the envelope phases is expected to increase, when the voice source changes from a modal (ideal) voice to a more breathy one.

3 Stable Part-Tones of a Pulsed Excitation

To demonstrate the generation of self-consistent part-tones of a non-stationary voiced acoustic object, a sequence of synthetic glottal pulses with a chirped instantaneous frequency is chosen as example. For simplicity the input pulses are chosen as constant amplitude saw teeth with a power spectrum, which is roughly similar to the one of the glottal excitation. The pulse shape is described by a coupling function of the form

$$G(\psi'_t) = \min(\mod(\psi'_t, 2\pi), s(2\pi - \mod(\psi'_t, 2\pi))) . \tag{4}$$

where ψ'_t represents the instantaneous phase of the fundamental drive. The parameter s (chosen to be 6) determines the ratio of the modulus of the downhill slope of the glottal pulses to the uphill one. The chirp of the glottal oscillator is described by a time dependent phase velocity $\omega'(t) = \psi'(t)$ which is chosen in analogy to equation

(2b), however, with potentially different chirp rate c' and initial phase velocity ω_0'. The fundamental phase ψ' is obtained by integrating the analogue of equation (2b) with respect to time t (replacing index k)

$$\psi'(t) = \omega_0'(t + c' t^2 / 2) \tag{5}$$

3.1 Time Scale Separation

In the situation of signal analysis, the filter-frequency contour of the bandpass filter of part-tone j has to be adapted algorithmically to the frequency contour of a suitable input process. As a characteristic feature of voiced signals this can be done iteratively by adapting the filter frequency contour to the respective part-tone output, starting from an appropriate initial filter frequency contour. For reasons of algorithmic stability it is advantageous to incorporate the *a priori* knowledge that the reconstructed frequency contour has a minimal degree of smoothness. In accordance to chapter 2.2 the smoothing step of each iteration is based on the assumption that the frequency contour can be approximated (within the current analysis window) by a linear trend (chirp) as described in equation (2b). To reduce the dependence of the estimated parameters on the size and position of the window of analysis (and/or to avoid the adaptation of the window length to the "instantaneous period length"), the linear trend ansatz is extended by a 2π periodic function $P_j(\varphi_{j,t} / h_j)$ of the respective normalized part-tone phase

$$\dot{\varphi}_{j,t} / h_j = \alpha_j t + P_j(\varphi_{j,t} / h_j) \ . \tag{6}$$

The 2π periodic function $P_j(\varphi)$ accounts for the oscillations of the part-tone phase velocity around the long term trend which result from the characteristic auto phase-locking. The oscillations can be assumed to be periodic with respect to the formant- or part-tone specific fundamental (normalized) phase and can therefore be approximated by an appropriate finite order Fourier series. The Fourier coefficients as well as the trend parameter α_j of time-scale separation ansatz (6) are obtained by multiple linear regression.

3.2 Graphical Adaptation of the Filter Chirp

With the exception of the first analysis window within a voiced segment of speech, the start value $\omega_{j,0}$ of the linear filter frequency contour can be assumed to be given as result of the adaptation of the filter chirp of the preceding analysis window. As a first step, we may therefore treat the latter parameter as given ($\omega_{j,0} = h_j \omega_0'$). In this situation the adaptation of the chirp parameter can be explained by a graph, which shows the trend parameter α_j of equation (6) for several part-tone indices j as function of the common filter chirp rate c. To make figure 1 suited for the graphical analysis it gives the estimates of the relative trend $\alpha_j / (\omega_0' c')$ for the indices $j = 2, 4, 6, 9$ (corresponding to the sequence of the fixed points from bottom to top) as function of the relative filter chirp rate c/c'. All chirp rates are given relative to the chirp rate of the input sawtooth process defined in equations (4, 5).

The adaptation of the chirp parameter of each filter-frequency contour can be read off from figure 1 by an iteration of two geometric steps: Project horizontally from one of the described curves to the diagonal of the first quadrant (which indicates the line where the fixed points of any iteration are situated) and project vertically down (or up) to the curve again. As can be seen from figure 1, the chirp parameters of all four part-tones have a stable fixed point (equilibrium) within a well extended basin of attraction of the chirp parameter. The fixed points indicate the final error of the filter chirp. Due to the simple least squares regression of equation (6), the modulus of the trend is systematically underestimated.

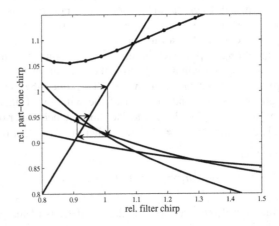

Fig. 1. Estimated relative part-tone chirp rates as function of the relative chirp rate of the centre filter frequentcies, given for the envelope phase of part-tone 9 (circles) and the three carrier phases of part-tones 2, 4, 6

The extended basins of attraction of the filter adaptation processes of figure 1 are not at all typical for the more general situation characterized by $\omega_{j,0} \neq h_j \omega_0'$ and by more complex voice sources. In general we have to expect the coexistence of different basins of attraction of the filter adaptation process. The stability regions of $\omega_{j,0}$ become necessarily smaller for higher part-tone indices. The number of stable fixed points with a macroscopic basin of attraction depends on the width of the power spectrum (or on the steepness parameter s of the slope) of the glottal pulse. Resonances of the secondary response are suited to enlarge the basin of attraction of the respective part-tones.

3.3 Circle Maps Relating Part-Tone Phases

The mutual phase locking of the self-consistently reconstructed part-tones is shown in figure 2. It demonstrates that the precision of reconstructed synchronization manifolds is hardly influenced by the deficient estimate of the filter chirp. The top row shows synchronization manifolds in the state space spanned by the part-tones 5 or 6 (being indicated on the ordinate) and a fundamental drive (being indicated on the ordinate). The perfectly linear one dimensional manifolds are obtained by showing the projections in the direction of the respective phases. The fundamental phase (with arbitrary initial phase) has been derived from the velocity of the carrier phase of part-tone 4. Care has been taken that the wrapping of all phases happens simultaneously. The bottom row shows the corresponding phase diagrams for the *envelope* phases of the part-tones 6 and 7.

In case of the circle maps, which relate exclusively carrier phases (top row), the phase relations are precisely time invariant and result in precisely linear synchronization manifolds. In case of circle maps which relate mixed type phases (bottom row), the time invariance is achieved only approximately (by an open loop group delay correction) and the circle maps become curved, the shape being dependent on the mentioned smoothing and sublinear scaling of the modulation amplitudes [18-21, 24]. When appropriately smoothed, the envelope phases are suited to be included into the cluster analysis of the phase velocity contours and potentially also to be used for a rough estimate of the phase velocity of the FD. They are, however, less suited for the precise reconstruction of the fundamental phase over an extended voiced speech segment. The more strict relation between the carrier phases is obviously advantageous for the precise adaptation and selection of the part-tone filters. The importance of an operational description of the adaptation of the centre filter frequencies to a specific voice and in particular the special role of the carrier phases of the *a posteriori* resolvable part-tones for a precise adaptation appear to have been underestimated by conventional psychoacoustics [2, 24].

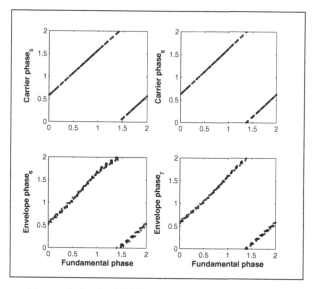

Fig. 2. Circle maps (phase relations) of different part-tone phases which are more or less suited to retrace the causal connection to the fundamental drive. Both carrier phases are harmonically normalized. All phases are given in units of π.

4 Multi Part-Tone Stable Acoustic Objects

It is well known that human pitch perception can be trained to switch between analytic listening to spectral pitch and synthetic listening to virtual pitch [2, 18]. It is plausible to interprete the described single part-tone stable acoustic objects with a macroscopic basin of attraction of the filter frequency contour (parameters) and with formant type underlying acoustic modes as potential candidates of *spectral* pitch perception. From psychoacoustic experiments it is also known that *virtual* pitch is a more universal and robust percept than spectral pitch [2, 18]. Due to the characteristic auto phase-locking mechanisms of voiced speech it is plausible that an observed (carrier or envelope) phase velocity of one part-tone might be used to adjust the centre filter frequency of other part-tones. This encourages the introduction of a more robust multi part-tone adaptation strategy.

4.1 Definition

In analogy to the single part-tone stability of the last section we define multi part-tone stability of an acoustic object by the existence of a common fundamental phase velocity contour which can be obtained as stable invariant set (fixed point) of the iteration of four cascaded mappings, where the first mapping relates a preliminary fundamental phase velocity contour to a set of filter-frequency contours, the second mapping uses the set of filter-frequency contours to generate a corresponding set of part-tone phase velocity contours, the third mapping executes the smoothing step and the forth mapping uses a subset of the smoothed part-tone phase velocity contours to update the fundamental phase velocity contour. The first mapping makes use of the fact that optimally adapted centre filter frequency contours of at least a subset of the part-tones can be assumed as winding number multiples of the frequency contour of the common drive ($\omega_{j,k} = h_j \, \omega_{0,k}$ with integer or small denominator rational h_j). The second mapping uses filter (1), the third mapping refers to the estimation of time scale separation (6) and the fourth mapping uses some kind of cluster analysis to identify a mutually consistent set of winding number normalized part-tone phase velocity contours $\{\dot{\varphi}_{j,k} / h_j \mid k = 0,1,....,t\}$ which are suited to reconstruct the phase velocity of the common drive.

As indicated above, the existence of a cluster of at least three mutually phase locked part-tones can be interpreted as a confirmation of topological equivalence of the respective part-tones to underlying acoustic modes in the vocal tract of the transmitter being synchronized to a common formant- or glottal oscillator. However, this confirmation relies on the *a priori* independence of those part-tones. It is therefore essential that the set of centre filter frequencies (of the part-tones taking part in the cluster analysis) is pruned in the non-resolvable frequency range of the part-tone decomposition. On the other hand it is allowed that single part-tones enter the cluster analysis with different hypothetical harmonic numbers (winding numbers) being used to normalize the part-tone phases. A typical cluster analysis might result in the following set of harmonic numbers $\{h_j\} = \{1,2,...,6,8,10,12,15,...\}$.

4.2 Relation to EMD and to the Perception of Virtual Pitch

In spite of the rather different generation mechanism, the described filter-stable part-tone decomposition has some similarity to the empirical mode decomposition being introduced by Huang et al. [27] and being applied to speech signals as part of the present volume [28]. Both decompositions are aimed at the extraction of intrinsic modes from strongly non-stationary signals. The present approach might be interpreted as an intrinsic mode decomposition which has been evolutionarily optimized for the analysis of voiced speech. For such signals the lower-harmonic filter-stable part-tones are optimally chosen to reconstruct topologically equivalent images of underlying physical modes. The topological equivalence of filter stable part-tones gives a more solid basis for the physical interpretation of the intrinsic modes. Due to their focus on the precise reconstruction of the instantaneous phase velocity, the topologically equivalent part-tones are better suited for the hypothetically relevant phase-modulation transmission protocol of voiced speech.

The indicated reconstruction of the phase velocity of the FD has been based on the assumption that virtual pitch perception plays the role of a near optimal instrument of basic causality analysis of a voiced signal. Virtual pitch perception of stationary signals has long been studied empirically and theoretically [18, 19]. In particular it has been established that the respective acoustic correlate depends not only on the phase velocities of the part-tones but also on their amplitudes. A corresponding modification of the fourth (cluster analysis) step of the iteration procedure can be expected to improve the robustness of the reconstruction of the fundamental phase.

The multi part-tone adaptation is also expected to be complicated by co-existence of different basins of attraction of the filter parameters. Apart from the octave ambiguity, different basins of attraction should now be interpreted in terms of different voice sources. More precisely, the choice of different start positions in different basins of attraction should correspond to an attention switching between different hypothetical voice sources as part of an auditory scene. The parameters of a perception equivalent acoustic correlate of non-stationary pitch should therefore also be chosen in view of numerous (psycho-acoustic) results from (monotic) auditory scene analysis.

4.3 Reconstruction of the Fundamental Drive

As a further remarkable feature of the unexpectedly subtle voice transmission protocol, the reconstruction of the phase velocity of the formant type acoustic modes and/or the FD can typically be achieved for considerably larger speech segments than the one being used for the described confirmation of topological equivalence between part-tones and respective acoustic modes of the vocal tract. Whereas the piecewise detection of phase synchronization clusters is preferentially performed in a time window of about 30 – 40 ms, the reconstruction of a coherent (continuous) fundamental phase can hypothetically be achieved for time segments, which corres-pond to an uninterrupted voiced segment of a syllable, i.e. for a time span of typically more than 100 ms [1, 21]. For voiced segments, which are composed of different phonemes, it is typical that the set of part-tones being used for the piecewise reconstruction of the phase velocity contour of the common drive changes in succeeding analysis windows.

According to a comparatively strict phonological rule [9], uninterrupted voiced segments of speech contain one vowel nucleus which carries the main accent of the sylable. This nucleus can be used to gauge the (wrapped up) fundamental phase with respect to the glottal closure event and can thus be used to remove the arbitrariness of the initial phase of the FD of a voiced segment. In fact it turns out that a high time resolution building block of the acoustic correlate of loudness perception is well suited to calibrate the wrapped up fundamental phase with respect to the glottal closure event [13].

The coherent reconstruction of the fundamental phase turns out to be particularly useful for the analysis and synthesis of sustainable voiced consonants. For the acoustic correlates of the latter phones the simple source-filter interpretation in terms of a plane wave source in an unbranched vocal tract looses its validity and the non-linearity of the aero-acoustic dynamics becomes more apparent [5-7]. Nasals are characterized by a sudden apparent time or fundamental phase shift of the glottal closure event induced pulse (due to a sudden increase of the group delay of the acoustic transmission path from the glottis to the receiver) [20, 21]. Voiced fricatives (as the English /z/ like in "zoom") are characterized by an acoustic source in the vicinity of a second constriction of the vocal tract, which generates an intermittently turbulent jet. The conversion of the kinetic energy of this pulsatile jet into acoustic energy (e.g. at the edge of the teeth) happens with a characteristic time delay, which results from the comparatively slow subsonic convection speed of the relevant jet [7]. The phoneme specific time shift of the second acoustic source with respect to the glottal closure event generates phase shifts of the instantaneous part-tone phases which are no longer explicable by resonances of a stationarily coupled secondary response. Such excessive phase shifts can be interpreted as further examples of topological invariants of voiced speech which are comparatively insensitive to variations of the acoustic communication channel.

Once the fundamental phase of a NAO has been reconstructed with the help of filter-stable part-tones, two different paths can be chosen to continue the analysis of NAOs. If the aim is given as a complete analysis, (optional transformation) and re-synthesis cycle there is probably no other choice than to determine also the amplitude of the FD and to estimate the parameters of the initially indicated two-level cascaded drive-response model with a given FD and a largely general fundamental phase triggered primary response. As has been explained elsewhere [13], the reconstruction of the fundamental amplitude can be based on the assumption that loudness perception plays the role of a complementary instrument of causality analysis [10-13].

4.4 Phase Related Acoustic Cues

However, if the aim is restricted to the *analysis* of a voiced signal (like in the case of the auditive pathway) the detailed knowledge of the filter-stable part-tones can directly be used to determine a favourable acoustic feature vector of voiced speech. The main idea of this shortcut is that the frequency dependent resonant amplification or damping of the acoustic modes during the passage trough the vocal tract cannot only be analysed by looking at the *amplitudes* of the different part-tones or formants but more directly by looking at their characteristic phase shifts. In case of a resonant amplification, the phase of the part-tone response lags the one of the excitation and precedes it in case of a resonant damping. As a second advantage of the phase related cues, the magnitude of the phase shifts are proportional to the time derivative of the corresponding amplitudes which is known to play a major role in the acoustic feature vector of conventional speech recognition [1].

The phase related acoustic cues are in open conflict to the conventional psycho-acoustic theory originating from Ohm and Helmholtz, which states that the *amplitudes* of subbands represent the primary acoustic cues [2, 24]. To explain the superior communication channel insensitivity of human acoustic perception (and the efferent enervation of the cochlea) it is hypothesized that the deviations of the carrier phases of self-consistently determined part-tones from the synchronization manifold of the ideal δ-function type pulsed excitation (triggered by a vowel nucleus anchored fundamental phase) have a comparable or higher relevance for acoustic perception than the corresponding amplitudes [20]. In particular it is expected that the rational winding numbers of self-consistently determined part-tones and the phone specific fundamental phase shifts of the receiver side reconstruction of the glottis induced pulses of nasals and other sustainable voiced consonants represent favorable cues which are suited to improve the distinction of the speakers as well as of their (hypothetically intended) voiced phonemes [13].

In this context it is important to remind that many phones are so far defined exclusively by human perception of minimal differences between syllables. Whereas vowels can alternatively be defined acoustically using the LTI model, this does not apply to many of the non-vocalic voiced continuants like nasals and sustainable voiced fricatives. For these phones the shift of the glottal closure event induced pulses with respect to the (wrapped up) fundamental phase generates a phone specific long range correlation or "co-articulation effect" which cannot be described by using a single LTI model. Together with the gliding part-tone coordination of the glides, such phones can only be described by NAOs with non-stationarily coupled responses. As doubly non-stationary NAOs the acoustic correlates of such "elementary" phones belong to the same complexity class as voiced syllables. From the point of view of acoustics either singly non-stationary acoustic objects which are consistent with a stationarily coupled response cascade or doubly non-stationary acoustic objects, which are suited to represent complete voiced sections of syllables, appear as the more natural atoms of voiced speech.

5 Conclusion

A transmission protocol of non-stationary voiced acoustic objects is outlined, which are generated as response of a non-stationary fundamental drive and which can be analysed as a superposition of time-frequency atoms with non-stationary, partially phase-synchronized instantaneous frequencies. For sustained voiced phones the partially synchronized set of time-frequency atoms can be extracted by part-tone filters with centre frequency contours which are iteratively adapted to the instantaneous frequencies of the respective part-tones (filter outputs). Sets of mutually phase synchronized filter-stable part-tones can be interpreted as topologically equivalent images of underlying acoustic modes of the transmitter and are thus suited for the reconstruction of the phase velocity of the FD. The latter properties qualify the non-stationary, part-tone stable (voiced) acoustic objects as most elementary atoms (symbols) of a voice transmission protocol being characterized by a time-scale separation which offers a precise and robust decoding option.

The minimal acoustic description of the phone specific "co-articulation effects" of sustainable voiced fricatives and nasals requires doubly non-stationary voiced acoustic objects which do not only result from a non-stationary fundamental drive but also from a non-stationary coupling of the primary and/or secondary response. The incorporation of appropriate acoustic cues, suited to describe these "co-articulation effects", into present day automatic speech recognition (LTI cue based discrete Hidden state Markov Models) represents a non-trivial task.

Acknowledgements

The author would like to thank M. Kob, B. Kröger, C. Neuschaefer-Rube and R. Schlüter, Aachen, J. Schoentgen, Brussels, A. Lacriox and K. Schnell, Frankfurt and M. Schiek and K. Ziemons, Jülich for helpful discussions.

References

1. Gold, B., Morgan, N.: Speech and audio signal processing. John Wiley & Sons, Chichester (2000)
2. Moore, B.C.J.: An introduction to the psychology of hearing. Academic Press, London (1989)
3. Rabiner, L.R., Schafer, R.W.: Digital Processing of Speech Signals. Prentice Hall, NJ, Englewood Cliffs (1978)
4. Kantz, H., Schreiber, T.: Nonlinear time series analysis. Cambridge Univ. Press, Cambridge (1997)
5. Herzel, H., Berry, D., Titze, I.R., Saleh, M.: Analysis of vocal disorders with methods from nonlinear dynamics. J. Speech Hear. Res. 37, 1008–1019 (1994)
6. Teager, H.M., Teager, S.M.: Evidence for nonlinear sound production in the vocal tract. In: Proc NATO ASI on Speech Production and Speech Modelling, pp. 241–261 (1990)
7. Jackson, P.J.B., Shadle, C.H.: Pitch scaled estimation of simultaneous voiced and turbulent-noise components in speech. IEEE trans. speech audio process 9, 713–726 (2001)
8. Schoentgen, J.: Stochastic models of jitter. J. Acoust. Soc. Am. 109(4), 1631–1650 (2001)
9. Grice, M.: Intonation. In: Brown, K. (ed.) Encyclopedia of Language and Linguistics, vol. 5, Elsevier, Oxford (2006)
10. Drepper, F.R.: A two-level drive-response model of non-stationary speech signals. In: Faundez-Zanuy, M., Janer, L., Esposito, A., Satue-Villar, A., Roure, J., Espinosa-Duro, V. (eds.) NOLISP 2005. LNCS (LNAI), vol. 3817, pp. 125–138. Springer, Heidelberg (2006)
11. Drepper, F.R.: Voiced excitation as entrained primary response of a reconstructed glottal master oscillator. In: Interspeech 2005, Lisboa, pp. 329–332 (2005)
12. Drepper, F.R.: Fortschritte der Akustik-DAGA 2006 (2006)
13. Drepper, F.R.: Voiced speech as response of a self-consistent fundamental drive. Speech Comm. 49, 186–200 (2007)
14. Rulkov, N.F., Sushchik, M.M., Tsimring, L.S., Abarbanel, H.D.I.:Generalized synchronization of chaos in directionally coupled systems. Phys. Rev. E 51, 980–994 (1995)

15. Afraimovich, V.S., Verichev, N.N., Rabinovich, M.I.: Stochastic synchronization of oscillation in dissipative systems. Radiophys. Quantum Electron. 29, 795 (1986)
16. Rameau, J.-P.: Generation harmonique. In: Jacobi, E. (ed.) Complete Theoretical Writings, vol. 3, American Institute of Musicology (1967)
17. Seebeck, A.: Über die Definition des Tones. Poggendorf's Annalen der Physik und Chemie LXIII, 353–368 (1844)
18. Terhardt, E., Stoll, G., Seewann, M.: Algorithm for extraction of pitch and pitch salience from complex tonal signals. J. Acoust. Soc. Am. 71, 679–688 (1982)
19. Goldstein, J.: An optimum processor theory for the central formation of the pitch of complex tones. J. Acoust. Soc. Am. 54, 1496–1516 (1973)
20. Paliwal, K.K., Atal, B.S.: Frequency-related representation of speech. In: Eurospeech 2003, Genf (2003)
21. Kawahara, H., Katayose, H., de Cheveigné, A., Patterson, R.: Fixed point analysis of frequency to instantaneous frequency mapping. EuroSpeech 99, 2781–2784 (1999)
22. McAulay, R., Quatieri, T.: Speech analysis/synthesis based on a sinusoidal representation. IEEE Trans. Acoust. Speech a. Signal Proc. ASSP 34(4), 744–754 (1986)
23. Heinbach, W.: Aurally adequate signal representation: The part-tone-time-pattern. Acustica 67, 113–121 (1988)
24. Patterson, R.D.: Auditory images: How complex sounds are represented in the auditory system. J. Acoust. Soc. Jpn (E) 21, 4 (2000)
25. Hohmann, V.: Frequency analysis and synthesis using a gammatone filterbank. Acta Acustica 10, 433–442 (2002)
26. Gabor, D.: Acoustic quanta and the theory of hearing. Nature 159, 591–594 (1947)
27. Huang, N.E., Shen, Z., Long, S.R., Wu, M.C., Shih, H., Zheng, Q., Yen, N.-C., Tung, C.C., Liu, H.H.: The empirical mode decomposition and the Hilbert spectrum for nonlinear and non-stationary time series analysis. Proc. R. Soc. Lond. A 454, 903–995 (1998)
28. Bouzid, A., Ellouze, N.: EMD analysis of speech signal in voiced mode. In: M. Chetouani et al. (Eds.): NOLISP 2007, LNAI 4885 (2007)

The Hartley Phase Cepstrum as a Tool
for Signal Analysis

Ioannis Paraskevas[1] and Maria Rangoussi[2]

[1] Centre for Vision Speech and Signal Processing (CVSSP),
School of Electronics and physical Sciences, University of Surrey,
Guildford GU2 7XH, Surrey, UK
paraskevas@env.aegean.gr
[2] Department of Electronics, Technological Education Institute of Piraeus,
250, Thivon str., Aigaleo-Athens, GR-12244, Greece
mariar@teipir.gr

Abstract. This paper proposes the use of the Hartley Phase Cepstrum as a tool for speech signal analysis. The phase of a signal conveys critical information, which is exploited in a variety of applications. The role of phase is particularly important for speech or audio signals. Accurate phase information extraction is a prerequisite for speech applications such as coding, synchronization, synthesis or recognition. However, signal phase extraction is not a straightforward procedure, mainly due to the discontinuities appearing in it (phase 'wrapping' effect). Several phase 'unwrapping' algorithms have been proposed to overcome this point, when extraction of the accurate phase values is required. In order to extract the phase content of a signal for subsequent utilization, it is necessary to choose a function that can efficiently encapsulate it. In this paper, through comparison of three alternative non-linear phase features, we propose the use of the Hartley Phase Cepstrum (HPC).

Keywords: Fourier Phase Cepstrum, Hartley Phase Cepstrum, Speech signal phase, Phase unwrapping algorithm.

1 Introduction

The phase of a signal as a function of frequency conveys meaningful information that is particularly useful for speech or audio signals. Accurate phase extraction is crucial in various speech processing applications, such as localization, synchronization, coding, etc. The major disadvantage of the computation of the phase spectrum via the Fourier transform is the heuristics employed for the compensation of the 'extrinsic' discontinuities arising in it (phase 'wrapping' ambiguities). The effect of these 'wrapping' ambiguities is more severe in the presence of additive noise. The phase spectrum obtained via the Hartley transform, on the other hand, is advantageous as (a) it does not exhibit 'extrinsic' discontinuities and (b) due to its structure, it is less affected by the presence of noise, as justified through comparison of the shapes of the respective probability distribution functions, [1].

M. Chetouani et al. (Eds.): NOLISP 2007, LNAI 4885, pp. 204–212, 2007.

As signal localization applications show, the phase content of a signal is more efficiently encapsulated in the Hartley Phase Cepstrum (HPC) rather than in the Fourier Phase Cepstrum (FPC) function. Interesting advantages of the HPC, such as localization capability and robustness to noise, are based on the properties of the respective spectra, which carry over to the cepstral domain thanks to the analytic relations holding between the two domains. As it will be presented in the following sections, the limited localization capability of the FPC as compared to the HPC is due to the ambiguities introduced by the use of the 'unwrapping' algorithm. The HPC advantage is preserved in the presence of additive noise, [1].

Another property of the HPC, of interest in speech synthesis, is its invertibility: the non-linear process for the evaluation of the HPC is invertible, because no phase 'unwrapping' algorithm is necessary.

Aiming towards a phase feature appropriate for accurate (noisy) signal localization, we examine here three alternatives, namely the FPC, the whitened FPC and the HPC. In conclusion, the HPC is proposed as a promising and viable substitute to its Fourier counterpart.

2   The Phase Cepstrum

In general, computation of the cepstrum of a discrete-time signal $x(n)$ belongs to a class of methods known as homomorphic deconvolution processes, [2]. The block diagram of such a process is given in Fig. 1:

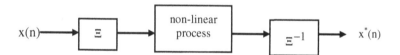

Fig. 1. Summary of the homomorphic deconvolution process

It is an invertible procedure, in which the signal $x(n)$ is transformed into another domain via an orthogonal transform Ξ, a non-linear process is applied to the transformed signal in the new domain, and the result is transformed back to the original domain, via the inverse transform, Ξ^{-1}. Discontinuities arising from the application of the non-linear processing step have to be compensated before the inverse transform Ξ^{-1} is applied. In the following paragraphs we will examine three alternative phase features produced by homomorphic deconvolution process, using either the Fourier or the Hartley direct and inverse transforms and phase computation as the non-linear step.

2.1   The Fourier Phase Cepstrum

If Ξ and Ξ^{-1} in figure 1 represent the Discrete-Time Fourier Transform (DTFT) and the Inverse Discrete-Time Fourier Transform (IDTFT), respectively, while the non-linear processing step is the evaluation of the Fourier phase spectrum,

$$\varphi(\omega) = \arctan\left(\frac{\Im(S(\omega))}{\Re(S(\omega))}\right) \tag{1}$$

where $\Re(S(\omega))$ and $\Im(S(\omega))$ are the real and imaginary components of the Fourier transform $S(\omega)$ of the signal $s(n)$, respectively, then we obtain the so-called Fourier Phase Cepstrum (FPC), $c_F(\tau)$:

$$c_F(\tau) = IDTFT(\varphi(\omega)) \tag{2}$$

The Fourier Phase Spectrum (FPS) $\varphi(\omega)$ experiences two types of discontinuities:

1. The first type, called 'extrinsic', is due to the use of the *arctan* function employed in equation (1) and is overcome using a phase 'unwrapping' algorithm, [3]. This step is necessary in order to apply the IDTFT and obtain the FPC. However, the heuristics involved in the extrinsic discontinuities unwrapping algorithm render the non-linear step non-invertible. This results in loss of the signal localization capability of the FPC, regardless of the SNR level. Indeed, experiments carried out on (noisy) synthetic signals containing one or more pulses, show that the FPC suffers loss of its signal localization capability, except for the ideal case of just one noise-free pulse (figure 2).
2. The second type of discontinuities, called 'intrinsic', originates from the spectral properties of the signal itself and is overcome by appropriate compensation algorithms, [4], [5].

2.2 The 'Whitened' Fourier Phase Cepstrum

An alternative for signal phase extraction, proposed among others in [6], is the use of the 'whitened' – rather than the conventional – Fourier (phase) spectrum in equation (1). The 'whitened' Fourier spectrum is implemented, by dividing the complex Fourier spectrum by its magnitude, for each frequency point:

$$WF(\omega) = \frac{S(\omega)}{\sqrt{\Re^2(S(\omega)) + \Im^2(S(\omega))}} \tag{3}$$

Consequently, the 'Whitened' Fourier Phase Cepstrum (WFPC) is obtained by evaluating the IDTFT of the 'whitened' Fourier spectrum, which is a complex quantity, by equation (3).

The advantage of whitening of the Fourier spectrum is that it yields the phase content of a signal without using the *arctan* function and therefore without any 'extrinsic' discontinuities (i.e., no 'wrapping' ambiguities arise). However, as to its 'intrinsic' discontinuities – still present due to the spectral properties of the signal – and due to the very same reason, there is no known method to overcome them, such as, e.g., adding / subtracting π (conventional FPS), or multiplying by -1 (HPS), [8].

2.3 The Hartley Phase Cepstrum

If in figure 1 we employ (i) the Discrete-Time Hartley Transform (DTHT), (ii) the evaluation of the Hartley Phase Spectrum [7], [8]:

$$Y(\omega) = \cos(\varphi(\omega)) + \sin(\varphi(\omega)) \tag{4}$$

and (iii) the Inverse Discrete-Time Hartley Transform (IDTHT), we then obtain the Hartley Phase Cepstrum (HPC), defined as:

$$c_H(\tau) = IDTHT(Y(\omega)) \tag{5}$$

The HPS $Y(\omega)$ of equation (4), unlike the conventional FPS $\varphi(\omega)$ of equation (1), does not need 'unwrapping' and hence, it does not suffer from the 'wrapping' ambiguities. Moreover, for the Hartley case, the homomorphic deconvolution process is invertible, since the 'unwrapping' algorithm is not used. The HPS experiences only the 'intrinsic' type of discontinuities, which can be compensated as in [8].

3 Comparison of the Three Alternative Cepstra on Synthetic Signals

In order to illustrate the relative merits of the two alternative cepstral phase features defined earlier (the WFPC is not considered after the comments in section 2.2), three signal cases are employed in this section, namely:

1. a single rectangular pulse signal (noise-free and noisy),
2. a sequence of five exponentially dumped sinusoidal pulses,
3. a sequence of rectangular pulses of varying widths and amplitudes, simulating a transmitter-receiver scenario.

Figure 2 (a) shows the location of a rectangular pulse in the time domain and figure 2 (b) shows the Fourier phase spectrum of the same signal. As can be seen, the Fourier phase spectrum is a ramp function. The gradient of this ramp depends on the location of the signal in the time domain. The amplitude of the cepstral function in figure 2 (c) has a linear relationship with the gradient of the FPS (after 'unwrapping' is applied) and consequently, corresponds to the location of the signal in the time domain. Hence, the maximum value (amplitude) of the cepstral function corresponds to the location of the pulse in the time domain. The amplitude of the cepstral function does not always correspond to the starting point of the signal in the time domain; the point it corresponds depends on the shape of the pulse in the time domain.

Figure 3 presents a rectangular pulse in the time domain in (a), along with the HPS and the HPC of the same pulse in (b) and (c) respectively. The shape of the HPS is a cosinusoidal signal; the rate of the zero crossings with respect to the ω-axis (frequency) corresponds to the signal location in the time domain. Thus, the higher the rate of the zero crossings of the Hartley phase function, the further the signal is shifted in the time domain. The location of the highest peak(s) in the HPC yields the location of the pulse in the time domain.

From figure 3 (c) it is clear that apart from the two dominant peaks, other peaks of lower amplitude appear in the HPC. The majority of these additional peaks are the result of the 'intrinsic' discontinuities that exist in the Hartley phase spectrum. These additional peaks can be removed from the Hartley phase cepstrum by compensating the 'intrinsic' discontinuities in the corresponding Hartley phase spectrum.

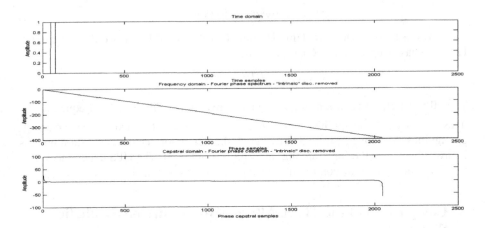

Fig. 2. (a) Time domain, (b) Frequency domain (FPS – 'intrinsic' discontinuities compensated) and (c) Cepstral domain (FPC) representation of a single rectangular pulse

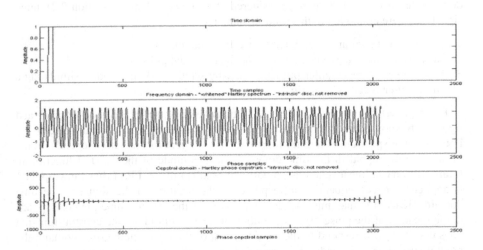

Fig. 3. (a) Time domain, (b) Frequency domain (HPS – 'intrinsic' discontinuities not compensated) and (c) Cepstral domain (HPC) representation of a single rectangular pulse

Figures 4(a) and 4(b) show the HPC before and after compensation of the intrinsic discontinuities, while figure 4(c) shows the reconstructed HPC after compensation. The number and amplitudes of additional peaks are significantly reduced in figure 4(c), as compared to figure 3(c). In the same figure, however, it is clear that the HPC peak(s) do not correspond to the endpoints of the pulse in the time domain; rather, they yield the middle or central point of the pulse. Hence, compensation may be useful or not depending on the application

The signal example employed next is a sequence of five exponentially dumped sinusoidal pulses – an example resembling the middle part of a voiced phoneme in

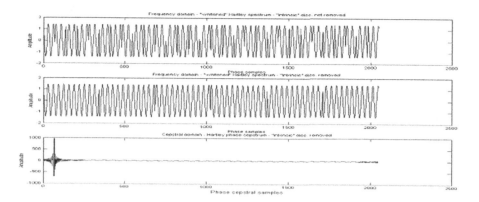

Fig. 4. (a) Frequency domain (HPS – 'intrinsic' discontinuities not compensated), (b) Frequency domain (HPS – 'intrinsic' discontinuities compensated) and (c) Cepstral domain (HPC) representation of a single rectangular pulse

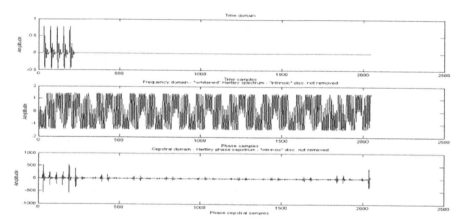

Fig. 5. (a) Time domain, (b) Frequency domain (HPS – 'intrinsic' discontinuities not compensated) and (c) Cepstral domain (HPC) representation of a sequence of five dumped sinusoids

speech signals. As shown in figure 5(c), peaks in the HPC indicate pulse positions along the time axis, while spurious peaks arise due to discontinuities still present. After compensation of the discontinuities, figure 6(c) show that, as expected, spurious peaks are suppressed; yet, HPC peaks correspond not to the individual pulses but to the central point of the pulse sequence.

The FPC cannot yield the location of more than one pulse, due to the heuristic and non-invertible nature of the 'unwrapping' algorithm, irrespective of the compensation of the spectral discontinuities. Thus, when more than one pulse exist in the time domain, the amplitude of the 0th cepstral coefficient of the FPC corresponds to an indefinite point within the support of the pulses in the time domain. Moreover, simulations carried out with additive noise (from SNR=20dB down to SNR=-11dB) for a single pulse (either exponentially dumped sine wave or rectangular pulse) show that, even for high SNRs, the amplitude of the 0th cepstral coefficient in the FPC does not correspond to the location of the pulse in the time domain, irrespective of the compensation of the 'intrinsic' discontinuities. This shows the sensitivity of the 'unwrapping' algorithm to the presence of even the lower possible noise level.

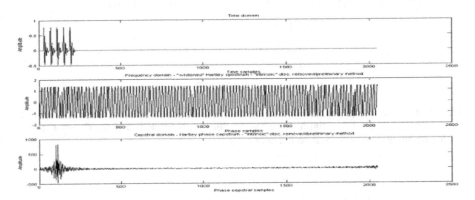

Fig. 6. (a) Time domain, (b) Frequency domain (HPS – 'intrinsic' discontinuities compensated) and (c) Cepstral domain (HPC) representation of a sequence of five dumped sinusoids

On the other hand, simulations on the synthetic signals mentioned above, indicate that the Hartley phase spectrum without the compensation of the 'intrinsic' discontinuities is more immune to noise compared to the Hartley phase spectrum with the compensation of the 'intrinsic' discontinuities. It is important to mention that the presence of noise in the time domain increases the amount of the 'intrinsic' discontinuities in the phase spectrum. Consequently, the task of the compensation of the 'intrinsic' discontinuities is more demanding in the case where noise is present in the time domain.

Concluding, the HPC compresses more efficiently than the FPC or the WFPC the signal's phase content and can therefore be used in speech processing applications such as compression or coding. Preliminary compression / coding experimentation on synthetic speech signals have already given encouraging results in [9].

3.1 The Hartley Phase Spectrum of a Rectangular Pulse Signal

The signal shown in figure 7 is produced by a rectangular pulse transmitted from a source. Multiple reflections are received with time delays and varying amplitudes, in a noisy environment.

As expected, the starting and finishing points of the pulse/reflection of the pulse in the time domain coincide with the highest cepstral peaks of the HPC.

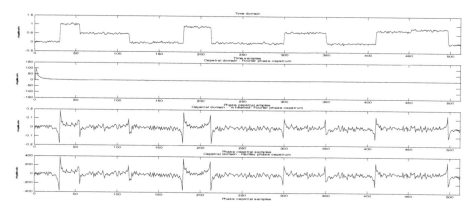

Fig. 7. Time domain signal (a) and cepstral domain signals: (b) FPC, (c) WFPC and (d) HPC, respectively, of the transmitted and reflected pulse

4   Conclusions

In this work we compare thre alternative non-linear (cepstral) phase features as to their noise robustness and phase content encapsulation efficiency merits. The feature proposed as advantageous in both aspects, with practical interest for (voiced) speech signal application is the Hartley Phase Cepstrum. The Hartley Phase Cepstrum may efficiently substitute the Fourier Phase Cepstrum in practical analysis of speech signals.

Acknowledgement

This research has been conducted within the framework of the "Environment-Archimedes II: Funding of research groups in TEI of Piraeus" project, co-funded by the European Union (75%) and the Greek Ministry of Education (25%).

References

1. Paraskevas, I.: Phase as a Feature Extraction Tool for Audio Classification and Signal Localisation, Ph.D. thesis, University of Surrey (2005)
2. Rabiner, L.R., Gold, B.: Theory and Applications of Digital Signal Processing, ch. 12. Prentice-Hall, Englewood Cliffs, New Jersey (1975)
3. Tribolet, J.: A new phase unwrapping algorithm", Acoustics, Speech, and Signal Processing [see also IEEE Transactions on Signal Processing]. IEEE Transactions on 25(2), 170–177 (1977)
4. Paraskevas, I., Chilton, E.: Combination of Magnitude and Phase Statistical Features for Audio Classification. Acoustics Research Letters Online (ARLO), Acoustical Society of America (July 2004)
5. Al-Nashi, H.: Phase Unwrapping of Digital Signals. IEEE Transactions on Acoustics, Speech and Audio Processing 37(11), 1693–1702 (1989)

6. Moreno, I., Kober, V., Lashin, V., Campos, J., Yaroslavsky, L.P., Yzuel, M.J.: Colour pattern recognition with circular component whitening. Optics Letters 21(7), 498–500 (1996)
7. Bracewell, R.N.: The Fourier Transform and Its Applications, ch. 19, 2nd edn. McGraw-Hill, New York (1986)
8. Paraskevas, I., Chilton, E., Rangoussi, M.: Audio Classification Using Features Derived From The Hartley Transform. In: 13th Int. Conference on Systems, Signals and Image Processing (IWSSIP 2006), Budapest, Hungary (September 2006)
9. Chilton, E., Hassanain, E.: Phase Estimation of Minimum Phase Systems using the Hartley Phase Cepstrum. In: Proceedings of the IASTED International Conference on Signal Processing, Pattern Recognition, and Applications (SPPRA 2006), Innsbruck, Austria, pp. 171–176 (February 2006)

Voiced Speech Analysis by Empirical Mode Decomposition

Aïcha Bouzid[1] and Noureddine Ellouze[2]

[1] Institut Supérieur d'Electronique et de Communication de Sfax,
Route Menzel Chaker Km 0.5, B. P. 868, 3018 Sfax, Tunisia
[2] Ecole Nationale d'Ingénieurs de Tunis, BP. 37, Le Belvédère 1002 Tunis, Tunisia
bouzidacha@yahoo.fr, N.Ellouze@enit.rnu.tn

Abstract. Recently Empirical Mode Decomposition has been proposed as a nonlinear tool for the analysis of non stationary data. This paper concerns Empirical Mode Decomposition (EMD) of speech signal into intrinsic oscillatory mode functions IMFs and their spectral analysis. EMD is applied on speech signal, spectrogram of speech and IMFs are analysed. The different modes explored, underline the band-pass structure of IMFs. LPC analysis of the different modes shows that formant frequencies of voiced speech signal are still preserved.

Keywords: Empirical mode decomposition, intrinsic mode functions, speech signal, spectral analysis.

1 Introduction

Basis decomposition techniques such as short time Fourier decomposition or wavelet decomposition have extensively been used to analyze non-stationary speech signals [1], [2], [3]. They are based on a complete and orthogonal decomposition of the signal into elementary components. The amplitudes of such components can be interpreted in terms of time-frequency or time-scale energy distribution. Spectrogram and scalogram which are respectively time-frequency and time-scale representation have been used in speech analysis. The main drawback of these approaches is that the basis functions are predetermined, and don't necessarily match varying nature of signals. Linear prediction coding applied on speech signal is widely used for formant estimation and voice source analysis. Recently, the Empirical Mode Decomposition (EMD) has been proposed as a new tool for data analysis [2]. This technique performs a time adaptive decomposition of a complex signal into elementary, almost orthogonal components that don't overlap in frequency. Practical applications of EMD are today broadly spread in numerous scientific disciplines and applied to a number of real life situations [5], [6], [7].

In this paper, we use the empirical mode decomposition (EMD), first introduced by N. E. Huang and al. in 1998 [4], in speech analysis. This technique, adaptively, decomposes a signal into oscillating components. The EMD is in fact a type of adaptive wavelet decomposition which sub-bands are built as needed to separate the different components of the signal.

M. Chetouani et al. (Eds.): NOLISP 2007, LNAI 4885, pp. 213–220, 2007.
© Springer-Verlag Berlin Heidelberg 2007

Motivated by the success of the EMD technique used in number of applications [6], [7] and [8], we are interested by the decomposition of natural speech signal in order to explore speech parameters.

The outline of the present paper is as follows. Second section presents the non linear decomposition EMD technique, EMD of composite synthesized signal is given as academic example. In the third section we analyze the spectral contribution of the first three IMFs of speech signal. Linear Prediction Coding (LPC) analysis of different intrinsic mode functions is presented in section 4. This analysis provides formant representation of speech. Last section concludes this work.

2 Empirical Mode Decomposition

The empirical mode decomposition is a signal processing technique, proposed to extract the oscillatory modes embedded in a signal without any requirement of stationarity or linearity of the data. The goal of this procedure is to decompose a time series into components with well defined instantaneous frequencies. This technique can empirically identify the physical time scales intrinsic to the data that is the time lapse between successive maxima and minima of the signal [9]. Each characteristic oscillatory mode extracted is named Intrinsic Mode Function (IMF). It satisfies the following properties: an IMF is symmetric, has unique local frequency, and do not exhibit the same frequency at the same time for different IMFs. In other words, the IMFs are characterized by having the number of maxima and minima equal to the number of zero crossings (or different at most by one).

The algorithm operates through the following steps [4]:

1) Identification of all the maxima and minima of input signal $x(k)$.
2) Generation of the upper and lower envelope via cubic spline interpolation among all the maxima and minima, respectively.
3) Point by point averaging of the two envelopes to compute a local mean series $m(k)$.
4) Subtraction of $m(k)$ from the data to obtain an IMF candidate $d(k) = x(k)-m(k)$.
5) Check the properties of $d(k)$:
   • If d is not an IMF (i.e: it does not satisfy the previously defined properties), replace $x(k)$ by $d(k)$ and repeat the procedure from step 1.
   • If d is an IMF, evaluate the residue $m(k) = x(k)-d(k)$.
6) Repeat the procedure from step 1 to step 5 by sifting the residual signal. The sifting process ends when the residue satisfies a predefined stopping criterion.

By construction, the number of maxima and minima decreases when going from one residual to the next (thus guaranteeing that the complete decomposition is achieved in a finite number of steps). The corresponding spectral supports are expected to decrease accordingly. Selection of modes rather corresponds to an automatic and signal dependent time variant filtering [9], [10], [11].

At the end, we have:

$$x(t) = \sum_{i=1}^{n} d_i(t) + m_n(t) \tag{1}$$

Here $m_n(t)$ is the residue and $d_i(t)$ is the intrinsic mode function relative to i. d_i has the same number of zero crossings and extrema; and is symmetric with respect to the local mean.

Another way to explain how the empirical mode decomposition works is that it picks out the highest frequency oscillation that remains in the signal. Thus, locally, each IMF contains lower frequency oscillations than the one extracted just before. This property can be very useful to pick up frequency changes, since a change will appear even more clearly at the level of an IMF [4].

Figure 1 shows EMD of composite signal. The signal taken in this example is composed by a superposition of a chirp and a sine wave.

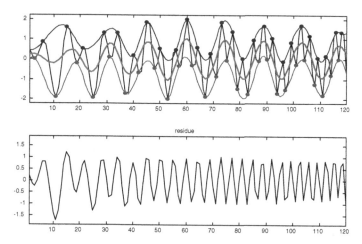

Fig. 1. At the top: the original signal composed by a chirp and a sine wave. Below: the first IMF witch is the chirp [12].

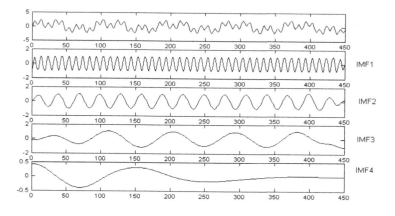

Fig. 2. EMD of a sum of 3 sine waves (100Hz, 300Hz and 900Hz)

Figure 2, shows another example where the analyzed signal is the sum of three sine waves having respectively 100 Hz, 300 Hz and 900 Hz as frequencies. The signal is composed by 450 samples at a sampling frequency of 9 kHz. EMD of this signal gives four IMFs and the residue. We can see that each IMF has the same number of zero crossings as maxima and minima, and is symmetric with respect to the zero line. We also note that the first mode which corresponds naturally to the highest frequency shows clearly that the 900 Hz frequency is present in the signal. Also, the second mode depicts 300Hz frequency and the third IMF shows the lowest frequency which is 100Hz.

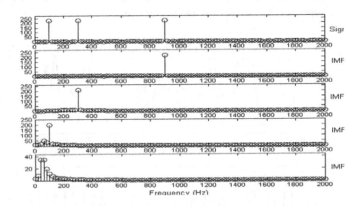

Fig. 3. Spectrums of a composite signal, (100Hz, 300 Hz and 900 Hz) and its 4 IMFs

Spectral analysis of the composite signal and its IMFs as depicted in figure 3, shows that the highest frequency is identified by the first IMF and the lowest one is given by the third IMF. This analysis permits to separate the composite signal into elementary components constituting the original signal.

3   EMD Analysis of Voiced Speech Signal

EMD is used to decompose the speech signal in order to analyze the formant frequencies characterizing the vocal tract. Speech signals used in this work are extracted from the Keele University database, sampled at 20 KHz [13].

For better comprehension and evaluation of IMF decomposition of speech signal, we compare the spectrogram of speech signal to spectrograms of the corresponding IMFs.

Figure 4 represents spectrogram of the sentence ''the north wind'' pronounced by the speaker f4 (given by Keele database) and spectrograms of the three first IMFs.

Spectrogram of speech is represented in figure 4a. Spectrogram of IMF1, IMF2 and IMF3 are respectively represented in figures 4b, 4c and 4d. Spectrogram of IMF1 (4b) shows highest frequencies of speech signal. The IMFs have band pass frequency structure; they are characterized by decreasing frequency bandwidth, and decreasing center frequency.

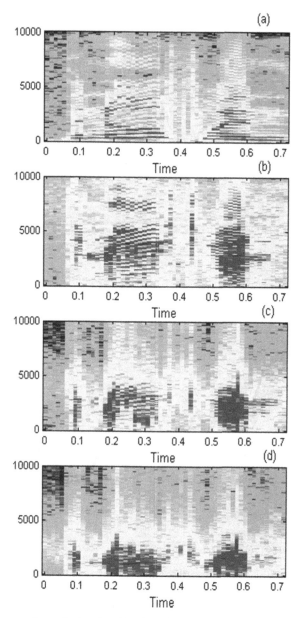

Fig. 4. Spectrograms of speech signal and its three first IMFs (a): spectrogram of speech signal, (b) spectrogram of IMF1, (c) spectrogram of IMF2, (d) spectrogram of IMF3

4   LPC Analysis of Intrinsic Mode Functions

For more exploration of IMFs, we operate LPC analysis of IMFs. We take as an exa-mple of speech signal, a vowel /o/ pronounced by a female speaker f1 from Keele database.

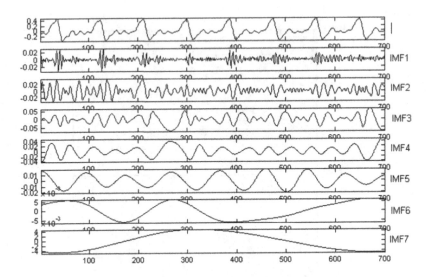

Fig. 5. Illustration of the EMD: vowel /o/ speaker f1 and the corresponding IMFs

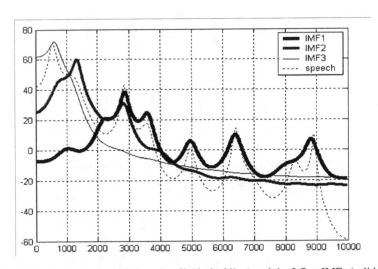

Fig. 6. LPC analysis of vowel /o/ speaker f1 (dashed line) and the 3 first IMFs (solid lines)

Figure 5 shows the different modes obtained from the empirical mode decomposition. Figure 6 represents LPC analysis of the signal and the three first IMFs. The LPC analysis of the first IMF fits approximately the speech signal for frequencies higher than 2.5 KHz. The first IMF does not depict the low frequencies of the signal, but the highest frequencies. These results can be interpreted as the frequency response of equivalent filters. As shown in figure 5, the collection of all such filters tends to estimate the different resonant frequencies of the vocal tract.

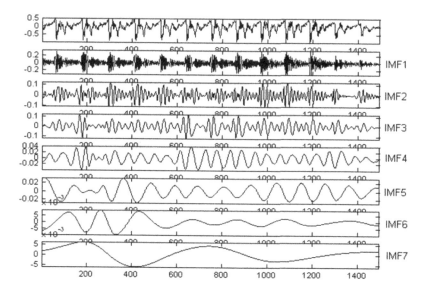

Fig. 7. Illustration of the EMD: vowel /a/, speaker m3 and the corresponding IMFs

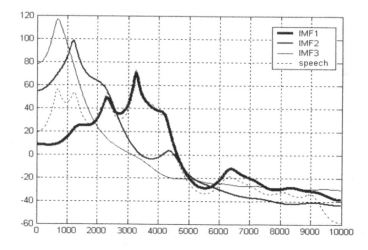

Fig. 8. LPC analysis of vowel /a/, speaker m3 (dashed line) and the 3 first IMFs (solid lines)

Even if EMD is a non linear processing technique, the formants of speech signal are preserved and these frequencies are correctly evaluated. We give a second example for the vowel /a/ expressed by a male speaker m2. The resulting EMD and the LPC analysis are respectively depicted in figures 7 and 8.

5 Conclusion

In this work, we have proposed a new method to decompose a speech signal into different oscillatory modes called empirical mode decomposition (EMD). Furthermore, we can look for a new time-frequency attributes obtained from the EMD analysis and based on an instantaneous frequency calculation of each component of the decomposition. LPC analysis of the first IMFs of speech signal, gives good estimation of formants, which represents resonant frequencies of the vocal tract. Perspectives of this work are noise reduction by EMD analysis, and parameter estimation of speech signal.

References

1. Flandrin, P.: Temps-Fréquence. Hermes (1993)
2. Cohen, L.: Time-Frequency Analysis. Prentice-Hall, Englewood Cliffs (1995)
3. Daubechies, I.: Ten Lectures on Wavelet. SIAM (1992)
4. Huang, N.E., Shen, Z., Long, S.R., Wu, M.L., Shih, H.H., Zheng, Q., Yen, N.C., Tung, C.C., Liu, H.H.: The Empirical Mode Decomposition and Hilbert Spectrum for Nonlinear and Non-Stationary Time Series Analysis. Proc. Roy. Soc. London A 454, 903–995 (1998)
5. Huang, N.E., Shen, S.S.P.: Hilbert–Huang Transform and Its Applications. World Scientific Publishing, Singapore (2005)
6. Fournier, R.: Analyse Stochastique Modale du Signal Stabilométrique. Application à l'Etude de l'Equilibre chez l'Homme. Thèse de Doctorat, Univ. Paris XII Val de Marne (2002)
7. Souza Neto, E.P., Custaud, M.A., Cejka, J.C., Abry, P., Frutoso, J., Gharib, C., Flandrin, P.: Assessment of Cardiovascular Autonomic Control by the Empirical Mode Decomposition. In: 4th Int. Workshop on Biosignal Interpretation, Como (I), pp. 123–126 (Juin 2002)
8. Balocchi, R., Menicucci, D., Santarcangelo, E., Sebastiani, L., Gemignani, A., Ghelarducci, B., Varanini, M.: Deriving the Respiratory Sinus Arrhythmia from the Heartbeat Time Series Using Empirical Mode Decomposition. Quantitative Biology (2003)
9. Flandrin, P., Gonçalvès, P.: Sur la Décomposition Modale Empirique. In: GRETSI 2003, Paris (2003)
10. Rilling, G., Flandrin, P., Gonçalvès, P.: On Empirical Mode Decomposition and its Algorithms. In: IEEE-EURASIP Workshop on Nonlinear Signal and Image Processing NSIP 2003, Grado (2003)
11. Flandrin, P., Rilling, G., Gonçalvès, P.: Empirical Mode Decomposition as a Filter Bank. IEEE Signal Processing Letters 11, 112–114 (2004)
12. http://perso.ens-lyon.fr/patrick.flandrin/emd.html (2007)
13. Plante, F., Meyer, G.F., Ainsworth, W.A.: A pitch extraction reference database. In: Proc. Eurospeech 1995, Madrid, pp. 837–840 (September 1995)

Estimation of Glottal Closure Instances from Speech Signals by Weighted Nonlinear Prediction

Karl Schnell

Institute of Applied Physics, Goethe-University Frankfurt
Max-von-Laue-Str. 1, 60438 Frankfurt am Main, Germany
schnell@iap.uni-frankfurt.de

Abstract. In this contribution, a method based on nonlinear prediction of speech signals is proposed for detecting the locations of the instances of glottal closures (GCI). For that purpose, feature signals are obtained from the nonlinear prediction of speech using a sliding window technique. The resulting feature signals show maxima caused by the glottal closures which can be utilized for the GCI detection. To assess the procedure, a speech database with corresponding EGG signals is analyzed providing GCIs as reference.

Keywords: speech analysis, nonlinear prediction, GCI detection.

1 Introduction

Speech analysis is often performed using linear models and statistics. However, nonlinear components are also contained in the speech signal [1]. The nonlinear components of speech signals are caused by several effects based on the speech production process and the excitation. The nonlinearity can be described more statistically by components which are not produced by a linear system excited with white Gaussian noise (WGN); this is especially valid, for example, for the voiced excitation. For speech analysis, nonlinear systems and operators, like the energy operator, are used [2, 3]. In this contribution, the nonlinearity of the speech signals is estimated by nonlinear prediction based on Volterra series. The estimation is performed by an LSE approach yielding the optimum coefficients for a speech segment analytically [4, 5]. In [5] speech features based on the prediction gain by nonlinear components are discussed. In this contribution, features based on individual nonlinear predictor coefficients are used and, additionally, a post-processing of the feature signals is carried out estimating the locations of the instances of glottal closures (GCI). The GCI detection from the speech signal is relevant for many applications; therefore, several methods exist [6]. One group of algorithms uses a first processing based on linear prediction or related methods with a sliding window to obtain feature signals, from which the GCIs are estimated [7, 8]. Other groups use, for example, wavelet-based methods or an analysis of the LPC residual [9]. The algorithm, proposed in this contribution, has a common ground with these of the first-mentioned group since it uses a sliding window technique, too. The contribution is organized in a way that, firstly, the nonlinear prediction and the feature signals are explained and, secondly, the GCI detection algorithm and its evaluation are discussed.

M. Chetouani et al. (Eds.): NOLISP 2007, LNAI 4885, pp. 221–229, 2007.
© Springer-Verlag Berlin Heidelberg 2007

2 Weighted Nonlinear Prediction

The nonlinear prediction based on Volterra series estimates a signal value $x(n)$ by a linear combination of last values and products of last values. The first line of eq. (1) shows the prediction error $e(n) = x(n) - \hat{x}(n)$ using the first and second Volterra kernels with the coefficients h_i and $h_{i,j}$, respectively. For a segment-wise analysis, attaching different weights to the error values can be appropriate leading to a weighted nonlinear prediction defined by the second line of eq. (1)

$$e(n) = x(n) - \sum_{i=1}^{N} h_i \cdot x(n-i) - \sum_{i=1}^{M} \sum_{j=1}^{i} h_{i,j} \cdot x(n-i)x(n-j)$$

$$w(n)e(n) = w(n)\left(x(n) - \sum_{i=1}^{N} h_i \cdot x(n-i) - \sum_{i=1}^{M} \sum_{j=1}^{i} h_{i,j} \cdot x(n-i)x(n-j) \right).$$

(1)

The weighting function $w(n)$ determines how strong the values are considered for the estimation depending on their positions within the segment. For the prediction of the segment values, the finite signals can be described by vectors leading to a vector-based description of eq. (1) represented by

$$e_w^{N,M} = \mathbf{u} - \sum_{i=1}^{N} h_i \cdot \mathbf{u}_i - \sum_{i=1}^{M} \sum_{j=1}^{i} h_{i,j} \cdot \mathbf{u}_{i,j}$$

with definitions:

$$e_w^{N,M} = \left(w(0) \cdot e(k), w(1) \cdot e(k+1), \ldots, w(L) \cdot x(k+L) \right)^T$$

(2)

$$\mathbf{u} = \left(w(0) \cdot x(k), w(1) \cdot x(k+1), \ldots, w(L) \cdot x(k+L) \right)^T$$

$$\mathbf{u}_i = \left(w(0) \cdot x(k-i), w(1) \cdot x(k+1-i), \ldots, w(L) \cdot x(k+L-i) \right)^T$$

$$\mathbf{u}_{i,j} = \left(w(0)x(k-i)x(k-j), w(1)x(k+1-i)x(k+1-j), \ldots \right)^T$$

implying the segment $\mathbf{x}_{k,k+L} = (x(k), x(k+1), \ldots x(k+L))$ with the length $l = L+1$. The vector $e_w^{N,M}$ includes the weighted prediction error values obtained from a prediction of orders N and M for the first and second kernel, respectively. Eq. (2) can be solved for the vector $\mathbf{u}$ resulting in eq. (3). The optimum predictor coefficients are given by the best possible approximation of the vector $\mathbf{u}$ by a linear combination of the vectors $\mathbf{u}_i$ and $\mathbf{u}_{i,j}$ minimizing the length of the error vector

$$\mathbf{u} = \sum_{i=1}^{N} h_i \cdot \mathbf{u}_i + \sum_{i=1}^{M} \sum_{j=1}^{i} h_{i,j} \cdot \mathbf{u}_{i,j} + e_w^{N,M}$$

(3)

$$\left| e_w^{N,M} \right| = \sqrt{\sum_n \left(e_w^{N,M}(n) \right)^2} \quad \rightarrow \quad \text{min.}$$

This optimization can be solved analytically by regression. An example of performing the regression is given in [5].

3 Nonlinear Feature Signals

The vector-based prediction algorithm of the previous section is used to estimate the coefficients h_i and $h_{i,j}$ from overlapping speech frames $x_{k,k+L}$. The coefficients corresponding to the frame $x_{k,k+L} = \left(x(k), x(k+1), \ldots x(k+L) \right)$ are denoted by the index k with $h_i(k)$ and $h_{i,j}(k)$; analogously, the same is valid for $e_w^{N,M}(k)$. For the analysis, a sliding window technique is used, since the positions of the frame boundaries affect the analysis results which is explained in the following. The voiced speech can be described by the output of the speech production system excited by the voiced excitation. The voiced excitation is highly affected by the glottal closures causing impulses in the excitation; in comparison to that, glottal openings have usually minor effects. In [7] a short rectangular window is used as sliding window, since in this case the prediction error can be assumed to be zero or minimum for windows within the closed glottis interval. In comparison to that, here, nonlinear prediction is used and, additionally, a special window function is integrated. Furthermore, the frame length is chosen longer modifying the argumentation slightly. The analysis results of the prediction are influenced by the numbers and locations of the glottal closures within in the frame. Therefore, the prediction results can be also very sensitive corresponding to the positions of the frame boundaries since a small shift of a boundary can decide whether a glottal closure is inside or outside of the frame. Hence, if the frame is shifted rightward, a glottal closure can be introduced at the right side and/or a glottal closure can be removed at the left side. To remove the escaping glottal closure at the left side gradually, an asymmetric window function w_a is used which can be seen in fig. 1. The left part (2/3 of the length) of w_a is equal to

Fig. 1. Asymmetric window function w_a

the left side of the Hann window. The window function is not included to eliminate spectral distortions since the estimation algorithm corresponds to the covariance method.

Feature signals are derived from the products of the nonlinear prediction which is explained in the following. Each frame $x_{k,k+L}$ yields a feature value F. Since the shifting of the frame is one sample, the series of features can be interpreted as a feature signal $F(k)$. For each feature value $F(k)$ a corresponding speech sample $x(k+d)$ can be assigned with $0 \le d \le L$. To synchronize the speech and feature signal, $d = L$ is reasonable for the asymmetric window w_a since it describes the right window side. In [5] the prediction gain by the nonlinear components is used to define the feature signal $F_{\text{gain}}^{N,M}(k)$ of eq. (4) describing a measure of nonlinearity; the numerator contains the error by the linear prediction whereas the denominator contains the error by the nonlinear prediction. The analyses indicate that the prediction gain yields best results for order $M = 1$ of the second kernel; however, it yields not reliably good results. One reason lies in the fact that the voiced excitation comprises components in addition to the glottal closures. Therefore, the feature signal $F_{i,j}^{N,M}(k)$ is proposed based on an individual nonlinear coefficient $h_{i,j}$ and its sign depends on the polarity of the analyzed signal

$$F_{\text{gain}}^{N,M}(k) = \log\left(\frac{\left|e_w^{N,0}(k)\right|}{\left|e_w^{N,M}(k)\right|}\right)$$

(4)

$$F_{i,j}^{N,M}(k) = \pm h_{i,j}'(k).$$

The feature signal $h_{i,j}'(k)$ is a mean-balanced and power-balanced version of $h_{i,j}(k)$. For the calculation of $h_{i,j}'(k)$, the short-time mean of $h_{i,j}(k)$ is subtracted to each value $h_{i,j}(k)$, after that, each value is divided by a short-time estimation of the power of the feature signal resulting in the feature signal $h_{i,j}'$.

4   Detection of GCI

To asses GCI detection algorithms, the GCIs obtained from the EGG signal can be used as reference. The locations of the GCI can be associated with the positive peaks of the DEGG signal which is the derivative of the EGG. Since the EGG signals can be a little bit noisy, the EGG signals are smoothed prior to applying the derivative. For the GCI detection from speech, the feature signals of the last section are used. In the following, the order selection and differences between the features signals for GCI detection are treated. The analyses indicate that the feature signals with small prediction orders yield mostly better or equal results than with higher prediction orders. The features with smallest prediction orders are $F_{1,1}^{1,1}$ and $F_{1,1}^{0,1}$; the latter feature considers only nonlinear components. Fig. 2 shows the feature signals and the EGG-based signals for a speech segment uttered by a female speaker. The speech segment is from the Keele database which is converted to a sampling rate of 8 kHz. The frame length for the analysis is $l = 150$. It can be seen that the peaks of the DEGG correspond to peaks of the feature signals $F_{\text{gain}}^{1,1}$ and $F_{1,1}^{1,1}$. Therefore, GCI candidates can be recognized by the maxima of these feature signals. The feature signal based on prediction gain shows additional maxima which complicates the choosing of the true GCIs from the candidates. Since the additional maxima have mostly a negative sign for the feature $F_{1,1}^{1,1}$, the feature $F_{1,1}^{1,1}$ has advantages. This circumstance is based on the fact that the prediction gain depends only on the absolute value of $h_{1,1}$ provided that the coefficient is optimum. Although the resulting feature signal $F_{1,1}^{1,1}(k)$ in fig. 2 is suitable, the analyses of different speakers indicate that the choice of a male speaker deteriorates often the results. In this point, the feature signal $F_{1,1}^{0,1}$ seems to be favorable since it delivers good results for female and male voices.

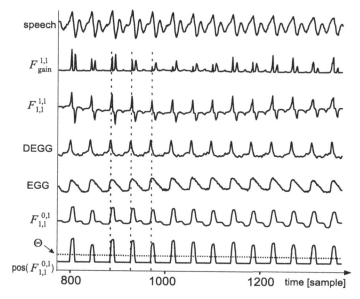

Fig. 2. Analyzed speech with corresponding feature signals and EGG signal

4.1 Algorithm for GCI Detection

In the following, an automatic GCI detection algorithm based on the feature signal $F_{1,1}^{0,1}$ is explained. In comparison to $F_{1,1}^{1,1}$, the glottal closures are estimated by crossing a threshold θ from beneath. The threshold is determined by a percentage of the maximum value of the feature signal; the calculation of θ is performed adaptively resulting in $\theta(k)$. The estimation of GCI candidates is defined by

$$F_{1,1}^{0,1}(k) \le \theta(k) \quad \text{and} \quad F_{1,1}^{0,1}(k+1) > \theta(k) \quad \Rightarrow \quad k+d \text{ is GCI candidate}$$

$$\text{with} \quad \theta(k) = \alpha \cdot \max\left(F_{1,1}^{0,1}(k-W), F_{1,1}^{0,1}(k-W+1), \dots F_{1,1}^{0,1}(k+W)\right). \tag{5}$$

The factor α of the maximum is chosen with $\alpha = 0.3$ and W determines the neighborhood for the calculation of the threshold $\theta(k)$; this threshold is shown in fig. 2 with the positive values of the feature signal representing the threshold for $\alpha = 0$; the function $\text{pos}(F)$ yields the feature value F for $F > 0$ and 0 for $F \le 0$. After determining the GCI candidates, a post-processing is performed estimating a realistic sequence of GCIs. Only GCI candidates are chosen which have distances between themselves which are greater than a minimum distance. This minimum distance is equal for all analyses, however, different for male and female speakers. Each GCI candidate is weighted by the sum S of the following consecutive feature values which are greater than the threshold. This value S can be used to decide between two or more possible GCI candidates which are close together. The algorithm starts with two adjoining GCI candidates describing the initial conditions. From the difference of the positions of the two candidates a provisional pitch period length p is estimated. Then, in a region of the position of the right GCI candidate plus p the GCI candidate with maximum S is chosen as next GCI position. If no GCI candidate is in that region, GCI candidates are used obtained with the threshold $\theta = 0$ ($\alpha = 0$). This is repeated till no candidate can be found. The same is performed on the left side. The initial condition of the algorithm is varied for all possible two adjoining GCI candidates and the resulting GCI positions are arranged in the final set of GCI positions considering the minimum distance. The final set of detected GCI positions is denoted with $\gamma_k(F_{1,1}^{0,1})$ whereas the GCI positions obtained from the EGG signal is denoted with $\gamma_i(\text{EGG})$.

4.2 Analysis of Speech Database

The automatic GCI detection algorithm based on the feature signal $F_{1,1}^{0,1}$ is used to estimate the GCIs of the speech signals from the Keele database. The Keele database contains utterances from five male and five female speakers [6]. Each utterance consists of the same text providing phonetically balanced English. For the analysis, the sampling rate of the speech and EGG signals are converted to 8 kHz. To analyze only voiced speech parts, firstly, the voiced parts of the speech signals are aligned. For the voice detection, the short-time energy of the speech (low-passed) is used. Then, the GCIs are automatically determined from the speech and the EGG signals resulting in the GCI positions $\gamma_k(F_{1,1}^{0,1})$ and $\gamma_i(\text{EGG})$, respectively. It should be mentioned that the $\gamma_i(\text{EGG})$ are actually obtained from the DEGG signal. For comparing the GCIs of $\gamma_k(F_{1,1}^{0,1})$ and $\gamma_i(\text{EGG})$, each EGG-based GCI position is assigned to a feature-based GCI: $\gamma_i(\text{EGG}) \rightarrow \gamma_{\upsilon(i)}(F_{1,1}^{0,1})$ with $\upsilon(i)$ on condition that the absolute value the difference $\delta = \gamma_{\upsilon(i)}(F_{1,1}^{0,1}) - \gamma_i(\text{EGG})$ of two positions is smaller or equal ε; the constant ε is the allowed deviation. This means that, if $|\delta| > \varepsilon$ is true, the EGG-based glottal closure is declared as not detected. Additionally, no unassigned $\gamma_k(F_{1,1}^{0,1})$ should exist between two adjacent $\gamma_i(\text{EGG})$. In this way, the percentage ϑ of correctly detected GCIs can be computed. This percentage $\vartheta(\varepsilon)$ of correct detections depends on the permitted deviation ε. Table 1 shows the resulting averaged values for the analysis of the Keele database depending on ε. The values $\overline{\delta}$ and $\overline{|\delta|}$ are the means of the differences δ and their absolute values representing the bias of the detection and the averaged distance to the reference

GCI, respectively. Since the first and last GCIs of each voiced segment are sometimes imperfect, the values are also computed ignoring these GCIs; this is denoted by ($*$). The resulting values of table 1 are averaged over all analyzed voiced segments of the speakers and, then, averaged for five female and four male speakers, respectively. The 4th male speaker of the Keele database is ignored since the EGG-based GCI detection was not reliable; however, this was not valid for the feature-based GCI detection. The voiced parts of the analyzed nine speakers of the Keele database yield about 26000 EGG-based GCIs which are considered for the evaluation. From table 1, it can be seen that the GCI detection yields better estimations for female speakers. This is also valid for the individual subjects, for example, the percentage of correctly estimated GCIs for $\varepsilon = 1$ ms is 96.5, 96.9, 96.9, 94.2, and 91.7 % for the five female speakers and 87.8, 87.7, 87.4, and 80.9 % for the four male speakers. The averaged offset $\bar{\delta}$ of the GCI detection is different for male and female speakers. This can be seen also for the individual subjects of the speakers, for example for $\varepsilon = 1$ ms, the offsets is 0.13, 0.18, 0.13, 0.35, and 0.16 ms for the female speakers and -0.11, -0.18, -0.11, and -0.27 ms for the male speakers. It should me mentioned that for the calculation of the percentage of the correctly estimated GCIs, the offset is not considered. By a consideration of an offset, the estimation results would be improved.

The averaged values give an evaluation respecting the whole database; however, an inspection of individual segments is necessary to judge several effects. Fig. 3 shows some individual examples cutting out from analyzed segments. Fig. 3 (a) shows that the algorithm works usually also for in-stationary speech regions; however, if the regions are very corrupted with abrupt changes of the pitch, the GCI detection can produce false detections. Fig. 3 (d) shows that multiple candidates can be produced by the threshold ($\alpha = 0.3$); for this case, the candidates are unambiguous with the threshold with $\alpha = 0$. The EGG and DEGG signals don't yield in all cases unambiguous and precise GCIs [10]. The figs. 3 (b),(c) and (e) show examples concerning the use of the EGG signal for the reference GCIs. In some cases the EGG signal has a region which is very

Table 1. Comparisons between estimated and reference GCIs obtained from Keele database: δ is the deviation between EGG-based and feature-based GCIs, $\vartheta(\varepsilon)$ is the percentage of correctly estimated GCIs with $|\delta| \leq \varepsilon$, $\overline{\delta(\varepsilon)}$ and $\overline{|\delta(\varepsilon)|}$ are the means of the deviations of the correctly estimated GCIs. ($*$) means ignoring the first and last GCI of each voiced segment.

ε [ms] / [samples]			ϑ [%] female/male	$\overline{|\delta|}$ [ms] female/male	$\overline{\delta}$ [ms] female/male
0.375 /	3		83.7 / 63.7	0.19 / 0.18	0.157 / -0.016
0.375 /	3	($*$)	85.7 / 67.5	0.19 / 0.18	0.163 / -0.014
0.625 /	5		93.3 / 76.6	0.22 / 0.25	0.185 / -0.092
0.625 /	5	($*$)	95.3 / 80.4	0.22 / 0.24	0.19 / -0.086
1.0 /	8		95.3 / 85.9	0.24 / 0.31	0.19 / -0.167
1.0 /	8	($*$)	97.0 / 89.6	0.23 / 0.31	0.2 / -0.157
1.5 /	12		96.2 / 90.9	0.25 / 0.37	0.2 / -0.22
1.5 /	12	($*$)	98.0 / 93.7	0.24 / 0.35	0.21 / -0.2
2.0 /	16		96.6 / 93.6	0.25 / 0.41	0.25 / -0.25
2.0 /	16	($*$)	98.3 / 95.6	0.25 / 0.38	0.21 / -0.22

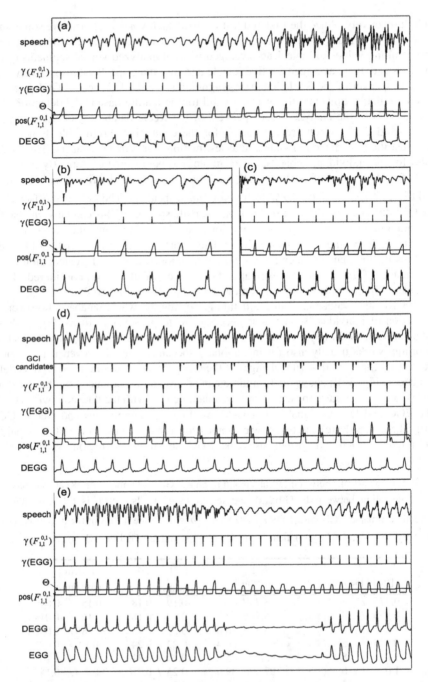

Fig. 3. Examples of analyzed speech segments: (a) in-stationary speech segment, (b) and (c) DEGG signal with double peaks, (d) multiple GCI candidates for threshold with $\alpha = 0.3$, (e) distorted EGG/DEGG signal

low-level and blurred, as shown in fig. 3 (e). In comparison to that, the GCI detection based on the feature signal works for these regions usually as good as for the other regions. The increasing regions of the EGG describing the GCIs can be relatively long. Additionally, this increasing part of one glottal cycle of the EGG can produce more than one peak in the DEGG, which is shown in the figs. 3 (b) and (c). This means, that the evaluation by EGG-based GCIs is a good method; however, it produces not continuously exact evaluations, especially, for a precise calculation of the deviations between the estimated and true GCIs.

5 Conclusions

In this paper a GCI detection algorithm based on nonlinear prediction is proposed. For that purpose, different speech features are discussed concerning the detection of GCIs. The analyses show that small prediction orders are favorable and that, for the feature definition, individual nonlinear coefficients are advantageous over the prediction gain. The proposed algorithm is evaluated by the analysis of the Keele database showing that the nonlinear statistics can be utilized for GCI detection.

Acknowledgments. The author would like to thank C. D'Alessandro for discussion.

References

1. Faundez, M., et al.: Nonlinear Speech Processing: Overview and Applications. Int. J. Control Intelligent Syst. 30(1), 1–10 (2002)
2. Maragos, P., Quatieri, T., Kaiser, J.: Speech Nonlinearities, Modulations, and Energy Operators. In: Proc. ICASSP 1991, pp. 421–424 (1991)
3. Atlas, L., Fang, J.: Quadratic Detectors for General Nonlinear Analysis of Speech. In: Proc. ICASSP 1992, pp. 9–12 (1992)
4. Thyssen, J., Nielsen, H., Hansen, S.D.: Non-linear Short-term Prediction in Speech Coding. In: Proc. ICASSP 1994, pp. 185–188 (1994)
5. Schnell, K., Lacroix, A.: Weighted Nonlinear Prediction Based on Volterra Series for Speech Analysis. In: Proc. EUSIPCO 2006, Florence (2006)
6. Mousset, E., Ainsworth, W., Fonollosa, J.A.R.: A Comparison of Several Recent Methods of Fundamental Frequency and Voicing Decision Estimation. In: Proc. ICSLP 1996, Philadelphia, pp. 1273–1276 (1996)
7. Wong, D.Y., Markel, J.D., Gray, A.H.: Least Squares Inverse Filtering from the Acoustic Speech Waveform. IEEE Trans. ASSP. ASSP-27, 350–355 (1979)
8. Strube, H.W.: Determination of the Instant of Glottal Closures from the Speech Wave. J. Acoust. Soc. Am. 56, 1625–1629 (1974)
9. Ananthapadmanabha, T.V., Yeganananarayana, B.: Epoch Extraction from linear prediction residual for identification of closed glottis interval. IEEE Trans. on ASSP. ASSP-27(4), 309–318 (1979)
10. Henrich, N., D'Alessandro, C., Doval, B., Castellengo, M.: On the use of the derivative of electroglottographic signals for characterization of nonpathological phonation. J.A.S.A. 115(3), 1321–1332 (2004)

Quantitative Perceptual Separation of Two Kinds of Degradation in Speech Denoising Applications

Anis Ben Aicha and Sofia Ben Jebara

Unité de recherche Techtra
Ecole Supérieure des Communications de Tunis, 2083 Cité El-Ghazala/Ariana,
Tunisie
anis_ben_aicha@yahoo.fr, sofia.benjebara@supcom.rnu.tn

Abstract. Classical objective criteria evaluate speech quality using one quantity which embed all possible kinds of degradation. For speech denoising applications, there is a great need to determine with accuracy the kind of the degradation (residual background noise, speech distortion or both). In this work, we propose two perceptual bounds $UBPE$ and $LBPE$ defining regions where original and denoised signals are perceptually equivalent or different. Next, two quantitative criteria $PSANR$ and $PSADR$ are developed to quantify separately the two kinds of degradation. Some simulation results for speech denoising using different approaches show the usefulness of proposed criteria.

Keywords: Objective criteria, speech denoising, $UBPE$, $LBPE$, $PSANR$, $PSADR$.

1 Introduction

Evaluation of denoised speech quality can be done using subjective criteria such as MOS (Mean Opinion Score) or DMOS (Degradation MOS) [1]. However, such evaluation is expensive and time consuming so that, there is an increasing interest in the development of robust quantitative speech quality measures that correlate well with subjective tests. Objective criteria can be classified according to the domain in which they operate. We relate, for example, the Signal to Noise Ratio (SNR) and segmental SNR operating on time domain [2], the Cepstral Distance (CD) and Weighted Slope Spectral distance (WSS) operating in frequency domain [2] and Modified Bark Spectral Distortion ($MBSD$) operating in perceptual domain [3]. Perceptual measures are shown to have the best chance of predicting subjective quality of speech and other audio signals since they are based on human auditory perception models.

The common point to all objective criteria is their ability to evaluate speech quality using a single parameter which embed all kinds of degradation after any processing. Indeed, speech quality measures are basing their evaluation on both original and degraded speeches according to the following application C:

$$C : \mathbb{E}^2 \longrightarrow \mathbb{R}$$
$$(x, y) \longmapsto c \tag{1}$$

M. Chetouani et al. (Eds.): NOLISP 2007, LNAI 4885, pp. 230–245, 2007.

where $\mathbb{E}$ denotes the time, frequency or perceptual domain. x (resp. y) denotes original speech (resp. observed speech altered by noise or denoised speech after processing) and c is the score of the objective measure.

Mathematically, C is not a bijection from $\mathbb{E}^2$ to $\mathbb{R}$. It means that it is possible to find a signal y' which is perceptually different from y but has the same score as the one obtained with y ($c(x, y) = c(x, y')$). We relate, for example, the case of an original signal x which is corrupted by an additive noise to construct the signal y. Then, x is coded and decoded using a CELP coder to obtain the signal y'. It is obvious that the degradation noticed in both y and y' are not the same. Degradation of y is heard as a background noise and the degradation of y' is perceptually heard as signal distortion.

We aim improving speech quality evaluation by separating two kinds of degradation which are the additive residual noise and the speech distortion. Each degradation will be evaluated using its adequate criterion so that the non bijection C will be avoided and replaced by a bijection one characterized by a couple of outputs instead of a single output. Moreover, thanks to the advantage of perceptual tools in the evaluation of speech quality, the new couple of criteria will be based on auditor properties of human ear.

2   Study Context: Speech Denoising

Before defining novel criteria of speech quality evaluation, let's define the different kinds of degradation altering speech. Without loss of generality, we consider the speech denoising application and we use spectral denoising approaches. They are viewed as a multiplication of noisy speech spectrum $Y(m, k)$ by a real positive coefficient filter $H(m, k)$ (see for example [5]). The estimated spectrum of clean speech is written

$$\hat{S}(m, k) = H(m, k)Y(m, k), \tag{2}$$

where m (resp. k) denotes frame index (resp. frequency index).

The estimation error spectrum $\xi(m, k)$ is given by

$$\xi(m, k) = S(m, k) - \hat{S}(m, k). \tag{3}$$

We assume that speech and noise are uncorrelated. Thus, the estimated error power spectrum is given by

$$E\{|\xi(m, k)|^2\} = [H(m, f) - 1]^2 E\{|S(m, k)|^2\} + H(m, k)^2 E\{|N(m, k)|^2\}, \tag{4}$$

where $|N(m, k)|^2$ denotes the noise power spectrum.

Since $0 < H(m, k) < 1$, the first term of Eq. 4 expresses the 'attenuation' of clean speech frequency components. Such degradation is perceptually heard as a distortion of clean speech. However, the second term expresses the residual noise which is perceptually heard as a background noise. Since, it is additive, it is possible to formulate it as an 'accentuation' of clean speech frequency components.

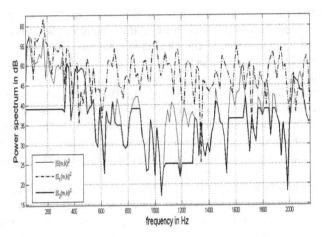

Fig. 1. Power spectrum of two signals degraded differently

3   Classical Criteria Limitations

To show the limitations of classic criteria for evaluating the denoised signal quality in terms of degradation nature i.e.; residual background noise or distortion
of clean speech, we construct the two following signals [4]:

− $s_1(n)$ is a corrupted version of the clean speech $s(n)$ by an additive white
Gaussian noise with $SNR_{seg} = 15$ dB. $s_1(n)$ is perceptually heard as the clean
speech drowned in background noise without any noticeable distortion of the
clean speech itself. The background noise heard in $s_1(n)$ express the residual
noise after the denoising process.

− $s_2(n)$ is constructed in the short time spectral domain. To simulate the speech
distortion, we artificially attenuate some frequency components of clean speech
signal. $s_2(n)$ is heard as a distorted version of the clean speech $s(n)$ without any
noticeable residual background noise.

We represent in Fig. 1, the power spectrum of the two signals. They are
completely different because of their different construction process. The power
spectrum of the first signal $|S_1(m,k)|^2$ is above the clean one. It can be seen
as an 'accentuation' of the clean speech power spectrum. However, the power
spectrum of the second signal $|S_2(m,k)|^2$ is below the clean one. Hence, it is
considered as an 'attenuation' of the clean speech power spectrum.

Regarding Fig. 1, the two signals $s_1(n)$ and $s_2(n)$ must be evaluated differently
using classic criteria. To asses the speech quality of $s_1(n)$ and $s_2(n)$, we use the
SNR_{seg} as temporal criterion, the WSS as frequency criterion and $MBSD$ as
perceptual criterion. Tab. 1 summarize the assessment scores obtained by the
mentioned criteria. In terms of SNR_{seg} and WSS scores, the two signals are
similar which means that they are supposed to have the same quality. However,
according to listening tests and to Fig. 1, this is can't be true. Thus, for the same
score obtained by an objective criterion, it is possible to find many signals which

Table 1. Objective evaluation of $s_1(n)$ and $s_2(n)$

	SNR_{seg} (dB)	WSS	$MBSD$
$s_1(n)$	3.5	34.3	0.92
$s_2(n)$	3.6	31.0	0.02

are perceptually different. This fact shows the non bijection of classical objective criteria. In terms of $MBSD$, the best score is obtained for the distorted signal. However, subjective tests show that the degradation of the signal $s_2(n)$ is more annoying than the degradation of signal $s_1(n)$.

Thus, using a single parameter to evaluate the speech quality, it is not possible to separate the two kinds of degradation.

4   Proposed Perceptual Characterization of Audible Degradation

We aim to perceptually characterize the degradation altering denoised speech. Hence, auditory properties of human ear are considered. More precisely, the masking concept is used: a masked signal is made inaudible by a masker if the masked signal magnitude is below the perceptual masking threshold MT. In our case, both degradation can be audible or inaudible according to their position regarding the masking threshold. We propose to find decision rules to decide on the audibility of residual noise and speech distortion by using the masking threshold concept. If they are audible, the audibility rate will be quantified according to the proposed criterion. There are many techniques to compute masking threshold MT, we use in this paper Johnston model which is well known for its simplicity and well used in coding context [6].

4.1   Perceptual Characterization of Audible Noise

According to MT definition, it is possible to add to the clean speech power spectrum, the MT curve (considered as a 'certain signal') so that the resulting signal (obtained by inverse FFT) has the same audible quality than the clean one. The resulting spectrum is called *Upper Bound of Perceptual Equivalence* "*UBPE*" and is defined as follows

$$UBPE(m, k) = \Gamma_s(m, k) + MT(m, k), \tag{5}$$

where $\Gamma_s(m, k)$ is the clean speech power spectrum.

When some frequency components of the denoised speech are above $UBPE$, the resulting additive noise is heard.

4.2   Perceptual Characterization of Audible Distortion

By duality, some attenuations of frequency components can be heard as speech distortion. Thus, by analogy to $UBPE$, we propose to calculate a second curve which expresses the lower bound under which any attenuation of frequency components is heard as a distortion. We call it *Lower Bound of Perceptual Equivalence "LBPE"*. To compute *LBPE*, we used the audible spectrum introduced by Tsoukalas *and al* for audio signal enhancement [7]. In such case, audible spectrum is calculated by considering the maximum between clean speech spectrum and masking threshold.

When speech components are under MT, they are not heard and we can replace them by a chosen threshold $\sigma(m,k)$.
The proposed *LBPE* is defined as follows

$$LBPE(m,k) = \begin{cases} \Gamma_s(m,k) & \text{if } \Gamma_s(m,k) \geq MT(m,k) \\ \sigma(m,k) & \text{otherwise .} \end{cases} \quad (6)$$

The choice of $\sigma(m,k)$ obeys only one condition $\sigma(m,k) < MT(m,k)$. We choose it for example equal to 0 dB.

4.3   Usefulness of *UBPE* and *LBPE*

Using *UBPE* and *LBPE*, we can define three regions characterizing the perceptual quantity of denoised speech: frequency components between *UBPE* and *LBPE* are perceptually equivalent to the original speech components, frequency components above *UBPE* contain a background noise and frequency components under *LBPE* are characterized by speech distortion. This characterization constitutes our idea to identify and detect audible additive noise and audible distortion. As illustration, we present in Fig. 2 an example of speech frame power spectrum and its related curves *UBPE* (upper curve in bold line) and *LBPE* (bottom curve in dash line). The clean speech power spectrum is, for all frequencies index, between the two curves *UBPE* and *LBPE*. We remark that the two curves are the same for most peaks. It means that for these frequency intervals, any kind of degradation altering speech will be audible. If it is over *UBPE*, it will be heard as background noise. In the opposite case, it will be heard as speech distortion.

5   Audible Degradation Estimation

5.1   Audible Additive Noise PSD Estimation

Once *UBPE* is calculated, the superposition of denoised signal power spectrum and *UBPE* leads to separate two cases. The First one corresponds to the regions of denoised speech power spectrum which are under *UBPE*. In such case, there is no audible residual noise. In the second case, some denoised speech frequency components are above *UBPE*, the amount above *UBPE* constitutes the audible residual noise. As illustration, we represent in Fig.3 an example of denoised speech power spectrum and its related *UBPE* curve calculated from clean speech. The used denoising approach is spectral subtraction [5]. From Fig.3, we

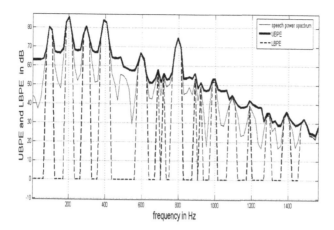

Fig. 2. An example of $UBPE$ and $LBPE$ in dB of clean speech frame

notice that frequency regions between 1 kHz and 2 kHz are above $UBPE$, they hence contain residual audible noise. In terms of listening tests, such residual noise is annoying and constitutes in some cases the musical noise. Such musical noise is very popular and constitutes the main drawback of spectral subtraction approaches.

Once the $UBPE$ is calculated, it is possible to estimate the audible power spectrum density of residual noise using a simple subtraction when it exists. Hence, the residual noise power spectrum density PSD is written

$$\Gamma_n^p(m,k) = \begin{cases} \Gamma_{\hat{s}}(m,k) - UBPE(m,k) & \text{if } \Gamma_{\hat{s}}(m,k) > UBPE(m,k) \\ 0 & \text{otherwise ,} \end{cases} \tag{7}$$

where $\Gamma_{\hat{s}}(m,k)$ denotes the PSD of denoised speech and the suffix p designs the perceptually sense of the PSD.

5.2 Audible Speech Distortion PSD Estimation

We use the same methodology as the one used for residual background noise. We represent in Fig.4 an example of denoised speech power spectrum and its related curve $LBPE$ calculated from the clean speech. We notice that some regions are under $LBPE$ (for example regions between 1.5 kHz and 2 kHz), they hence constitute the audible distortion of the clean speech. In terms of listening tests, they are completely different from residual background noise. They are heard as a loss of speech tonality.

It is possible to estimate the audible distortion PSD Γ_d^p as follows

$$\Gamma_d^p(m,k) = \begin{cases} LBPE(m,k) - \Gamma_{\hat{s}}(m,k) & \text{if } \Gamma_{\hat{s}}(m,k) < LBPE(m,k) \\ 0 & \text{otherwise .} \end{cases} \tag{8}$$

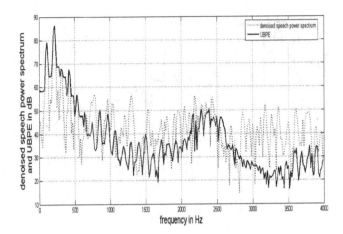

Fig. 3. Superposition of a denoised speech power spectrum and its related clean speech *UBPE*

6   Audible Degradation Evaluation

In this section, we detail the proposed approach to quantify separately the two kinds of degradation. The assessment of the denoised speech quality by means of two parameters permits to overcome the problem of non bijection of classic objective evaluation and to better characterize each kind of speech degradation. Hence, instead of the application defined in Eq. 1, we develop a novel application from perceptual domain to $\mathbb{R}^2$

$$C : \mathbb{E}^2 \longrightarrow \mathbb{R}^2$$
$$(x, y) \longmapsto (PSANR, PSADR) \tag{9}$$

where $PSANR$ and $PSADR$ are two parameters related respectively to the residual noise and the distortion.

The definition of $PSANR$ and $PSADR$ is inspired from the SNR definition which is the ratio between signal energy and noise energy. Thanks to Parseval theorem it can be calculated in frequency domain. Moreover, since the $UBPE$ and $LBPE$ are perceptually equivalent to the original signal, the proposed definition uses the energy of $UBPE$ and $LBPE$ instead of the energy of the clean speech. The time domain signal related to $UBPE$ is called "upper effective signal" whereas the time domain signal related to $LBPE$ is called "lower effective signal". In the following subsection, we define the proposed criteria.

6.1   Perceptual Noise Criterion PSANR

The perceptual residual noise criterion is defined as the ratio between the upper effective signal which is the $UBPE$ and the audible residual noise. The Perceptual Signal to Audible Noise Ratio $PSANR(m)$ of frame m is calculated in frequency domain (due to the Parseval theorem) and it is formulated as follows

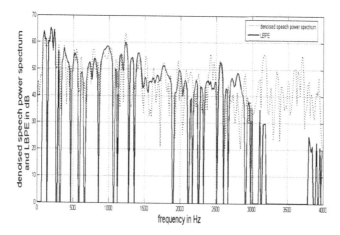

Fig. 4. Superposition of a denoised speech frame and its related clean speech $LBPE$

$$PSANR(m) = \frac{\sum_{k=1}^{N} UBPE(m,k)}{\sum_{k=1}^{N} \Gamma_n^p(m,k)}, \tag{10}$$

where N denotes the total number of frames.

6.2   Perceptual Distortion Criterion PSADR

By the same manner, we define the Perceptual Signal to Audible Distortion Ratio $PSADR(m)$ of frame m as a ratio between the lower effective signal which is $LBPE$ and the audible distortion. The $PSADR(m)$ is given by:

$$PSADR(m) = \frac{\sum_{k=1}^{N} LBPE(m,k)}{\sum_{k=1}^{N} \Gamma_d^p(m,k)}. \tag{11}$$

6.3   PSANDR Criteria

To compute the global $PSANR$ and $PSADR$ of the total speech sequence, we are referred to the segmental SNR (SNR_{seg}) thanks to its better correlation with subjective tests when compared to the traditional SNR. The principle of segmental SNR consists in determining the SNR for each frame $SNR(m)$ and then calculating their geometric mean over the total number of frames $SNR_{seg} = \sqrt[M]{\prod_m^M SNR(m)}$ [2]. Moreover, since the SNR and SNR_{seg} are usually expressed in dB. The geometric mean is equivalent to the arithmetic mean in log domain.

Using this approach, we compute the global $PSANR$ and $PSADR$ for a given sequence of speech. Next, the couple ($PSANR,PSADR$) defines the new criterion to evaluate both kinds of degradation. We call it *Perceptual Signal to Audible Noise and Distortion Ratio "PSANDR"*.

7   Experimental Results for Artificial Degradations

7.1   Case of Artificial Additive Noise

To show the ability of $PSANDR$ to take into account the perceptual effect of an additive noise, we add to a clean speech an artificial noise, constructed from the masking threshold by multiplying it with a factor $\alpha \geq 0$:

$$y(n) = s(n) + \alpha MT(n). \tag{12}$$

In Fig.5, we represent the evolution of SNR_{seg}, $PSANR$ and $PSADR$, versus α, calculated between clean speech $s(n)$ and the noisy one $y(n)$. We notice the following interpretations.

- For the range of α between 0 and 1, SNR_{seg} decreases as α increases which means that there is a degradation of speech quality. This fact is true in terms of signal to noise ratio. In fact, the noisy speech temporal form is different from the clean speech temporal form. In perceptual sense, the power of the added artificial noise doesn't overtake the masking threshold MT. So, the additive noise is not audible because it is masked by the clean speech. With $PSANR$, we confirm that the amount of audible noise is null (see Eq. 7) and the $PSANR$ is infinite. In our simulation, we choose to truncate it to value 35 dB.
- For $\alpha > 1$, the background noise becomes audible because its power overtakes MT. Thus, when α increases, the $PSANR$ decreases showing that the additive noise is audible and more annoying. However, for all ranges of α, the $PSANR$ remains above the SNR_{seg}. This is explained by the ability of the clean speech to mask a certain portion of the added noise.
- We notice that for any value of α, the second term $PSADR$ is always constant and is equal to 35 dB. In fact, there is no distortion of the clean speech and the only audible degradation is the background noise.

7.2   Case of Artificial Distortion

We propose to show the ability of $PSADR$ to take into account the perceptual effect of the distortion impairing the denoised speech. For simplicity reasons, we deal with the case where the distortion is inaudible. For such reason, we built an artificial signal obtained from the clean one by multiplying its power spectrum which is under the MT by a factor γ $(0 \leq \gamma \leq 1)$.

$$Y'(m,k) = \begin{cases} \gamma \cdot S(m,k) & \text{if } |S(m,k)|^2 < MT(m,k) \\ S(m,k) & \text{otherwise .} \end{cases} \tag{13}$$

We hence define the distortion as the attenuation of frequency components of clean speech. When we superpose the clean speech power spectrum and it's related masking threshold MT, frequency components under MT are not audible.

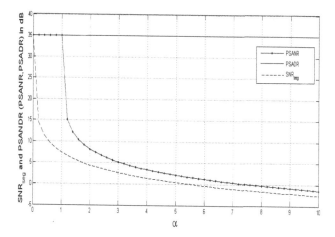

Fig. 5. Evolution of SNR_{seg}, $PSANR$ and $PSADR$ versus α in case of additive noise

By multiply these non audible components by a factor $\gamma \leq 1$, we will not touch on the perceptual quality of the clean speech.

In Fig.6, we represent the evolution of SNR_{seg} and $PSADR$ versus γ calculated between clean speech $s(n)$ and the distorted one $y'(n)$. We notice the following interpretations.

- For the range of $0 \leq \gamma < 1$, SNR_{seg} decreases as γ decreases which involves the presence of a certain degradation. However, because of the perceptual transparency of the transformation from $s(n)$ to $y'(n)$, the two signals have the same perceptual quality. Therefore, the detected degradation in SNR_{seg} has no significant mean in perceptual sense.
- $PSADR$ is constant, for all ranges of $0 \leq \gamma < 1$, which means that although the modification of the speech spectrum, the resulting signal is still perceptual equivalent to the original one. This experience confirms once again that there are some distortions which are not audible but detected by classic objective criteria as noticeable distortion.

8   Experimental Results with Subtractive Denoising Techniques

8.1   Overview

In order to show advantages of the proposed criterion for evaluating quality of denoised speech in real cases, we propose to assess the performances of power subtraction technique using $PSANR$, $PSADR$ and traditional criteria.

We recall that the denoised speech power spectrum is obtained from the noisy one using the following relationship [8]:

$$|\hat{S}(m,k)|^2 = \begin{cases} |Y(m,k)|^2 - \beta|\bar{N}(m,k)|^2 & \text{if } |Y(m,k)|^2 > |\bar{N}(m,k)|^2 \\ \beta'|\bar{N}(m,k)|^2 & \text{otherwise .} \end{cases} \qquad (14)$$

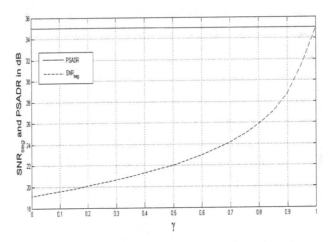

Fig. 6. Evolution of SNR_{seg} and $PSADR$ versus γ in case of artificial distortion

where $|\hat{S}(m,k)|^2$ (resp. $|Y(m,k)|^2$) denotes the denoised speech power spectrum (resp. the noisy speech power spectrum). $|\bar{N}(m,k)|^2$ is the estimated noise power spectrum, obtained by averaging the noise spectra from several frames of "silence" during pause intervals. m (resp. k) designs frame index (resp. frequency index). β is the over subtraction factor and β' is the spectral flooring factor.

The phase of noisy speech is not modified. Thus, the enhanced speech signal is obtained with the following relationship.

$$\hat{s}(m,k) = IFFT\left(\hat{S}(m,k) \cdot e^{\theta(m,k)}\right), \tag{15}$$

where $IFFT$ is the Inverse Fast Fourier Transformation and $\theta(m,k)$ is the phase of noisy speech.

8.2   Perceptual Effect of β and β'

The choice of the two parameters β and β' in Eq. (14) must obey the classical tradeoff between residual noise and speech distortion. In fact, the parameters β and β' operates as follows :

- The parameter β controls the amount of noise to be reduced. If $0 < \beta < 1$, the noise power spectrum is underestimated and the denoised speech power spectrum is little modified. Intuitively, we can expect high level of residual noise with low distortion. when β is chosen larger than 1, the noise is overestimated and $\beta|N(m,k)|^2$ is subtracted. Thus, the denoised speech is more attenuated with introduction of unavoidable distortion. Subjective tests confirm that if $0 < \beta < 1$, the denoised speech is heard as a clean speech drowned in background noise without noticeable distortion. If $\beta \gg 1$ the denoised speech is heard as pure distorted version of clean speech with little amount of residual noise.

- β' is a parameter to control the amount of residual noise when the first condition of Eq. (14) is not satisfied. When β' increases, the background noise level increases. In our study, we choose it equal to zero.

8.3   Influence of β on Objective Criteria

In this section, we propose to study the influence of the factor β on the quality of the denoised speech using $PSANR$, $PSADR$ and classic criteria. We seek to demonstrate that the proposed criterion can predict the impact of varying β on the denoised speech quality when classic criteria are not able to do it.

We summarize, in Tab. 2, the evolution of WSS and $MBSD$ versus the factor β.

- In terms of WSS criterion the best score is obtained when $\beta = 0$ i.e., for the noisy speech. When β increases the quality of the denoised speech decreases until $\beta = 6$. Next, the speech quality is improved again. This behaviour is unexpected and didn't give any idea about speech degradation nature (background noise or speech distortion).
- Using $MBSD$ criterion, performances are improved when β increases. It means that the denoised speech is well enhanced when β is large. However, according to previous paragraphs, the denoised speech is highly distorted.

In Fig. 7, we represent the evolution of $PSANR$, $PSADR$ and SNR_{seg} in terms of β. We notice the following interpretations :

Table 2. Evolution of WSS and $MBSD$ versus β

β	0	1	2	3	4	5	6	7	8	9	10
WSS	45.8	55.56	72.65	110.3	170.2	222.8	229.6	200.3	158.3	123	98.17
$MBSD$	2.30	1.74	1.28	0.92	0.65	0.46	0.31	0.20	0.14	0.09	0.06

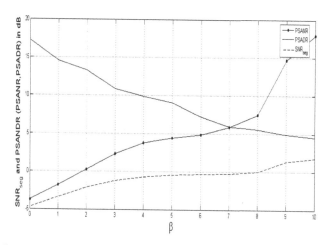

Fig. 7. Evolution of SNR_{seg}, $PSANR$ and $PSADR$ versus β in case of subtraction techniques

- SNR_{seg} is improved slightly when β increases which means that the denoised speech quality is slightly enhanced.
- $PSANR$ increases when β increases. It means that the audible residual noise is well reduced when we increase the amount of residual noise. However, we must take into account the second parameter $PSADR$ which quantify the audible distortion. $PSADR$ shows that the high reduction of noise is accompanied by the increasing of the audible distortion. These results are well glued with subjective tests and intuitive analysis.

9   Experimental Results with Perceptual Denoising Techniques

9.1   Perceptual Techniques Overview

Let's now compare some perceptual denoising techniques by means of the new objective criteria. We propose to denoise a corrupted signal, by Gaussian noise with $SNR = 0$ dB, using the following techniques:

- Classical wiener filtering [5]. It consists on filtering the noisy speech with a time-varying linear filter depending on the characteristics of the noisy signal spectrum and the estimated noise spectrum. The Wiener filter is given by the following equation:

$$H_w(m,k) = \frac{SNR_{prio}(m,k)}{1 + SNR_{prio}(m,k)}, \tag{16}$$

where $SNR_{prio}(m,k)$ is the *a priori* Signal to Noise Ratio [9]

$$SNR_{prio}(m,k) = (1-\tau)P(SNR_{post}(m,k)) + \tau \frac{(H_w(m-1,k)|Y(m-1,k)|)^2}{|\bar{N}(m,k)|^2}, \tag{17}$$

where τ is a real constant, $P(x) = \frac{1}{2}(x + |x|)$, $|\bar{N}(m,k)|^2$ is the noise power spectrum estimated during pause intervals and $SNR_{post}(m,f)$ is the *a posteriori* Signal to Noise Ratio calculated as follows:

$$SNR_{post}(m,k) = \frac{|Y(m,k)|^2}{(m,k)} - 1. \tag{18}$$

The major drawback of Wiener technique is the presence of a musical residual noise with unnatural structure in the enhanced speech. Indeed, an over or a sub estimation of noise power spectrum at a given frequency leads to the occurrence of an artificial tone which is called musical tone. Such residual noise becomes in some cases more annoying than the original noise.

- Perceptual filtering proposed by Gustafsson *and al* in [10] which consists on masking the residual noise and allowing variable speech distortion. Indeed, according to Eq. (4), the residual noise power spectrum $|\xi(m,k)|^2$ is given by:

$$|\xi(m,k)|^2 = H_G(m,k)^2 \cdot E\{|\bar{N}(m,k)|^2\}, \tag{19}$$

where $H_G(m,k)$ is the considered denoising filter.
To make the residual noise inaudible, $H_G(m,k)$ must verify the following equation:

$$H_G(m,k)^2 \cdot E\{|\bar{N}(m,k)|^2\} \leq MT(m,k). \tag{20}$$

By taking into account that $H_G(m,k)$ must be between 0 and 1, the perceptual filter is given by:

$$H_G(m,k) = \min\left(\sqrt{\frac{\widehat{MT}(m,k)}{|\bar{N}(m,k)|^2}}, 1\right), \tag{21}$$

where $\widehat{MT}(m,k)$ is the estimation of the clean speech masking threshold. $\widehat{MT}(m,k)$ is calculated from a denoised version of noisy speech using traditional power subtraction technique.
This method is popular thanks to its ability to reduce residual noise and musical noise. However, because the non accuracy of the estimation of both noise power spectrum and clean masking threshold, the level of speech distortion is high comparing to that of Wiener technique.

- Modified wiener technique [11]. It is an approach for detection and reduction of musical noise appearing in Wiener denoising technique. The goal of this approach is to make the musical noise perceptually white, which means less annoying to listeners and more comfortable. This method is based on detection and reduction of musical tones thanks to their unnatural characteristics in frequency domain:

$$\begin{aligned} 6\text{dB} \leq h \leq 9\text{dB} \\ 90\text{Hz} \leq w \leq 110\text{Hz}, \end{aligned} \tag{22}$$

where h is the amplitude difference between the musical peaks and its neighbors and w is the width of musical tones.
The reduction of musical noise is done by multiplying the power spectrum of the detected musical tones by a factor α ($0 < \alpha < 1$) which controls the shape attenuation. It leads to the improvement of many quantitative criteria temporal, spectral and perceptual characteristics. These results are confirmed by subjective tests.

9.2   Performances Comparison

Evaluation of denoising quality is done using classical objective criteria (segmental $SNR, WSS, MBSD$) and the proposed $PSANDR$. Results are resumed in Tab.3.

- In terms of SNR_{seg}, the used techniques are comparable even if there is a little improvement noticed with perceptual technique. But, subjective tests show that the denoised signals are completely different.

- Using WSS criterion, the best score is obtained with perceptual technique and it is nearly equal to the noisy speech score. Although, subjective tests show that the two signals are perceptually different. Indeed, the denoised speech using perceptual technique is heard as distorted version of clean speech and not as clean speech with background noise.
- In terms of $MBSD$, the perceptual technique is also the best. However, this technique is characterized by a loss of the speech tonality comparing to wiener technique. Thus, we can see that classic evaluation tools don't give any idea about the kind and nature of the degradation of the signals.
- $PSANR$, which gives an idea about residual noise, shows that perceptual technique is the best one regarding noise attenuation. $PSADR$, which determines the distortion of the denoised signals, shows that the important distortion is obtained using perceptual technique. These observations are confirmed by subjective tests.

Table 3. Evaluation of denoised signals

	SNR_{seg} (dB)	WSS	$MBSD$	$PSANR$ (dB)	$PSADR$ (dB)
noisy speech	-4.30	46.07	2.32	-3.90	17.27
wiener technique	1.05	74.25	0.28	5.04	**7.53**
modified wiener	1.13	69.63	0.19	5.54	7.01
perceptual technique	**1.62**	**45.41**	**0.15**	**12.71**	6.93

10   Conclusion

The spectral and perceptual analysis of the degradation, in the case of denoised speech, imposes to separate between residual noise and signal distortion. We first propose two curves $UBPE$ and $LBPE$ to calculate the audible residual noise and audible distortion. Next, two parameters $PSANR$ and $PSADR$ characterizing the two kinds of degradation are developed. Simulation results comparing different denoising approaches and classical objective measures, show a better characterization of degradation nature of denoised signal. The calculation of the degree of correlation of the proposed criteria with MOS criterion constitutes the perspectives of our work.

References

1. Recommandation UIT-T P.800. Méthodes d'évaluation subjective de la qualité de transmission (1996)
2. Hansen, J.H.L., Pellom, B.L.: An effective quality evaluation protocol for speech enhancement algorithms. In: Int. Conf. on Spoken Language Processing ICSLP, Austria (1998)

3. Yang, W., Benbouchta, M., Yantorno, R.: Performance of the modified bark spectral distortion as an objective speech measure. In: ICASSP. Proc. Int. Conf. on Acoustics, Speech and Signal Processing, vol. 1, pp. 541–544 (1988)
4. Benaichaet, A., Ben Jebara, S.: Caractérisation perceptuelle de la dégradation apportée par les techniques de débruitage de la parole. Traitement et Analyse de l'Information Méthodes et Applications TAIMA, Tunisia (2007)
5. Lim, J.S., Oppenheim, A.V.: Enhancement and Bandwidth Compression of Noisy Speech. In: Proc. IEEE, vol. 67, pp. 1586–1604 (1979)
6. Johnston, J.D.: Transform coding of audio signal using perceptual noise criteria. IEEE J. Select. Areas Commun. 6, 314–323 (1988)
7. Tsoukalas, D.E., Mourjopoulos, J., Kokkinakis, G.: Speech enhancement based on audible noise suppression. IEEE Trans. Speech and Audio Processing 5(6), 497–514 (1997)
8. Beruoti, M., Schwartz, R., Makhoul, J.: Enhancement of speech corrupted by acoustic noise. In: Proc. IEEE ICASSP, pp. 208–211 (1979)
9. Ephraim, Y., Malah, D.: Speech enhancement using a mean square error short-time spectral amplitude estimator. IEEE Trans. Acoust., Speech, Signal Processing 32, 1109–1121 (1984)
10. Gustafsson, S., Jax, P., Vary, P.: A novel psychoacoustically motivated audio enhancement algorithm preserving backround noise characteristics. In: Proc. Int. Conf. Acoustics, Speech, and Signal Processing, Seattle, WA, pp. 397–400 (May 1998)
11. Ben Aicha, A., Ben Jebara, S., Pastor, D.: Speech denoising improvement by musical tones shape modification. In: ISCCSP. International Symposium on Communication, Control and Signal Processing, Morocco (2006)

An Efficient VAD Based on a Generalized Gaussian PDF

O. Pernía, J.M. Górriz, J. Ramírez, C.G. Puntonet, and I. Turias

E.T.S.I.I.T, Universidad de Granada
C/ Periodista Daniel Saucedo, 18071 Granada, Spain
gorriz@ugr.es

Abstract. The emerging applications of wireless speech communication are demanding increasing levels of performance in noise adverse environments together with the design of high response rate speech processing systems. This is a serious obstacle to meet the demands of modern applications and therefore these systems often needs a noise reduction algorithm working in combination with a precise voice activity detector (VAD). This paper presents a new voice activity detector (VAD) for improving speech detection robustness in noisy environments and the performance of speech recognition systems. The algorithm defines an optimum likelihood ratio test (LRT) involving Multiple and correlated Observations (MCO). An analysis of the methodology for $N = \{2, 3\}$ shows the robustness of the proposed approach by means of a clear reduction of the classification error as the number of observations is increased. The algorithm is also compared to different VAD methods including the G.729, AMR and AFE standards, as well as recently reported algorithms showing a sustained advantage in speech/non-speech detection accuracy and speech recognition performance.

1 Introduction

The emerging applications of speech communication are demanding increasing levels of performance in noise adverse environments. Examples of such systems are the new voice services including discontinuous speech transmission [1,2,3] or distributed speech recognition (DSR) over wireless and IP networks [4]. These systems often require a noise reduction scheme working in combination with a precise voice activity detector (VAD) [5] for estimating the noise spectrum during non-speech periods in order to compensate its harmful effect on the speech signal.

During the last decade numerous researchers have studied different strategies for detecting speech in noise and the influence of the VAD on the performance of speech processing systems [5]. Sohn *et al.* [6] proposed a robust VAD algorithm based on a statistical likelihood ratio test (LRT) involving a single observation vector. Later, Cho *et al* [7] suggested an improvement based on a smoothed LRT. Most VADs in use today normally consider hangover algorithms based on empirical models to smooth the VAD decision. It has been shown recently [8,9] that incorporating long-term speech information to the decision rule reports

M. Chetouani et al. (Eds.): NOLISP 2007, LNAI 4885, pp. 246–254, 2007.
© Springer-Verlag Berlin Heidelberg 2007

benefits for speech/pause discrimination in high noise environments, however an important assumption made on these previous works has to be revised: *the independence of overlapped observations*. In this work we propose a more realistic one: *the observations are jointly gaussian distributed with non-zero correlations*. In addition, important issues that need to be addressed are: *i*) the increased computational complexity mainly due to the definition of the decision rule over large data sets, and *ii*) the optimum criterion of the decision rule. This work advances in the field by defining a decision rule based on an optimum statistical LRT which involves multiple and *correlated* observations. The paper is organized as follows. Section 2 reviews the theoretical background on the LRT statistical decision theory. Section 4 considers its application to the problem of detecting speech in a noisy signal. Finally in Section 4.1 we discuss the suitability of the proposed approach for pair-wise correlated observations using the experimental data set AURORA 3 subset of the original Spanish SpeechDat-Car (SDC) database [10] and state some conclusions in section 6.

2   Multiple Observation Probability Ratio Test

Under a two hypothesis test, the optimal decision rule that minimizes the error probability is the Bayes classifier. Given an observation vector $\hat{\mathbf{y}}$ to be classified, the problem is reduced to selecting the hypothesis (H_0 or H_1) with the largest posterior probability $P(H_i|\hat{\mathbf{y}})$. From the Bayes rule:

$$L(\hat{\mathbf{y}}) = \frac{p_{\mathbf{y}|H_1}(\hat{\mathbf{y}}|H_1)}{p_{\mathbf{y}|H_0}(\hat{\mathbf{y}}|H_0)} \begin{array}{c} > \\ < \end{array} \frac{P[H_0]}{P[H_1]} \Rightarrow \begin{array}{c} \hat{\mathbf{y}} \leftrightarrow H_1 \\ \hat{\mathbf{y}} \leftrightarrow H_0 \end{array} \tag{1}$$

In the LRT, it is assumed that the number of observations is fixed and represented by a vector $\hat{\mathbf{y}}$. The performance of the decision procedure can be improved by incorporating more observations to the statistical test. When N measurements $\hat{\mathbf{y}}_1, \hat{\mathbf{y}}_2, \ldots, \hat{\mathbf{y}}_N$ are available in a two-class classification problem, a multiple observation likelihood ratio test (MO-LRT) can be defined by:

$$L_N(\hat{\mathbf{y}}_1, \hat{\mathbf{y}}_2, ..., \hat{\mathbf{y}}_N) = \frac{p_{\mathbf{y}_1, \mathbf{y}_2, ..., \mathbf{y}_N|H_1}(\hat{\mathbf{y}}_1, \hat{\mathbf{y}}_2, ..., \hat{\mathbf{y}}_N|H_1)}{p_{\mathbf{y}_1, \mathbf{y}_2, ..., \mathbf{y}_N|H_0}(\hat{\mathbf{y}}_1, \hat{\mathbf{y}}_2, ..., \hat{\mathbf{y}}_N|H_0)} \tag{2}$$

This test involves the evaluation of an N-th order LRT which enables a computationally efficient evaluation when the individual measurements $\hat{\mathbf{y}}_k$ are independent. However, they are not since the windows used in the computation of the observation vectors $\mathbf{y}_k$ are usually overlapped. In order to evaluate the proposed MCO-LRT VAD on an incoming signal, an adequate statistical model for the feature vectors in presence and absence of speech needs to be selected. The joint probability distributions under both hypotheses are assumed to be jointly gaussian independently distributed in frequency and in each part (real and imaginary) of vector with correlation components between each pair of frequency observations:

$$L_N(\hat{\mathbf{y}}_1, \hat{\mathbf{y}}_2, ..., \hat{\mathbf{y}}_N) =$$
$$\prod_{p \in \{R,I\}} \{\prod_\omega \frac{p_{y_1^\omega, y_2^\omega, ..., y_N^\omega | H_1}(\hat{y}_1^\omega, \hat{y}_2^\omega, ..., \hat{y}_N^\omega | H_1)}{p_{y_1^\omega, y_2^\omega, ..., y_N^\omega | H_0}(\hat{y}_1^\omega, \hat{y}_2^\omega, ..., \hat{y}_N^\omega | H_0)}\}_p \tag{3}$$

This is a more realistic approach that the one presented in [9] taking into account the overlap between adjacent observations. We use following joint gaussian probability density function (jGpdf) for each part:

$$p_{\mathbf{y}_\omega | H_s}(\hat{\mathbf{y}}_\omega | H_s)) = K_{H_s,N} \cdot \exp\{-\frac{1}{2}(\hat{\mathbf{y}}_\omega^T (C_{\mathbf{y}_\omega, H_s}^N)^{-1}\hat{\mathbf{y}}_\omega)\} \tag{4}$$

for $s = 0, 1$, where $K_{H_s,N} = \frac{1}{(2\pi)^{N/2}|C_{\mathbf{y}_\omega, H_s}^N|^{1/2}}$, $\mathbf{y}_\omega = (y_1^\omega, y_2^\omega, ..., y_N^\omega)^T$ is a zero-mean frequency observation vector, $C_{\mathbf{y}, H_s}^N$ is the N-order covariance matrix of the observation vector under hypothesis H_s and $|.|$ denotes determinant of a matrix. The model selected for the observation vector is similar to that used by Sohn $et~al.$ [6] that assumes the discrete Fourier transform (DFT) coefficients of the clean speech (S_j) and the noise (N_j) to be asymptotically independent Gaussian random variables. In our case the observation vector consist of the real and imaginary parts of frequency DFT coefficient at frequency ω of the set of m observations.

3   Evaluation of the LRT

In order to evaluate the MCO-LRT, the computation of the inverse matrices and determinants are required. Since the covariances matrices under $H_0 \& H_1$ are assumed to be tridiagonal symmetric matrices[1], the inverses matrices can be computed as the following:

$$[C_{\mathbf{y}_\omega}^{-1}]_{mk} = [\frac{q_k}{p_k} - \frac{q_N}{p_N}]p_m p_k \quad N - 1 \geq m \geq k \geq 0 \tag{6}$$

where N is the order of the model and the set of real numbers q_n, p_n $n = 1 \ldots \infty$ satisfies the three-term recursion for $k \geq 1$:

$$0 = r_k(q_{k-1}, p_{k-1}) + \sigma_{k+1}(q_k, p_k) + r_{k+1}(q_{k+1}, p_{k+1}) \tag{7}$$

with initial values:

---

[1] The covariance matrix will be modeled as a tridiagonal matrix, that is, we only consider the correlation function between adjacent observations according to the number of samples (200) and window shift (80) that is usually selected to build the observation vector. This approach reduces the computational effort achieved by the algorithm with additional benefits from the symmetric tridiagonal matrix properties:

$$[C_{\mathbf{y}_\omega}^N]_{mk} = \begin{bmatrix} \sigma_{y_m}^2(\omega) \equiv E[|y_m^\omega|^2] & if & m = k \\ r_{mk}(\omega) \equiv E[y_m^\omega y_k^\omega] & if & k = m + 1 \\ 0 & other & case \end{bmatrix} \tag{5}$$

where $1 \leq i \leq j \leq N$ and $\sigma_{y_i}^2(\omega)$, $r_{ij}(\omega)$ are the variance and correlation frequency components of the observation vector $\mathbf{y}_\omega$ (denoted for clarity σ_i, r_i) which must be estimated using instantaneous values.

$$p_0 = 1 \quad \text{and} \quad p_1 = -\frac{\sigma_1}{r_1}$$
$$q_0 = 0 \quad \text{and} \quad q_1 = \frac{1}{r_1} \tag{8}$$

In general this set of coefficients are defined in terms of orthogonal complex polynomials which satisfy a Wronskian-like relation [11] and have the continued-fraction representation[12]:

$$\begin{bmatrix} q_n(z) \\ p_n(z) \end{bmatrix} = \frac{1}{(z - \sigma_1)-} \ominus \frac{r_1^2}{(z - \sigma_2)-} \ominus \ldots \ominus \frac{r_{n-1}^2}{(z - \sigma_n)} \tag{9}$$

where $\ominus$ denotes the continuos fraction. This representation is used to compute the coefficients of the inverse matrices evaluated on $z = 0$. In the next section we show a new VAD based on this methodology for $N = 2$ and 3, that is, this robust speech detector is intended for real time applications such us mobile communications. The decision function will be described in terms of the correlation and variance coefficients which constitute a correction to the previous LRT method [9] that assumed uncorrelated observation vectors in the MO.

4   Application to Voice Activity Detection

The use of the MCO-LRT for voice activity detection is mainly motivated by two factors: i) the optimal behaviour of the so defined decision rule, and ii) a multiple observation vector for classification defines a reduced variance LRT reporting clear improvements in robustness against the acoustic noise present in the environment. The proposed MCO-LRT VAD is described as follows. The MCO-LRT is defined over the observation vectors $\{\hat{\mathbf{y}}_{l-m}, \ldots, \hat{\mathbf{y}}_{l-1}, \hat{\mathbf{y}}_l, \hat{\mathbf{y}}_{l+1}, \ldots, \hat{\mathbf{y}}_{l+m}\}$ as follows:

$$\ell_{l,N} = \sum_\omega \frac{1}{2} \left\{ \mathbf{y}_\omega{}^T \Delta_N^\omega \mathbf{y}_\omega + \ln \left[\frac{|C_{\mathbf{y}_\omega, H_0}^N|}{|C_{\mathbf{y}_\omega, H_1}^N|} \right] \right\} \tag{10}$$

where $\Delta_N^\omega = (C_{\mathbf{y}_\omega, H_0}^N)^{-1} - (C_{\mathbf{y}_\omega, H_1}^N)^{-1}$, $N = 2m + 1$ is the order of the model, l denotes the frame being classified as speech (H_1) or non-speech (H_0) and $\mathbf{y}_\omega$ is the previously defined frequency observation vector on the sliding window.

4.1   Analysis of jGpdf Voice Activity Detector for $N = 2$

In this section the improvement provided by the proposed methodology is evaluated by studying the most simple case for $N = 2$. In this case, assuming that squared correlations ρ_1^2 under $H_0 \& H_1$ and the correlation coefficients are negligible under H_0 (noise correlation coefficients $\rho_1^n \to 0$) vanish, the LRT can be evaluated according to:

$$\ell_{l,2} = \frac{1}{2} \sum_\omega L_1(\omega) + L_2(\omega) + 2\sqrt{\gamma_1 \gamma_2} \left[\frac{\rho_1^s}{\sqrt{(1 + \xi_1)(1 + \xi_2)}} \right] \tag{11}$$

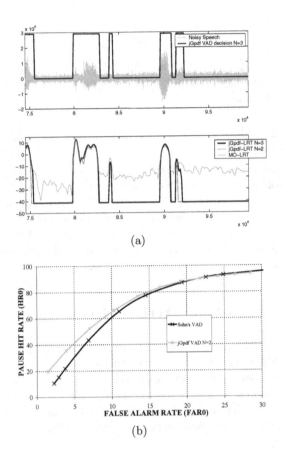

Fig. 1. a) jGpdf-VAD vs. MO-LRT decision for $N = 2$ and 3. b) ROC curve for jGpdf VAD with $l_h = 8$ and Sohn's VAD [6] using a similar hang-over mechanism.

where $\rho_1^s = r_1^s(\omega)/(\sqrt{\sigma_1^s \sigma_2^s})$ is the correlation coefficient of the observations under H_1, $\xi_i \equiv \sigma_i^s(\omega)/\sigma_i^n(\omega)$ and $\gamma_i \equiv (y_i^\omega)^2/\sigma_i^n(\omega)$ are the SNRs a priori and a posteriori of the DFT coefficients, $L_{\{1,2\}}(\omega) \equiv \frac{\gamma_{\{1,2\}}\xi_{\{1,2\}}}{1+\xi_{\{1,2\}}} - \ln(1 + \xi_{\{1,2\}})$ are the independent LRT of the observations $\hat{\mathbf{y}}_1, \hat{\mathbf{y}}_2$ (connection with the previous MO-LRT [9]) which are corrected with the term depending on ρ_1^s, the new parameter to be modeled, and l indexes to the second observation. At this point frequency ergodicity of the process must be assumed to estimate the new model parameter ρ_1^s. This means that the correlation coefficients are constant in frequency thus an ensemble average can be estimated using the sample mean correlation of the observations $\hat{\mathbf{y}}_1$ and $\hat{\mathbf{y}}_2$ included in the sliding window.

4.2   Analysis of jGpdf Voice Activity Detector for $N = 3$

In the case for $N = 3$ the properties of a symmetric and tridiagonal matrix come out. The likelihood ratio can be expressed as:

$$\ell_{l,3} = \sum_\omega \ln \frac{K_{H_1,3}}{K_{H_0,3}} + \frac{1}{2}\hat{\mathbf{y}}_\omega^T \Delta_3^\omega \hat{\mathbf{y}}_\omega \tag{12}$$

where $\ln \frac{K_{H_1,3}}{K_{H_0,3}} = \frac{1}{2}\left[\ln\left[\frac{1-(\rho_1^2+\rho_2^2)^{H_0}}{1-(\rho_1^2+\rho_2^2)^{H_1}}\right] - \ln\left[\prod_{i=1}^3(1+\xi_i)\right]\right]$, and Δ_3^ω is computed using the following expression under hypotheses $H_0 \& H_1$:

$$\hat{\mathbf{y}}_\omega^T(C_{\mathbf{y}_\omega,H_s}^3)^{-1}\hat{\mathbf{y}}_\omega = \frac{1}{1-(\rho_1^2+\rho_2^2)}\left[\frac{1-\rho_2^2}{\sigma_1}(y_1^\omega)^2 + \frac{(y_2^\omega)^2}{\sigma_2}\cdots\right]$$
$$\left[+\frac{1-\rho_1^2}{\sigma_3}(y_3^\omega)^2 - 2\rho_1\frac{y_1^\omega y_2^\omega}{\sqrt{\sigma_1\sigma_2}} - 2\rho_2\frac{y_2^\omega y_3^\omega}{\sqrt{\sigma_2\sigma_3}} + 2\rho_1\rho_2\frac{y_1^\omega y_3^\omega}{\sqrt{\sigma_1\sigma_3}}\right] \tag{13}$$

Assuming that squared correlations under $H_0 \& H_1$ and the correlations under H_0 vanish, the log-LRT can be evaluated as the following:

$$\ell_{l,3} = \frac{1}{2}\sum_\omega\sum_{i=1}^3 L_i(\omega) + \frac{2\sqrt{\gamma_1\gamma_2}\rho_1^s}{\sqrt{(1+\xi_1)(1+\xi_2)}}$$
$$+\frac{2\sqrt{\gamma_2\gamma_3}\rho_2^s}{\sqrt{(1+\xi_2)(1+\xi_3)}} - \frac{2\sqrt{\gamma_1\gamma_3}\rho_1^s\rho_2^s}{\sqrt{(1+\xi_1)(1+\xi_2)^2(1+\xi_3)}} \tag{14}$$

5   Experimental Framework

The ROC curves are frequently used to completely describe the VAD error rate. The AURORA 3 subset of the original Spanish SpeechDat-Car (SDC) database [10] was used in this analysis. The files are categorized into three noisy conditions: quiet, low noisy and highly noisy conditions, which represent different driving conditions with average SNR values between 25dB, and 5dB. The non-speech hit rate (HR0) and the false alarm rate (FAR0= 100-HR1) were determined in each noise condition.

Using the proposed decision functions (equations 14 and 11) we obtain an almost binary decision rule as it is shown in figure 1(a) which accurately detects the beginnings of the voice periods. In this figure we have used the same level of information in both methods ($m = 1$). The detection of voice endings is improved using a hang-over scheme based on the decision of previous frames. Observe how this strategy cannot be applied to the independent LRT [6] because of its hard decision rule and changing bias as it is shown in the same figure. We implement a very simple hang-over mechanism based on contextual information of the previous frames, thus no delay obstacle is added to the algorithm:

$$\ell_{l,N}^h = \ell_{l,N} + \ell_{l-l_h,N} \tag{15}$$

where the parameter l_h is selected experimentally. The ROC curve analysis for this hang-over parameter is shown in figure 2(a) for $N = 3$ where the influence of hang-over in the zero hit rate is studied with variable detection threshold. Finally, the benefits of contextual information [9] can be incorporated just averaging the decision rule over a set of multiple observations windows (two observations for each window). A typical value for $m = 8$ produces increasing levels of detection

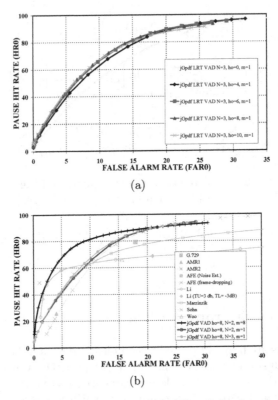

Fig. 2. a) ROC curve analysis of the jGpdf-VAD ($N = 3$) for the selection of the hang-over parameter l_h. b) ROC curves of the jGpdf-VAD using contextual information (eight MO windows for $N = 2$) and standards and recently reported VADs.

accuracy as it is shown in the ROC curve in figure 2(b). Of course, these results are not the optimum ones since only pair-wise dependence is considered here. However for a small number of observations the proposed VAD presents the best trade-off between detection accuracy and computational delay.

6   Conclusion

This paper showed a new VAD for improving speech detection robustness in noisy environments. The proposed method is developed on the basis of previous proposals that incorporate long-term speech information to the decision rule [9]. However, it is not based on the assumption of independence between observations since this hypothesis is not realistic at all. It defines a statistically optimum likelihood ratio test based on multiple and correlated observation vectors which avoids the need of smoothing the VAD decision, thus reporting significant benefits for speech/pause detection in noisy environments. The algorithm has an optional inherent delay that, for several applications including robust speech recognition, does not represent a serious implementation obstacle. An analysis based on the ROC curves unveiled a clear reduction of the classification error for second and third order model. In this way, the proposed VAD outperformed, at the same conditions, the Sohn's VAD, as well as the standardized G.729, AMR and AFE VADs and other recently reported VAD methods in both speech/non-speech detection performance.

6.1   Computation of the LRT for $N = 2$

From equation 4 for $N = 2$ we have that the MCO-LRT can be expressed as:

$$\ell_{1,2} = \sum_{\omega} \ln \frac{K_{H_1,2}}{K_{H_0,2}} + \frac{1}{2} \hat{\mathbf{y}}_\omega^T \Delta_2^\omega \hat{\mathbf{y}}_\omega \tag{16}$$

where:

$$\ln \frac{K_{H_1,2}}{K_{H_0,2}} = \frac{1}{2} \ln \left(\frac{|C_{\mathbf{y}_\omega,H_0}^N|}{|C_{\mathbf{y}_\omega,H_1}^N|} \right) = \frac{1}{2} \frac{\sigma_1^{H_0} \sigma_2^{H_0} - (r_1^{H_0})^2}{\sigma_1^{H_1} \sigma_2^{H_1} - (r_1^{H_1})^2} \tag{17}$$

and $C_{\mathbf{y}_\omega}$ is defined as in equation 5. If we assume that the voice signal is observed in additive independent noise, that is for $i = 1, 2$:

$$\begin{aligned} H_1: & \quad \sigma_i^{H_1} = \sigma_i^n + \sigma_i^s \\ H_0: & \quad \sigma_i^{H_0} = \sigma_i^n \end{aligned} \tag{18}$$

and define the correlation coefficient $\rho_1^{H_s} \equiv \dfrac{r_1^{H_1}}{\sqrt{\sigma_1^{H_1} \sigma_2^{H_1}}}$ and the a priori SNR $\xi_i \equiv \dfrac{\sigma_i^s}{\sigma_i^n}$, we have that:

$$\ln \frac{K_{H_1,2}}{K_{H_0,2}} = \frac{1}{2} \left[\ln \left(\frac{1 - (\rho_1^{H_0})^2}{1 - (\rho_1^{H_1})^2} \right) - \ln \left(\prod_{i=1}^{2} (1 + \xi_i) \right) \right] \tag{19}$$

On the other hand, the inverse matrix is expressed in terms of the orthogonal complex polynomials $q_k(z), p_k(z)$ as:

$$(C_{\mathbf{y}_\omega,H_s}^2)^{-1} = \left(\begin{array}{cc} \left[\frac{q_0}{p_0} - \frac{q_2}{p_2}\right] p_0 p_0 & \left[\frac{q_1}{p_1} - \frac{q_2}{p_2}\right] p_0 p_1 \\ \left[\frac{q_1}{p_1} - \frac{q_2}{p_2}\right] p_0 p_1 & \left[\frac{q_1}{p_1} - \frac{q_2}{p_2}\right] p_1 p_1 \end{array} \right)_{H_s} \tag{20}$$

where $p_0 = 1$, $q_0 = 0$, $p_1 = -\sigma_1/r_1$ and $q_2/p_2 = \sigma_2/(r_1^2 - \sigma_1\sigma_2)$ under hypothesis H_s. Thus the second term of equation 16 can be expressed as:

$$\hat{\mathbf{y}}_\omega^T \Delta_2^\omega \hat{\mathbf{y}}_\omega = (y_1^\omega)^2 (\Delta_2^\omega)_{00} + (y_2^\omega)^2 (\Delta_2^\omega)_{11} + 2 y_1^\omega y_2^\omega (\Delta_2^\omega)_{01} \tag{21}$$

where $(\Delta_2^\omega)_{00} = \dfrac{\sigma_2^{H_0}}{\sigma_2^{H_0} \sigma_1^{H_0} - (r_1^{H_0})^2} - \dfrac{\sigma_2^{H_1}}{\sigma_2^{H_1} \sigma_1^{H_1} - (r_1^{H_1})^2}$, $(\Delta_2^\omega)_{11} = \dfrac{\sigma_1^{H_0}}{\sigma_2^{H_0} \sigma_1^{H_0} - (r_1^{H_0})^2} - \dfrac{\sigma_1^{H_1}}{\sigma_2^{H_1} \sigma_1^{H_1} - (r_1^{H_1})^2}$ and $(\Delta_2^\omega)_{01} = \dfrac{r_1^{H_0}}{(r_1^{H_0})^2 - \sigma_2^{H_0} \sigma_1^{H_0}} - \dfrac{r_1^{H_1}}{(r_1^{H_0})^2 - \sigma_2^{H_0} \sigma_1^{H_0}}$. Finally, if we define the a posteriori SNR $\gamma_i \equiv (y_i^\omega)^2/\sigma_i^n(\omega)$ and neglect the squared correlation functions under both hypotheses we have equation 11.

References

1. Benyassine, A., Shlomot, E., Su, H., Massaloux, D., Lamblin, C., Petit, J.: ITU-T Recommendation G.729 Annex B: A silence compression scheme for use with G.729 optimized for V.70 digital simultaneous voice and data applications. IEEE Communications Magazine 35(9), 64–73 (1997)
2. ITU, A silence compression scheme for G.729 optimized for terminals conforming to recommendation V.70, ITU-T Recommendation G.729-Annex B (1996)
3. ETSI, Voice activity detector (VAD) for Adaptive Multi-Rate (AMR) speech traffic channels, ETSI EN 301 708 Recommendation (1999)
4. ETSI, Speech processing, transmission and quality aspects (STQ); distributed speech recognition; advanced front-end feature extraction algorithm; compression algorithms, ETSI ES 201 108 Recommendation (2002)
5. Bouquin-Jeannes, R.L., Faucon, G.: Study of a voice activity detector and its influence on a noise reduction system. Speech Communication 16, 245–254 (1995)
6. Sohn, J., Kim, N.S., Sung, W.: A statistical model-based voice activity detection. IEEE Signal Processing Letters 16(1), 1–3 (1999)
7. Cho, Y.D., Al-Naimi, K., Kondoz, A.: Improved voice activity detection based on a smoothed statistical likelihood ratio. In: ICASSP. Proc. of the International Conference on Acoustics, Speech and Signal Processing, vol. 2, pp. 737–740 (2001)
8. Górriz, J.M., Ramírez, J., Segura, J.C., Puntonet, C.G.: An effective cluster-based model for robust speech detection and speech recognition in noisy environments. Journal of Acoustical Society of America 120(470), 470–481 (2006)
9. Górriz, J.M., Ramirez, J., Segura, J.C., Puntonet, C.G.: An improved mo-lrt vad based on a bispectra gaussian model. Electronic Letters 41(15), 877–879 (2005)
10. Moreno, A., Borge, L., Christoph, D., Gael, R., Khalid, C., Stephan, E., Jeffrey, A.: SpeechDat-Car: A Large Speech Database for Automotive Environments. In: Proceedings of the II LREC Conference (2000)
11. Akhiezer, N.I.: The Classical Moment Problem. Oliver and Boyd, Edimburgh (1965)
12. Yamani, H., Abdelmonem, M.: The analytic inversion of any finite symmetric tridiagonal matrix. J. Phys. A: Math Gen. 30, 2889–2893 (1997)

Estimating the Dispersion of the Biometric Glottal Signature in Continuous Speech

Pedro Gómez, Agustín Álvarez, Luis Miguel Mazaira, Roberto Fernández, Victoria Rodellar, Rafael Martínez, and Cristina Muñoz

Facultad de Informática, Campus de Montegancedo, s/n
E-28660, Boadilla del Monte, Madrid, Spain
pedro@pino.datsi.fi.upm.es

Abstract. The biometric voice signature may be derived from voice as a whole, or from the separate vocal tract and glottal source after inverse filtering extraction. This last approach has been used by the authors in early work, where it has been shown that the biometric signature obtained from the glottal source provides a good description of speaker's characteristics as gender or age. In the present work more accurate estimations of the singularities in the power spectral density of the glottal source are obtained using an adaptive version of the inverse filtering to carefully follow the spectral changes in continuous speech. Therefore the resulting biometric signature gives a better description of intra-speaker variability. Typical male and female samples chosen from a database of 100 normal speakers are used to determine certain gender specific patterns useful in pathology treatment availing. The low intra-speaker variability present in the biometric signature makes it suitable for speaker identification applications as well as for pathology detection and other fields of speech characterization.

Keywords: Speaker's biometry, glottal signature, glottal source estimation.

1 Introduction

The biometric signature obtained from the glottal source after careful removal of the vocal tract function by inverse filtering gives good descriptions of the speaker's identity and characteristics as gender, age or pathology [1, 2, 3]. Earlier implementations [4] required frame-based pitch-synchronous processing of the glottal source by phonation cycles for the estimation of the signature parameters. This requirement is difficult to be met with sounds of dynamic nature (consonants and glides). To solve this problem a new methodology is proposed using the accurate estimation of the glottal source by the adaptive removal of the vocal tract transfer function, and the robust detection of the glottal spectral singularities. In what follows an overview of the adaptive estimation of the glottal source and the vocal tract is briefly summarized, followed by a description of the glottal biometric signature estimation from the glottal source power spectral density. The normalized singularities detected on the envelope of the spectral distributions (maxima and minima) are used as biometric descriptors as these are strongly related to vocal fold

M. Chetouani et al. (Eds.): NOLISP 2007, LNAI 4885, pp. 255–262, 2007.

biomechanics [5]. In section 4 signatures from male and female voice show that these singularities present gender specificities. Intra-speaker variability is explored in section 5, where a study case is shown on the use of intra-speaker variability in pathology treatment assessment. Conclusions and future lines are given in section 6.

2 Glottal Source Adaptive Estimation

The key for the accurate estimation of the glottal source is to obtain a good representation of the vocal tract transfer function, and vice-versa [6, 7]. Traditionally the profile of the glottal source power spectral density has not been considered of relevance for biometric purposes. Nevertheless this profile is strongly influenced by vocal fold biomechanics and can be used in applications such as the speaker's biometrical description [8] or in pathology detection [3].

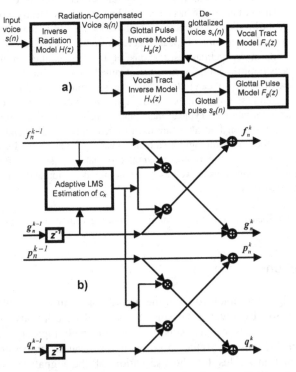

Fig. 1. a) Iterative estimation of the vocal tract transfer function $F_v(z)$ and the glottal pulse residual $s_g(n)$. b) Paired adaptive-fixed lattice section to implement parallel function estimation and removal.

The extraction method is based on the iteration of the following loop as shown in Figure 1.a:

1. Estimate the inverse glottal source model $F_g(z)$ from input voice using an order-2 gradient adaptive lattice (upper lattice in Figure 1.b).

2. Remove the glottal source model from input voice by a paired fixed lattice (lower lattice in Figure 1.b) using the parameters obtained in step 1. The resulting trace $s_v(n)$ will be an estimate of the vocal tract impulse response.
3. Estimate the vocal tract transfer function $F_v(z)$ from this last trace using another adaptive lattice (typically of order 20-30).
4. Remove the vocal tract transfer function from input voice using a fixed lattice using the filter parameters from step 3. The resulting trace $s_g(n)$ will be an estimate of the glottal residual.

This iteration is repeated till estimates of the vocal tract transfer function are almost free from glottal source information, and vice-versa. The glottal signals from utterances of the vowel /a/ by typical male and female speakers are shown in Figure 2.

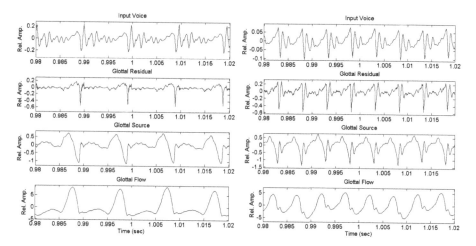

Fig. 2. Typical male (left) and female (right) utterances of vowel /a/ and derived glottal traces. From top to bottom: input voice, glottal residual after adaptive inverse removal of the vocal tract, glottal source, and glottal flow.

An initialization lap and two more iterations were enough for good vocal tract removal. A gradient adaptive lattice was implemented whose details may be found in [9]. Both male and female glottal source traces show clear L-F [10] patterns as an avail of the extraction method accuracy.

3   Estimating the Biometric Signature of Voiced Speech

The FFT power spectral density of the glottal source after normalization is used to obtain the positions of envelope singularities as follows:

*   512 sample 2-msec sliding frames of the glottal source power spectral density in logarithmic (dB) scale are used as shown in Figure 3 for the same male and female speakers.
*   On each frame the power spectral density envelopes are estimated (dot line).

- The envelope maxima (*) and minima (◊) in amplitude and frequency are estimated as ordered pairs with order index k: $\{T_{Mk}, f_{Mk}\}$ and $\{T_{mk}, f_{mk}\}$.
- The largest of all maxima (T_{Mm}, f_{Mm}) is used as a normalization reference both in amplitude and in frequency as given by:

$$\left.\begin{array}{l} \tau_{Mk} = T_{Mk} - T_{Mm} \\ \tau_{mk} = T_{mk} - T_{Mm} \end{array}\right\}; \quad 1 \le k \le K \tag{1}$$

$$\left.\begin{array}{l} \varphi_{Mk} = \dfrac{f_{Mk}}{f_{Mm}} \\ \varphi_{mk} = \dfrac{f_{mk}}{f_{Mm}} \end{array}\right\}; \quad 1 \le k \le K \tag{2}$$

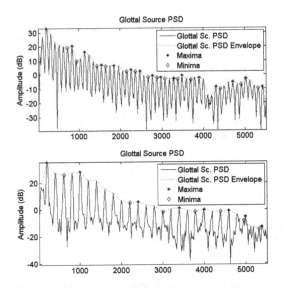

Fig. 3. Short-term Power Spectral Density of Glottal Signals. Top: Glottal Source) from a typical male speaker (vowel /a/) showing superimposed singularities. Bottom: idem for a typical female speaker (vowel /a/). Horizontal axes given in Hz.

The *slenderness* factor is a parameter derived from each "V" trough profile formed by each minimum and the two neighbour maxima as:

$$\sigma_{mk} = \frac{f_{Mm}\left(2T_{mk} - T_{Mk+1} - T_{Mk}\right)}{2\left(f_{Mk+1} - f_{Mk}\right)}; \quad 1 \le k \le K \tag{3}$$

The set of normalized ordered pairs and the derived slenderness parameters constitute the proposed biometric signature. The normalized singularity profiles for both reference male and female traces are plotted in Figure 4.

4 Materials and Methods

To study the properties of the biometric signature a set of 100 normal speakers equally distributed by gender was used. Subject ages ranged from 19 to 39, with an average of 26.77 years and a standard deviation of 5.75 years. The normal phonation condition of speakers was determined by electroglottographic, video-endoscopic and GRBAS [11] evaluations. The recordings consisted in three utterances of the vowel /a/ produced in different sessions of about 3 sec per record at a sampling rate of 44,100 Hz, a 0.2 sec segment derived from the central part for use in the experiments. For presentation purposes the traces were re-sampled at 11,025 Hz. This database was fully parameterized to obtain the singularity biometric signature described in section 3. The most representative male and female speakers in this database were selected for the study, their biometric signatures being plotted in Figure 4.

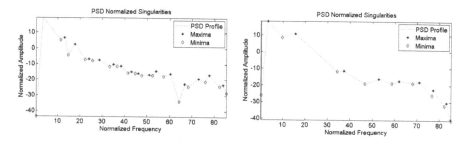

Fig. 4. Normalized singularity profiles for the male (left) and female (right) records

A first inspection shows that the male speaker's signature exhibits more and deeper "V" troughs than the female case. This is consistent with the biomechanical explanation of the nature of peaks and troughs, as these are based on the mechanical resonances and anti-resonances of the systems of masses and springs describing vocal fold vibration. In general, female vocal folds show more stiff links among body and cover masses, and this would explain why they show lower amount of less sharp anti-resonances (see [4] and [12] for a wider explanation).

5 Intra-speaker Variability

The robustness of the estimates depends in large extent on intra-speaker variability. The processing of the 0.2 sec segments in 512-sample windows sliding in 2 msec steps produce around 76 estimates per segment. The positions of the 8 minima and maxima for the typical male and female speakers (plus the origin value) vs time are given in Figure 5. It may be observed that lower order singularities show more stable values and positions than higher order ones. This finding is consistent under biomechanical considerations. Lower frequency troughs and peaks are due to larger vocal fold masses, which for a given articulation and vocal tract load do not change substantially during the phonation frame observed, whereas higher order singularities are due to irregular small mass distributions on the cord, which may suffer important alterations during phonation and are more sensitive to vocal tract coupling effects. In

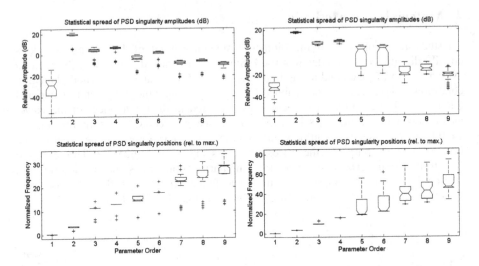

Fig. 5. Statistical distribution of the first 8 singularity points and the origin for a 0.2 sec segment of the male (left) and female (right) samples referenced. From top to bottom: Amplitudes and Singularity Orders.

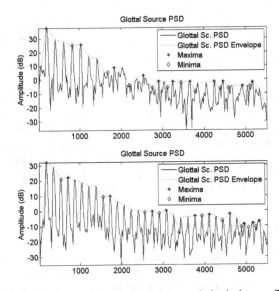

Fig. 6. Glottal Source Power Spectral Signature for a pathological case: Top: pre-treatment. Bottom: post-treatment. Horizontal axes given in Hz.

general it may be said that singularities in the male case are deeper and mainly appear at lower frequencies than in the female case. Low frequency singularities are less spread over than high frequency ones (which show stronger skewness), this fact being more evident in the female case.

To explore the applicability of the glottal signature proposed a study has been conducted on a specific pathologic case as the one shown in Figure 6, corresponding to the pre- and post-treatment glottal source signatures from a non-smoking 34-year old female after suffering a four-year lasting vocal production limitation.

The patient reported chronic disphonia, vocal fatigue, changes in loudness and soaring during speaking or singing. After medical examination a gelatine-type small polyp affecting the free lip of the medial third of the left vocal fold, substrate-attached and mildly edematous was diagnosed. This resulted in incomplete glottal closure during phonation and in a reduction and asymmetry on the mucosal wave appearing on the vocal cord affected. The pre-treatment signature shows that the harmonic structure between 1.6 kHz and 3.3 kHz was completely altered or distorted and that natural phonation was tenser and at a higher pitch.

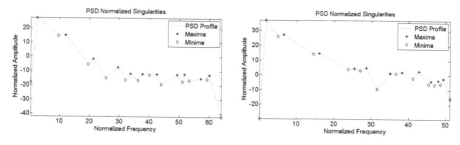

Fig. 7. Normalized singularity profiles for the pre-treatment (left) and post-treatment (right) records

The post-treatment signature (3 months after the surgical removal of the polyp) shows a restoration of the distorted harmonic band and the production of a glottal signature closer to normal female voicing conditions as confirmed by the plots in Figure 7. Comparing these plots against the one in Figure 4 (right) it may be seen that the glottal signature between normalized frequencies of 5 and 20 in the pre-treatment case shows an average decay slope of 12.9 dB/oct vs an equivalent slope of 8.0 dB/oct in the post-treatment case, this last one being more in correspondence with the average 5.4 dB/oct for the normal female case. This behavior avails the usefulness of the glottal signature as a biometrical description of pathologic voice.

6 Conclusions

The work presented is a generalization of prior studies using non-adaptive estimations of the vocal tract on short segments of vowels where it was shown that estimates from the glottal source could be used in the determination of the biomechanical parameters of the vocal fold. The use of adaptive estimations allow a higher accuracy in the estimates of the vocal tract, and consequently on the glottal signals and the underlying biomechanics. The extension of the glottal spectra singularities to time-varying conditions allow a better description of the non-stationary processes appearing in vocal fold vibration even in the production of sustained sounds. As an example a study case from pre- and post-treatment of a specific mild pathological case has been exposed. Both the harmonic structure and the biometric signature of the glottal source confirmed the success of the treatment and the recovery of normal phonation conditions. This has to be attributed to the tracking accuracy of the adaptive methods used. This methodology will help in conducting more careful studies about inter-speaker and intra-speaker variability to extend the use of the glottal source spectral signature to speaker identification and characterization applications as well as in voice quality measurements, pathology detection and treatment assessment.

Acknowledgments. This work is funded by grants TIC2003-08756, TEC2006-12887-C02-00 from Plan Nacional de I+D+i, Ministry of Education and Science, CCG06-UPM/TIC-0028 from the Plan Regional de Investigación Científica e Investigación Tecnológica de la Comunidad de Madrid, and project HESPERIA from the Program CENIT, CDTI, Ministry of Industry, Spain.

References

1. Gómez, P., Rodellar, V., Álvarez, A., Lázaro, J.C., Murphy, K., Díaz, F., Fernández, R.: Biometrical Speaker Description from Vocal Cord Parameterization. In: Proc. of ICASSP 2006, Toulouse, France, pp. 1036–1039 (2006)
2. Whiteside, S.P.: Sex-specific fundamental and formant frequency patterns in a cross-sectional study. J. Acoust. Soc. Am. 110(1), 464–478 (2001)
3. Godino, J.I., Gomez, P.: Automatic detection of voice impairments by means of short-term cepstral parameters and neural network based detectors. IEEE Trans Biomed. Eng. 51, 380–384 (2004)
4. Gómez, P., Godino, J.I., Díaz, F., Álvarez, A., Martínez, R., Rodellar, V.: Biomechanical Parameter Fingerprint in the Mucosal Wave Power Spectral Density. In: Proc. of the ICSLP 2004, pp. 842–845 (2004)
5. Gómez, P., Martínez, R., Díaz, F., Lázaro, C., Álvarez, A., Rodellar, V., Nieto, V.: Estimation of vocal cord biomechanical parameters by non-linear inverse filtering of voice. In: Faundez-Zanuy, M., Janer, L., Esposito, A., Satue-Villar, A., Roure, J., Espinosa-Duro, V. (eds.) NOLISP 2005. LNCS (LNAI), vol. 3817, pp. 174–183. Springer, Heidelberg (2006)
6. Alku, P.: An Automatic Method to Estimate the Time-Based Parameters of the Glottal Pulseform. In: Proc. of the ICASSP 1992, pp. II/29-32 (1992)
7. Akande, O.O., Murphy, P.J.: Estimation of the vocal tract transfer function with application to glottal wave analysis. Speech Communication 46(1), 1–13 (2005)
8. Nickel, R.M.: Automatic Speech Character Identification. IEEE Circuits and Systems Magazine 6(4), 8–29 (2006)
9. Haykin, S.: Adaptive Filter Theory, 4th edn. Prentice-Hall, Upper Saddle River, NJ (2001)
10. Fant, G., Liljentcrants, J., Lin, Q.: A four-parameter model of glottal flow. STL-QSPR 4, 1–13 (1985), Reprinted in Speech Acoustics and Phonetics: Selected Writings, G. Fant, pp. 95–108. Kluwer Academic Publishers, Dordrecht (2004)
11. Hirano, M., Hibi, S., Yoshida, T., Hirade, Y., Kasuya, H., Kikuchi, Y.: Acoustic analysis of pathological voice. Some results of clinical application. Acta Otolaryngologica 105(5-6), 432–438 (1988)
12. Berry, D.A.: Mechanisms of modal and non-modal phonation. J. Phonetics 29, 431–450 (2001)

Trajectory Mixture Density Networks with Multiple Mixtures for Acoustic-Articulatory Inversion

Korin Richmond

Centre for Speech Technology Research
Edinburgh University, Edinburgh, United Kingdom
korin@cstr.ed.ac.uk

Abstract. We have previously proposed a trajectory model which is based on a mixture density network (MDN) trained with target variables augmented with dynamic features together with an algorithm for estimating maximum likelihood trajectories which respects the constraints between those features. In this paper, we have extended that model to allow diagonal covariance matrices and multiple mixture components in the trajectory MDN output probability density functions. We have evaluated this extended model on an inversion mapping task and found the trajectory model works well, outperforming smoothing of equivalent trajectories using low-pass filtering. Increasing the number of mixture components in the TMDN improves results further.

1 Introduction

Mainstream speech technology, such as automatic speech recognition and concatenative speech synthesis, is strongly focused on the acoustic speech signal. This is natural, considering the acoustic domain is where the speech signal exists in transmission between humans, and we can conveniently measure and manipulate an acoustic representation of speech. However, an articulatory representation of speech has certain properties which are attractive and which may be exploited in modelling. Speech articulators move relatively slowly and smoothly, and their movements are continuous; the mouth cannot "jump" from one position to the next. Using knowledge of the speech production system could improve speech processing methods by providing useful constraints. Accordingly, there is growing interest in exploiting articulatory information and representations in speech processing, with many suggested applications; for example, low bit-rate speech coding [1], speech analysis and synthesis [2], automatic speech recognition [3,4], animating talking heads and so on.

For an articulatory approach to be practical, we need convenient access to an articulatory representation. Recent work on incorporating articulation into speech technology has used data provided by X-ray microbeam cinematography and electromagnetic articulography (EMA). These methods, particularly the latter, mean we are now able to gather reasonably large quantities of articulatory data. However, they are still invasive techniques and require bulky

M. Chetouani et al. (Eds.): NOLISP 2007, LNAI 4885, pp. 263–272, 2007.

and expensive experimental setups. Therefore, there is interest in developing a way to recover an articulatory representation from the acoustic speech signal. In other words, for a given acoustic speech signal we aim to estimate the underlying sequence of articulatory configurations which produced it. This is termed acoustic-articulatory inversion, or the inversion mapping.

The inversion mapping problem has been the subject of research for several decades. One approach has been to attempt analysis of acoustic signals based on mathematical models of speech production [5]. Another popular approach has been to use articulatory synthesis models, either as part of an analysis-by-synthesis algorithm [6], or to generate acoustic-articulatory corpora which may be used with a code-book mapping [7] or to train other models [8]. Much of the more recent work reported has applied machine learning models to human measured articulatory data, including artificial neural networks (ANNs) [9], codebook methods [10] and GMMs [11].

The inversion mapping is widely regarded as difficult because it may be an ill-posed problem; multiple evidence exists to suggest the articulatory-to-acoustic mapping is many-to-one, which means that instantaneous inversion of this mapping results in a one-to-many mapping. If this is the case, an inversion mapping method must take account of the alternative articulatory configurations possible in response to an acoustic vector.

In previous work [12,9], we have successfully employed the mixture density network (MDN) [13] to address this problem. The MDN provides a probability density function (pdf) of arbitrary complexity over the target articulatory domain which is conditioned on the acoustic input. In [14], we began to extend this work to provide a statistical trajectory model, termed the Trajectory MDN, along similar lines as the HMM-based speech production model of [15] and the GMM-based inversion mapping of [11]. This was achieved by augmenting the static articulatory target data with dynamic delta and deltadelta features and incorporating the maximum likelihood parameter generation (MLPG) algorithm [16]. This allows to calculate the maximum likelihood estimate of articulatory trajectories which respect the constraints between the static and derived dynamic features.

This paper seeks to further the work in [14] with three specific aims: 1) to evaluate an extension to the TMDNs in [14] (which were limited to using spherical covariance matrices) that allows mixture models with diagonal covariance matrices. 2) to evaluate the new implementation of TMDN on the full set of articulator channels, and in comparison with a low-pass filtering approach previously reported. 3) to evaluate TMDNs with multiple mixture components.

2   The Trajectory Mixture Density Network Model

We give here a very brief introduction to the MDN, and describe how it may be extended with the MLPG algorithm to give a trajectory model. For full details of the MDN and MLPG, the reader is referred to [13] and [16] respectively. To avoid introducing unnecessary confusion, we have attempted to retain the original notation as far as possible.

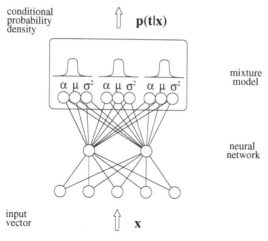

conditional probability density

p(t|x)

mixture model

α μ σ²   α μ σ²   α μ σ²

neural network

input vector

x

Fig. 1. The mixture density network combines a mixture model and a neural network

2.1 Mixture Density Networks

The MDN combines a mixture model with an ANN. Here, we will consider a multilayer perceptron and Gaussian mixture components. The ANN maps from the input vector $\mathbf{x}$ to the control parameters of the mixture model (priors α, means μ and variances σ^2), which in turn gives a pdf over the target domain, conditioned on the input vector $p(\mathbf{t}|\mathbf{x})$. The toy-example MDN in Figure 1 takes an input vector $\mathbf{x}$ (dimensionality 5) and gives the conditional probability density of a vector $\mathbf{t}$ (dimensionality 1) in the target domain. This pdf takes the form of a GMM with 3 components, so it is given as:

$$p(\mathbf{t}|\mathbf{x}) = \sum_{j=1}^{M} \alpha_j(\mathbf{x})\phi_j(\mathbf{t}|\mathbf{x}) \tag{1}$$

where M is the number of mixture components (in this example, 3), $\phi_j(\mathbf{t}|\mathbf{x})$ is the probability density given by the jth kernel, and $\alpha_j(\mathbf{x})$ is the prior for the jth kernel.

In order to constrain the GMM priors to within the range $0 \leq \alpha_j(\mathbf{x}) \leq 1$ and to sum to unity, the *softmax* function is used

$$\alpha_j = \frac{\exp(z_j^\alpha)}{\sum_{l=1}^{M} \exp(z_l^\alpha)} \tag{2}$$

where z_j^α is the output of the ANN corresponding to the prior for the jth mixture component. The variances are similarly related to the outputs of the ANN as

$$\sigma_j = \exp(z_j^\sigma) \tag{3}$$

where z_j^σ is the output of the ANN corresponding to the variance for the jth mixture component. This avoids the variance becoming ≤ 0. Finally, the means are represented directly:

$$\mu_{jk} = z_{jk}^{\mu} \tag{4}$$

where z_{jk}^{μ} is the value of the output unit corresponding to the kth dimension of the mean vector for the jth mixture component.

Training the MDN aims to minimise the negative log likelihood of the observed target data points

$$E = -\sum_n \ln \left\{ \sum_{j=1}^{M} \alpha_j(\mathbf{x}^n) \phi_j(\mathbf{t}^n|\mathbf{x}^n) \right\} \tag{5}$$

given the mixture model parameters. Since the ANN part of the MDN provides the parameters for the mixture model, this error function must be minimised with respect to the network weights. The derivatives of the error at the network output units corresponding separately to the priors, means and variances of the mixture model are calculated (see [13]) and then propagated back through the network to find the derivatives of the error with respect to the network weights. Thus, standard non-linear optimisation algorithms can be applied to MDN training.

2.2   Maximum Likelihood Parameter Generation

The first step to an MDN-based trajectory model is to train an MDN with target feature vectors augmented with dynamic features (i.e. deltas and deltadeltas), derived from linear combinations of a window of static features. For the sake of simplicity we will first consider MDNs with a single Gaussian distribution and a single target static feature c_t at each time step. Given the output of this MDN in response to a sequence of input vectors, in order to generate the maximum likelihood trajectory, we aim to maximize $P(\mathbf{O}|\mathbf{Q})$ with respect to $\mathbf{O}$, where $\mathbf{O} = [\mathbf{o}_1^T, \mathbf{o}_2^T, ..., \mathbf{o}_T^T]^T$, $\mathbf{o}_t = [c_t, \Delta c_t, \Delta\Delta c_t]$ and $\mathbf{Q}$ is the sequence of Gaussians output by our MDN. The relationship between the static features and those augmented with derived dynamic features can be arranged in matrix form

$$\mathbf{O} = \mathbf{WC} \tag{6}$$

where $\mathbf{C}$ is a sequence of static features and $\mathbf{W}$ is a transformation matrix composed of the coefficients of the delta and deltadelta calculation window and 0. Under the condition expressed in Eq. 6, maximising $P(\mathbf{O}|\mathbf{Q})$ is equivalent to maximising $P(\mathbf{WC}|\mathbf{Q})$ with respect to $\mathbf{C}$. By setting

$$\frac{\partial \log P(\mathbf{WC}|\mathbf{Q})}{\partial \mathbf{C}} = 0 \tag{7}$$

a set of linear equations is obtained (see [16] for the details)

$$\mathbf{W}^T \mathbf{U}^{-1} \mathbf{WC} = \mathbf{W}^T \mathbf{U}^{-1} \mathbf{M}^T \tag{8}$$

where $\mathbf{M}^T = [\mu_{q_1}, \mu_{q_2}, ..., \mu_{q_T}]$ and $\mathbf{U}^{-1} = diag[\mathbf{U}_{q_1}^{-1}, \mathbf{U}_{q_2}^{-1}, ..., \mathbf{U}_{q_T}^{-1}]$ (μ_{q_T} and $\mathbf{U}_{q_t}^{-1}$ are the 3×1 mean vector and 3×3 (diagonal) covariance matrix respectively). Solving Eq. 8 for $\mathbf{C}$ computes the maximum likelihood trajectory.

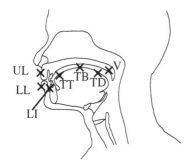

label	articulator	label	articulator
UL	Upper lip	TT	Tongue tip
LL	Lower lip	TB	Tongue body
LI	Lower incisor	TD	Tongue Dorsum
V	Velum		

Fig. 2. Placement of EMA receiver coils in the MOCHA database for speaker `fsew0`. Coil placement abbreviations may be suffixed with "_x" and "_y" to designate the x- and y-coordinate for a given coil in the midsagittal plane respectively.

To extend the MLPG algorithm to the case of a sequence of pdfs with multiple mixture components, we make use of an iterative EM method described in [16]. Essentially, for each time frame at each iteration, instead of using the means and covariances of a single Gaussian in (8), we use a weighted sum of these parameters of the multiple mixture components, weighed by their occupancy probabilities (i.e. posterior probability of each component given the augmented observation sequence $\mathbf{O}$). Hence, we first choose an initial static feature trajectory $\mathbf{C}$ and use this to calculate the occupancy probabilities using the forward backward algorithm. We can then solve (8) using the weighted means and covariances to obtain an updated feature trajectory $\mathbf{C}'$, which is then used to calculate updated occupancy probabilities. This two stage iteration is repeated until convergence.

3   Inversion Mapping Experiment

3.1   MOCHA Articulatory Data

The multichannel articulatory (MOCHA) dataset [17] used for the experiments in this paper gives the acoustic waveform recorded at the same time as electromagnetic articulograph (2D EMA) data. The sensors shown in Figure 2 provide x- and y-coordinates in the midsagittal plane at 500Hz sample rate. Speakers were recorded reading a set of 460 short, phonetically-balanced British-TIMIT sentences. Female speaker `fsew0` was used for the experiments here. This is the same data set as used previously [9,14], and so enables comparison with those and similar results reported in the literature (e.g. [11]).

Data Processing. The acoustic data was converted to frames of 20 melscale filterbank coefficients using a Hamming window of 20ms with a shift of 10ms. These were z-score normalised and scaled to the range [0.0,1.0]. The EMA trajectories were downsampled to match the 10ms shift rate, then z-score normalised and scaled to the range [0.1,0.9] using the normalisation method described in [12]. Frames of silence at the beginning and end of the files were discarded, using the labelling provided with MOCHA.

368 utterances were used for the training set, and the validation and test sets contained 46 utterances each (the same subsets as [9,14]). A context window of 20 consecutive acoustic frames was used as input to the TMDN, which increased the order of the acoustic vector paired with each articulatory vector to 400.

3.2 Method

We trained TMDNs with 1, 2 and 4 mixture components for each of the 14 EMA channels, making a total of 42 models trained. In [14], we trained separate MDNs for the static, delta and deltadelta features for each articulatory channel, because the implementation limited output pdfs to spherical covariance. Here, in contrast, our implementation has been extended and now allows diagonal covariance matrices, and so the three feature streams for each articulator channel were trained in a single network. All networks contained a hidden layer of 80 units. The scaled conjugate gradients non-linear optimisation algorithm was run for a maximum of 4000 epochs, and the separate validation set was used to identify the point at which an optimum appeared to have been reached. The validation error was calculated in terms of RMS error between the target trajectories and those resulting from the Trajectory MDN. This differs from using simply the likelihood of the target data given the pdfs output by the MDN. To generate output trajectories from the TMDN, we simply ran the input data for an utterance through the TMDNs for each articulatory channel, and then ran the MLPG algorithm on the resulting sequences of pdfs over the static and dynamic feature spaces.

To evaluate the Trajectory MDN, we compared the resulting trajectories with those of the output units corresponding to the mean of the static feature alone. This output is in theory approximately equivalent to that of an MLP (with linear output activation function) trained with a standard least-squares error function[1]. In this way, we can directly observe the effect of using the augmented features without considering the effects of two systems having been trained differently. Finally, we also low-pass filtered the static mean trajectories as a smoothing step which has been shown in the past to improve inversion results [12,11], and compared those smoothed trajectories with the TMDN output.

4 Results

Table 1 lists the results of 14 TMDNs trained on each articulatory channel separately, using an output pdf containing a single Gaussian. Two error metrics have been used: correlation between the target and output trajectories, and root mean square error (RMSE) expressed in millimetres. The table also lists the results previously reported in [9], which used an MLP with exactly the same dataset, for comparison. It can be seen that the improvement is substantial. By way of further comparison with other studies, [11] reported an average RMS error of 1.45mm for MOCHA speaker fsew0.

---

[1] Although the MLP component of the TMDN here has been trained with augmented target features, which from comparison with previous results, e.g. [9], seems beneficial

Table 1. Comparison of results for Trajectory MDNs (TMDN) with a single Gaussian with the MLP described in [9]. Exactly the same training, validation and testing datasets have been used. Average RMSE(mm) in [9] was 1.62mm, compared with 1.4mm here.

Channel	Correlation MLP	Correlation TMDN	RMSE(mm) MLP	RMSE(mm) TMDN	RMSE(mm) reduction %
ul_x	0.58	0.68	0.99	0.90	9.5
ul_y	0.72	0.79	1.16	1.05	9.9
ll_x	0.60	0.69	1.21	1.10	9.2
ll_y	0.75	0.83	2.73	2.27	16.8
li_x	0.56	0.63	0.89	0.82	8.1
li_y	0.80	0.85	1.19	1.03	13.3
tt_x	0.79	0.85	2.43	2.12	12.9
tt_y	0.84	0.90	2.56	2.08	18.7
tb_x	0.81	0.85	2.19	1.96	10.4
tb_y	0.83	0.89	2.14	1.76	17.6
td_x	0.79	0.84	2.04	1.85	9.5
td_y	0.71	0.82	2.31	1.89	18.2
v_x	0.79	0.86	0.42	0.35	15.6
v_y	0.77	0.83	0.41	0.37	10.2

Table 2. Channel-specific cutoff frequencies used for low pass filtering

	ul	ll	li	tt	tb	td	v
_x	3 Hz	3 Hz	3 Hz	6 Hz	6 Hz	7 Hz	5 Hz
_y	5 Hz	8 Hz	7 Hz	9 Hz	7 Hz	6 Hz	5 Hz

Table 3. Comparison of correlation and RMS error (in millimetres) for Trajectory MDN model ("TMDN") with the static mean MDN output only ("static only") and low-pass filtered static mean ("static lpfilt"). The TMDN here has a single Gaussian.

Channel	Correlation static only	Correlation static lpfilt	Correlation TMDN	RMSE(mm) static only	RMSE(mm) static lpfilt	RMSE(mm) TMDN	RMSE(mm) reduction %
ul_x	0.63	0.67	0.68	0.93	0.90	0.90	0.6
ul_y	0.74	0.77	0.79	1.13	1.06	1.05	1.5
ll_x	0.64	0.69	0.69	1.17	1.11	1.10	1.0
ll_y	0.81	0.83	0.83	2.40	2.31	2.27	1.6
li_x	0.57	0.62	0.63	0.88	0.84	0.82	2.4
li_y	0.83	0.84	0.85	1.07	1.05	1.03	1.5
tt_x	0.82	0.84	0.85	2.26	2.14	2.12	1.0
tt_y	0.88	0.89	0.90	2.19	2.12	2.08	1.8
tb_x	0.83	0.85	0.85	2.05	1.99	1.96	1.2
tb_y	0.87	0.89	0.89	1.88	1.80	1.76	1.8
td_x	0.81	0.83	0.84	1.95	1.88	1.85	2.1
td_y	0.78	0.81	0.82	2.04	1.92	1.89	1.7
v_x	0.84	0.85	0.86	0.37	0.36	0.35	1.2
v_y	0.80	0.82	0.83	0.39	0.37	0.37	1.6

In order to investigate the effect of using dynamic features and the MLPG algorithm within the Trajectory MDN, we have compared these results for TMDNs with a single Gaussian with those obtained using low-pass filtering, as described in [12,11]. Table 3 compares three conditions: *"TMDN"*, *"static only"* and *"static lpfilt"*. For the *"static only"* condition, we have used the TMDN's output corresponding to the mean for the static target feature as the output trajectory. For the *"static lpfilt"* condition, we have further low-pass filtered the static mean above using the cutoff frequencies listed in Table 2. These channel-specific cutoff frequencies were determined empirically in [12], and are very similar to those given in [11]. As expected, it can be seen that low-pass filtering improves results for all channels. However, using the dynamic features and the MLPG algorithm in the Trajectory MDN results in the best performance, with improvements varying between 0.6 and 2.4% over low-pass filtering.

The improvements over using low-pass filtering shown in Table 3, although consistent, are not huge. However, in contrast to low-pass filtering, the TMDN is able to make use of multiple mixture components, which can potentially increase performance further. Table 4 performs this comparison, by the addition of results for TMDNs with 2 and 4 mixture components. We see that in the majority of cases increasing the number of mixture components improves results, e.g. by up to 8.3% in the case of the tt_y channel using 4 mixture components.

Table 4. Comparison of RMS error (in millimetres) between using the low-pass filtered static feature mean ("static lpfilt") and Trajectory MDNs with 1, 2 or 4 mixture components. Average (min) RMSE=1.37mm.

Channel	static lpfilt	TMDN 1 mix	TMDN 2 mix	TMDN 4 mix	opt # mixes	% best reduction
upper lip x	0.90	0.90	0.90	0.91	1	0.6
upper lip y	1.06	1.05	1.03	1.06	2	3.3
lower lip x	1.11	1.10	1.10	1.12	1	1.0
lower lip y	2.31	2.27	2.20	2.22	2	4.7
lower incisor x	0.84	0.82	0.80	0.81	2	4.2
lower incisor y	1.05	1.03	1.04	1.03	1	1.5
tongue tip x	2.14	2.12	2.09	2.10	2	2.1
tongue tip y	2.12	2.08	1.98	1.94	4	8.3
tongue body x	1.99	1.96	1.97	1.98	1	1.2
tongue body y	1.80	1.76	1.73	1.78	2	3.5
tongue dorsum x	1.88	1.85	1.81	1.83	2	4.1
tongue dorsum y	1.92	1.89	1.85	1.88	2	3.6
velum x	0.36	0.35	0.35	0.35	2	3.3
velum y	0.37	0.37	0.36	0.37	2	2.8

Finally, Figure 3 gives a qualitative demonstration of the nature of this improvement. In these plots we compare the tt_y trajectory estimated by the TMDN with 4 mixture components (bottom plot) with the low-pass filtered static mean (top plot). It can be seen in several places that the TMDN with 4 mixtures is substantially closer to the real target trajectory.

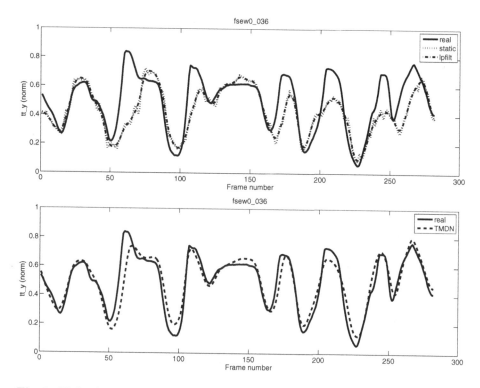

Fig. 3. "Only the most accomplished artists obtain popularity." (fsew0_036). Comparison of TMDN output trajectory with low-pass filtered static mean output trajectory.

5   Conclusion

The results of this paper show we have successfully extended the Trajectory MDN first described in [14] to allow diagonal covariance matrices. For all 14 articulator channels tested, the TMDN with a single Gaussian output pdf performed better than low-pass filter smoothing. Increasing the number of mixture components improved results further. This is a unique advantage of the TMDN model over smoothing single trajectories using, for example, low-pass filters.

Acknowledgments

Many thanks to Junichi Yamagishi for useful discussion pertaining to implementation. This work was supported by EPSRC grant EP/E027741/1.

References

1. Schroeter, J., Sondhi, M.M.: Speech coding based on physiological models of speech production. In: Furui, S., Sondhi, M.M. (eds.) Advances in Speech Signal Processing, pp. 231–268. Marcel Dekker Inc., New York (1992)

2. Toda, T., Black, A., Tokuda, K.: Mapping from articulatory movements to vocal tract spectrum with Gaussian mixture model for articulatory speech synthesis. In: Proc. 5th ISCA Workshop on Speech Synthesis (2004)
3. King, S., Frankel, J., Livescu, K., McDermott, E., Richmond, K., Wester, M.: Speech production knowledge in automatic speech recognition. Journal of the Acoustical Society of America 121(2), 723–742 (2007)
4. Wrench, A., Richmond, K.: Continuous speech recognition using articulatory data. In: Proc. ICSLP 2000, Beijing, China (2000)
5. Wakita, H.: Estimation of vocal-tract shapes from acoustical analysis of the speech wave: The state of the art. IEEE Trans. Acoust. Speech Signal Process. ASSP-27, 281–285 (1979)
6. Shirai, K., Kobayashi, T.: Estimating articulatory motion from speech wave. Speech Communication 5, 159–170 (1986)
7. Atal, B.S., Chang, J.J., Mathews, M.V., Tukey, J.W.: Inversion of articulatory-to-acoustic transformation in the vocal tract by a computer sorting technique. J. Acoust. Soc. Am. 63, 1535–1555 (1978)
8. Rahim, M.G., Kleijn, W.B., Schroeter, J., Goodyear, C.C.: Acoustic-to-articulatory parameter mapping using an assembly of neural networks. In: Proceedings of the IEEE International Conference on Acoustics, Speech, and Signal Processing, pp. 485–488 (1991)
9. Richmond, K., King, S., Taylor, P.: Modelling the uncertainty in recovering articulation from acoustics. Computer Speech and Language 17, 153–172 (2003)
10. Hogden, J., Lofqvist, A., Gracco, V., Zlokarnik, I., Rubin, P., Saltzman, E.: Accurate recovery of articulator positions from acoustics: New conclusions based on human data. J. Acoust. Soc. Am. 100(3), 1819–1834 (1996)
11. Toda, T., Black, A., Tokuda, K.: Acoustic-to-articulatory inversion mapping with Gaussian mixture model. In: Proc. 8th International Conference on Spoken Language Processing, Jeju, Korea (2004)
12. Richmond, K.: Estimating Articulatory Parameters from the Acoustic Speech Signal. PhD thesis, The Centre for Speech Technology Research, Edinburgh University (2002)
13. Bishop, C.: Neural Networks for Pattern Recognition. Oxford University Press, Oxford (1995)
14. Richmond, K.: A trajectory mixture density network for the acoustic-articulatory inversion mapping. In: Proc. Interspeech, Pittsburgh, USA (September 2006)
15. Hiroya, S., Honda, M.: Estimation of articulatory movements from speech acoustics using an HMM-based speech production model. IEEE Transactions on Speech and Audio Processing 12(2), 175–185 (2004)
16. Tokuda, K., Yoshimura, T., Masuko, T., Kobayashi, T., Kitamura, T.: Speech parameter generation algorithms for HMM-based speech synthesis. In: Proc. ICASSP, Istanbul, Turkey, pp. 1315–1318 (June 2000)
17. Wrench, A.: The MOCHA-TIMIT articulatory database (1999), http://www.cstr.ed.ac.uk/artic/mocha.html

Application of Feature Subset Selection Based on Evolutionary Algorithms for Automatic Emotion Recognition in Speech

Aitor Álvarez, Idoia Cearreta, Juan Miguel López, Andoni Arruti,
Elena Lazkano, Basilio Sierra, and Nestor Garay

Computer Science Faculty (University of the Basque Country)
Manuel Lardizabal 1, E-20018 Donostia (Gipuzkoa), Spain
aitor.alvarez@ehu.es

Abstract. The study of emotions in human-computer interaction is a growing research area. Focusing on automatic emotion recognition, work is being performed in order to achieve good results particularly in speech and facial gesture recognition. In this paper we present a study performed to analyze different machine learning techniques validity in automatic speech emotion recognition area. Using a bilingual affective database, different speech parameters have been calculated for each audio recording. Then, several machine learning techniques have been applied to evaluate their usefulness in speech emotion recognition, including techniques based on evolutive algorithms (EDA) to select speech feature subsets that optimize automatic emotion recognition success rate. Achieved experimental results show a representative increase in the success rate.

Keywords: Affective computing, Machine Learning, speech features extraction, emotion recognition in speech.

1 Introduction

Human beings are eminently emotional, as their social interaction is based on the ability to communicate their emotions and perceive the emotional states of others [1]. Affective computing, a discipline that develops devices for detecting and responding to users' emotions [2], is a growing research area [3]. The main objective of affective computation is to capture and process affective information with the aim of enhancing the communication between the human and the computer. Within the scope of affective computing, the development of affective applications is a challenge that involves analyzing different multimodal data sources. In order to develop such applications, a large amount of data is needed in order to include a wide range of emotionally significant material. Affective databases are a good chance for developing affective recognizers or affective synthesizers. In this paper different speech paralinguistic parameters have been calculated for the analysis of the human emotional voice, using several audio recordings. These recordings are stored in a bilingual and multimodal affective database. Several works have already been done in which the use of Machine Learning paradigms takes a principal role.

M. Chetouani et al. (Eds.): NOLISP 2007, LNAI 4885, pp. 273–281, 2007.

2   Related Work

As previously mentioned affective databases provide a good opportunity for training affective applications. This type of databases usually record information such as images, sounds, psychophysiological values, etc. There are some references in the literature that present affective databases and their characteristics [4],[5],[6]. Many studies have been focused on the different features used in human emotional speech analysis [7],[8]. The number of voice features analysed varies among the studies, but basically most of these are based in fundamental frequency, energy and timing parameters, such as speech rate or mean phone duration. Works where the use of Machine Learning paradigms take a principal role can also be found in the literature [9],[10]. The work by [4] is related with this paper in the sense of using a Feature Selection method in order to apply a Neural Network to emotion recognition in speech, although both, the methods to perform the FSS and the paradigms used, are different. In this line it has to be pointed out the work by [11] which uses a reduced number of emotions and a greedy approach to select the features.

3   Study of Automatic Emotion Recognition Relevant Parameters Using Machine Learning Paradigms

3.1   RekEmozio Database

The RekEmozio bilingual database was created with the aim of serving as an information repository for performing research on user emotion, adding descriptive information about the performed recordings, so that processes such as extracting speech parameters and video features could be carried out on them. Members of different work groups involved in research projects related to RekEmozio have performed several processes for extracting speech and video features; this information was subsequently added to the database. The emotions used were chosen based on [12], and the neutral emotion was added. The characteristics of the RekEmozio database are described in [13]. The languages that are considered in RekEmozio database are Spanish and Basque.

3.2   Emotional Feature Extraction

For emotion recognition in speech, one of the most important questions is which features should be extracted from the voice signal. Previous studies show that it is difficult to find specific voice features that could be used as reliable indicators of the emotion present in the speech [14]. In this work, RekEmozio database audio recordings (stereo wave files, sampled at 44100 Hz) have been processed using standard signal processing techniques (windowing, Fast Fourier Transform, auto-correlation...) to extract a wide group of 32 features which are described below. Supposing that each recording in the database corresponds to one single emotion, only one global vector of features has been obtained for each recording by using some statistical operations. Parameters used are calculated over entire recordings. Selected features are detailed next (in italics):

- **Fundamental Frequency (F0):** The most common feature analyzed in several studies [7],[8]. For F0 estimation we used Sun algorithm [15] and statistics are computed: *Maximum, Minimum, Mean, Range, Variance, Standard deviation and Maximum positive slope in F0 contour.*
- **RMS Energy:** The mean energy of speech quantified by calculating root mean square (RMS) value and 6 statistics: *Maximum, Minimum, Mean, Range, Variance and Standard Deviation.*
- **Loudness:** *Absolute loudness* based on Zwicker's model [16].
- **Spectral distribution of energy:** Each emotion requires a different effort in the speech and it is known that the spectral distribution of energy varies with speech effort [7]. We have computed energy in *Low band*, between 0 and 1300 Hz, *Medium band*, between 1300 and 2600 Hz and *High band* from 2600 to 4000 Hz [17].
- **Mean Formants and Bandwidth:** Energy from the sound source (vocal folds) is modified by the resonance characteristics of the vocal tract (formants). Acoustic variations dues to emotion are reflected in formants [18]. The *first three mean Formants*, and their corresponding *mean Bandwidths.*
- **Jitter:** *Perturbation in vibration of vocal chords.* It is estimated based on the model presented by [19].
- **Shimmer:** *Perturbation cycle to cycle of the energy.* Its estimation is based on the previously calculated absolute loudness.
- **Speaking Rate:** Rhythm is known to be an important aspect in recognition of emotion in speech. Progress has been made on a simple aspect of rhythm, the alternation between speech and silence [7]. The speaking rate estimation has been divided in 6 values based on their duration with respect to the whole elocution: *Duration of voice part, Silence part, Maximum voice part, Minimum voice part, Maximum silence part and Minimum silence part.*

3.3   Machine Learning Standard Paradigms Used

In the supervised learning task, a classification problem has been defined where the main goal is to construct a model or a classifier able to manage the classification itself with acceptable accuracy. With this aim, some variables are to be used in order to identify different elements, the so called predictor variables. For the current problem, each sample is composed by the set of 32 speech related values, while the label value is one of the seven emotions identified. The single paradigms used in our experiments that come from the family of Machine Learning (ML) are briefly introduced:

- **Decision trees:** A decision tree consists of nodes and branches to partition a set of samples into a set of covering decision rules. In each node, a single test or decision is made to obtain a partition. The starting node is usually referred as the root node. In each node, the goal is to select an attribute that makes the best partition between the classes of the samples in the training set [20],[21]. In our experiments, two well-known decision tree induction algorithms are used, ID3 [22] and C4.5 [23].

- **Instance-Based Learning:** Instance-Based Learning (IBL) has its root in the study of nearest neighbor algorithm [24] in the field of machine learning. The simplest form of nearest neighbor (NN) or k-nearest neighbor (k-NN) algorithms simply stores the training instances and classifies a new instance by predicting the same class its nearest stored instance has or the majority class of its k nearest stored instances have, respectively, according to some distance measure as described in [25]. The core of this non-parametric paradigm is the form of the similarity function that computes the distances from the new instance to the training instances, to find the nearest or k-nearest training instances to the new case. In our experiments the IB paradigm is used, an inducer developed in the *MLC++* project [26] and based on the works of [27] and [28].

- **Naive Bayes classifiers:** The Naive-Bayes (NB) rule [29] uses the Bayes theorem to predict the class for each case, assuming that the predictive genes are independent given the category. To classify a new sample characterized by d genes $X = (X_1, X_2, ... , X_d)$, the NB classifier applies the following rule:

$$c_{NB} = arg\ max\ p(c_j) \prod_{i=1}^{d} p(x_i|c_j) \tag{1}$$

where c_{NB} denotes the class label predicted by the Naive-Bayes classifier and the possible classes of the problem are grouped in $C = c_1, ... , c_l$. A normal distribution is assumed to estimate the class conditional densities for predictive genes. Despite its simplicity, the NB rule obtains better results than more complex algorithms in many domains.

- **Naive Bayesian Tree learner:** The naive Bayesian tree learner, NBTree [30], combines naive Bayesian classification and decision tree learning. It uses a tree structure to split the instance space into sub-spaces defined by the paths of the tree, and generates one naive Bayesian classifier in each sub-space.

Feature Subset Selection by Estimation of Distribution Algorithms. The basic problem of ML is concerned with the induction of a model that classifies a given object into one of several known classes. In order to induce the classification model, each object is described by a pattern of d features. Here, the ML community has formulated the following question: are all of these d descriptive features useful for learning the 'classification rule'? On trying to respond to this question, we come up with the Feature Subset Selection (FSS) [31] approach which can be reformulated as follows: given a set of candidate features, select the 'best' subset in a classification problem. In our case, the 'best' subset will be the one with the best predictive accuracy. Most of the supervised learning algorithms perform rather poorly when faced with many irrelevant or redundant (depending on the specific characteristics of the classifier) features. In this way, the FSS proposes additional methods to reduce the number of features so as to improve the performance of the supervised classification algorithm. FSS can be viewed as a search problem [32], with each state in the search space specifying a subset of the possible features of the task. Exhaustive evaluation of possible feature subsets is usually unfeasible in practice due to the large amount of computational effort required. In this way, any feature selection method must determine the nature of the search process. In the experiments performed, an Estimation of Distribution Algorithm (EDA) has been used which has the model accuracy as fitness function. To assess the goodness of each proposed gene subset for a specific classifier, a wrapper approach is applied. In the same way as supervised classifiers when no gene selection is applied, this wrapper approach estimates, by using the 10-fold crossvalidation [33] procedure, the goodness of the classifier using only the variable subset found by the search algorithm.

Other Feature Subset Selection Approaches. Several approaches have been developed to search a good attribute selection. On Filter Based approach the attribute selection takes a statistical measure of each variable and sorts them according to the obtained value. Among them, Principal Component analysis takes a measure of the correlation and covariance among the predictor variables and the class. Transformation based Feature Selection is a second approach which transforms the representation space to obtain a reduced one. For instance, Singular Value Decomposition transforms the classification problem in another one after projecting the variables through a Matrix, while the number of singular selected values determines the dimension (size) of the vectors.

Another Feature Subset Selection technique, the one used in this paper, is the so called Wrapper approach in which a subset of variables is selected based on the accuracy of the classifier itself. Two simple ways to perform this selection are the following:

- **Forward:** starts with an empty set of variables and adds to the set, at each step, the variable which most increases the obtained accuracy, until no increase is obtained.
- **Backward:** starts with all the variables and deselects variables while no decrease is produced.

These approaches are outperformed by a more powerfull method based on Evolutionary Algorithms; such as EDA. As it can be seen, the rest of the approaches are local guided, while the used one is a more sophisticated search engine, which is supposed to outperform the rest of the approaches. In fact, this happens with any greedy search when compared to an evolutionary one when applied to the same search problem.

4   Experimental Results

The above mentioned methods have been applied over the crossvalidated data sets using the *MLC++* library [26]. Each dataset corresponds to a single actor. Experiments were carried out with and without FSS in order to extract the accuracy improvement introduced by the feature selection process. Tables 1 and 2 show the classification results obtained using the whole set of variables, for Basque and Spanish languages respectively. Each column represents a female (Fi) of male (Mi) actor, and mean values corresponding to each classifier/gender are also included. Last column presents the total average for each classifier.

Results don't seem very impressive. ID3 best classifies the emotions for female actresses, for both Basque and Spanish languages, while C4.5 outstands for Basque male actors and IB for Spanish male actors. Results obtained after applying FSS are more appealing, as can be seen in Tables 3 and 4. There, classifier IB appears as the best paradigm for all the categories, female and male, and Basque and Spanish languages. Moreover, the accuracies outperform the previous ones in more than 15%. It must also be highlighted that FSS improves the well classified rate for all the ML paradigms, as it can be seen in Figure 1.

Table 1. 10-fold crossvalidation accuracy for Basque language using the whole variable set

	Female				Male					Total
	F1	F2	F3	mean	M1	M2	M3	M4	mean	
IB	35.4	48.8	35.2	39.8	44.2	49.3	36.9	40.9	42.8	41.5
ID3	38.7	45.5	44.7	**43.0**	46.7	46.9	43.3	51.1	47.0	45.3
C4.5	41.5	52.2	35.0	42.9	60.4	53.3	45.1	49.5	**52.0**	**48.1**
NB	42.9	45.8	37.7	42.1	52.2	44.1	36.2	41.4	43.5	42.9
NBT	42.3	39.8	35.2	39.1	53.1	46.2	45.2	43.3	46.9	43.6

Table 2. 10-fold crossvalidation accuracy for Spanish language using the whole variable set

	Female						Male						Total
	F1	F2	F3	F4	F5	mean	M1	M2	M3	M4	M5	mean	
IB	34.6	43.6	54.6	54.6	38.2	45.1	25.5	33.6	51.8	47.7	33.6	**38.4**	**41.8**
ID3	36.4	52.7	49.1	47.3	42.7	**45.6**	20.9	30.9	40.9	47.3	40.0	36.0	40.8
C4.5	30.9	50.0	46.4	43.6	42.7	42.7	29.1	31.8	46.4	42.7	35.5	37.1	39.9
NB	38.2	42.7	49.1	40.0	42.7	42.5	24.6	30.9	49.1	45.5	34.6	36.9	39.7
NBT	42.7	43.6	49.1	50.0	39.1	44.9	18.2	27.3	40.9	48.2	42.7	35.5	40.2

Table 3. 10-fold crossvalidation accuracy for Basque language using FSS

	Female				Male					Total
	F1	F2	F3	mean	M1	M2	M3	M4	mean	
IB	63.0	68.0	59.3	**63.5**	72.7	67.4	61.0	62.8	**65.9**	**64.9**
ID3	62.7	60.5	65.5	62.9	72.7	62.0	56.5	62.7	63.4	63.2
C4.5	60.2	66.0	60.0	62.1	71.8	62.8	60.1	63.6	64.6	63.5
NB	64.5	64.6	48.9	59.3	74.6	62.5	62.7	60.0	64.9	62.5
NBT	58.6	61.1	54.8	58.1	74.4	59.9	62.7	59.4	64.1	61.6

Table 4. 10-fold crossvalidation accuracy for Spanish language using FSS

	Female						Male						Total
	F1	F2	F3	F4	F5	mean	M1	M2	M3	M4	M5	mean	
IB	61.8	66.4	75.5	71.8	68.2	**68.7**	42.7	57.3	69.1	63.6	60.9	**58.7**	**63.7**
ID3	59.1	66.4	66.4	60.0	61.8	62.7	42.7	51.8	66.4	61.8	60.0	56.5	59.6
C4.5	57.3	62.7	64.6	65.5	63.6	62.7	43.6	56.4	65.5	64.6	56.4	57.3	60.0
NB	54.6	59.1	68.2	65.5	60.0	61.5	40.9	48.2	64.6	59.1	51.8	52.9	57.2
NBT	53.6	66.4	63.6	58.2	60.0	60.4	38.2	47.3	60.0	63.6	59.1	53.6	57.0

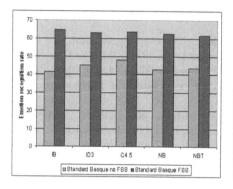 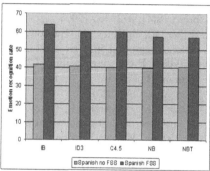

Fig. 1. Improvement in Basque and Spanish languages using FSS in all classifiers

5 Conclusions and Future Work

RekEmozio database has been used to training some automatic recognition systems. In this paper we have shown that applying FSS enhances classification rates for the ML paradigms that we have used (IB, ID3, C4.5, NB and NBTree). An analysis of the selected features by FSS is required. Moreover, the speech data should be combined with visual information. This combination could be performed by means of a multiclassifier model [34].

References

1. Casacuberta, D.: La mente humana: Diez Enigmas y 100 preguntas, Océano, Barcelona, Spain (2001)
2. Picard, R.W.: Affective Computing. The MIT Press, Cambridge, Massachusetts (1997)
3. Tao, J., Tan, T.: Affective computing: A review. In: Tao, J., Tan, T., Picard, R.W. (eds.) ACII 2005. LNCS, vol. 3784, pp. 981–995. Springer, Heidelberg (2005)
4. Cowie, R., Douglas-Cowie, E., Cox, C.: Beyond emotion archetypes: databases for emotion modelling using neural networks. Neural Network 18(4), 371–388 (2005)
5. Humaine, Retrieved (January 10, 2007),
   http://emotion-research.net/wiki/databases

6. López, J.M., Cearreta, I., Fajardo, I., Garay, N.: Validating a multilingual and multimodal affective database. In: Proc. HCII, Beijing, China. LNCS, vol. 4560, pp. 422–431. Springer, Heidelberg (2007)

7. Cowie, R., Douglas-Cowie, E., Tsapatsoulis, N., Votsis, G., Kollias, S.D., Fellenz, W.A., Taylor, J.G.: Emotion recognition in human-computer interaction. Signal Processing Magazine, IEEE 18(1), 32–80 (2001)

8. Schröder, M.: Speech and emotion research: An overview of research frameworks and a dimensional approach to emotional speech synthesis. PhD thesis, Institute of Phonetics, Saarland University (2004)

9. Dellaert, F., Polzin, T., Waibel, A.: Recognizing emotions in speech. In: Proc. ICSLP 1996, Philadelphia, PA, vol. 3, pp. 1970–1973 (1996)

10. Taylor, J.G., Scherer, K.R., Cowie, R.: Neural network. Special issue: Emotion and brain 18(4), 313–455 (2005)

11. Huber, R., Batliner, A., Buckow, J., Noth, E., Warnke, V., Niemann, H.: Recognition of emotion in a realistic dialogue scenario. In: Proc. Int. Conf. on Spoken Language Processing, Beijing, China, vol. 1, pp. 665–668 (October 2000)

12. Ekman, P., Friesen, W.V.: Pictures of facial affect. Consulting Psychologist Press, Palo Alto, CA (1976)

13. López, J.M., Cearreta, I., Garay, N., López de Ipiña, K., Beristain, A.: Creación de una base de datos emocional bilingüe y multimodal. In: Redondo, M.A., Bravo, C., Ortega, M. (eds.) Proceeding of the 7th Spanish Human Computer Interaction Conference, Interacción 2006, Puertollano, pp. 55–66 (2006)

14. Laukka, P.: Vocal Expression of Emotion: Discrete-emotions and Dimensional Accounts. PhD thesis, Comprehensive Summaries of Uppsala Dissertations from the Faculty of Social Sciences (2004)

15. Sun, X.: Pitch determination and voice quality analysis using subharmonic-to-harmonic ratio. In: Proc. of IEEE International Conference on Acoustics, Speech, and Signal Processing, Orlando, Florida (2002)

16. Fernandez, R.: A Computational Model for the Automatic Recognition of Affect in Speech. PhD thesis, Massachusetts Institute of Technology (2004)

17. Kazemzadeh, A., Lee, S., Narayanan, S.: Acoustic correlates of user response to errors in human-computer dialogues. In: Proc. IEEE ASRU, St. Thomas, U.S. Virgin Islands (December 2003)

18. Bachorowski, J.-A., Owren, M.J.: Vocal expression of emotion: acoustic properties of speech are associated with emotional intensity and context. Psychological Science 6(4), 219–224 (1995)

19. Rothkrantz, L.J.M., Wiggers, P., van Wees, J.W.A., van Vark, R.J.: Voice stress analysis. In: Sojka, P., Kopeček, I., Pala, K. (eds.) TSD 2004. LNCS (LNAI), vol. 3206, pp. 449–456. Springer, Heidelberg (2004)

20. Martin, K.: An exact probability metric for decision tree splitting and stopping. Mach. Learn. 28(2-3), 257–291 (1997)

21. Mingers, J.: A comparison of methods of pruning induced rule trees, Technical Report, Coventry, England: University of Warwick, School of Industrial and Business Studies (1988)

22. Quinlan, J.R.: Induction of decision trees. Mach. Learn. 1(1), 81–106 (2003)

23. Quinlan, R.R.: C4.5: programs for machine learning. Morgan Kaufmann Publishers Inc., San Francisco (1993)

24. Dasarathy, B.V.: Nearest Neighbor (NN) Norms: NN Pattern Recognition Classification Techniques. IEEE Computer Society Press, Los Alamitos (1991)

25. Ting, K.M.: Common issues in Instance-Based and Naive-Bayesian classifiers. PhD thesis, Baser Department of Computer Science, The University of Sidney, Australia (1995)
26. Kohavi, R., Sommerfield, D., Dougherty, J.: Data mining using MLC++: A machine learning library in C++. In: Tools with Artificial Intelligence, pp. 234–245. IEEE Computer Society Press, Los Alamitos (1996)
27. Aha, D.W., Kibler, D., Albert, M.K.: Instance-based learning algorithms. Machine Learning 6(1), 37–66 (1991)
28. Wettschereck, D.: A study of distance-based machine learning algorithms. PhD thesis, Adviser-Thomas G. Dietterich (1994)
29. Minsky, M.: Steps towards artificial intelligence. In: Feigenbaum, E.A., Feldman, J. (eds.) Computers and Thought, pp. 406–450. McGraw-Hill, New York (1963)
30. Kohavi, R.: Scaling up the accuracy of naive-Bayes classifiers: a decision-tree hybrid. In: Proceedings of the Second International Conference on Knowledge Discovery and Data Mining, pp. 202–207 (1996)
31. Liu, H., Motoda, H.: Feature Selection for Knowledge Discovery and Data Mining. Kluwer Academic Publishers, Dordrecht (1998)
32. Inza, I., Larrañaga, P., Etxeberria, R., Sierra, B.: Feature subset selection by bayesian network-based optimization. Artificial Intelligence 123(1-2), 157–184 (2000)
33. Stone, M.: Cross-validatory choice and assessment of statistical procedures. Journal of the Royal Statistical Society 36, 111–157 (1974)
34. Gunes, V., Menard, M., Loonis, P., Petit-Renaud, S.: Combination, cooperation and selection of classifiers: A state of the art. International Journal of Pattern Recognition 17, 1303–1324 (2003)

Author Index

Lecture Notes in Artificial Intelligence (LNAI)

Vol. 4676: M. Klusch, K.V. Hindriks, M.P. Papazoglou, L. Sterling (Eds.), Cooperative Information Agents XI. XI, 361 pages. 2007.

Vol. 4667: J. Hertzberg, M. Beetz, R. Englert (Eds.), KI 2007: Advances in Artificial Intelligence. IX, 516 pages. 2007.

Vol. 4660: S. Džeroski, L. Todorovski (Eds.), Computational Discovery of Scientific Knowledge. X, 327 pages. 2007.

Vol. 4659: V. Mařík, V. Vyatkin, A.W. Colombo (Eds.), Holonic and Multi-Agent Systems for Manufacturing. VIII, 456 pages. 2007.

Vol. 4651: F. Azevedo, P. Barahona, F. Fages, F. Rossi (Eds.), Recent Advances in Constraints. VIII, 185 pages. 2007.

Vol. 4648: F. Almeida e Costa, L.M. Rocha, E. Costa, I. Harvey, A. Coutinho (Eds.), Advances in Artificial Life. XVIII, 1215 pages. 2007.

Vol. 4635: B. Kokinov, D.C. Richardson, T.R. Roth-Berghofer, L. Vieu (Eds.), Modeling and Using Context. XIV, 574 pages. 2007.

Vol. 4632: R. Alhajj, H. Gao, X. Li, J. Li, O.R. Zaïane (Eds.), Advanced Data Mining and Applications. XV, 634 pages. 2007.

Vol. 4629: V. Matoušek, P. Mautner (Eds.), Text, Speech and Dialogue. XVII, 663 pages. 2007.

Vol. 4626: R.O. Weber, M.M. Richter (Eds.), Case-Based Reasoning Research and Development. XIII, 534 pages. 2007.

Vol. 4617: V. Torra, Y. Narukawa, Y. Yoshida (Eds.), Modeling Decisions for Artificial Intelligence. XII, 502 pages. 2007.

Vol. 4612: I. Miguel, W. Ruml (Eds.), Abstraction, Reformulation, and Approximation. XI, 418 pages. 2007.

Vol. 4604: U. Priss, S. Polovina, R. Hill (Eds.), Conceptual Structures: Knowledge Architectures for Smart Applications. XII, 514 pages. 2007.

Vol. 4603: F. Pfenning (Ed.), Automated Deduction – CADE-21. XII, 522 pages. 2007.

Vol. 4597: P. Perner (Ed.), Advances in Data Mining. XI, 353 pages. 2007.

Vol. 4594: R. Bellazzi, A. Abu-Hanna, J. Hunter (Eds.), Artificial Intelligence in Medicine. XVI, 509 pages. 2007.

Vol. 4585: M. Kryszkiewicz, J.F. Peters, H. Rybinski, A. Skowron (Eds.), Rough Sets and Intelligent Systems Paradigms. XIX, 836 pages. 2007.

Vol. 4578: F. Masulli, S. Mitra, G. Pasi (Eds.), Applications of Fuzzy Sets Theory. XVIII, 693 pages. 2007.

Vol. 4573: M. Kauers, M. Kerber, R. Miner, W. Windsteiger (Eds.), Towards Mechanized Mathematical Assistants. XIII, 407 pages. 2007.

Vol. 4571: P. Perner (Ed.), Machine Learning and Data Mining in Pattern Recognition. XIV, 913 pages. 2007.

Vol. 4570: H.G. Okuno, M. Ali (Eds.), New Trends in Applied Artificial Intelligence. XXI, 1194 pages. 2007.

Vol. 4565: D.D. Schmorrow, L.M. Reeves (Eds.), Foundations of Augmented Cognition. XIX, 450 pages. 2007.

Vol. 4562: D. Harris (Ed.), Engineering Psychology and Cognitive Ergonomics. XXIII, 879 pages. 2007.

Vol. 4548: N. Olivetti (Ed.), Automated Reasoning with Analytic Tableaux and Related Methods. X, 245 pages. 2007.

Vol. 4539: N.H. Bshouty, C. Gentile (Eds.), Learning Theory. XII, 634 pages. 2007.

Vol. 4529: P. Melin, O. Castillo, L.T. Aguilar, J. Kacprzyk, W. Pedrycz (Eds.), Foundations of Fuzzy Logic and Soft Computing. XIX, 830 pages. 2007.

Vol. 4520: M.V. Butz, O. Sigaud, G. Pezzulo, G. Baldassarre (Eds.), Anticipatory Behavior in Adaptive Learning Systems. X, 379 pages. 2007.

Vol. 4511: C. Conati, K. McCoy, G. Paliouras (Eds.), User Modeling 2007. XVI, 487 pages. 2007.

Vol. 4509: Z. Kobti, D. Wu (Eds.), Advances in Artificial Intelligence. XII, 552 pages. 2007.

Vol. 4496: N.T. Nguyen, A. Grzech, R.J. Howlett, L.C. Jain (Eds.), Agent and Multi-Agent Systems: Technologies and Applications. XXI, 1046 pages. 2007.

Vol. 4483: C. Baral, G. Brewka, J. Schlipf (Eds.), Logic Programming and Nonmonotonic Reasoning. IX, 327 pages. 2007.

Vol. 4482: A. An, J. Stefanowski, S. Ramanna, C.J. Butz, W. Pedrycz, G. Wang (Eds.), Rough Sets, Fuzzy Sets, Data Mining and Granular Computing. XIV, 585 pages. 2007.

Vol. 4481: J. Yao, P. Lingras, W.-Z. Wu, M.S. Szczuka, N.J. Cercone, D. Ślęzak (Eds.), Rough Sets and Knowledge Technology. XIV, 576 pages. 2007.

Vol. 4476: V. Gorodetsky, C. Zhang, V.A. Skormin, L. Cao (Eds.), Autonomous Intelligent Systems: Multi-Agents and Data Mining. XIII, 323 pages. 2007.

Vol. 4460: S. Aguzzoli, A. Ciabattoni, B. Gerla, C. Manara, V. Marra (Eds.), Algebraic and Proof-theoretic Aspects of Non-classical Logics. VIII, 309 pages. 2007.

Vol. 4457: G.M.P. O'Hare, A. Ricci, M.J. O'Grady, O. Dikenelli (Eds.), Engineering Societies in the Agents World VII. XI, 401 pages. 2007.

Vol. 4456: Y. Wang, Y.-m. Cheung, H. Liu (Eds.), Computational Intelligence and Security. XXIII, 1118 pages. 2007.

Vol. 4455: S. Muggleton, R. Otero, A. Tamaddoni-Nezhad (Eds.), Inductive Logic Programming. XII, 456 pages. 2007.

Vol. 4452: M. Fasli, O. Shehory (Eds.), Agent-Mediated Electronic Commerce. VIII, 249 pages. 2007.

Vol. 4451: T.S. Huang, A. Nijholt, M. Pantic, A. Pentland (Eds.), Artifical Intelligence for Human Computing. XVI, 359 pages. 2007.

Vol. 4442: L. Antunes, K. Takadama (Eds.), Multi-Agent-Based Simulation VII. X, 189 pages. 2007.

Vol. 4441: C. Müller (Ed.), Speaker Classification II. X, 309 pages. 2007.

Vol. 4438: L. Maicher, A. Sigel, L.M. Garshol (Eds.), Leveraging the Semantics of Topic Maps. X, 257 pages. 2007.